Korean Studies of the Henry M. Jackson School of International Studies

EDITED BY CLARK W. SORENSEN,
University of Washington

Heritage Management In Korea and Japan

The Politics of Antiquity and Identity

HYUNG IL PAI

UNIVERSITY OF WASHINGTON PRESS | *Seattle and London*

This publication was supported in part by the Korea Studies
Program of the University of Washington in cooperation with
the Henry M. Jackson School of International Studies.

The University of Washington Press gratefully acknowledges
the support of the Northeast Asia Council (NEAC) of the
Association for Asian Studies, Inc. (AAS) and the Academy of
Korean Studies (AKS), which provided assistance through their
book subvention programs.

University of Washington Press
PO Box 50096, Seattle, WA 98145, USA
www.washington.edu/uwpress

Library of Congress Cataloging-in-Publication Data
Pai, Hyung Il.
Heritage management in Korea and Japan : the politics of antiquity and
    identity / Hyung Il Pai. — First [edition].
pages cm. — (Korean studies of the Henry M. Jackson School of International
    Studies)
ISBN 978-0-295-99304-1 (hardback) — ISBN 978-0-295-99305-8 (pbk.)
1. Cultural property—Protection—Korea (South) 2. Cultural property—
Protection—Japan. I. Title.
NA109.K6P35 2013   951.95—dc23   2013017057

For my parents, Dr. Pai Soo Tong and Park Kyung Duk,
for inspiring me with their world travels.

CONTENTS

ACKNOWLEDGMENTS

In the course of researching and writing this book, the following mentors, colleagues, sponsors, and friends extended unwavering support and encouragement. It is my pleasure to finally express my gratitude in print.

First, I would like to thank professors Inaga Shigemi and Yamada Shōji for inviting me to the Research Center for Japanese Studies, better known as Nichibunken in Kyoto. The former invited me as a visiting research professor in 2000–2001, and the latter in 2007–8 to participate as one of the core members of his research team project called "The Ownership and Spread of Culture." At Nichibunken, I also participated in several international symposiums organized by senior archaeologists such as Uno Takao, Akazawa Takeru, and Senda Minoru. Their insights, support, and encouragement gave me new perspectives into their respective fields of expertise—the Kofun period, human evolution, and environmental archaeology. Former staff members Okuno Yukiko, Sasaki Ayako, and Ishida Miho, who coordinated everyday matters and planned outings in and around scenic Kyoto, made my life at Nichibunken the most memorable of all of my foreign trips. The staff of the Nichibunken Library and Information Services also provided invaluable assistance with scanning the numerous figures included in this book.

Of all of the specialists in Kyoto who have assisted me in more ways than I can do justice to here, I am most indebted to the members of the Mokuyō Club, whose biweekly seminars opened my eyes to the history of modern Japanese archaeology. I always looked forward to our after-seminar drinking sessions, held at out of the way *izakayas* in old residential neighborhoods in Kyoto and Nara that only locals would be familiar with. I have depended extensively on the club's journal, *Nihon kōkogakushi kenkyū*, published annually by founding members Uchida Yoshiyaki (Kyoto City Buried Cultural Properties Center) and Hirose Shigeaki (Shinyōsha Publishing Company) since 1996. The articles are devoted to unearthing the lives, careers, and achievements of the earliest pioneers of Japanese archaeology, and have set new standards for archaeological scholarship in Japan, which is unknown outside of small circles.

I remember fondly our memorable road trip together to the Torii Ryūzō Memorial Museum located in Tokushima, Shikoku. Inhaling the fresh, crisp winter sea air on a cold February day in 2001, I paid respects at the grave of the first prehistoric archaeologist to survey Korea in 1911. To my surprise and delight, Torii and his wife were interred under a monumental Korean table-style dolmen. The club's members also invited me to accompany them to the laboratory of Fujii Keisuke, professor of Japanese architecture at the University of Tokyo. I want to thank Professor Fujii personally for taking the time to show us Sekino Tadashi's original writings, drawings, sketches, and even his handwritten undergraduate thesis, now archived at the Department of Architecture library.

The late Arimitsu Kyōichi, retired professor of Korean archaeology at Kyoto University who passed away on May 15 2011, at the age of 103, was an inspiring figure who urged me to write this book. He was the last Japanese director of the former Colonial Government Museum, whose collections were turned over to the new Korean director, Kim Chae-wŏn (1909–92) following the liberation of Korea on August 1945 (for more about this, see the conclusion). In April 2001, despite his advanced age of ninety-four, Arimitsu agreed to be interviewed. Professor Yoshii Hideo of Kyoto University and the members of the Mokuyō Club played a critical role in Arimitsu's agreeing to the interview. They also participated in our question-and-answer session, which was subsequently summarized in volume ten of the *Nihon kōkogakushi kenkyū* (Mokuyō Club 2003, 3–30). During our three-hour session, Arimitsu responded to all of my inquiries with good humor and incredible recall regarding the daily activities of a field archaeologist in the 1930s. His many vivid recollections and anecdotes were remarkable in detail, and he provided me with personal insights concerning the inner workings of the Committee on Korean Antiquities, museum management, and staffing that are unattainable through published colonial sources.

Kim Ri-na, the daughter of Kim Chae-wŏn (1909–90), the first director of the National Museum of Korea (1945–70) and now a retired professor of Hongik University's Department of Art History in Seoul, was also one of my informants. She inherited her father's archives, and I interviewed her informally on two separate occasions regarding her father's life and career. The first time was in Kyoto in February 2000 at a publication party celebrating Arimitsu's very belated excavation report of two tombs he excavated in Kyŏngju in the early 1930s. The party was organized by UNESCO's Tokyo office and the Tōyō Bunkō (Oriental Library). The second time was in March 2001 at the international symposium "Establishing a Discipline: The Past, Present, and Future of Korean Art History" cosponsored by the Los Angeles County Museum and the University of California, Los Angeles.

I feel privileged to call professor Yoshii Hideo of Kyoto University's Department of Archaeology a good friend and colleague. He invited me to his laboratory as a Japan Foundation visiting foreign researcher for six months, from August 2004 to February 2005. Although he began his archaeological career as a specialist of the Tumulus, or Kofun, period in Japan, by sheer luck he also shares my interest in the intellectual history of archaeology. In my mind, Yoshii is indeed a worthy successor to the long line of Kyoto University–trained luminaries who have guided Japan's oldest department of archaeology, which was founded by Hamada Kōsaku (1881–1938) in 1910. As curator of the university museum archaeological lab collections and archives dating back to the early Taishō period, Yoshii obtained permission for me to photograph many original maps, illustrations, and teaching collections dating from the museum's early days. Yoshii also introduced me to his university library collections, which house Japan's largest and oldest archaeological archives, covering two centuries' worth of field excavation reports, ranging from Troy (Heinrich Schliemann) to India (James Ferguson) to the Far Eastern Archaeological Society (Tōhō Kōkogaku Gakkai). Browsing through the stacks in the winter of 2004–5 was a privilege and a joy and gave me a rare glimpse into the truly international scope of prewar Japanese archaeology.

In Tokyo, the staff and research curators at the Tokyo National Research Institute of Cultural Properties (Tōbunken), especially Hiroyuki Suzuki and Emiko Yamanishi, were instrumental in helping me search for the colonial-era photographs, postcards, and art catalogues I consulted for this book. At the University of Tokyo Institute of Oriental Culture, professor Hirase Takao, and Inoue Naomi and Xu Su-bin (Tianjin University Graduate School of Architecture) arranged for me to access the stacks of the closed library so that I could work in the archives of Torii Ryūzō and Sekino Tadashi, and have access to related prewar anthropological and archaeological reports published by the university. In Nara, Walter Edwards, Akira Matsui, and Mitsutani Takumi (Nara Institute of Cultural Properties) were instrumental in alerting me to the groundbreaking research, dating methods, conservation techniques, and restoration activities conducted over the years at the Nara Institute of Cultural Properties. Finally, I am deeply indebted to my friend and colleague, Taylor Atkins (Northern Illinois University), whose close reading of my manuscript helped make this book a reality.

Several grant agencies, research institutions, and people made the writing and the publication of the manuscript possible. First, research funds and salaries received from two separate Nichibunken visiting professorships (2000–2001 and 2007–8) and the Japan Foundation Senior Grant (2004–5) supported my travel and research to museums, monuments, and archives in Japan. Second, a Korea Foundation Advanced Research Grant (2004) paid for student assistants for cataloguing and scanning, and for preparing the digital artwork and bibliography needed for the publication of the manuscript. Third, the Academy of Korean Studies and the Northeast Asia Council of the Association of Asian Studies provided publications subventions for the book's production.

I also want to thank my former students and graduate students, especially Shantoba Carew, David Hull, and Amelia Bowen, for their research and computer skills. Amy Feng at Johns Hopkins University came to my aid in packing many heavy boxes of books when I was leaving my apartment in Tokyo one cold winter, for which I will be eternally grateful. During the final stages of revisions in 2010, Yuri Takahashi was especially helpful with preparing the Excel tables and charts. At the University of California Instructional Development Office, I want to thank Dottie McClaren, who assisted me with my digital maps.

Last, but not least, I want to thank the staff at the Harvard University libraries—Harvard/Yenching, Houghton, Tozzer, Rubel, and Widener—who over the years were invaluable in assisting me with tracking down obscure reports, maps, newsletters, and unpublished resources. Alain Bain, the former archivist and director of the Archives Division, Smithsonian Institution Archives, on special detail to the National Anthropological Archives, deserves credit for alerting me to the existence of the Eugene I. Knez papers. In Korea, I would also like to express my appreciation to the staff of the Korean Tourism Organization Office library and the Ministry of Culture and Tourism Annex library. Professor Kim Su-ta'e (History Department at Ch'ungnam University) deserves special mention, since he was the first to encourage me to study Korean history when I was a college freshman at Sŏgang University. He also played a valuable role in me getting access to in-house reports and archives produced by the Cultural Heritage Administration (CHA).

The following are the many conference sponsors, mentors, and colleagues who have provided me with opportunities to present many of my research ideas in their formative stages. Listed here are individuals and institutions in alphabetical order: Noriko Aso (University of California Santa Cruz); Lionel Barbiz (formerly Maison Franco-Japonaise, Tokyo, now University of Sydney); Gina Barnes (Society of East Asian Archaeology); Mark Byington (Harvard University Early Korea Institute); Ellie Choi (formerly Harvard University Korea Institute and currently at Cornell University); Getty Research Institute, Los Angeles; Wu Hung and Katherine Mino (University of Chicago Art Institute); Laurel Kendall (Museum of Natural History, New York); Burglind Jungman and Timothy Tangherlini (University of California, Los Angeles); Moon Ok-pyo (Academy of Korean Studies); Daniel Shapiro (International Journal of Cultural Properties); Indra Sengupta (German Historical Institute, London); Ned Shultz (Center for Korean Studies, University of Hawai'i); Social Science Research Council (New York); Xu Su-bin (Tianjin University Graduate School of Architecture); Sem Vermeesh (Kyujangak Institute, Seoul National University); Yamamoto Chie (Kyoto Japan Foundation Office); and Yamanishi Emiko (Tokyo National Research Institute of Cultural Properties).

Arguments developed in chapters 4, 5, and 6 first appeared in the following publications: "Collecting Japan's Antiquity in Colonial Korea: The Tokyo Anthropological Society and the Cultural Comparative Perspective," *Moving Objects: Time, Space, and Context*, 57–72, Twenty-Sixth

International Symposium on the Preservation of Cultural Property Series, sponsored by the Tokyo National Research Institute of Cultural Properties; "Sinhwasŏk kot'o pogwŏn ŭl wihan yujŏk t'amsaek (Reclaiming the ruins of imagined imperial terrains: Meiji archaeology and art historical surveys in the Korean Peninsula [1900–1916])," *Ilbon ŭi palmyŏng kwa kŭndae* (The discovery of "Japan" and modernity), 247–84; and "Travel Guides to the Empire: The Production of Tourist Images in Colonial Korea," in conference volume *Consuming Korean Tradition in Early and Late Modernity*, ed. by Laurel Kendall (Honolulu: University of Hawai'i Press), 67–87.

PREFACE

Critical Perspectives on Archaeology, Heritage, and Tourism

Neither by the public, nor by those who have the care of the public monuments, is the true meaning of *restoration* understood. It means the most total destruction which a building can suffer: a destruction out of which no remnants can be gathered: a destruction accompanied by a false description of the thing destroyed. Do not let us deceive ourselves in this important matter; it is impossible to raise the dead, to restore anything that has ever been great or beautiful in architecture.

—John Ruskin, *The Seven Lamps of Architecture* (Roth et al. 1997, 18)

The finding of an object is in fact a refinding of it.

—Sigmund Freud, cited in *Irresistible Decay: Ruins Reclaimed* (Roth et al. 1997, 41)

The term "heritage" is conventionally used in the contemporary world by international organizations such as the United Nations Educational, Scientific, and Cultural Organization's (UNESCO) World Heritage Committee, as well as by national heritage industries (for example, heritage centers, parks, museums, products, and so on), to refer to a nation's or a people's past that has been passed on in the sense of an "inheritance." So, it is possible to have a built heritage, a natural heritage, or a cultural heritage.[1] The general understanding is that "heritage" means more than just history; it's a sense of past events or old objects that belong, can be inherited, and are therefore relevant to the present (Baker 1988, 141). According to the first article of the Convention Concerning the Protection of the World Cultural and Natural Heritage, UNESCO lists the world's "cultural heritage" as (1) "monuments: architectural works, works of monumental sculpture and painting, elements or structures of an archaeological nature, inscriptions, cave dwellings and combinations of features, which are of outstanding universal value from the point of view of history, art or science;" (2) "groups of buildings: groups of separate or connected buildings which, because of their architecture, their homogeneity or their place in the landscape, are of outstanding universal value from the point of view of history, art or science;" and (3) "sites: works of man or the combined works of nature and man, and areas including archaeological sites which are of outstanding universal value from the historical, aesthetic, ethnological or anthropological point of view."

Article two of the convention defines "natural heritage" as: (1) "natural features consisting of physical and biological formations or groups of such formations, which are of outstanding universal value from the aesthetic or scientific point of view;" (2) "geological and physiographical formations and precisely delineated areas which constitute the habitat of threatened species of animals and plants of outstanding universal value from the point of view of science or conservation;" and (3) "natural sites or precisely delineated natural areas of outstanding universal value from the point of view of science, conservation or natural beauty."[2]

The convention document goes on to emphasize the many historical, scientific, and environmental reasons why organizations, governments, and citizens should make a concerted effort to protect and conserve the heritage categories designated above for the benefit of all mankind. However, in today's postmodern society, the most conspicuous aspect of the "heritage industry" is that it has not only come to represent a nation's past collective identity, but it is situated at the forefront of the hyperconsumerists' tourist industry characterized by image making, packaging, and marketing (Rowan, Yorke, and Baram 2004; Selwyn 1996). Beginning in the 1970s, affordable jet travel made tourism available to the masses, who could now afford to fly to destinations to experience alpine scenery, adventure safaris, and ancient ruins next to leisure resorts in virtually every corner of the globe, from the mountains of Switzerland to the glaciers of Alaska and Antarctica (MacCannell 1999; Zimmer 1998). Consequently, national cultural administrative organizations, tourism boards, and developers are more invested than ever before in the training of specialists and bureaucrats dedicated to the protection, preservation, and promotion to a world audience of "authentic" natural and cultural assets. At many universities worldwide, cultural resource management (CRM), the hospitality industry, and tourism have all become very popular majors, with faculty teaching marketing strategies, business marketing, hotel management, resort development, and anthropology (V. Smith 1977).

The explosive growth in the symbolic, educational, and commercial value of heritage monuments has also paralleled the formation of preservation trusts, museums, research institutions, and local historical societies, which are now found in all communities, large and small. These museums, committees, and organizations, both public and private, allocate the bulk of their resources, man power, and funds to study, preserve, and restore historical landmarks for both domestic and international audiences (Hevia 2001). Currently, this notion of stewardship and the "shared" cultural heritage of humanity, in which all of the world's citizens are responsible for the protection and conservation of man-made and natural heritage, reflects the core mission of the UNESCO Convention Concerning the Protection of Cultural and Natural World Heritage (Stone and Molyneaux 1994; World Heritage Committee 1993). When the UNESCO convention was first adopted in 1972, the committee members' most immediate concern was to prevent the further destruction of natural and cultural monuments threatened by economic and industrial development, for example, salvaging Egyptian temple sites from inundation due to construction of the Aswan High Dam. However, over the decades, national cultural bureaucracies and their representatives have competed fiercely to be included on the prestigious list of World Heritage monuments, since the World Heritage logo confers instant celebrity status and the badge of authenticity necessary to market heritage sites to tourists and to international investors and developers.[3]

The staggering number of 962 World Heritage properties currently listed on the home page of the World Heritage Centre demonstrates the successful lobbying efforts of the UNESCO commissions' national representatives, who sponsor annual open workshops at designated World Heritage Cities, such as Cardigan, Columbia; Chiengmai, Thailand; and Kyŏngju, South

Korea (World Heritage Committee 1993). International heritage workshops are organized by the members of the International Council on Monuments and Sites, or ICOMOS, an organization made up of archaeologists, art historians, architects, and museum curators, as well as bureaucrats and professionals working in the fields of CRM. Media companies from popular magazines such as *National Geographic* and *Smithsonian,* and cable networks such as the Discovery Channel and the History Channel, are also actively engaged in raising the profile of well-funded public campaigns promoting the future potential of nominated sites—from Nepal's "holiest" shrines to Mayan ruins to numerous folk villages in the Republic of Korea—to lure tourists to their regional destinations.[4]

With the emergence of what have been called the "dragon" and "tiger" economies of Hong Kong, Singapore, the Republic of Korea, Taiwan, Thailand, Malaysia, and India—and, recently, the People's Republic of China—these nations' tourist destinations have become the most anticipated growth area for attracting global capital investments, municipal funds, and real estate developers (Picard and Wood 1997; T. Oakes 1997). Today, many Asian governments are ever eager to attract foreign investors and visitors to remote and inaccessible locations in order to build airports, theme parks, resort casinos, and shopping malls tailored to the jaded tourist who seeks ever more exotic experiences but is not willing to give up the familiar creature comforts offered by hotel chains, from the Holiday Inn to more luxurious establishments such as the Grand Hyatt and InterContinental Hotels. At the same time, the major stumbling block for the governments of poorer developing countries is finding a way to meet the many UNESCO-mandated conservation guidelines for reporting, monitoring, and maintaining the buffer zones demarcated to preserve the structural integrity of the proposed site from damage and pollution in the case of tourist development.[5] These ICOMOS forums are where local participants and specialists share information and ideas about "sustainable tourism," such as how to resurrect traditional building materials while at the same time adopting new technological improvements to ensure that the historicity, beauty, and authenticity of the monuments are protected against manmade and natural disasters, such as theft, looting, pollution, floods, fires, and too many eager tourists. Today, World Heritage sites are promoted by tourism boards, transportation companies, and travel magazines, as well as e-businesses—not only to sell package tours but also to market the latest movies, fashion, festivals, and international mega-events, such as the 2008 Beijing Olympics.

The close geographic proximity of World Heritage icons such as the Taj Mahal, Angkor, and Borobudur have also made their tourist bureaus quite conscious that they are in constant competition with one another for the same circulating groups of well-heeled tourists (Edensor 1998). This keen awareness of the existence of a neighboring country's potential tourist destination that is at most a three-hour plane ride away is the primary reason that every country has devoted its economic resources to building and promoting unique "heritage destinations" that will stand out. Such national agendas have in recent years spurred the creation of spectacular tourist attractions ranging from the colossal Tomb of China's First Emperor (c. 221 BCE) in Xian, an open-air museum highlighting an ongoing archaeological excavation pit preserved in situ, to the laser-show dioramas of Samurai in battle at Japan's Osaka Castle to Singapore's soaring Jurong Bird Park African Waterfall Aviary—not to mention the transplanted American theme parks, such as the Disneylands in Tokyo and Hong Kong, and Osaka's Universal Studios. The desire to see, experience, and be entertained at an "imagined" ancestral "folk village" (see fig. 1.6) or revel at patriotic war memorials dedicated to real and fictitious heroes and warriors (see figs. 1.1 and 1.2) are not just confined to visiting foreign tourists but are fueled by local citizens' nostalgia and fears that their past cultural traditions—including artistic achievements, village customs, folk religions, and festivals—are rapidly disappearing for good under the onslaught of urbanization, industrialization, and globalization (Hendry 2000a, 2000b; Gluck 1998). And their fears aren't unfounded, since on any given day in metropoles and countrysides throughout Asia, one can encounter old buildings, historical remains, and even whole city blocks being bulldozed to make way for highways, factories, high-rise apartments, and office complexes. Due to the pressures of modern society; in general, government developmental policies have prioritized the building of infrastructure and transportation services, such as rails, freeways, roads, bridges, and airports, over preservation projects. Therefore, in terms of drawing up national legislation, the norm in most countries has been toward transferring private ownership from churches, religious orders, and private estates to state control so that the government can steer the developmental agenda (Handler 1985, 1988).

During the formative stages of cultural properties legislation in the late nineteenth and early twentieth centuries, nationalist ideologues and politicians determined the preservation agenda. Spectacular monuments such as mausoleums, palatial estates, religious sites, churches, fortresses, and battlefields glorifying conquering kings, warriors, saints, and mythical heroes were preserved and restored for historical edification, so as to confer a sense of place in the national and colonial imaginary (Dirks 2001; Lewis 1975; Pelizzari 2003; Schwartz and Ryan 2003, 19–95; A. Smith 1986). In particular, the real or imagined threat of the loss of a nation's heritage is key to understanding the irresistible attraction and emotional pull of archaeological and historical remains (Reid 2002; Roth et al. 1997; Silberman 1982, 1989). This fascination with ruins from antiquity in Europe and the Middle East on the part of the general public dates back to the eighteenth century, when their "picturesque" visages began appearing in landscape paintings, prints, and theatre sets, as well popular romance novels of the day (Beaulieu and Roberts 2002).

The physical documentation of ruins, whether by artists, antiquarians, or photographers, as sketches on paper or as printed photographs (see figs. 3.3, 5.1, 5.3, 5.4, and 5.6), is an act of arresting time to preserve an image of a once-glorious past, reveal the origins of the present, and thereby confer a sense of immortality, belonging, and nostalgia on the beholder (Roth et al. 1997, 25). That is why monumental ruins—the Acropolis, the Pyramids, the Great Wall, Machu Picchu, Notre Dame Cathedral, and Angkor Wat, to name the most prominent few—are today some of the most recognized national icons representing the antiquity, beauty, and cultural patrimony of the world's oldest bygone civilizations.

In Europe, the evolution of the concept of museum treasures and of categories of national heritage paralleled the heyday of territorial, economic, and cultural expansion when empire-building politicians, scientists, merchants, archaeologists, and architects pioneered the establishment of fine arts and ethnographic museums, libraries, botanical gardens, zoos, and the staging of world fairs around the world (Bennett 1995; Barringer and Flyn 1998). By the 1880s, the most successful imperial regimes, represented by the British and French enterprises, as well as small-scale mercantile companies from far-flung colonies such as India and Australia, were sending their most valuable discoveries, arts, curios, and products to international expositions for competitive display and consumption.[6] These products constituted a wide range of natural and raw materials (tea, wool, rubber, cotton), manmade inventions, foods and liquor (wine, Indian tea), arts and crafts, and even live natives peoples brought in for education and entertainment (Geary and Webb 1998; Maxwell 1999). The myriad products were judged by appointed imperial commissioners for their retail merits, such as utilitarian uses, decorative functions, cheap prices, and sheer popularity as recorded by the numbers of curious visitors who visited national pavilions (Briggs 1989; Hoffenberg 2001, 63–98).

At about the same time, national trusts in England, Germany, and France also began commissioning architects and art historians, not only in their own countries but also dispatching them to far-off colonies in Egypt, Palestine, Greece, and India, to survey, map, and collect new discoveries to fill their newly built museums and art galleries (Abu El-Haj 2001; Marchand 1996; Reid 2002). In France, the team members of La Mission Héliographique, who conducted the first systematic surveys of abbeys and churches in 1851, were classically trained architects whose recording methodology involving sketch surveys, line drawings, and photographs left a lasting effect on the selection of which remains were worthy of representing the French national past (Boyer 2003). These aesthetic restoration techniques employed by these architects in the preservation and promotion of France's cultural patrimony would later influence the curriculum and training of painters, architects, art historians, and photographers at academic institutions from America to Japan (N. Murakata 2002; Nihon Kenchiku Gakkai 1972; J. Oakes 2009). Arts education in Europe since the eighteenth century was also dominated by generations of classically trained art historians who insisted that the intensive study of ancient scripts, ruins, sculpture, and objects, preferably from Greece and Rome, was the most useful for artists and architects to advance cultural knowledge as well as their careers (Marchand 1996, xxi). It is not an exaggeration to state that, to this day, "Graecophilia" continues to influence the core curriculum offered by departments of archaeology, architecture, and art history; the methodology of drawing, measuring, and classifying stylistic and period elements in order to date objects, recovered and reconstructed from the ground up, remains predominant (Inoue Shōichi 1994; Marchand 1996; Roth et al. 1997, 7–11).

In academia today, "heritage" studies is distinguished by the very inter-disciplinary nature of the concept, which encompasses intersections of history, archaeology, museology, art history, architecture, music, dance, and natural resources. This multifacted approach dates back to the early 1990s and the publication of two seminal works, *The Invention of Tradition* (Hobsbawm and Ranger 1996) and *Imagined Communities* (Anderson 1992). In the former work, Eric Hobsbawm and Terence Ranger expertly demonstrate how long-accepted tropes, customs, and rituals symboliz-ing "English heritage," such as Scottish tartans and Victorian-era royal parades, were in fact "traditions" invented and marketed by nationalistic politicians, government committees, enterprising merchants, and globe-trotting dealers of the past two centuries. In *Landscape and Identity: Geographies of Nation and Class in England*, Wendy Darby has also demon-strated that, from the inception of English national trusts and legislations in the early nineteenth century, the state has attempted to assert control over public access to potential natural and tourist resources from nature parks, commons, and even mountain hiking trails (Darby 2000, 108–11). Consequently, we now know that the quintessential "English" countryside of wind-swept moors, rolling hills, and lush gardens depicted in some of the most popular historical epics produced by BBC television were and remain highly romanticized landscapes engineered by state-owned media for entertainment, profit, and propaganda.

Similarly, historians of modern Japan have tackled the topic of the inven-tion of national symbols (see figs. 2.8, 3.2, and 7.1) and national traditions set against the background of staged "authenticity" and imperial legitimacy dating back to the early Meiji era (Fujitani 1996; Gluck 1985, 1998). Here, the *Mirror of Modernity* (Vlastos 1998) warrants particular mention, for the volume contributors, including Carol Gluck, Harry Harootonian, Jennifer Robertson, and Jordan Sand, have tackled topics such as the proliferating Edo Village, the national sport of judo, the aesthetics of domestic architec-ture, and the imagined concept of the "folk" propagated by Japan's first pro-fessional folklorist, Yanagita Kunio (1875–1962). In Japanese academia, the subject of the multinational as well as multiinstitutional origins of Japan's modern cultural heritage management policies and its art history as state-endorsed disciplines was pioneered by Takagi Hiroshi of Kyoto University's Humanities Research Institute, or Jinbunken, and Satō Dōshin of the Tokyo University of Fine Arts (Satō 1999; Takagi Hiroshi 1995). Most significantly,

Takagi's scholarship takes a very long historical view in analyzing how the politics of Meiji nation building and emperor image making were critically tied to the rewriting of a mythohistory of the imperial household that were dubbed *banzai ikkei* or "ten thousand successive generations"–old imperial traditions.[7] Takagi's anthology, *A Study of Modern Japanese Imperial Cultural Policies (Kindai tennosei no bunkashiteki kenkyū)*, documents the central role played by the Imperial Household Agency–appointed bureaucrats and specialists who were charged with micromanaging tomb rituals, parades, temples, the registration of national treasures, and the preservation of imperial relics at Shōsōin (Matsuoka 1935; Takagi Hiroshi 2000). Takagi's meticulously researched articles represent a major methodological breakthrough in the field of Japanese historiography in demystifying the inner workings of the secretive Imperial Household Ministry (Kunaishō), which has retained the sole guardianship of Japan's imperial relics and tombs for more than a century (Matsuoka 1935). In this sense, Takagi's approach echoes that of Fujitani's *Splendid Monarchy: Power and Pageantry in Modern Japan*, which exposed how imperial rituals and parades were critical to the legitimization of the Meiji imperial regime and were consecrated by the accession of the fictitious first Emperor Jimmu in mythical times (Fujitani 1996).

In addition, postcolonial studies in the past decade have also focused on how sacred objects, customs, places, aboriginal peoples, and natural landscapes first discovered by colonial-era explorers, collectors, and ethnologists were codified as markers of national patrimony by nation-building politicians, preservation committees, museums, and national and imperial cultural institutions from Afria to the Middle East to India (Barringer and Flynn 1998; Coombes 1994; Dirks 2001; Gupta and Ferguson 2001; Handelman and Handelman 1990). The topic of imperialism and its effect on the political, economic, social, and cultural transformation of former colonies was notably pioneered by the late Edward Said (1935–2003). Said is widely acknowledged as the inspirational figure who created the field of "cross-cultural terrains" of knowledge (Bhaba 1994; Segal 1992; Said 1979, 1993, 1995), an approach that focuses on the discourse about how power relationships have influenced not only the colonized but also the colonizer (Chatterjee 1993; Dirks 2001). In the past decade, prominent authors such as Nadia Abu El-Haj, Mary Louise Pratt, Nicholas Dirks, Catherine Lutz, Jane

Collins, and Winichakul Thongchai have also proposed new and creative ways of dissecting colonial power relationships that have redrawn the geographic, literary, visual, material, ethnic, and cultural boundaries of the imagined past, from Latin America to the Middle East to India to Java to Thailand (Abu El-Haj 2001; Anderson 1992; Dirks 2001; Lutz and Collins 1993; Pratt 1992; Thongchai 1998). Currently, the most-often-cited theoretical contributions are attributed to the Subaltern Studies Group, who have attempted to frame the cultural contexts of European territorial expansion, civilization discourse, and discussions about how the accumulation of colonial knowledge has contributed to national narratives in Asia, Africa, India, China, and South America (Bhaba 1994; Chatterjee 1993; Guha and Spivak 1988; Duara 1995; Prakash 1995). These pioneers have attempted to understand why such disparate groups as Marxist revolutionaries, nation-building politicians, intellectuals, artists, and journalists came to appropriate their colonial forbearers' ruling apparatuses, laws, institutions of learning, and cultures, as well as the transformation of colonial architectural monuments into national tourist spaces (Cohn 1986; Edensor 1998).

Their works have documented that field explorations in the colonies, from India and the Middle East to Africa and the Pacific, also resulted in the accumulation of an entirely different body of knowledge, distinguished from previous sources of travel information recorded by "untrained" observers such as soldiers and missionaries (Pratt 1992). Researchers were now required to document their finds in a systematic manner. The task of trained specialists, usually graduates of a university department or museum staff, was to record the precise locations, descriptions, measurements, and images of remains in order to study the decline of indigenous peoples, as well as the decay or destruction of monuments, using detailed sketches, maps, and photographs (Roth et al. 1997; Pelizzari 2003; Pai 2011). The ostensible purpose, then, was "scientific" documentation in field notes, sketches, maps, and photographs, which usually accompanied the collection of material objects from the field (Coombes 1994; Stocking 1988; Thomas 1994). In order to satisfy government agencies, learned societies, and museums whose operating budgets in many cases depended on the generosity of rich donors and eccentric patrons, field data became a requisite part of reports submitted by explorers and scholars. The necessity of inventorying, preserving, classifying, studying, and exhibiting this vast body of materials was the impetus for the establishment of modern cultural and research institutions and museums dedicated to the study and preservation of "heritage" (Bennett 1995; Chapman 1988; Hooper-Greenhill 1992; Pearce 1991, 1992). Consequently, the specific locations and standing physical structures, as well as their reproductions—either as landscape paintings, architectural line drawings, field notes, photographs, or museum pieces preserved in documented archives and collections—make up today's vast collective of national and global patrimony.

In the early twentieth century, the emerging global tourist industry represented the new vanguard of colonial modernity around the world (Lofgren 1999; MacCannell 1999). The invention of mechanical vehicles such as steamships, railways, and buses capable of transporting hundreds of passengers, combined with the marketing power of national tourist bureaus and commercial travel agencies, were the two main driving forces in the launching of transcontinental and oceanic voyages in the mid-nineteenth century. The opening of the two main transoceanic water routes, the Suez (1867) and Panama (1914) Canals, as well as the introduction of new communications networks, such as telegrams and telephones, also facilitated world circumnavigation. Next to regular and reliable transportation, the introduction of photography and the availability of cheap print media were the other two technological innovations that allowed the mass production of newspapers, maps, guidebooks, and postcards (see figs. 6.2 and 6.3), giving the average consumer a glimpse of far-off lands for the first time (Schwartz and Ryan 2003; Geary and Webb 1998). During the 1860s, with the invention of the portable camera for the amateur, photography became the most important tool to record, catalogue, and arrange peoples, architectural remains, and objects as "empirical evidence" in the classification of the ethnographic "Other" (E. Edwards 1992; Maxwell 1999). The expansion of European colonies to every corner of the globe also inspired the brave amateur to make expeditions to unexplored terrain in order to record permanent images of yet undiscovered peoples and exotic places, and in search of adventure, romance, fame, and profit (Ryan 1997).

The great photographs taken by both commercial photographers and anthropologists that were printed in academic field reports and museum catalogues were often reproduced and repackaged as postcards and popular illustrated magazines such as *National Geographic* (Geary and Webb 1998;

Lutz and Collins 1993). Historians of orientalism have pointed out that sociopolitical conditions that are highly dependent upon the changing fashions, tastes, and collecting behaviors of a few well-heeled and eccentric travelers, writers, artists, and globe-trotting curio dealers and collectors have also influenced the global spread of "orientalists" aesthetics from England to Japan (Beaulieu and Roberts 2002; Bourdieu 1984; Brandt 1997; Christ 2000; Guth 2000; Sand 2000; Takagi Yōko 2002). The late nineteenth century's fascination with paintings and postcard images of the "noble naked male savages" and "desirable dancing island women" living at the margins of their empires in Africa, the Middle East, the South Pacific, the Americas, and Asia have thus left us an enduring legacy of "who" and "what" continue to be objectified as vanishing cultures and races on the verge of extinction (Desmond 1999; Jackson 1992; Yoshida and Mack 1997). Among academics, archaeologists, and anthropologists, art historians in the past century have exerted the most influence on who and what have been selected as the "Exotic Other" by the camera's eye (E. Edwards 1992; Pai 2009). This is because Victorian-era field researchers operated under the assumption that the more "authentic" and "antiquated" remains of man's past were to be found in the newly discovered remote lands in the far corners of Africa, India, South America, and the Pacific, where "native" peoples incapable of progress lived a "timeless" existence (Stocking 1985, 1988, 1991).

By the early twentieth century, postcards, posters, and guidebooks portraying panaromic views of decaying cairns, castles, and churches framed by vistas of majestic mountains, valleys, and waterfalls were distributed worldwide by commercial photographers, the print media, world fair organizers, and the leisure tourist industry to promote travel to the masses (Cook 1938, 1998; Geary and Webb 1998; Tomita 2005). The familiar images of natives posed among ruins of ancient civilizations—for instance, Balinese court dancers framed by red temple gates, and beautiful courtesans strolling amid palace gardens (see fig. 6.4)—have thus become the most instantly recognizable tangible symbols of antiquity, civilizational continuity, and national identity. The transformation of ruins into national markers for display and consumption, therefore, relied on the sites' physical monumentality, their visualty, and the aesthetic appeal of decay and destruction (see figs. 5.3 and 5.6). Thus, in the past two centuries, ruins of antiquity and their ubiquitous images have demarcated the geographic, cultural, and natural boundaries of national tourist landscapes.[8]

Following World War II, many nations and cities in Europe and the war-torn former colonies were faced with widespread physical devastation of the natural and cultural landscapes. With few remaining intact monuments or historical urban centers that had escaped firebombings, scavengers, and looters, cultural resource management became an integral component of long-range economic development plans at all levels of government and municipalities, determining the profile of CRM as we know it today (Cleere 1989, 20). By far the majority of national heritage management services, from national museums to local preservation societies, are now compelled by legal, political, and budget constraints to operate through some form of selection process, especially at large-scale archaeological sites, since all recognize that they cannot protect and preserve everything. National trusts and preservation societies have thus asked specialists to come up with standardized systems for selecting, ranking, and registering which cultural properties to destroy, preserve, or promote as World Heritage sites. Of all of the innumerable heritage categories subject to the regulations of governments and of international bodies such as ICOMOS, in most areas of the world archaeological heritage management laws have had the longest and most complex history and, consequently, best reflect the cultural, political, and economic trajectories unique to each nation's heritage management history (Cleere 1989).

As before, ruins and relics as objects of study as well as objects of collection, contemplation, and exhibition continue to be given top priority by national governments and archaeologists in particular. This is because the discipline of archaeology and its practice of field excavations are widely perceived as "scientific efforts to unearth the past" (Hodder, et al. 1995). From the perspective of the individual archaeologist, one's reputation, authority, and even pocketbook are dependent on deciphering buried objects and interpreting their origins, meanings, and functions for a public composed of educated citizens, students, museum visitors, tourists, and, increasingly, the media (as we have recently witnessed with the notorious case of the powerful former minister of antiquities for Egypt, Zahi Hawass [b.1947]). Respected as authorities and speakers for the ancient past, experts rely on years of intensive field training in one world area or cultural phase, which qualifies them to identify, dig up, and plot material artifacts, archaeological sites, and objects across the landscape, to be recorded in excavation reports, photographs, and survey maps. Therefore, of all field specialists, archaeologists and art historians serving on national cultural committees, museums, and research institutions dedicated to the identification, preservation, and reconstruction of the past have exerted the greatest influence on designing and implementing national preservation laws governing standards of beauty, authenticity, and antiquity around the world.

Consequently, for over two centuries, academic institutions, colonial governments, rich patrons, imperial museums, and, increasingly, media companies from the National Geographic, Discovery, and History Channels have funded or supported expensive expeditions led by professional archaeologists and art historians whose main job is to authenticate, explain, and reconstruct remnants of past nations and ethnic groups for public consumption and education (Kohl and Fawcett 1995; Shennan 1989; Stone and Molyneaux 1994). This continuing fascination and romance with archaeological records and its practitioners also derives from the widely held assumption on the part of the public that ruins constitute the remnants of past nations and ethnic groups to be identified and plotted across the landscape as "distinctly demarcated archaeological cultures" (Abu El-Haj 2001, 3). At the same time, the critical mission of the recovery of a heritage has been complicated by the question of ownership, since many of the world's leading institutions—such as the Royal Anthropological Institute, the British Museum, the Louvre, and the Smithsonian—have inherited their core collections from eccentric donors, enterprising businessmen, and rapacious plunderers masquerading as scientists and scholars.

Today, the complex job of unravelling the social, cultural, and historical biographies of objects and monuments has been entrusted to archaeologists, curators, and cultural anthropologists, who are all confronted with the immense task of sorting through untold number of boxes of specimens, materials, arts, and visual collections (Akazawa 1991, 1992; Appadurai 1986). The task of establishing the provenance, context, and dates of discovery, and discovering by what means and dubious channels ownership was transferred, determines what can be taken out of storage and restored for public viewing (E. Edwards 1996). This is because, in contrast to past practices, the main goal of the curating is not only to ensure the authenticity of the object but also to confirm that it was not looted or illegally obtained, and thus must be returned to its rightful owners (Brown 2003; O'Keefe 1999; Messenger 1989). In the process of reconstructing the biography of objects and collections, museum historians and anthropologists have proven beyond a doubt that the search for "scientific data" from curios, natural specimens, photographs, and souvenirs in the past two centuries has advanced the documentation of selected primitive peoples and archaeological civilizations from Africa to Asia to the South Pacific (Clifford and Marcus 1986; Coombes 1994; Pai 2009; Thomas 1994). It is therefore not a coincidence that the fields of ethnography and archaeology, which benefited most from nineteenth-century European, North American, Russian, and Japanese territorial expansion and colonial domination, have left us an indelible cultural, visual, and material legacy (Minpaku 1990; Stocking 1991; Walraven 1999; Yoshida and Mack 1997).

In the continuing effort to build up a nation's sense of solidarity and belonging, newly formed postwar national regimes have also continued to rely on the so-called archaeological record in the rewriting of a nation's ethnic and cultural identity (Abu El-Haj 2001; Lewis 1975; Pai 2000; Reid 2002; Silberman 1982, 1989; Shennan 1989). The identification and ownership of art and artifacts recovered from the ground, therefore, have been and remain to this day the most contested symbols of nationhood. Thus, for more than two centuries the empirical search for a "unique" prehistoric past and an unbroken ethnic and cultural continuity is the most powerful impetus for archaeological and ethnographic field surveys around the world.

Despite the exponential growth in the multiplicity of perspectives involved—from human rights issues, economic arguments, environmental protection, and conflict between development and heritage preservation—it is unfortunate that the majority of case studies so far have been confined to European states and their former colonies. In contrast, this book is devoted to contextualizing the ethnographic, archaeological, and heritage-related knowledge produced in Japan and Korea, the two most oft-cited model nations manifesting the successes of centralized management of heritage resources outside of Europe. For more than a century, well-preserved Buddhist monuments, imperial tombs, and palatial remains from Nara, Kyoto, and Kyŏngju have not only attracted scholars, conservators, and heritage specialists, but also developers, vendors, movie producers, and millions of tourists, both domestic and foreign. The immense national pride of ownership that citizens of Japan and Korean take in their cultural institutions, museums, and thousands of registered national, municipal, and provincial cultural properties can be seen in the record attendance whenever there are special exhibitions featuring national treasures (see fig. 7.1). However, no study in any language has analyzed how concepts of race and ethnicity, categories of antiquities, and the ranking of treasures, historical sites, and monuments were codified through national or colonial legislation, fine art museums' collections or inventories, or tourist publications in an East Asian regional context.

While both Korean states have used art objects and archaeological monuments to depict themselves as the sole rightful heir to a glorious Korean past, the chapters that follow will only address the case of Republic of Korea and its Cultural Heritage Administration (Munhwajae Ch'ŏng, hereafter CHA) ministry, formerly known as the Office of Cultural Properties (Munhwajae Kwalliguk, hereafter KSMKG), whose data sources are more reliable.[9] The goal of this study is to unravel how Japanese racial, cultural, and tourist policies, driven by ideologies of nationalism, mercantilism, and imperialism, have determined the fate of art and of the archaeological remains currently displayed in public and private museums, art galleries, and tourist sites in the Republic of Korea as well as Japan. I believe that this is the first attempt to address one of the most culturally sensitive and still politically charged topics of postwar Korea-Japan diplomatic relations— that is, the contested history of shared museum treasures and cultural properties.

The first part of the book focuses on prewar Japan because it was the first modern nation in the region to emulate European imperial powers by actively staging world fairs (see figs. 2.1, 2.2, and 2.3), building museums, conducting art and archaeological surveys, promulgating national treasure laws, and developing a modern tourist industry (Japan Bunkachō 1960; Leheny 1998; Shiina Shintarō 1977). In a remarkably short and productive period of three decades, from 1871 to 1900 (see table 4), the Imperial Household Ministry, the Education Ministry, and the Home Ministry worked together to set up a nationwide heritage management bureaucracy and network of three imperial museums (Kuroita Hakushi Kinenkai 1953;

Tanaka 1982; Yoshida Kenji 2001). A new generation of imperial university-educated bureaucrats and scholars were appointed to coordinate site reports, material collections, and guide art and architectural preservation activities at research institutions, prefectural offices, local police stations, and museums. Thus, beginning in the early Meiji era, only state-sanctioned institutions were permitted to conduct archaeological surveys and excavations, register treasures, and manage buried properties throughout the prefectures of Japan. These three decades also overlapped with the emergence of Japan not only as a modern nation but also an unrivalled military and naval power in Northeast Asia (Jansen 1995).

Following its victories in the Sino-Japanese (1894–95) and Russo-Japanese (1904–5) Wars, the newly acquired colonies in Taiwan, on the Liaodong peninsula, and on the Korean peninsula (see tables 5 and 6) also became the sites of archaeological and anthropological fieldwork, art collections, and museum building, as well as being developed as tourist destinations (Pai 2006, 2009, 2010a, 2010b, 2011). The following narrative thus takes a long view of the major ideological, economic, and political agendas that have framed the development of preservationist legislation, cultural institutions, and field disciplines in the past one hundred and fifty years. Its focus is mainly on but not confined to the creation of legal standards and bureaucratic procedures for authenticating, classifying, and ranking heritage remains, museum antiquities, and tourist sites (*meishō*) in contemporary South Korea, and traces their institutional, aesthetic, and disciplinary genealogies back to the Meiji-era expansion into Korea in the 1900s.

Here, an explanatory note on the organization and presentation of archival sources cited and listed in the reference material is necessary. As with most surviving CRM data today, the material collections, annual administrative reports, inventories, excavations, exhibitions, and photographic catalogues consulted for this work were for the most part produced and circulated by museums, national cultural research institutions, tourism boards, and heritage committees. As a result, they are now housed at former imperial university libraries and national cultural research institutions in Japan and in the Republic of Korea. The arrangement of the chapters reflects the author's approach to organizing this vast body of accumulated heritage resource materials with four main archival goals in mind: the framing of institutional histories; the processes of documentation; the disciplinary goals and classificatory agendas of prominent preservationists; and the development of heritage tourism.

In each chapter, if only in a cursory manner, I have attempted to explain the institutional backgrounds of national preservation committees, learned societies, museums, exposition committees, preservation trusts, and individual scholars whose collecting and taxonomic efforts have determined the preservation agenda. For major national institutions, the discussion has relied on primary sources such as in-house records and museum histories penned by resident experts and curatorial staff (Ch'oe Sŏk-yŏng 2001; Kaneko Atsushi 2001; Shiina Noritaka 1988, 1989). The main institutional sources consulted are listed here (in chronological order): exposition catalogues published or reprinted by nationally sanctioned sponsors (e.g., Alcock 1878; Japan-British Exposition 1911); official museum chronicles published by the Tokyo National Museum (Former Imperial Museum of Japan or Tokyo Teishitsu Hakubutsukan) commemorating its bicentennial (Tokyo Teishitsu Hakubutsukan 1938), its centennial in 1976, and its hundred and twentieth anniversary in 1992 (Tokyo Kokuritsu Hakubutsukan 1976, 1992), as well as Japan's Cultural Ministry or Bunkachō (Tanaka 1982); Handbooks, manuals, and national treasures registries published by the Ministry of Culture (Japan Bunkachō 1960, 1997). Many of these institutions' current publications are accessible now online at http://www. bunka.go.jp. For the history of the Tokyo Anthropological Society, I have consulted the early issues of the Tokyo Anthropological Society journals (Tokyo Jinrui Gakkai), which began publishing in 1886 and continues to this day.

First, for the postwar history of the National Museum of Korea and the Office of Cultural Properties, I relied on three main sources: the thirty-year history of the Republic of Korea's Ministry of Culture and Information (Korea [South] KS Munhwakongbopu 1979); the CHA monthly newsletter series and journal *Munhwajae* (1965–present); and the monthly newsletters of the National Museum of Korea (Korea [South] Kungnip Chungang Pangmulgwan 1973–present), as well as online resources from annual meeting reports, national registries, and the home page of the Cultural Heritage Administration, or CHA, at http://www.cha.go.kr/.

Second, to assess the documentation process and reconstruct case studies, I consulted excavation reports, maps, photographs, personal correspondence, and cultural properties' inventories and rankings submitted by state-appointed field specialists. The cataloguing of many colonial-era survey records are still in progress, being carried out by historians, archaeologists, and architectural historians based at Tokyo University, Kyoto University, the Nara Institute of Cultural Properties, and the National Museum of Korea. For example, the bulk of the original Meiji-era architectural survey sketches, photographs, and restoration data recorded by Sekino Tadashi (1868–1935) are archived at his alma mater, the Tokyo University Museum and the architecture department library (Fujii et al. 2005; Shimizu 2003). Sekino's architectural plans and standardized forms for registering locations, dimensions, age, states of preservation or decay, and preservation methods remain invaluable today for "authentication" and restoration purposes.[10]

Third, to understand the disciplinary goals and collecting agendas of art historians, archaeologists, and collectors, I have consulted the personal archives left by Ernest Fenollosa (1853–1908) and his former student Okakura Kakuzō (or Tenshin, 1863–1913), and the diaries of Edward Morse (1838–1925), the three towering figures (see fig. 2.4) in the annals of Meiji-era connoisseurship. Fenollosa's manuscripts are now housed at his alma mater Harvard University's Houghton Library. For Japanese-language sources, I have relied on the anthologies compiled by Yamaguchi Seiichi (1982) and Murakata Akiko (1980, 1982a, 1982b), whose studies of Fenollosa's career include Japanese translations of unpublished handwritten lecture notes, covering a broad range of topics, from art appreciation to the relationships between art and society, nature, literature, and poetry.[11]

Finally, my analysis of the heritage and tourist industry depends on a wide array of guidebooks, tourist maps, pamphlets, postcards, and exhibition catalogues produced for the general public, which, in addition to museum treasures, souvenir objects, ethnographic images (*fūzoku shashin*), and famous tourist destinations (*meishō*), have played a vital role in the dissemination of knowledge about the heritage of Korea. Due to the sheer number of players and producers, including public and private transportation companies that were actively engaged in promoting the heritage and tourist trade, chapter 6 concentrates on only a handful of the most widely circulated photo albums, art catalogues, travel guides, and

postcards dating from the 1920s and 1930s. I have also consulted publications issued by corporations such as the Bank of Chōsen (Chōsen Sōtokufu,
Chōsen Ginkō 1919), the Japan Tourist Bureau (Japan Nihon Kōtsu Kōsha;
see fig. 6.1), and the South Manchuria Railroad Company (SMR, Minami
Tetsudō Kabushiki Kaisha), all of which were actively involved in the
financing and development of the tourist industry throughout the empire.
This mass-produced tourist literature and visual media, which show off the
decaying ruins of Buddhist temple caves, royal tombs, prehistoric dolmens,
and shell mounds, are significant because they were the first to alert the
outside world to the existence of thousand-year-old ruins in Korea (Pai
2010a, 2010b, 2011).

Last, but not least, it is important to note here that, despite the millions
of train schedules, pamphlets, and guidebooks estimated to have been distributed at major piers, train stations, and department stores throughout
the empire, only a minute fraction survive today, in private and library collections. This is because tourist literature as a paper medium was by nature
a disposable consumer item. Consequently, the items most likely to have
been preserved in research libraries, personal collections, and museum
archives in Japan, Korea, and the United States have tended to be sturdy
pocket guidebooks or attractive postcards that were collected as souvenirs
of trips and commemorative events (Haraguchi 2002; Hayashi 2004a,
2004b). I also want to emphasize here that all of the CRM data and tourist
media sources from the colonial era I have been able to track down so far
were printed either in Japanese or in Western languages (English, French,
Russian, or German), indicating that the colonial-era tourist industry was
mainly interested in attracting foreigners with deep pockets. I am assum-
ing that the absence of any Korean-language tourist brochures meant that
by the late 1920s, the new generations of assimilated (*dōka*) colonized subjects—which included resident settlers, school children (see fig. 6.7), and
soldiers (both of the latter were admitted free of charge at museums)—were
already familiar with the tourist regulations and manners to be observed
in public spaces.

The final chapter concludes with a discussion of the contentious debates
surrounding the question "Who is to blame for the plunder of Korean
treasures?" and the unresolved issues of the "return of cultural treasures,"
which have hindered the normalization of post–World War II bilateral rela-

tions between the Republic of Korea and Japan. My discussion is mainly based on interviews, personal correspondence, and published autobiographies of the intertwined careers of three key figures who salvaged Korea's museum treasures and monuments during the chaotic period encompassing the surrender of Japan (August 15, 1945), the arrival of American occupation forces, and the end of the Korean War in 1953. These are the former Japanese director of the Government-General of Chōsen Museum (CST; Chōsen Sōtokufu Hakubutsukan), Arimitsu Kyōichi (1907–2011); the first Korean director of the National Museum of Korea (Kungnip Chungang Pangmulgwan), Kim Chae-wŏn (1909–90); and Eugene Knez (1916–2010), a young army captain who served as liason between the Ministry of Education and US Armed Forces in Korea (USAMGIK). It is generally unknown outside of museum staff circles that the trio helped salvage and protect tens of thousands of CST Museum artifact collections under wartime conditions following the evacuations of Seoul, the invading armies, and the repeated bombings between 1945–53. The book's aim is to demonstrate that the selection process of designating national treasures, ethnic categories, and tourist destinations in Japan and Korea was never a neutral activity but rather one driven by overlapping and competing political, social, and economic imperatives such as nation building, territorial claims, civilizing missions, curatorial schemes, and the promotion of diplomacy, trade, and commerce.

CONVENTIONS

The following conventions regarding the romanization and translation of proper nouns (including place names, people, events, and institutions, as well as publications) were adopted throughout this book for consistency and historical accuracy:

The names of authors and major historical figures cited in this work follow the Korean/Japanese convention of putting the family names first. The Korean romanization system follows the McCune-Reischauer system and not the current system used by the Republic of Korea. The Japanese romanization convention follows the style sheet of the long-running journal series *Monumenta Nipponica*. Well-known public figures such as Syngman Rhee, Park Chung-hee, and Chun Doo-hwan are given according to their common usage in the media.

For historical accuracy, some famous place names and publication titles—such as Formosa (Taiwan), Keelung (Jilong), Keijō (Seoul), and Dairen (Dalian)—follow early twentieth-century spellings and usage. When first appearing in the text, their current names will be included in brackets. Lesser-known tourist destinations and place names are written as they are currently used in Korea—such as Pusan (J. Fusan), Kyŏngju (J. Keishū), and Taegu (Taikyū)—instead of the names used in the colonial area (given in brackets). Names of historical periods and archaeological entities were kept as close as possible to the forms given in the original colonial-era reports in Japanese; for example, the Han dynasty commandery site of Lelang (in Pinyin) is referred to as Rakurō, the name most often used in colonial-period archaeological literature. When a name first appears in text, the original Chinese or Korean pronunciation is cited in brackets.

For English translations of the names of prewar Japanese colonial institutions, I have relied on Asami Noboru's 1924 work, "The Japanese Colonial Government" (PhD diss., Columbia University). All other translations of original texts and most of the translations of reference titles are my own unless otherwise noted.

Archaeological and art historical dates used throughout this work relied on the following two widely used reference sources:

Yamasaki Shigehisa. 1981. *Chronological Table of Japanese Art.* Tokyo: Geishinsha.
Kim, Wŏl-lyong. 1986. *Han'guk kogohak kaesŏl* (Introduction to Korean Archaeology). 3rd. ed. Seoul: Ilchisa.

For English translations of archaeological vocabulary, I have used these dictionaries:

Kim Kwang-ŏn et al. 2004. *Han'guk munhwa Yong-ŏ sajŏn* (Dictionary of Korean art and archaeology). Seoul: Hallim Ch'ulp'ansa.
Tokyo Bijutsu. 1990. *Wa-ei Taishō Nihon bijutsu yōgo jiten henshū iinkai / A Dictionary of Japanese Art Terms.* Bilingual Japanese and English edition. Tokyo: Tokyo Bijutsu.
Yamamoto Tadanao. 2001. *Eiwa taichō Nihon kōkogaku yōgeiyaku jiden kōhon* (Dictionary of Japanese archaeological terms). Tokyo: Tokyo Bijutsu.

Tables 4, 5, and 6, which document the chronology of Japanese ethnography and archaeology, heritage laws and regulations, and its tourist industry, were compiled by consulting the following resources:

Fujita Ryōsaku. 1933. "Chōsen no koseki chōsa to hozon no enkaku" (The process of the preservation and research of Korean ancient monuments). In *Chōsen sōran* (Korean almanac), 1027–47. Keijō: Chōsen Sōtokufu.

Nihon Kōtsu Kōsha (Japan Tourist Bureau, JTB). 1982. *Nihon kōtsu kōsha nanajūnenshi* (Seventy years of the Japan Tourist Bureau). Tokyo: Nihon Kōtsu Kōsha.

Saitō Tadashi. 2001. *Nihon kōkogakushi nenpyō* (A chronology of Japanese archaeology). Kyoto: Gakuseisha Insatsu, 16–17.

Sasaki Kōmei, ed. 1993. *Torii Ryūzō no mita Ajia* (Asia photographed by Torii Ryūzō). Tokushima: Tokushima Kenritsu Hakubutsukan (Tokushima County Museum) / Ōsaka Kokuritsu Minzoku Hakubutsukan (National Museum of Ethnology). Tokyo: Nakanishi

Tokyo Kokuritsu Hakubutsukan. 1992. *Me de miru hyakunijūnen* (Visual records of the hundred and twenty years of the Tokyo National Museum), appendix, 107–11. Tokyo: Tokyo Bijutsu Publishing.

ABBREVIATIONS

The following abbreviations were used for the most frequently cited institutions, museums, journals, learned societies, and preservation committees for convenience's sake. For major institutions (such as national museums and cultural research organizations), I've adopted the abbreviated usage as spoken by professionals in their respective countries and fields; for example, Tōhaku refers to the Tōkyō Kokuritsu Hakubutsukan (Tokyo National Museum), Nabunken to the Nara Bunkazai Kenkyūjō (National Research Institute of Cultural Properties), and Tōbunken to Tokyo National Research Institute of Cultural Properties. In some cases (such as postwar institutions in the Republic of Korea and Japan), the English language initials on the official website home page has been adopted; for example, NRICP stands for the National Research Institute of Cultural Properties of the Republic of Korea (Kungnip Munhwajae Yŏn'guso). The abbreviations are listed in alphabetical order in the chart below.

CHA	Cultural Heritage Administration (of the Republic of Korea; Munhwajae Ch'ŏng)
CSHKMT	Chōsen Sōtokufu Hōmotsu Koseki Meishō Tennen Kinen Butsu (Committee on the Preservation of Treasures, Ancient Remains, Scenic Places, and Natural Monuments)
CSKCIK	Chōsen Sōtokufu, Koseki Chōsa Iinkai/Kenkyūkai (Committee on the Investigation of Korean Antiquities)
CST-Chōsen Sōtokufu	Government-General Office of Chōsen
CSTTK	Chōsen Sōtokufu Tetsudō Kyoku (Chōsen Sōtokufu Railways)

GGC	Government-General of Korea
JIGR	Japan Imperial Government Railways (Teikoku tetsudō)
JNTO	Japan National Tourism Organization
JTB	Japan Tourist Bureau
KCPIA	Korean Cultural Properties Investigation Administrative Research Association
KS Pangmulkwan	Korea (South) (Kungnip Chung'ang Pangmulgwan National Museum of Korea)
KSMKG	Korea (South) Munhwajae Kwalliguk (Office of Cultural Properties of the Republic of Korea)
KTO	Korean Tourism Organization
MCST	Ministry of Culture, Sports, and Tourism (of the Repubic of Korea)
Nabunken	Nara Bunkazai Kenkyūjō (National Research Institute of Cultural Properties, Japan)
NRICP	National Research Institute of Cultural Properties (Republic of Korea)
NYK	Nippon Yūsen Kaisha (Japan Mail Steamship Company)
SMR	South Manchuria Railroad Company
Tōbunken	Tokyo Bunkazai Kenkyūjō (Tokyo National Research Institute of Cultural Properties)
Tōhaku	Tōkyō Kokuritsu Hakubutsukan (Tokyo National Museum)
TJGK	Tokyo Jinrui Gakkai (Tokyo Anthropological Society)

Heritage Management In Korea and Japan

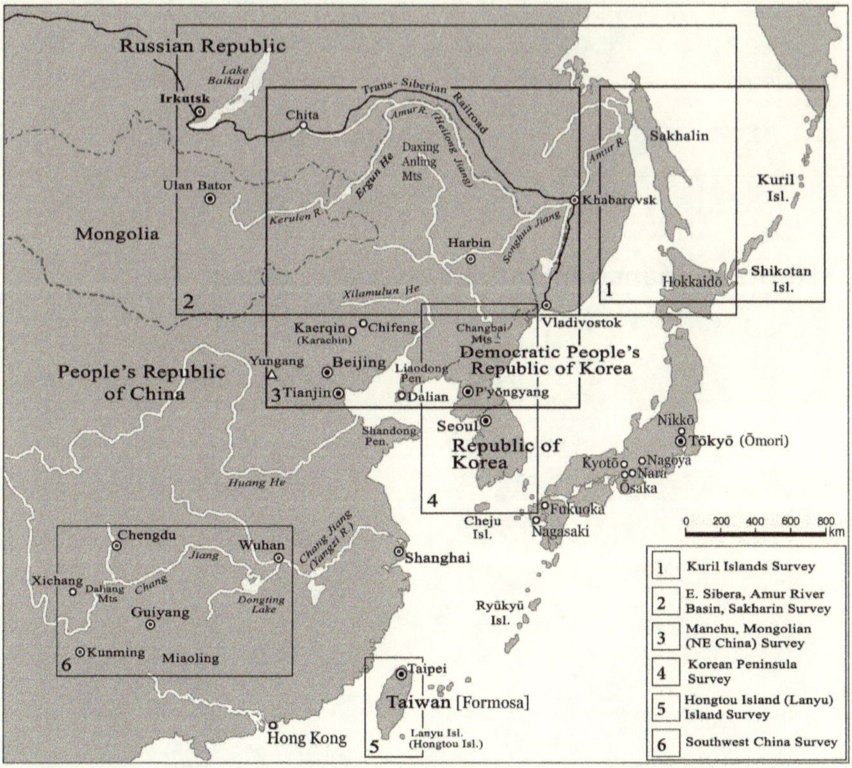

Russian Republic

Lake Baikal

Irkutsk

Chita

Trans-Siberian Railroad

Amur R. (Heilong Jiang)

Daxing Anling Mts

Ergun He

Kerulen R.

Ulan Bator

Mongolia

Songhua Jiang

Harbin

Khabarovsk

Amur R.

Sakhalin

Kuril Isl.

Shikotan Isl.

Hokkaidō

1

Vladivostok

Xilamulun He

2

Kaerqin (Karachin)

Chifeng

Changbai Mts

Democratic People's Republic of Korea

People's Republic of China

Yungang

Beijing

Liaodong Pen.

3 Tianjin

Dalian

P'yŏngyang

Shandong Pen.

Seoul

Republic of Korea

Nikkō

Tōkyō (Ōmori)

Kyoto

Nagoya

Nara

Ōsaka

Huang He

4

Cheju Isl.

Fukuoka

Nagasaki

Chengdu

Wuhan

Chang Jiang (Yangzi R.)

Jiang

Shanghai

Xichang

Dahang Mts

Chang

Dongting Lake

Guiyang

Kunming

Miaoling

6

Ryūkyū Isl.

Taipei

Taiwan [Formosa]

Hong Kong

Lanyu Isl. (Hongtou Isl.)

5

0 200 400 600 800 km

1	Kuril Islands Survey
2	E. Sibera, Amur River Basin, Sakharin Survey
3	Manchu, Mongolian (NE China) Survey
4	Korean Peninsula Survey
5	Hongtou Island (Lanyu) Island Survey
6	Southwest China Survey

MAP 1. Japanese anthropological surveys in Asia, 1895–1911, showing principal areas to which Torii Ryūzō was dispatched by the Tokyo Anthropological Society.

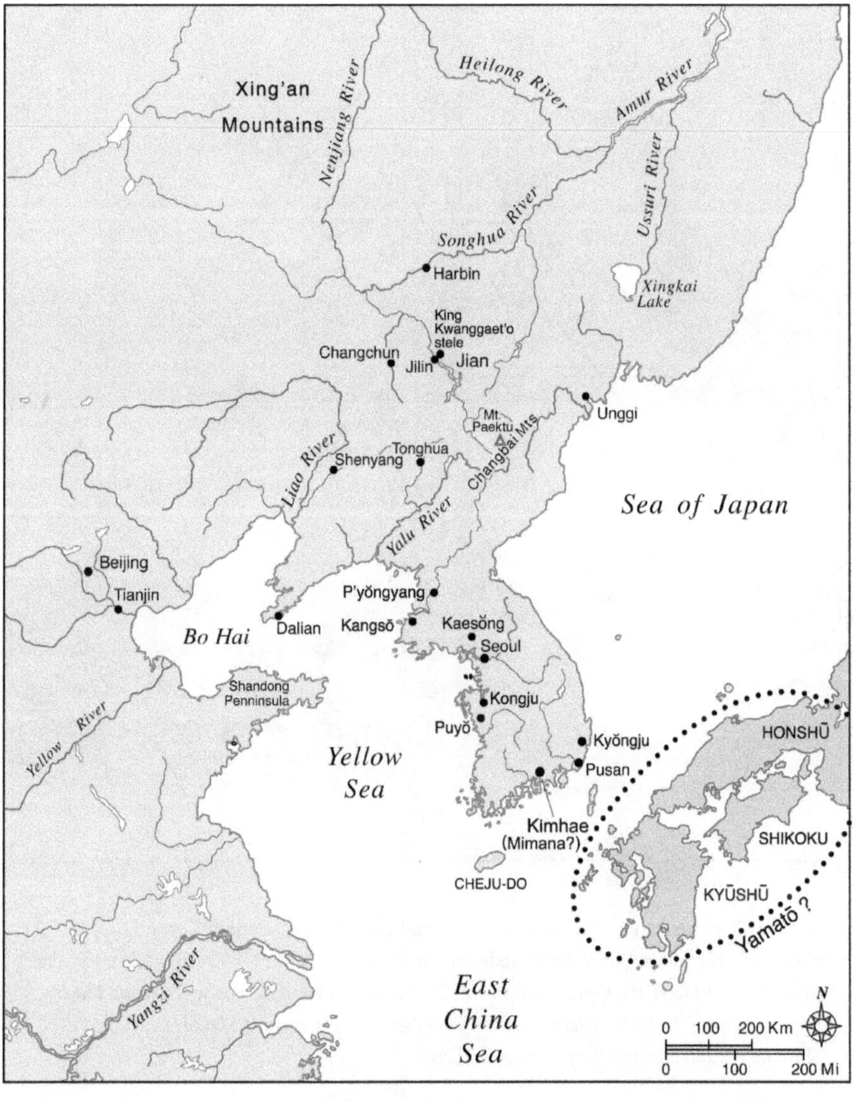

MAP 2. Sites of major excavations conducted by the CST in colonial Korea, 1910–45. The dotted circle indicates the sphere of Yamato influence as estimated by Gina Barnes (1988, fig. 3).

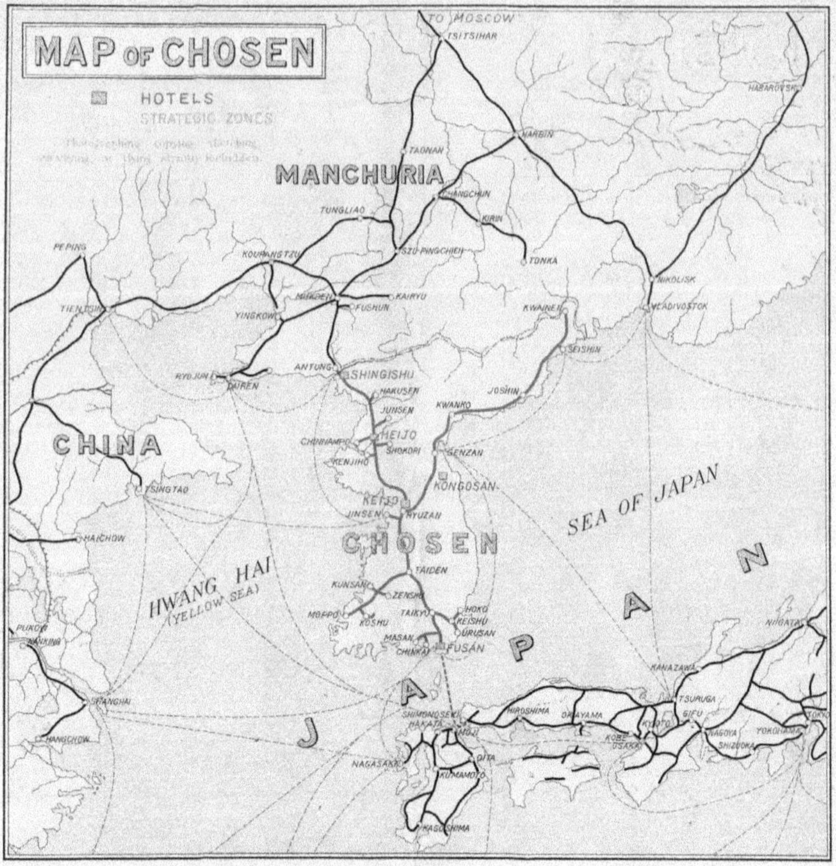

MAPS 3. Transportation links, station hotels, and tourist destinations in Korea, 1930s.*
*The CSTTK managed six station hotels and one station restaurant in Korea in the 1930s: the Pusan Station Hotel, the Keijō Station/grill, the Chōsen Hotel in Keijō, the Diamond Mountain (Kongōsan) Hotels in Changanri and Onjŏngni, the P'yŏngyang Station Hotel, and the Shinŭiju Station Hotel. Source: *Hotels in Chōsen*.

CHAPTER 1

RANKING "KOREAN" PROPERTIES

Heritage Administration, South Gate, and Salvaging Buried Remains

The Cultural Heritage Administration, or the Munhwajae Chŏng (hereafter CHA, 1998–present), formerly the Office of Cultural Properties (Munhwajae Kwalliguk, hereafter KSMKG, 1961–98), has played the major role in transforming the cultural and tourist landscape of the Republic of Korea. For more than three decades, its committee members and staff have worked hand in hand with the Ministry of Culture, Sports, and Tourism (MCST; Munhwa Ch'eyuk Kwan'gwangbu) and the Korean Tourism Organization (KTO; Han'guk Kwan'gwang Kongsa) to promote Korea to a world audience. Beginning with the successful staging of the Seoul 1988 Olympics, these national institutions have constructed museums, monuments, and shrines, as well as erected tens of thousands of signs and markers promoting cultural properties throughout the peninsula.[1] They have also deployed media outlets, including newsletters, newspapers, television, and the Internet, to advertise Korea's latest World Heritages sites— royal palaces, tombs, temples, Yangban Villages architecture, and ancient walled towns such as Suwŏn (fig. 1.1) and Kyŏngju (see figs. 5.5, 5.6, 5.7, 6.5, and 6.7)—to both the domestic audience as well as foreign visitors (KS Korean National Commission for UNESCO 2001, 2002). Consequently, from the densely populated urban enclaves of Seoul to remote mountainous locations only hikers frequent, one can come across green-painted railings fencing off state-designated cultural properties and heritage zones. As we can see in figure 1.1, heritage sites are demarcated by "Korean-style" columns decorated with red-stained gabled roofs framing large, shiny metal plaques inscribed with the name of the monument and its registered classification or ranking category as a world heritage site, national treasure, treasure, historical site, natural monu-

5

FIG. 1.1. Tourists in front of a large multilingual (Korean, English, Japanese, and simplified Chinese) information board, 2010. The board marks the West Command Post (Sŏjangdae), one of the lookout stations located inside the fortress of Hwasŏng, better known as Suwŏn-sŏng. Built during the reign of King Chŏngjo (1752–1800), it was registered as a World Heritage site in 1997. Photo by author.

ment, or provincial-government-designated property. In recent years, in an attempt to greet all visitors, these information boards and tourist maps have been translated into English, Japanese, and, increasingly, simplified Chinese.

Because of the perceived inherent value of cultural properties as immutable tangible relics demonstrating Korea's antiquity, ancestral achievements, and the unbroken continuity of its civilization, more than in any other country, state-employed archaeologists, architects, curators, academics, and research staff in Korea have micromanaged every aspect of heritage management (including excavations, collections, documentations, registrations, museum exhibitions, and restoration projects) for tourists in the past century. Although in 2011 the CHA commemorated its fiftieth anniversary as the supreme arbiter of state-directed cultural initiatives, very few (except for a handful of historians and insiders working for the CHA) are aware that the institutional foundations of Korea's cultural heritage management system dates back much earlier, to the early colonial period in the 1910s (Pai 2001). Like many political, military, economic, and cultural institutions introduced by Japan's empire-building colonialists and administrators, the CHA inherited its hierarchical working structure and property-ranking criteria directly from the Government-General of Chōsen (Chōsen Sōtokufu, hereafter CST) Preservation Laws Governing Antiquities and Relics that were first promulgated in 1916, and, therefore, it is not without much controversy (Pai 1994, 2006). For example, the bulk of Korea's most representative national treasures (*kukpo*)—such as Pulguksa Temple (see figs. 5.6 and 5.7), Sŏkkuram Grotto (see figs. 5.5 and 6.5), and archaeological remains dating back to the Three Kingdoms era (c. 3rd–8th century CE)—were first surveyed, excavated, and reconstructed for tourists by Japanese scholars, engineers, and developers (Pai 1994, 2010a, 2010b, 2011). Therefore, the CHA's naming and ranking systems for Korea's national treasures inventory have sometimes been challenged as relics of colonial practices that have distorted the "true" identity, age, and artistic worth of Korea's core body of ruins and relics.

Since the first Cultural Properties Preservation Act (Munhwajae Pohobŏp) was promulgated in 1962, the term "state-designated heritage" (*chijŏng munhwajae*) has been broadly defined as consisting of natural and man-made objects designated as having important archaeological, prehistorical, historical, literary, artistic, and technological importance. The CHA Ministry, currently ranks national cultural properties into the following seven categories:[2]

1. National treasures (*kukpo*): Heritage of a rare and significant value in terms of human culture with an equivalent to "treasures."
2. Treasures (*pomul*): Tangible Cultural heritage (*yuhyŏng munhwajae*) of important value, such as historic architecture, ancient books and documents, paintings, sculpture, handicrafts, archaeological materials, and armory.
3. Historic sites (*sajŏk*): Places and facilities of great historic and academic value that are worthy of commemoration (e.g., prehistoric settlements, fortresses, ancient tombs, kiln sites, dolmens, temple sites, and shell mounds).
4. Scenic places (*myŏngsŭng*): Places of natural beauty with great historic, artis-

tic, or scenic values, which feature distinctive uniqueness and rarity originated from their formation process.

5. Natural monuments (*ch'ŏnyŏn kinyŏmmul*): Animals, plants, minerals, caves,
   geological features, biological products, and special natural phenomena carrying great historic, cultural, scientific, aesthetic, or academic values, through
   which the history of a nation or the secrets of the creation of the earth can be
   identified or revealed.

6. Important intangible cultural heritage (*muhyŏng munhwajae*): Drama, music,
   dance, and craftsmanship carrying great historic, artistic, or academic values.
   The list includes the following: (a) living artisans who, as "possessors of
   traditional arts and crafts" (*poyuja*), are represented by craftsmen, wine makers, singers, and musicians; (b) religious customs such as Confucian ancestor
   ceremonies and shaman exorcism rituals; (c) regional theaters and musical
   and village dances; and (d) folksongs and folktales.

7. Important folklore materials (*chungyo minsok charyo*): Clothing, implements,
   and houses used for daily life and business, transportation, communication,
   entertainment and social life, and religious or annual events that are valuable
   for understanding people's lifestyles and more. This category includes subsistence strategies such as food-preparation techniques, cooking recipes, local
   agricultural festivals, rituals (sixtieth birthday party, ancestral worship, and
   shaman rituals), local customs, games (kites, wrestling, and the like), religious
   customs (shaman paintings), and costumes.

The application forms submitted for formal consideration must include
detailed information such as the name and address of the owner of the
property where the artifact was reported, its location, its discoverer, its
measurements, legends, related stories, and the state of preservation—all
of which are recorded side by side with an attached photograph. The registration requiring specialists' survey records, supporting historical records,
and collections of associated legends supervised by CHA staff is a complex
and time-consuming bureaucratic process. Once an item is deemed worthy
of serious investigation, one of the CHA committee members is dispatched
to the site to verify its status and report it to their respective committees.
Currently, CHA-appointed specialists (*munhwajae wiwŏn*) meet monthly,
as nine separate committees (*punkwa wiwŏnhoe*): (1) Architectural

Heritage; (2) Movable Cultural Properties Division; (3) Historic Sites and Monuments; (4) Historic Cities Division; (5) Archaeological Heritage; (6) Natural Heritage; (7) Intangible Cultural Properties; (8) Modern Cultural Heritage; and (9) Heritage Security. The final decision to register a cultural property is handed down by the minister of CHA, who awards a certificate of authenticity (*munhwajae taejang*). In addition, on occasion the committees will decide which state-designated inventories (*munhwajae mongnok*) are to be reshuffled between categories, appended, or delisted, depending on reports of new discoveries and major restorations, either due to natural or man-made disasters in the previous year.[3] The class and ranking of a cultural property is particularly significant, because it determines not only the amount of government funding granted for its preservation, study, and promotion but also its monetary value in the international art market.[4] The fact that the 2010 budget for the CHA amounted to 521.2 billion Korean won (about 500 million dollars) indicates how much the government invests in long-term efforts to preserve and promote for posterity the tangible symbols of Korea's natural and cultural identity.

According to the CHA search engine, as of 2011 the number of nationally registered cultural properties totaled 3,385 items (see appendix, table 1), including a wide array of both tangible and intangible properties from prehistoric sites, such as shell mounds and rock reliefs; burial goods of bronze weapons and gold crowns; architecture such as Buddhist cave temple sculptures; tumuli, Chosŏn dynasty (1392–1910) royal burials, and shrines; palaces, battle sites and fortresses; natural monuments (plants, trees, animals, and mountains); and skilled artists and craftsmen designated as "living treasures" or "possessors of tradition" (*poyuja*). Once a site is registered, it is the duty of the CHA to inform the general public of the status of the ever-growing list of national treasures, historical sites, and folk resources. Although previously the bulk of heritage information was disseminated in school textbooks, published catalogues, and national or municipal government-issued monthly newsletters, today anyone can visit the CHA home page to access the latest news and statistics of discoveries, excavations, and restoration projects, as well as tourist information about transportation access and a wide array of visitors' facilities (see appendix, table 2). The recent addition of an English-language search function indicates that cultural properties are being valued as increasingly vital components in "branding" the cultured image of the country for a world audience. In recent years, the CHA has also actively courted "netizens" input by sponsoring online competitions with a sizable amount of prize money (US $1,000–3, 000) awarded for the best essays, tourist photos, posters, videos, and even academic papers addressing new ways to promote heritage venues to tourists, including festivals and cultural events held at royal palaces, temples, historical sites, and ancient capitals such as Kyŏngju and Puyŏ (see fig. 1.6).[5]

In contrast to such outreach efforts, CHA committee membership has historically been reserved for well-connected academics who have served at least ten years as professors at leading universities, or for curatorial staff at national museums. Over the decades, CHA-appointed experts have expanded to include a wide range of disciplines, including archaeology, anthropology, art history, architecture, ancient history, ethnomusicology, ethnology, botany, zoology, and geology. That is, their expertise has qualified them to evaluate which geological formations, natural species, objects, monuments, talents, and skills should represent the body of "Korean" identity and heritage. Most notably, out of the hundreds of academics who have served as committee members over the past five decades, the most prestigious posts (such as the directorships of the network of eleven national museums) have been dominated by archaeologists and art historians who were appointed as the "authentic" speakers of Korea's most ancient past. For example, the first director of the National Museum of Korea was Kim Chae-wŏn (directorship, 1945–70), an art historian and archaeologist who received his degree from the University of Munich (Kim Chae-wŏn 1992).

He was succeeded by Kim Wŏl-lyong (r. 1970–71), another art historian and archaeologist, trained at Seoul National University, with graduate degrees from New York University and the University College London. Kim Wŏl-lyong is also often referred to as the father of native Korean archaeology because he founded the Department of Art and Archaeology at Seoul National University (Kogo Misul Sahakwa). Kim was the influential author of *Introduction to Korean Archaeology* (Han'guk kogohak kaesŏl), which has been published in a dozen revised versions and has served as the bible for students of Korean archaeology since its first edition appeared in 1973 (Kim Wŏl-lyong 1986). The third director, Hwang Su-yŏng (1972–74), was also an art historian, with degrees from Tokyo University, and is recognized as the preeminent expert on the Buddhist art and sculpture of the Three Kingdoms period (Hwang 1989).

The fourth director of the CHA was Yi Kŏn-mu (2008–11), another Seoul National University–trained archaeologist of prehisty who earned his pedigree excavating under his mentor, Kim Wŏl-lyong. Yi's other positions included the directorship of the Kwangju National Museum and of the National Museum of Korea.[6] In 2011, he was replaced by Ch'oe Kwangsik (2011–12), another scholar of ancient history and former director of the Korea University Museum. As we can see, over the past fifty years, a small core of state-appointed bureaucrats and academics trained at elite universities have exerted enormous influence in defining what, who, and in which order something or someone represents the ever-growing body of "Korean patrimony."

The current structure and ranking system of the CHA bureaucracy can be traced back to the year 1961, when its predecessor, the Office of Cultural Properties (Korea [South] Munhwajae Kwalliguk; hereafter KSMKG) was founded under the auspices of the Ministry of Education. The OCP's official journal, *Journal of the Office of Cultural Properties* (Munhwajae), was launched in 1965 and is still published today. The following mission statement in the journal's inaugural issue states the raison d'être of the KSMKG as follows:

> The goal of the office and its promulgation of cultural preservations laws and regulations is to preserve, manage, and reconstruct our cultural properties so as to hold on to our most precious ancestral heritage and keep them with us for eternity.... Furthermore, we have to make up for the systematic destruction and plunder of Korean art and architecture perpetrated by the Japanese. Our mission is also an urgent one because Korea's cultural properties are currently being threatened daily by the onslaught of Western culture with the stationing of American soldiers in the postwar period. (KSMKG *Munhwajae* 1965b, 1–6)

The patriotic sentiments expressed in this directive clearly reflect the overwhelming pride of ownership of museum officials, curators, and KSMKG committee members, who have often referred to themselves as "the creators of Korean Culture" (*minjok munhwa ch'angjo*; KSMKG 1965b, 1).

The amorphous slogan dubbed the "Korean spirit" (*Chosŏn chŏngsin*) was the most-often-cited criteria considered by the committees when deciding which objects, historical sites, and monuments ought to represent Korea's racial identity and cultural lineage (Pai 2001, 76).

Needless to say, the patriotic direction of the KSMKG's policy mandates during the 1960s through the 1980s was also heavily influenced by the personal ambitions of past presidents, who ruled with an iron fist for more than three decades. President Park Chung-hee (r. 1961–79)—a former colonel in the Japanese army who masterminded a coup in 1961 following the chaos of the student revolt that overthrew the lame-duck President Syngman Rhee (1875–1965)—is widely acknowledged as the first president to use "history" as a political tool in a systematic manner (Park S. 2010; Park Sang-mi 2010). According to the broad outlines of Park's 1972 Yusin Constitution's ideology of national restoration that was propagated in school textbooks and the media, the trajectory of Korea's history was driven by the spirit of national resistance (*t'uchaengsa*) in order to preserve the Korean people and its unique culture from invading foreign armies. In this overarching narrative, Korea's unique identity and independent spirit were forged over two millennia, in resistance to successive invasions by Chinese conquerors, beginning with Han Emperor Wu-di (c. 108 BCE) and continuing with the dynasties of the Sui and Tang (6th–7th century), the Mongols (13th century), the Khitans (17th century), the Japanese (16th–20th century), the Manchus (17th century), the US Army (1945–48), and, finally, the communist North during the Korean War (1950–53) (Kal 2008). The turning points in the struggle for national independence were not only marked by epic battles but also by the appearance of self-sacrificing martyrs such as Admiral Yi Sun-sin (1545–98), who saved the people from the rampaging armies of Japanese warlord Toyotomi Hideyoshi (1536–98) during the Imjin Wars (1592–98). Handpicked as Korea's hero par excellence Admiral Yi under President Park's directive, the KSMKG commissioned the construction of several war monuments to consecrate the bitter memories of the seven-year period of the Imjin War, including the Hyŏnch'ungsa Shrine (1966–75) and a floating replica of Yi's "turtle boat" in white stucco placed in an inlet of Hansando Island, where Yi famously defeated the Japanese navy (Korea [South] Munhwa Kongbobu 1979, 288–89). Today, reproductions of turtle boats are ubiquitous; they appear as artwork etched into wall

FIG. 1.2. Children dodging water streams sprouting from fountains lining the paved pathways in front of Admiral Yi Sun-shin's statue, 2009. Commissioned by president Park Chung-hee, the statue is 6.5 meters tall, weighs eight tons, and was erected on April 27, 1968. Photo by author.

reliefs adorning the halls of the Yongsan National War Memorial, as well as in many lesser-known war memorials scattered throughout the peninsula (Jager 1999). They are also sold in souvenir shops in the form of miniaturized toys, drawings, and puzzles (Park Yŏng-mu 1971). The most famous relic dating from Park's Yusin era is the colossal bronze statue of the admiral that still towers over the renovated Kwanghwamun Plaza (fig. 1.2), which has now been transformed into a family-friendly destination complete with fountains, an underground museum complex, and a gigantic gold-plated statue of a seated King Sejong (r. 1418–50).[7]

Beginning in the early 1970s, Park became adept at deploying the then relatively new technology of broadcast television to push for his own political agenda and economic developmental plans for the nation (Park S. 2010). One anecdote attributed to Park appears in the memoirs of Cho Yu-jŏn (1942–), the long-time field archaeologist who served as the director of the excavation team at Kyŏngju's Hwangnyong-sa Temple ruins in the 1970s and 1980s. In his vivid account, Cho recalls that Park chose to land in the middle of ongoing archaeological sites via military helicopter, no doubt to project an image of himself as a strong military leader. Cho also commented that journalists from major national newspapers and networks were informed beforehand so that they would not miss any photo ops. On occasion, Park also requested that Cho hand-deliver new tomb finds to the presidential residence, the Blue House, for his personal inspection and appreciation (Cho Yu-jŏn 1996, 104–7). In 1971, not long after these headline-grabbing visits were broadcast, Park personally launched "The Kyŏngju Tourism Comprehensive Development Plan" and set aside large government subsidies dedicated to restoring the ancient glories of the Silla Kingdom for foreign tourists. A development company, Kyŏngju Kaebal Kongsa, was given the charge of remaking Kyŏngju into "the greatest, most elegant, dynamic, and leisurely ancient city in the peninsula," including the construction of high-rise hotels and golf resorts built around an artificial man-made lake of the Pomun Resort development complex, as well as the sponsoring of annual Silla festivals, parades, and other cultural events (Korea [South] Munhwa Kongbobu 1979, 285; Oppenheim 2008). After Park's assassination in 1979, his successors, Presidents Chun Doo-hwan (r. 1980–86) and Roh Tae-woo (r. 1986–92), did not deviate from Park's tried-and-true strategy of glorifying kings and military heroes, since they were also keen to legitimize their oppressive regimes—for they, too, had been former military officers who had risen to the highest office (Shin 1998, 148–65).

Thus, the KSMKG has devoted the bulk of its construction budget over the past four decades to building shrines, monuments, altars, and cemeteries—including Tan'gun's Shrine (Kanghwa-do Manisan), the Tomb of the Seven Hundred Righteous Soldiers (Ch'ilbaek ŭich'ong; 1975–76), Chinju-sŏng (Chinju Fortress), and Tongnae-sŏng (Tongnae Fortress)—in order to showcase legendary founders and sites of foreign resistance, both real and imagined (Pai 2000, 57–95). In a similar vein, the CHA continues to celebrate a rotating list of national heroes and heroines, which now includes Confucian philosophers, artists, literary figures, religious leaders, inventors, colonial-era anti-Japanese resistance fighters, and even a handful of virtuous women and wise mothers. Calendars and brochures promoting local festivals celebrating birthplaces, shrines, and monuments are always included on the "must-see" itinerary of patriotic destinations for school-led educational tours every fall and spring.

In 1998, due to its ever-expanding roster of nationwide projects, the KSMKG was upgraded to independent status and renamed the Ministry of Culture Heritage Administration or CHA (Munhwajae-ch'ŏng). Currently, its high-rise headquarters in Taejŏn boasts a working staff of over eight hundred employees who oversee a vast administrative structure, including the following affiliated museums, research institutions, and monuments: the National Research Institute of Cultural Properties, or NRICP (Kungnip Munhwajae Yŏn'guso), founded in 1975; National Palace Museum of Korea; the National Maritime Museum (Kungnip Haeyang Pangmulkwan), overseeing the following sites: Royal Palaces and Royal Shrines Management Office Kyŏngbok Palace, Ch'angdŏkkung, Tŏksukkung, Ch'anggyŏnggung, the Chongmyo Confucian shrine, and the Royal Tombs Office; and the Shrine Office of Hyŏnch'ungsa dedicated to Yi Sun-sin and the Ch'ilbaek ŭich'ong Shrine Office. The CHA ministry also manages the Korean National University of Cultural Heritage (Munhwajae Taehakkyo), located in Puyŏ, the former capital of the Paekche dynasty (c. 1st century BCE–7th century CE). The ministry works closely with the two central museums: the National Museum of Korea (Kungnip Chungang Pangmulgwan; 1909–present), and the National Folk Museum (Kungnip Minsok Pangmulgwan; 1975–present) in Kyŏngbok Palace. In addition, there is an extended network of ten national museums (Kyŏngju, Kwangju, Chŏnju, Ch'ŏngju, Puyŏ, Kongju, Taegu, Kimhae, Ch'unch'ŏn, and Cheju) located in the former dynastic capitals (Kyŏngju, Puyŏ, Kongju) and major provincial cities (Kwangju, Chŏnju, Ch'ŏngju, Taegu, Kimhae, Ch'unch'ŏn), and on the island of Cheju.

For close to forty years, the top-down authoritarian management style of the KSMKG heritage management policies went unchallenged for two main reasons. First, as mentioned above, the exclusive nature of the CHA committees membership, which was mostly composed of elite university-trained academics, archaeologists, historians, art historians, architects, curators, and anthropologists, meant that very few outside of the CHA were aware of their biased preference for ancient heroes and martyrs. Second, this uncritical situation was in keeping with the character of the three decades of military rule (1961–92), when the specter of government censorship loomed over all university campuses, institutions, and media outlets. Detailed censorship laws were especially enforced for all print and broadcast media, extending even to quotas on imported foreign films and the kinds of plays performed in theatres.

With the belated arrival of a working democratic government in the late 1990s and the easing of authoritarian government control and censorship, the situation is quite different today, for in the past decade dozens of public debates have been waged in the blogosphere by Internet-savvy citizens, or netizens, in Korea. Here, we will look at two headline-grabbing controversies that have directly challenged the CHA's historical role as the sole arbiter and executor of Korea's heritage.

No one would argue that the most serious public-relations dilemma in the history of the CHA was the massive fire that burned down Seoul's iconic symbol, South Gate (Namdaemun) on the night of February 10, 2008 (Park Sang-mi 2010,1). Although a small fire was initially reported around 8 pm, in less than five hours the six-hundred-year-old structure had been reduced to a pile of broken timber and ashes (fig. 1.3). Live-streaming online video images of the burning gate thus marked a tragic coda to the fate of South Gate, which had been constructed in 1398 by the newly installed Yi dynastic regime as the gateway to their new capital of Hansŏng. Two days later, interviews with the shell-shocked citizens, Seoul City officials, politicians, and leading intellectuals who had congregated around the rubble were featured as top news stories in international media outlets, from NHK, Japan's national broadcasting corporation, to cable television channels such as BBC and CNN.

The citizens of Seoul were even more outraged when the arsonist apprehended three days later turned out to be a seventy-year-old "mentally unstable" man who, upon interrogation, said that he had simply scaled a ladder

방화로 소실된 국보1호 숭례문 〔2008〕

〔사진출처 최진연〕

FIG. 1.3. The caption to this photograph reads, "National Treasure Number One, Sungnye-mun, lost to arson fire." February 11, 2008. Photo by Ch'oe Chin-yŏn. Source: Seoul Design Foundation, *Kyŏng-gye rŭl nŏmŏ kiri hŭrŭnda: Seoul Sŏnggwak sajinjŏn* (Pathway flows beyond boundaries—Photography exhibition on project of Seoul Sŏnggwak) (Seoul: Seoul Design Foundation, Seoul Metropolitan Government Publication, 2009).

to get access to the roof. He confessed that his act of vandalism was an act of revenge for the unfair treatment and lack of adequate cash compensation he had received when he was forced to sell his land to the government many years ago. The journalists who covered every angle of this sorry tale for several weeks blamed the CHA and the Seoul Metropolitan Government for the following unforgivable failures in management: (1) the absence of a twenty-four-hour security guard; (2) the lack of an automatic sprinkler system (the only antifire prevention measures on-site were eight canisters of fire retardant); (3) the fact that motion sensors and closed-circuit television cameras monitored only the main gate entrance and not the entire grounds; and (4) that the emergency response team did not receive any prior training and was not in possession of building plans or instructional manuals issued by the CHA.[8] The firemen, without the proper training or manuals for putting out fires at national treasures the size and stature of South Gate, were not aware that their hoses should have been directed at the base of the burning roof beams, where in all likelihood live embers remained smoldering after the firefighters left the scene. Once the journalists exposed this appalling state of negligence—the absence of even a basic primer on disaster prevention and the lack of protection of cultural properties from vandalism or theft—suspicions were raised about the state of other acclaimed wooden structures, including the World Heritage sites located in and outside of the capital, including Chongmyo Shrine, Ch'angdŏk Palace, Haeinsa Temple, Pulguksa Temple, and Sŏkkuram Grotto.

Less than a week after the fire, under mounting media pressure, the then head of the CHA, minister Yu Hong-jun (1949–), was forced to hand in his resignation. In his public letter of apology posted on the CHA home page, Yu acknowledged that he had failed in his assigned duty as the chief caretaker of Korea's national assets. In retrospect, his fall from grace was doubly ironic, since Yu was a well-known celebrity author who had catapulted to fame based largely on the popularity of his best-selling travelogues, nostalgically titled *My Travels to Cultural Remains* (Naŭi munhwa yusan tapsaki), which continue to sell millions of copies (Yu 1993).

With all the hype surrounding the fire, there was a distinct sense of déjà vu within the CHA, for this was not the first time that the media had challenged the long-standing authority of the CHA concerning its misman-agement of South Gate (KSMKG 1997a, 73–74, 77). Although not as well publicized, ten years earlier many editorials featured in national dailies such as the *Han'guk Ilbo*, *Tong-a Ilbo*, *Chosŏn Ilbo*, *Kyŏnghyang Sinmun*, and *Han'gyŏre* had requested that the CHA reevaluate whether South Gate was really worthy of its moniker as the premier national treasure. They called on CHA officials to investigate Japanese colonial-era records to find out if the gate had not been "arbitrarily" registered in 1934. They wanted to know if the Japanese had either imposed their own "distorted values" (*kach'i waegok*), leading to "mistaken names" (*munhwajae chich'ing*) or "mislabeled ranks" (*munhwajae tŭnggŭp*), amongst the 503 cultural properties listed in the colonial inventory. Reflecting the widespread anti-Japanese sentiments of the times, the editors called on the KSMKG to "scrape off the rotten vestiges of Japanese imperialism" (*ilche chan'jae ch'ŏngsan*), and to reinstate Korea's pride and reputation (*myŏngye hoebok*) so that the public would be assured that the top 503 items reassigned in 1962 by the KSMKG indeed represented "true Korean values" (KSMKG 1997a, 67–84).

In order to diffuse the volatile situation and preserve its national image as the self-anointed steward of Korea's past, the KSMKG conducted a survey of 135 cultural committee members and their staff to determines how best to restructure the current cultural properties rankings. In 1997, the specialist committee that had been formed to reevaluate the colonial inventories reported its findings in a publication titled "Report on the Re-Evaluation of Cultural Properties Designated during the Japanese Colonial Era" (KSMKG 1997a). According to this report, a majority of specialists (59.2 percent), KSMKG staff members, and other cultural brokers opposed any drastic reforms and advocated keeping the status quo. Their cited reasons were as follows:

1. The registry of cultural properties is numbered in sequence and not by any absolute aesthetic or historical criteria.
2. There are no superior or inferior cultural properties, and their value may change over time.
3. If we were to change our national treasure number one from the Japanese-designated South Gate to something else, we would have to keep on readjusting the registry every year. This would result in uneconomical expenditures, since we would have to reregister all of the thousands of cultural properties in books, on signposts, and in tourist advertisements, causing much confusion on the part of the public. (KSMKG 1997a, 138–39)

On November 1996, the KSMKG contracted a pollster, the Kŭkdong Agency, to conduct a nationwide survey eventually recruiting one thousand citizens over twenty years old who had visited a museum, historical site, or cultural remain in the past two years. A large portion of citizens surveyed (67.6 percent) voted to keep the current national properties registry intact. Interestingly, the only surveyed citizens who deviated from this pattern were students attending Seoul National University (SNU), notoriously the most progressive-minded body of students among the hundreds of university campuses. Fifty-seven percent of the 262 students questioned (including both undergraduates and graduate students enrolled in the liberal arts and engineering schools) replied that national treasure number one should be reassigned. An overwhelming 78 percent of those opposed to South Gate picked *Hunmin Chŏngŭm* (The correct sounds to educate the people)—an original document dating to 1466 that is widely acknowledged as the first training manual for the Korean alphabet—as the most unique (*koyu*) achievement of Korean civilization. Only 8 percent of the SNU students surveyed believed that South Gate was a representative example of a Korean national treasure (KSMKG 1997a, 77).

Thus, after more than a year of media debates, commonsense- and budget-minded administrators seem to have prevailed over anti-Japanese sentiments. In conjunction with this nationwide citizen survey, the KSMKG sponsored an academic conference titled "A Seminar on the Re-Evaluation of Japanese Registered Cultural Properties" in December 1996. The conference invitees were asked to report on the findings of a specially formed cultural committee made up of thirty-four members divided into fourteen different groups, such as "transportable cultural properties" (*tong-san munhwajae*), "historical remains" (*sajŏk*), and "architectural monuments" (*kinyŏmmul*). The committee's assigned mission was to dig up all prior documentation for evidence of mistaken classifications (*munhwajae myŏngch'ing*), ranking status (*tŭnggŭp chae chojŏng*), and "Japanese-style reference labels" (*ilbonsik p'yohyŏn*). The goal was to expose any underlying "Japanese" motives that may have contributed to distorting the Korean past (*yŏksa waegok;* KSMKG 1997a, 5). After looking into the 503 registered items inherited from the colonial registry, the committee made the following changes: First, the most distorted item they identified on the list was Suwŏn Fortress (national treasure number three), which has since been renamed Hwasŏng after its original Chosŏn dynastic name (see fig.1.1). Second, the committee recommended that the eight forts attributed to

Hideyoshi's invasion forces be labeled "of Japanese origin" (*waesŏng*) and demoted from the status of "national" historical sites to the lesser rank of provincial cultural properties (*chibang chijŏng munhwajae*). Third, six treasures (*pomul*) were upgraded to national treasure (*kukpo*), and one pagoda was demoted from "treasure" rank to that of "provincial cultural property." An additional six items were relabeled with slightly revised names underlined as follows: (1) South Gate (Namdaemun) to revert back to its Yi dynasty name of Gate of Exalted Ceremonies or Sungnyemun (national treasure number one); (2) Pongsŏn Honggyŏng Temple Stele (*Kalbi*) to Pongsŏn Honggyŏngsa Sajŏk (historical site) Kalbi (stele) ; (3) Seoul's East Gate (Tongdaemun) to revert back to its Yi dynasty name of Gate for Raising Human-Heartedness or Hŭnginjimun (treasure number one); (3) stele from Wŏn'gak Temple (Wŏn'gaksabi) to Taewŏngaksabi (treasure number three); (4) the stele of Chungch'ang from Pogwang Temple to Chin'gwangsa Taejin Kwangsŏnsabi (treasure number 107); and (5) the Repository of the Haeinsa Tablets (Changyŏng P'an'go-Haeinsa) to the Repositories of the Tripataka Koreana woodblocks (Taewŏngaksabi Changgyŏng P'anjŏn; national treasure number fifty-two).[9]

In the final analysis, despite the six months the committee specialists spent mulling over 130 proposed items (including twenty-six items to be reranked, and seven delisted), they could make up their minds on only the twenty-two items mentioned above, a mere 4 percent of the suspect 503 items on the colonial inventory (KSMKG 1997a, 6–10). This dismal failure (by any measure) on the part of KSMKG specialists to reinscribe what they called a "new order of Korea's Cultural Properties" (*Munhwa yusan yŏksa paro seugi*) demonstrates that when the KSMKG founders reassigned the early Shōwa era (1925–89) colonial inventories on December 20, 1962, they had basically replicated the Japanese colonial-era classification system, ranking criteria, and naming system, listing items in more or less the same order. For example, out of the 591 items listed in the colonial inventory dating back to 1943 (the last year the colonial-era listings were updated), the top 503 items were incorporated into the KSMKG registry as follows: 69 national treasures (*kukpo*); 271 treasures (*pomul*); 98 historical sites (*sajŏk*); 63 natural monuments (*ch'ŏnnyŏn kinyŏmmul*); and 3 historical sites or scenic places (*sajŏk/myŏngsŭng*). The 88-item discrepancy accounts for some minor revisions, including delisted items, many of which permanently reverted to North Korea after the Korean War, while others had been destroyed or had simply vanished following the bombings and looting during the bloody war.

What stood out most prominently in the case of South Gate, was that the KSMKG-appointed specialists skated around the fact that South Gate had been first registered by the CST as Korea's premier national landmark on August 27, 1934. At that time, the CST had selected the gate for its central location, situated between the Old City populated by Koreans in the north and the New Town (Shin Machi), which was being developed by the CST military to accommodate an increasing number of Japanese soldiers, merchants, and settlers (Henry 2008). The CST engineers and the Department of Public Works also devoted years to building up the area to serve as a main traffic hub, where one could transfer from the Chōsen Government Railways (CSTTK) to local buses, trams, and rickshaws (see fig. 6.2). Therefore, colonial developers and merchants remade South Gate and its market area into the iconic gateway to Chōsen, designed to be seen by the millions of inbound train passengers disembarking from the Keifu (Keijō-Pusan) trunkline to conduct business at nearby Mitsukoshi Department Store (now Shinsegye), the Central Post Office, or the Bank of Chōsen, or to dine at the Chōsen or Bando Hotels. South Gate's image also appeared in many editions of travel guides and on postcards distributed by the millions throughout the empire (Pai 2010b).

In addition, according to the 1933 *Treasures, Ancient Sites, Famous Places, and Natural Monuments* (Hōmotsu koseki meishō kinenbutsu) catalogue, items were listed in the sequence of CST administrative units, beginning with monuments located in central Seoul, then followed by the provinces of Kyŏnggi, North Ch'ungch'ŏng and South Ch'ungch'ŏng, North Chŏlla and South Chŏlla, North Kyŏngsang and South Kyŏngsang, Kangwŏn-do, Hwanghae-do, North P'yŏngan and South P'yŏngan, and North Hamgyŏng and South Hamgyŏng. Newly discovered items were subsequently appended to the 1934 listings, as they are today (CST 1937). To this day, it remains unclear why the KSMKG did not choose to simply share with Seoul's citizens and journalists the fact that the current method listing of cultural properties was derived from a bureaucratic accounting system. However, we cannot deny that, over the course of eight decades, the national treasures classification and numbering system came to represent the order of "Korean" things, and ultimately led to the general public perception that the smaller the number, the more antiquated and authentic an object or monument must be (Pai 2001).

Another case study involves ongoing debates about contested claims for buried properties that continue to embroil developers, local governments, and local citizens on a daily basis (KS-NRICP 1997; Pai 1999b; Bale 2008). The "undiscovered" and "unknown" buried remains were recognized as the nation's most valued assets in 1962 with the promulgation of the KSMKG's cultural preservation laws (KS-NRICP 1997, 91). Buried cultural remains (*maejang munhwajae*) are currently defined as any artifact or structure beneath Korean soil, waters, or buildings (according to Buried Cultural Properties Laws, number 43). This definition includes underground finds of tangible cultural properties (buildings, old documents, paintings, sculpture, arts, and crafts); monuments (shell mounds, tumuli, fortresses, palaces, temple sites, and kilns); archaeological features (stratigraphic layers); and other related historical sites (ibid., 163). The first article of the Buried Cultural Properties Laws (number 42) stipulates mandatory reporting to the local police by any individual or institution upon discovery of sites or artifacts. Individuals caught excavating without a permit can be jailed for up to five years (Pai 1999b, 621). In cases in which the owner (of an object of value that is either reported or found) can be identified, the government will purchase the artifact after having consulted with the staff of a national museum. This monetary compensation is euphemistically referred to as a "reward" (*posanggŭm*) but is in fact a "finder's fee." As indicated by its name, the practice ensured that an honest patriotic citizen would be encouraged by the reward to turn buried finds over to the government.[10]

However, in the past forty years, critics of the cash-reward system have argued that low cash reimbursements for artifacts have instead encouraged looters and smugglers, who prefer to deal with shady black marketers who are willing to pay full market price (KSMKG 1967, 8–9). The CHA also maintains databases of all Korean collections abroad, as well as properties lost, stolen, and, on rare occasions, retrieved from antiquities dealers (KSMKG 1997a, 193–96). With the introduction of government-ministry home pages, one can also fill out a form to report a theft online through the CHA website. These archival records documenting lost and stolen antiquities date back to the early years of the KSMKG and serve one of the more important functions of the National Research Institute of Cultural Properties founded in 1975 (NRICP 1992).

The current framework of Korea's buried properties laws can be traced to the 1967 amendments to the Cultural Preservation Act, in which the main objective was to deter widespread looting of buried sites exposed during the rush to industrialize and development Korea's infrastructure that was launched by the construction of Park Chung-hee's pet project, the Seoul-Pusan Highway (KSMKG 1967; Munhwa Kongbopu 1979). Since the late 1960s, the intense political pressure to make room for bulldozers has not let up by any means, as witnessed by the hundreds of salvage excavations carried out on an annual basis (see appendix, table 3). However, because the stated goal of all heritage management is original and authentic preservation and restoration, to this day the most important contracts for major excavations continue to be assigned to national research institutions, universities, and a few private museums that have historically retained their role as the sanctioned caretakers of Korea's buried past (Pai 1999b; Shōda 2008, 203–9). Despite the overwhelming responsibility given to these government institutions and staff, who have unearthed tens of thousands of sites over the decades, in reality each typically has had at most one or two professionally trained archaeologists capable of supervising any kind of excavation. As a result, most excavations are carried out by a large number of day laborers, while the intricate and time-consuming tasks of mapping, recording, cataloguing, analyzing, and writing up excavation reports are assigned to a handful of graduate students and undergraduates who are not up to the task (fig.1.4).

In sum, the typical Korean excavation is still a salvage project carried out during a short two-month summer-vacation period and conducted haphazardly without adequately trained staff or sufficient funds. Considering the daunting task facing many Korean archaeologists, it comes as no surprise that only the most urgent, media-grabbing, or highly visible sites are investigated in any systematic manner. For instance, a small sample of calculations based on KSMKG records from the 1990s reveal that out of a total of 966 excavations, 585 were salvage projects, 236 were reconstruction or restoration projects, and 145 were research projects (KSMKG 1997a, 188–89). Most salvage projects in the past two decades have resulted from the construction of massive high-rise apartment housing projects, road

FIG. 1.4. Typical view of Seoul National University Museum staff, students, and laborers hard at work on a hot summer's day, moving dirt and rocks to reveal the inner structure of a stone-mounded tomb, c. 1983. Photo by author .

construction, office construction, the building of factory complexes, and infrastructure development such as the building of dams, ports, and airports (Pai 1999b).

The failings of KSMKG archaeological heritage management practices to protect Korea's buried properties was addressed in a systematic manner for the first time at a conference titled "Fifty Years of Buried Cultural Properties" held in June 1997 (KS-NRICP 1997). The conference was sponsored by the National Research Institute of Cultural Properties (KS-NRICP) and offered a forum for discussing opinions and recommendations for overhauling field operations. The presenters who were invited represented a "who's who in the field of archaeology," including professors and directors with leading universities and museums, and excavation teams, who gave their frank assessment of the state of the field. Archaeologists agreed that the first major challenge requiring attention was the contract-bidding process, which virtually guaranteed that the lowest bidder would receive the permit to excavate the site. This practice was seen as shortsighted for various reasons. First, since archaeological remains are underground, it is almost impossible to predict in advance how much an excavation will cost. Second, as pointed out by professor Yi Kang-sŭng (of Ch'ungnam University) and Yi Kŏn-mu (then director of the Kwangju National Museum), under the present system systematic site surveys were not required prior to excavation. Third, the archaeologists noted that the decision to hire the cheapest contractor assured mediocrity, since the pressure of keeping under budget obstructed creativity and research.

The second major challenge, addressed by Cho Yŏng-hyŏn (curator of the Kyemyŏng University Museum), was the lack of a standardized accounting system for projecting excavation budgets. Cho argued that there was a dire need to develop a uniform calculation format for expenses—such as average daily costs for transportation, lodgings, equipment, labor, and insurance fees—that archaeologists could then use to compute efficient excavation costs based on the kind, size, depth, or length of the excavation and surveys (KS-NRICP 1997, 55–98). All agreed that the lack of accounting standards and transparency was a deplorable situation, considering that accurate financial and time budgeting are critical for any dig working one step ahead of bulldozers and dynamite. In addition, such a lackadaisical approach to public funds spent in the field also led to accusations of corruption, collusion, and fleecing of tax payers' money on the part of excavation team leaders, many of whom were once-respected professors of archaeology at major universities. These latter, who were entrusted with tens of millions of won provided by the KSMKG, the municipal government, and construction companies to salvage the nation's increasingly threatened buried remains, were thus not living up to their obligations.

Third, archaeologists complained that the proper excavation of archaeological sites was made even more difficult by the fact that the KSMKG was loath to exercise its authority in halting projected construction schedules. Furthermore, the Ministry of Transportation had been reluctant to reimburse the developers' lost revenue if the recommended field season lasted longer than planned due to unforeseen events.

Lastly, conference participants blamed the top-heavy bureaucratic process for producing a chaotic field situation in which no one could be held accountable for the destruction of a site or the rejection of an advisory committee member's recommendation. If the local authority ignored the

KSMKG committee's decision to preserve a site, there was neither recourse nor any way to reverse the process. To remedy the situation, Pae Ki-dong (director of the Hanyang University Museum) suggested the creation of a committee that would exercise greater authority over field projects. As Pae observed on June 29, 1996, at the time only twelve of the 503 KSMKG employees held research positions. The rest were career bureaucrats who were constantly rotated throughout the vast system, never staying in one position long enough to accumulate the expertise and knowledge necessary to run an archaeological outfit (KS-NRICP 1997, 150). Furthermore, the few research jobs were notoriously hard to come by, and required passing a competitive comprehensive entrance exam that covered Korean history and English, and required a detailed knowledge of preservation laws and regulations. Archaeologists also pointed out that, despite the thirty-year-old national rhetoric emphasizing the training of specialists in fields related to Korean cultural preservation (Chŏng Chae-hun 1969), the average graduate of an archaeology program could not hope to find an entry-level job in the government sector but was forced to look elsewhere, and usually ended up leaving the field altogether.[11] And finally, as we have seen, in contrast to KSMKG rhetoric about valuing Korea's buried past, participants complained that the government had in fact devoted few resources and little talent to serious academic research excavations, as shown by the paltry numbers.

To solve such chronic logistical, bidding, and budgetary problems, a few archaeologists participating in the conference advocated ending the government monopoly on excavation permits.[12] They suggested instead an alternative approach, such as the establishment of professional organizations and commercial excavation enterprises throughout the country. One major outcome of this groundbreaking conference was the formation of the Korean Cultural Properties Investigation and Research Institute Association (Hang'uk Munhwajae Chosa Yŏn'gu Kigwan Hyŏphoe, hereafter KCPIA, the official home page name) to oversee the coordination of excavation units, evaluate qualified researchers, and publish archaeological reports. According to the data provided by the KCPIA, as of May 2008, 126 official organizations are engaged in general archaeological surveys and excavations, made up of 48 museums, 37 university museums, 13 national museums, and 28 other licensed specialized archaeological units (Shōda 2008, 202).

In principal, once the state-sanctioned institutions decide to excavate a site, the owner or manager of the property cannot refuse their request. When a site is excavated on public land, anything that is unearthed belongs to the state and must be deposited at a municipal institution or at the regional KS-NRICP branch for evaluation and authentication. However, even with these oversight committees in place, the continuing lack of transparency about how the CHA allocates funds to various agencies for excavation projects has resulted in conflicts of interest involving developers, farmers, archaeologists, museums, and local officials, because the outcome is tied directly to ongoing policy debates concerning the environment, reconstruction, and long-range plans for reviving the stagnant rural economy. According to Martin Bale, a Canadian archaeologist who has participated in salvage operations in the Yŏngnam River region, Kyŏngnam provincial authorities were faced with many construction delays between 1992 and 1997 when villagers and farmers staged antigovernment demonstrations decrying inadequate compensation schemes for their lands in projected inundation zones.[13] The protests also revolved around the exact boundaries of demarcated heritage areas to be studied prior to the expansion of the Chinyang Lake dam. Due to the breakdown of communications between the various factions and parties involved—including the Korea Water Resources Corporation; provincial government officials; the provincial bureau of the Ministry of Culture, Sports, and Tourism (MCST); and CHA committee members—by the time the Kyŏngnam University Museum team was notified, the sites had been destroyed.

The destruction of the Chinyang Lake sites is a clear indictment; the creation of another bureaucratic committee, the KCPIA, did not solve any of the chronic problems or deal with the lack of accountability or transparency of the KS-NRICP's or the KSMKG's management style or culture. Japanese archaeologist Shōda Shin'ya has examined the three main types of excavations (purely academic, reconstruction, and rescue) and tracked their absolute numbers (see appendix, table 3). As we can see, the proportion of rescue excavations jumped from 30 to 1,108 between 1991 and 2011, a nearly thirty-seven-fold increase in a span of twenty years.[14]

With such overwhelming odds favoring salvage archaeology at the expense of research, and with the CHA and MCST favoring the best-selling monuments on behalf of the state and tourist developers, we will

FIG. 1.5. Tourists buying handmade "palace" (Kungjung) rice cakes along the main streets of Insadong, Seoul. The vendor's name is licensed from the hit television series "Tallin" (literally, "those who have attained the Way"), devoted to broadcasting the most popular chefs, craftsmen, and showmen. January 18, 2011. Photo by author.

never know how many sites and relics were bulldozed to make way for dams, hotels, golf courses, airports, freeways, and casinos.[15] Thus, "less glamorous" prehistoric sites (shell mounds, subterranean dwellings, and so on), foreigners' concession buildings, churches, consulates, Japanese colonial architecture, and vernacular architecture have been sacrificed.[16] For example, as we can see in figure 1.5, only a tiny cluster of traditional Korean-style residences (*hanok*) preserved as "authentic" souvenir shops hawking traditional foods are all that remain of the once-vibrant urban lifestyle of the gentry (*yangban*) merchants, and the courtesans' (*kisaeng*) houses around Insadong and Pukch'on in Seoul (fig. 1.5).

Consequently, even if the newly formed specialty archaeological excavation units were successful in decreasing the burden on universities and museums, the general direction of archaeological heritage management is not going to change. This is because the field of archaeology as a whole, and most archaeologists in particular, have not yet come to terms with the effects of the heritage industry and tourist-development projects—the elephants in the room that were ignored by specialists at the 1997 conference. With the emergence of a domestic mass-tourist industry since the 1970s, with millions of cars on freeways and the recent launch of Korean high-speed rails (KTX), local governments, businesses, and consumers alike have placed big expectations on the future of commercially viable heritage sites inside and outside Seoul. Today, the ongoing competition that has pitted large-scale real-estate developers and conglomerates (*chaebŏl*) investors (from Lotte Group, Lucky-Goldstar, Hyundai, and the like) who are keen on developing ever more tourist facilities (luxury hotels, condos, casinos, golf courses, theme parks, beaches, and ski resorts, from Inch'ŏn to Cheju Island) has further complicated the issues of development rights and compensation paid for farmland. Today the ultimate goal of heritage management in the Republic of Korea, as articulated by the MCST, is to define core areas for intensive tourist development in both urban and rural areas. More importantly, these plans have selected a handful of "designated cultural centers" (*munhwakkwŏn*) revolving around "best-selling" souvenirs, monuments, and heritage sites (such as royal burial mounds, palaces, shrines, temple complexes, and folk villages) to attract both domestic and foreign visitors (Park Yŏng-mu 1971). In 1994, the tourist development office launched the first of its "Five-Year Plans" with the *1994 Visit Korea Year* (Han and Kim 1994), with strategic initiatives for the future development of tourism focusing on six core areas: (1) Seoul (Yi dynastic culture); (2) Puyŏ/Kongju (Paekche culture; 1st–3rd century); (3) Kyŏngju (Silla culture; 3rd–10th century); (4) Chungwŏn; (5) Pusan (Kaya culture; 1st–3rd century); and (6) Cheju Island (sports, leisure, ecotourism). The six proposed centers of culture were also selected on the basis of the number of cultural properties unique to the area, in descending order of national importance, as follows: (1) national monuments, such as major art historical sites, architecture, sculpture, archaeological remains, and museums; (2) lifestyles and subsistence strategies, such as the first occurrence of major events, such as sites of historical battles against foreign resistance (e.g., Chinju-sŏng, the site of anti-Hideyoshi resistance, and Hyŏnch'ungsa Shrine of Korea's most famous naval hero, Yi Sun-sin); (3) technological

FIG. 1.6. Actors in costume waiting to perform as palace guards at Paekche Culture Land, the latest theme park to open in Puyŏ, October 5, 2010. The October 2010 opening was part of a nationwide advertising campaign promoting the park as the shooting locale of the latest historical epic, *King Kŭnch'ogo of the Paekche Kingdom* (r. 346–75). This television drama was produced by the Korean Broadcasting Corporation, and aired in the spring of 2011. Photo by author.

and scientific achievements of the Korean people (e.g., the turtle boats at Hansan Island); (4) holy sites and sacred places (e.g., Kanghwa-do's Tan'gun Shrine to the first founding ancestor, Tan'gun; and (5) sites of myths and legends (Kim Hong-un 1995).

In 1997, after more than a decade of intense lobbying, the KSMKG announced the first five sites to be included on the prestigious list of UNESCO World Heritage sites: (1) Sŏkkuram Grotto and Pulguksa Temple; (2) the Tripitaka Koreana (P'alman Taejanggyŏng) at Haeinsa, dating to the Koryŏ period (13th century CE); (3) Chongmyo Confucian Shrine, the Yi dynasty ancestral shrine (c. late 13th century); (4) Ch'angdŏk Palace (c. 15th century) in Seoul; and (5) Hwasŏng Fortress (c. late 18th century) in Suwŏn (see fig. 1.1; Lee 1997).

More recent campaigns initiated by the Korean Tourism Organization (KTO; Han'guk Kwan'gwang Kongsa) to attract visitors to distant areas outside of Seoul have involved organizing festivals with events promoting local cuisine, seasonal festivals, beauty contests, trade expositions, the 2002 World Cup, and the building of ethnic theme parks and family entertainment destinations such as the Korean Folk Village in Yongin, the Kyŏngju Silla Millenium Park, and Paekche Culture Land (fig. 1.6).

In this era of globalization, we have to face the fact that the promotion of a viable heritage industry that will create jobs and lure investments while sustaining the local natural and cultural environment is the biggest challenge facing all regional and national governments, from England and China to Southeast Asia and the Pacific Islands (Baker 1988; Hevia 2001; T. Oakes 1988; Picard and Wood 1997; Rowan and Baram 2004). Because of the fierce competition with neighboring countries such as China and Japan, there is increasing pressure on local government agencies and developers to construct profitable heritage sites, ethnic theme parks, and folk villages. In many cases, in the overzealous adaptation of cultural resources to make heritage sites more accessible to "jaded" twenty-first-century tourists, franchise restaurants, high-rise hotels, duty-free souvenir shops, and massive parking lots that can accommodate gigantic tour buses are adversely affecting the structural integrity of old temples and scenic gardens.[17] The intrusive nature of these establishments cannot be ignored when their mere existence diffuses a site's "sense of place" and sometimes even obstructs the viewing of the monument, with street noise, milling crowds, and air pollution. The ever-present tourist is also a mixed blessing, since the majority of heritage sites cannot escape their dependence on ticket sales, which constitute the main source of revenue for the high cost of infrastructure maintenance (including roads, gates, security and fire prevention, plumbing, electricity, trash collection, toilet cleaning, and so on). Consequently, in most destinations the competition for tourist revenue has overtaken the main goal of the preservation of "original remains" and their surrounding environments for posterity. The popularity of a heritage site itself can ultimately undermine its own authentic value as unique cultural experience, which was its main attraction in the first place. The trajectory of tourism-development plans for the twenty-first century reveals that the complex web of ministries led by the CHA and the MCST, in cooperation with the

Korean Tourism Organization, have become even more involved in the daily planning, management, and marketing of archaeological remains, temples, and museums as must-see destinations, ultimately affecting their final transformations as national sites of common memory and nostalgia (Rowlands 1994, 133–36).

The following chapters are dedicated to tracing the administrative, disciplinary, and aesthetic legacies of this long-neglected but century-old shared body of heritage knowledge that, once codified through colonial and national legislation, has continued to affect how national treasures and tourist destinations are marketed to a world audience.

CHAPTER 2

COLLECTING JAPAN'S CURIOS

World Fairs, Imperial Tombs, and Preservation Laws

The idea of "national objects" being collected and catalogued as commodities for display and exhibition can be traced back to the mid-nineteenth century, when world fairs were staged in the capitals of Europe. Far-flung nations and colonized outposts of the British and French empires from India, Africa, Asia, and Australia competed with established colonial enterprises and lesser-known merchants to send to these world fairs their most valuable products, ranging from natural and raw materials to man-made inventions such as food products, wine, and curios. Even dioramas of "live" native peoples and their photographic reproductions on souvenir postcards were presented for the enlightenment, education, and entertainment of the masses (Geary and Webb 1998; Maxwell 1999). Imperial commissioners appointed by world-fair organizers judged submissions based on their utility, price, beauty, and popularity, as assessed by the sheer number of curious visitors who flocked to national pavilions.[1] The artisans and merchants of nations large and small who were awarded coveted winning medals were influential in creating new tastes and fashion trends, such as drinking tea and chocolate, and decorating homes with Oriental rugs, fabrics, and china (Briggs 1989; Hoffenberg 2001, 63–98).

The fascination with arts and crafts imported from the Far East among increasing numbers of middle-class consumers living in the capitals of Europe was also driven by the marketing skills of globe-trotting diplomats of the day, such as Sir Rutherford Alcock (1809–97), the first consul-general to open a British legation in Tokyo. Alcock has occupied a special position in the history of Japanese arts because he was the first foreign consultant to be commissioned by the shogun Tokugawa Iemochi (r. 1858–66) to represent

Japan at the Great London Exposition held in South Kensington in 1862 (Tokyo Kokuritsu Hakubutsukan 1976, 9–10). Alcock's personal recollections of Japan's first official showing appear prominently in his volume *Art and Art Industries in Japan*, which was published in 1878 and is recognized as one of the earliest treatises on the subject. In the preface, Alcock states that he was approached by the shogun himself to intervene on his behalf to obtain "contributions, illustrative of the arts and industries of Japan, either from Japanese themselves or from any of the foreign mercantile community willing to assist in the work." However, despite the open endorsement of officialdom, Alcock confessed that he had been very disappointed at the general lack of cooperation not only from the shogun himself but also from the powerful daimyo, whom Alcock accused of being interested only in preserving their "cherished isolation from foreign influences and interests." In response, Alcock, who was by no means a shy man, claimed that he had "no choice but to take upon himself the whole task, since he was determined that Japan not be un-represented."[2] Alcock achieved his mission by visiting all of the various magazines and shops in Yokohama, as well as in the smaller cities and trading quarters in Edo, where only diplomats were allowed access at that time. In these rich and busy quarters, Alcock bragged that he worked tirelessly to track down "those items the Japanese found most attractive or to find purchasers among foreigners." Much to his delight, every day he came upon "some new and interesting fabric to light, some original application to Art to industrial work of unrivalled beauty." Only a few years later, upon his return to London from Japan, Alcock was gratified to find that Japanese fabrics, silks, embroideries, lacquerwares, china, faience, bronzes, and enamels could be found for sale in all of the major shops of every capital of Europe. He therefore remained confident that there was indeed a bright future for Japanese goods, because of their "inherent beauty, grace and perfection of workmanship, variety of form, and novelty of design, as well as bargain prices far below that of European articles" (Alcock 1878, 1–3). Contemporary sources also confirm that the successful showing of Alcock's assemblage at the London Great Exposition inspired a more organized Japanese mission to the 1867 Paris International, where a pavilion featured a traditional house in which three kimono-clad ladies were on hand to serve tea (Takagi Yōko 2002, 25).

When news of the exciting and lucrative world of international fairs and museums reached Japan, "exhibitionary" complexes such as world fairs, zoos, botanical gardens, and museums were included in the official itineraries of diplomatic missions dispatched to the capitals of Europe and America between 1862 and 1867. According to Fukuzawa Yukichi (1835–1901), who served as the main translator and chronicler on the first of these "fact-finding" observation tours (*kenmon*) in 1862, the main goal was to bring back pertinent information on the latest scientific, commercial, industrial, and educational ventures from hospitals, schools, prisons, post offices, and factories, and so on, which would serve as reference guides in the modernization of Japan's new institutions.[3] Among the many centers of culture, industry, and commerce mentioned in these mission diaries, the entries for the month of April 1864 describing several official trips to the Smithsonian and the US Patent Office in Washington, DC, elicited the most rave reviews. The visitors' diary entries noted the imposing architecture of the Smithsonian Museum building itself, with its multistoried grandeur, elegant central hall, and radiating exhibition rooms crammed full of wonderful things from around the world. The main exhibitions in the hallways, which caught everyone's attention, included a model of a steam engine, a thousand-year-old Egyptian mummy, and a very large portrait of George Washington. The visitors also marveled at the innumerable plants, birds, animal specimens, machines, and crafts that they observed laid out in hundreds of glass cases arranged according to their utilitarian functions: scientific items, domestic objects, agricultural tools, and mechanical devices. One astute observer noted, for example, that the variety of agricultural tools and food products on display reminded him of the kinds of dried seafood produced by the northern Ezo or Ainu (Tokyo Kokuritsu Hakubutsukan 1976, vol. 1, 1–12; Shiina Noritaka 1988, 15–23).

The same mission diaries feature prominently in the annals of Japanese museum history, for they also contain the earliest documented use of the generic word for "museum" in the Japanese language, that is, *hakubutsukan*. There were actually two different Chinese character compounds used in the Meiji period for "museum," *haku* ("all things") and *hyaku* ("hundreds"), as in *hyakubutsukan*, which was often translated as "a building with a hundred different things" (Shiina Noritaka 1988, 28–30). Other popular character sets relating to museums included *tenjijō* ("display grounds"), *hōko* or *hōzō* ("treasure house" or "treasures registry"), and *kokibutsu shūkan* ("buildings for antiquities"). Relying on these observations, the centennial history of the Tokyo National Museum (hereafter Tōhaku), published in two large volumes, argues that the idea, function, and purpose of the museum as "a free-standing building for the public display of all kinds of objects" could be traced back as early as the 1860s in Japan (Tokyo Teishitsu Hakubutsu-kan 1938, 3; Tokyo Kokuritsu Hakubutsukan 1976, 1:1–12). In contrast to this official in-house narrative chronicling the introduction of the public museum in the late Tokugawa period, Shiina Noritaka, a historian of Meiji museums, does not believe that the young samurai who had been raised in the Tokugawa era would have truly understood the educational value or commercial purpose of museum exhibitions. In his widely read book on the development of Japanese museums, *The Historical Development of Japanese Museums* (Nihon hakubutsukan hattatsu shi), Shiina refers to Fukuzawa as the first Japanese intellectual who may have truly understood the function of a museum in modern society. As evidence, he cites Fuku-zawa's widely read travelogue *Observations of Western Countries* (Seiyō jijō), issued in three volumes (1866–69), in which the author defined the museum (*hakubutsukan*) as "a place where all the world's different objects, antiques (*kobutsu*), and curios (*chinbutsu*) are collected and displayed for the purpose of broadening people's knowledge (*kenmon*)" (Shiina Noritaka 1988, 1–31).

Not surprisingly, the 1862 mission returnees were asked to serve as advi-sors on the board of Japan's first Exposition Office (Hakurankai), which was established by the Education Ministry (see fig. 2.1) in January 1872 (Tokyo Teishitsu Hakubutsukan 1938, 1–3). As seasoned diplomats who had seen the world, these advisors' first recommendation to the committee was that their country would be better off exhibiting curios in Vienna, since they knew Japan, which was lacking in advanced machinery and technology, could not compete with other nations in Europe (Tokyo Teishitsu Hakubut-sukan 1938, 15; Guth 2000; Sand 2000). By selecting "Oriental" curios, china, and lacquerware, as well as consumer goods such as green tea and textiles that had already established a track record of proven sales at auc-tions in Europe, Meiji exposition planners had to compete with Indian and Chinese exhibitors (Barringer and Flynn 1998; Tokyo Kokuritsu Hakubut-sukan 1997, 2005). To drum up domestic support for building a grand pavil-ion in Vienna, the Education Ministry couched the staging of expositions in the popular rhetoric of "enlightenment" (*kaimei*), that is, "to further human knowledge and raise the level of Japanese civilization" (Tokyo Teishitsu Hakubutsukan 1938, 3; Shiina Noritaka 1988, 34; Takagi Hiroshi 2000). Despite government propaganda, in reality the stated mission the collection of large numbers of objects worthy of sending abroad was in jeopardy: once the exposition office planners looked into the national coffers, they quickly realized that their "few imperial jewels and crystals" were unlikely to satisfy a discriminating panel of international judges or generate positive product reviews in the competitive world marketplace (Hoffenberg 2001, 63–98). As a remedy, the Education Ministry decided to make an unprecedented nationwide plea for public donations. The ministry was especially keen on recruiting aristocratic family members, former officials, antiquarians, and anyone interested in lending, selling, or donating their heirlooms for international display. The office also made an effort to reach out to officials in prefectures and rural counties, asking them to send their local products (*meisan butsu*), both natural and man-made (*bussan*). The newly established Department of Agriculture and Commerce envisioned that exhibitions of plants, food, and animals would serve as models for improving breeding methods that would benefit the growing state agribusiness (Tokyo Teishitsu Hakubutsukan 1938, 19). As the first calculated public message designed to sell the benefits of world expositions to a domestic audience, the Education Ministry issued the following announcement two months prior to the opening of Yūshima Seiden Hakurankai, the first domestic exposition in March 1872 at the Main Hall (Taiseiden, more commonly known as Seidō) occupying the spacious temple grounds (fig. 2.1) of Yūshima near Tokyo Bay:[4]

> The purpose of the Hakurankai is to collect products/materials [*sanbutsu*], regardless of whether they are "nature or heaven made [*tenzō*] or man-made [*jinzō*]," and to correctly name them and explain their usage so as to further human knowledge. The reason we are making this announcement is that we want to arrange and display them for public viewing. We are looking forward to the day when representative collections from all over the country will be collected. At present, the oldest vessels that have been handed down reside in temples and shrines, and their numbers are small. In order to seek more exhibition goods, we also brought out the precious curios from our imperial storage, but they only amounted to a few jewels and crystals.[5] This is why we

are appealing to those who have in their possession either antiquities, natural materials, or imported curios from China or the West. Even if your objects are new, we are requesting citizens bring them for display [*shuppin*] so that these materials can enlighten the public's understanding of the difference between old and new. We sincerely ask for your cooperation in this matter.

(quoted in Tokyo Teishitsu Hakubutsukan 1938, 16)

FIG. 2.1. Exposition displays at Yūshima, 1873. *Top:* Commemoration photo of exposition committee members, c. 1871. The committee's first director, Machida Hisanari, is the sixth figure from the left. *Bottom left:* Yūshima Exhibition Halls. Source: Tokyo Kokuritsu Hakubutsukan 1992, p. 8. Reproduced courtesy of the Tokyo National Museum.

This unprecedented invitation, extended to all classes of citizens and all sectors of the government, to participate in a series of traveling expositions to the imperial capitals of Tokyo, Kyoto, and Nara, succeeded in attracting a new breed of entrepreneurs who understood that exposition venues could be used as social-climbing opportunities, where one's good taste and wealth could be put on display for a world audience (Bourdieu 1984). Soon, all kinds of interested parties—from municipal offices to individuals, from merchants to collectors, both large- and small-scale—began to vie for a chance to show off their collections and products at special booths and exhibition halls, and on the pages of printed exposition catalogues (Tokyo Teishitsu Hakubutsukan 1901; Japan-British Exhibition 1911). In less than two months, the government coffers had accumulated massive quantities of paintings, books, scrolls, pottery, cloisonné, lacquerware, and textiles—more than enough to fill a Japanese Pavilion at Vienna. The Yūshima Exposition attendance records tallied by the Imperial Museum Teishitsu Hakubutsukan indicate that, for the first time in Japanese history, three thousand visitors had passed through daily (Tokyo Teishitsu Hakubutsukan 1938). The final total exceeded 150,000 by the end of the two-month exhibition (Tokyo Kokuritsu Hakubutsukan 1992, 5).

The Exposition Office eventually dispatched over seventy people to Vienna, including forty-two officials, twenty-five architects and landscape gardeners, and six foreigners, as well as translators, to coordinate the technical and organizational feat of exhibiting this vast array of objects. The pavilion entrance was framed by an imposing shrine gate (*torii*) that opened into a scenic Japanese garden setting. The magnificent center display was a gigantic gold-plated mythological animal from Japanese folklore, the dragonfish (*shachihoko*) donated by Nagoya castle (fig. 2.2).

There was also a giant papier-mâché replica of the Great Buddha of Kamakura, one of the more popular tourist destinations featured in the souvenir photo albums sold by commercial photographic studios in the newly opened ports of Nagasaki, Yokohama, and Kobe. Although in Europe the successful staging of the Japanese Pavilion in Vienna launched the first wave of "Japonisme," or the love affair with all things Japanese (Takagi Yōko 2002), back home the fad introduced new agents who were given the charge of selecting and arranging exposition goods for the benefit of European judges, commissioners, and consumers.[6]

The Vienna exhibition organizers came up with a new taxonomy of "Japanese" objects for display, listed in the following order: (1) ritual vessels; (2) old jade and jewels; (3) stone bows and lightning axes; (4) old mirrors and bells; (5) bronze vessels; (6) old tiles; (7) weapons (swords, bows, banner flags, armor, horse equipment, halberds, small and large firearms,

65 名古屋城の金の鯱 ca.1880 愛知 Mythological dragon-fish roof ornament from Nagoya Castle, Aichi

1873年（明治6）開催のウィーン万国博覧会への出品準
備のため名古屋藩より貢納された金の鯱。左手後方には
沖縄からの出品か、大貝が見える。

FIG. 2.2. Photograph of the mythological dragonfish (*shachihoko*) sent to the 1873 Vienna International Exhibition. The sign reads, "Donated by Nagoya Castle." The large piece of shell to the left represents a product sent from Okinawa. The original albumen photograph, attributed to Uchida Kuichi (1844–75), is in the Museum of the Imperial Collection (Sanno-maru Shōzōkan), Tokyo. Source: Konishi and Hideo et. al. 2005, plate 65.

bullets, and war drums); (8) old documents and paintings; (9) old books and classics; (10) screens and paintings from shrines and Buddhist temples; (11) musical instruments; (12) rubbings from steles and bells; (13) old seals; (14) stationary (writing implements); (15) agricultural implements; (16) tools; (17) chariot parts; (18) households items; (19) old textiles; (20) costumes; (21) leather items; (22) coins; (23) precious metalwork; (24) pottery from around theworld; (25) lacquerware; (26) weights and measures; (27) toys; (28) dolls; (29) old Buddhist sculptures and Buddhist paraphernalia; and (30) animal and plant fossils (Tokyo Kokuritsu Hakubutsukan 1976, 2:221–22; Japan Bunkachō 1997, 197–98).

At a cursory glance, the list of objects appears true to its namesake of Hakurankai, that is, collecting and surveying all Japanese products amassed, from the principal donors, represented by the imperial family, shrines, temples, to purchases donated by collectors. However, upon closer inspection, we can discern distinct patterns reflecting the mixed bag of classificatory schemes adopted by European natural scientists, Edo-era antiquarian catalogues, and the casual collectors of the day. First, the broadest classification scheme for the Vienna exhibition arrangement divided items into the following categories: nature-made objects, animals, minerals, fossils, weapons, toys, pottery, tea implements, and coins. These divisions clearly mirror the museum arrangement schemes most famously pioneered by the two oldest university museums, founded exclusively for archaeological and ethnographical acquisitions, the Pitt-Rivers Museum at the University of Oxford and Harvard University's Peabody Museum of Archaeology and Ethnology.[7] At the same time, these categories also mirrored the tastes and preferences of an earlier generation of acquisitive collectors, namely former diplomats, teachers, merchants, and scientists, many of whom had been stationed in Nagasaki.

Philipp Franz von Siebold (1796–1866) was a well-known traveler, geographer, and doctor, as well as being one of the earliest proponents of the race theory of the Ainu. Trained as a physician in Germany, von Siebold spent a total of eight years in the Dutch East Indies in Batavia (Jakarta) and Dejima (Nagasaki), where he was posted in 1823. While he was stationed in Dejima, he was widely hailed for his work as mentor to the first generation of Japanese students trained in Western medicine.[8] Although von Siebold was a physician, he also possessed a thorough knowledge of pharmacology, and soon became respected as the first naturalist to investigate the flora and fauna of Japan. Emulating other Victorian-era scientists, such as Charles Darwin (1809–82), von Siebold spent much of his time coming up with his own classification system in order to arrange his specimens. In addition to botany, von Siebold was also fascinated by ethnography, which at that time only existed as a subfield of geography and was therefore not regarded as a scientific subject in its own right. Von Siebold's interest may also have been influenced by two of his predecessors, who had also been stationed in Nagasaki, Jan Cock Blomhoff (1779–1853; on Dejima from 1809 to 1813 and again from 1817 to 1823) and Johannes Overmeer Fisscher (1800–1848; on Dejima from 1819 to 1823), both of whom had also created their own classifications. Von Siebold, however, surpassed his predecessors because he had also collected documentary support, in the form of Japanese language books and of pictures depicting the use and meanings of the objects (Vos 2001, 40).

When von Siebold returned from Japan in 1830, the personal collections of ethnographic artifacts and botanical specimens that he had accumulated during his career as a doctor in the Dutch colonies were donated to the Rijksmuseum voor Volkenkunde in Leiden in 1831. In fact, in the early years, the museum was then known as the Museum Japonicum because of the substantial holdings from Japan. Rijksmuseum curator Ken Vos, who has studied the six thousand objects in von Siebold's collections, suggests that von Siebold's knowledge of botanical classifications may have influenced the arrangements of other ethnographic collections that were rapidly coming into vogue in Europe. A handwritten catalogue (dating to 1832 and 1837), attributed to von Siebold, was divided into four main classes and subdivisions:

Class I.   Scientific objects: (1) printed books, manuscripts, and woodcuts; (2) drawings and paintings; (3) coins, commemorative medals, and some antiquities.

Class II. Objects of classes and industries: (4) raw materials and products obtained by a simple manufacturing process; (5) products of art and industry largely made from a single material; (6) products of art and industry made from combinations of materials.

Class III. Models: (7) Models buildings and implements serving the comfort and security of man; (8) models of furniture and implements for agriculture, fishing, and other economic activities; (9) machines and instruments.

Class IV. Ethnographic objects from other areas.[9] (Vos 2001)

According to Vos, the beauty of von Siebold's hierarchical system was that, through ever-increasing refinement, one could eventually go down to specify categories of related objects. However, the drawback was that the existing semantic bias among the classes was exacerbated as material properties had to be further subdivided into social and functional categories, based apparently on traditional and "intuitive" classification that also appear in the Blomhoff and Fisscher collections (Vos 2001, 45). Citing a 1843 quote attributed to von Siebold, Vos has proposed that von Siebold's rationale for dividing his objects into "racial" and "cultural groupings" was that this arrangement gave the best impression of a "people's relative progress," the "condition of their arts," and the nature of past exchanges with other peoples (Chapman 1988, 24). Hence, the class divisions von Siebold applied to his Japanese collections may have represented the first documented case of ethnographic collections being arranged according to geographic and cultural regions, preceding Pitt-Rivers, who was responsible for popularizing ethnographic museum arrangements.

The exposition catalogue's secondary system numbered items from one to four— ritual vessels or "old vessels" (kogibutsu), bronzes bearing inscriptions (kinsekimon), jades (kogyoku), and stone objects (kamiseki)—popular objects that had long been favored by antiquarians regardless of country of origin. Needless to say, the circulation of antiquities prior to Meiji state intervention had been a haphazard affair, largely carried out by a close-knit network of dealers, collectors, and tomb raiders. It is well documented in the annals of Japanese archaeology that looting reached its peak in 1784, when a solid gold seal from China's later Han dynasty (c. 25–220 CE) was discovered on an island in Hakata Bay across from Fukuoka. Its discovery became the cause célèbre of the age for the following reasons.

Not only was it the first time an artifact unearthed from the ground had supported the records of the ancient kingdom of Wa, but the ruler may have maintained a close diplomatic and trade relationship with the Han Empire (Saitō 1982, 32–58). If the four-character inscription was read as "The Seal of the King of Na of Wa of Han" (Kan no Wa no Na no koku ō), and the seal was indeed a genuine Han dynasty make, then the dating of the inscription posed a major challenge to the veracity of the earliest historical accounts of Japan, previously known from only the *Accounts of the Eastern Barbarians* (Weizhi Dongyi zhuan) dating to the late-third-century textual records of the Wei dynasty (Inoue Hideo 1974). Despite the two-century gap between the dating of the seal and its story, which is linked to the *History of the Latter Han Dynasty* (Hou han shu), this seal proved to be the single most valuable find unearthed by native historians of the time.[10] Following this sensational discovery, the possibility that tantalizing and valuable ancient treasures could be unearthed from the ground led to even more widespread looting, with professional grave diggers and enthusiastic collectors venturing into remote areas far from the centers of learning and commerce in Kyoto, Osaka, and Edo in search of similar treasures (Ikawa-Smith 1982).

It is important to remind the reader here that, prior to the eighteenth century, the common belief was that stone weapons had been sent down from on high during the "age of the gods" (*kami jidai*), which predated the ascension of Emperor Jimmu. Before the advent of modern archaeology in Japan, which was introduced by foreign scientists (to be discussed further), strange-looking stones and artifacts were reputed to possess mysterious and magical powers. Although the term *kami jidai* originated in the *Nihon Shoki* (Chronicles of Japan) and the *Record of Ancient Matters* (*Kojiki*) in the eighth century, it came into wide usage in reference to "stone tools" (*kamiseki*) only during the Edo period (Uchida Yoshiaki 2004, 55). Corresponding names, such as "thunder stones" (stone celts) and "elf bolts" (stone projectiles), were also given to stone tools in medieval times in China, Korea, and Europe, where they were also widely collected (Trigger 1989, 28).

Arai Hakusei (1657–1725) is often referred to as Japan's "first native archaeologist" because he dug up unusual stones from tombs two centuries before the arrival of Edward Morse in 1878 (Oba 1935). Arai's collecting activities are well documented because he left behind two-hundred-year-old sketches of distinctive large keyhole mounds (*zenpō-kōen*) depicting keyholed burial shaped mounds surrounded by trees or tomb figurines (*haniwa*).[11] Arai was also known to have devised his own cataloguing scheme for stone tools, dividing them first into man-made stones (*jinjaku* or *jinkō*) and natural stones (*shizen no ishi* or *tennen no mono*), and then subdividing these into twenty-four different types. Archaeological terminology widely used today—such as *sekifu* (axe/adze), *sekizoku* (arrowhead), *sekken* (dagger), *ishiguwa* (stone hoe), *sekisō* (spearhead), *ishisaji* (stone scraper), and the more common *haniwa* (pottery figurine), and *magatama* (comma-shaped jade bead)—can in fact be traced to Arai's classification system.[12] Teshigawara Akira, a historian of Japanese archaeology, mentions that, as early as 1794, Arai had suggested that the Ezo (Ainu) tribes living in northeastern Japan (the locus of many stone arrowheads) may have descended from the same stone-weapon-making tribes as the Sushen recorded in Chinese textual sources (Teshigawara 1995, 19). Because of Arai's hypothesis that arrowheads originated in "ancient China," "foreign-made" stone arrowheads became coveted collectors' items (Uchida 2004, 60–63). Due to Arai's contributions, stone objects (*kamiseki*) began to acquire the reputation of being the oldest, but nonetheless skillfully crafted, man-made items. However, before the advent of modern archaeology, their function seems to have remained a mystery—even to the initiated.

After Arai, the best-known group of antiquarians (*aikōsha*) were the "Sekitei followers," who came from a wide swath of society (from the high-born samurai to middle-class doctors, monks, scholars, merchants, and even farmers). They began collecting everything—in cluding natural minerals, fossils, man-made stone, and jade objects (Saitō 1974, 13–72). The group's namesake, Kiuchi (or Kinouchi) Sekitei (1725–1808), a well-known Kyoto resident, was at one time reported to have amassed over two thousand stone objects, or *kamiseki* (Oba 1935, 411–12). The fad of collecting odd-shaped ancient jades and prehistoric stone tools peaked in the mid-eighteenth century, with many antiquarians holding joint exhibitions and circulating printed catalogues complete with measurements, descriptions, and illustrations based on their own classification systems of objects and sketches of tomb structures (Uchida Yoshiaki 2004, 59). Considering the centuries-old Edo belief that ancient stones and bronzes held magical powers, we can understand why exposition officials decided to place ritual bronze vessels prominently at the entrance leading up to the Vienna pavilion.[13] The vessels not only signaled the Meiji regime's official debut in the international arena but also attempted to send the message that the Japanese imperial lineage was substantially older than those of European royalty (Suzuki and Takagi 2000).

Last, but not least, the largest number of exhibition objects consisted of "everyday objects," such as tea bowls, lacquerware, toys, and dolls, reflecting the many leisure pursuits and hobbies of the descendants of the now-defunct aristocratic classes and samurai households who had inherited family heirlooms. Although formerly used for tea ceremonies and local festivals (*matsuri*), these items acquired universal cachet when their status was elevated to that of "national objects" by virtue of their being sent abroad, exhibited, and collected as fashionable status items flaunted by wealthy British merchants and collectors (Baird 2000; Earle 1986). Suzuki Hiroyuki has observed that the Meiji collectors' appreciation of old things was just one more aspect of the zeitgeist, enlightenment of civilization (*bunmei kaika*), and was characteristic of cultured and enlightened men well versed in "Western civilized ways" (Suzuki Hiroyuki 2003, 52). The competitive aspect of the evolving tastes of turn-of-the-century collectors was also noted by art historian Jordan Sand, who has pointed out that the Tokyo elites were remodeling Japanese-style homes with "Western-style" living rooms and high-priced exposition souvenirs (fig. 2.3), in imitation of popular Victorian trends of the day (Sand 2000; Tokyo Kokuritsu Hakubutsukan 2005).

FIG. 2.3. Japanese Meiji-era porcelain and pottery wares on display at the Japan-British Exposition held at White City in London, 1910. These gigantic elaborately inlaid and colorfully glazed decorative wares were produced for the European exposition circuit. Source: Japan-British Exhibition 1911, 271.

The exposition objects sent to Vienna thus reflected a hybrid mix of the "Edo antiquarians' classifications system," ethnographic museum arrangement schemes, Victorian tastes, and world fair marketing agendas—blending the tastes of the "East and West." Following the success of the Japanese Pavilion in Vienna, the returning collections were reassembled with much fanfare. A prominent place was reserved for imperial treasures, such as mirrors and swords from Ise Grand Shrine, samurai armor, and *ukiyo-e* prints of the period. Special invitations were reserved for foreign diplomats, guest educators, aristocrats, and municipal officials throughout the country. The invited guests included diplomats, high-ranking bureaucrats, and aristocrats, who were favored with the privilege of seeing the Meiji emperor and his entourage on opening day (Tokyo Teishitsu Hakubutsukan 1938, 25). Eventually, over ten thousand people, from the highest ministries down to the local levels of government—including officials from the Imperial Household Agency and Foreign Affairs Ministry, mayors of the capital, Tokyo, and of major cities such as Osaka, Kyoto, Saitama, Shinagawa, Chiba, and Shizuoka, and prefectural and county officials—showed up for the openings (Tokyo Teishitu Hakubutsukan 1938, 30).

In addition to high-ranking bureaucrats, all ranks of citizenry, both men and women, regardless of status, were encouraged to come and mingle in an urban environment. Contemporary prints and photographs produced for the event depict daily throngs of thousands of curious visitors from all walks of life lining up to get a glimpse of the eclectic mix of old and new paintings and hanging scrolls (with subject matter ranging from portraits and tigers to Oriental-style landscapes), kimono textiles, musical instruments, woven baskets, ceramics, lacquerware, and animal specimens such as birds, reptiles, snakes, and crabs (Hachizume 2005). One prominent guest was Edward Morse (1838-1925), whose observation demonstrates the extent to which the Meiji state had invested in exhibition spaces:

> The building included a long and spacious hall [which] was filled with an extensive and interesting collection of educational apparatus from Europe and America—modern schoolhouses in miniature, desks, inkstands, and the minutest details of closed school appliances abroad.... What a wide conception of the Japanese, entering as they were methods of education, that they should establish a museum to display the apparatus used in the work. Here

was a nation spending nearly a third of its annual budget on education, and
in contrast Russia spending a half of one percent on the same department.
(cited in Coaldrake 1994, 24)

Although it has not been confirmed whether Morse was accurate in his
estimates of the expositions portion of the overall Meiji education budget,
it does not seem implausible that he was, since a fortune was spent on staging expositions inside and outside of Japan before World War II (Tokyo
Kokuritsu Hakubutsukan 1976, 1992). Thus, the popularity of Meiji-era
expositions inside and outside of Japan marked a pivotal turning point but
also became an important source of state revenue from ticket sales and a
vehicle of nation building.

In order to prepare for this event, the Exposition Office was moved to the
Interior Ministry in 1873 so that the police could more efficiently monitor
the circulation of objects as well as coordinate the nationwide administration of a standardized registration system. To that end, the ministries'
officials agreed to monitor the large number of objects that were pouring in
from temples and shrines to private individuals and municipal authorities.
In order to track the flow of donations, officials set up a card-cataloguing
system (*daichō tōroku*) requiring new identification tags for accounting and
storage purposes, and estimated insurance fees for repair or replacement in
cases of loss or theft. Controlling thousands of people daily to protect exhibition goods and pavilions from damage, fire, and theft proved to be quite a
logistical nightmare for the exposition planners, who decided to introduce
detailed accounting and touring regulations for future exhibitions. First
and foremost, the Exposition Office decided to sell admission tickets at the
entrance gates. The tickets were then retrieved upon exiting, ensuring an
accurate headcount. Second, all visitors were required to follow designated
routes marked by clear signs, and written rules prohibiting smoking, loud
talking, trash, animals, and large bags. Third, separate rest areas were designated for relaxation and refreshments for smokers and viewers. Fourth,
in order to allow maximum viewing time, the exhibitions were open daily
from 9 am to 4 pm—except on major holidays (Tokyo Teishitsu Hakubutsukan 1938, 31). The sheer number of visitors instigated long-range plans
to build permanent museums and cultural spaces in Ueno and Nara, where
ground was broken in 1878 and 1881, respectively (16–17).

The conscious decision on the part of Meiji exposition organizers to concentrate on "decorative arts," catering to foreign buyers and tourists, also meant that Japanese exports were subject to the same market forces of supply and demand that had determined the monetary worth of objets d'art appraised by auction houses and antiquity dealers, much as exports had been with the trade in chinoiserie for centuries.[14] For example, Rutherford Alcock's 1862 submissions were resold at various auction venues, with a large number ending up at the Bowes Museum in Liverpool. The museum's founder, James Lord Bowes (1834–99), was a wealthy local businessman who had been appointed the first honorary consul for Japan in 1888. Bowes is known to have bought his collections from local dealers, such as the Holt shipping family, and at auctions between 1862 and 1874. Opening on June 19, 1890, this first museum devoted to the Japanese arts welcomed a record number of 11,229 visitors in the first five days. At the time, Liverpool was a busy international trading center plied by ship captains with ample opportunities to trade directly with the newly opened ports of Japan. The city's journals and directories of transaction records surviving from the 1870s and 1880s also confirm the popularity of Japanese arts. For example, the June 9, 1888, edition of the *Times* advertised the upcoming sale of Japanese goods as follows: "Hampton and Sons invite an inspection of their new stock 'including this year's latest novelties at never before seen low prices—Japanese decorated spears and porcelains" (cited in Baird 2000, 128). Records from another source, the Liverpool bill of entry (dated February 23, 1865), noted the import of a Japanese suit of armor. These items may have been shipped via China, since the ship is not recorded as having called at a Japanese port. According to contemporary Liverpool sales records, the most popular items being bought and sold were lacquerware, ceramics, woodblock prints, burial garments, kites, swords, and miniature sculptures (*netsuke*), which to this day are bought and sold by private museums and individual collectors in Europe and America (Baird 2000, 127–28; Earle 1986, 864). Therefore, we can see that, even before Japanese Pavilions became popular exposition venues, a diverse range of Japanese goods were being sent to Europe via various trading routes from East Asia.

By the late 1850s, secondhand shops (*furui dōguya*) eager to cater to the new influx of foreign customers and consumers had opened for business along the main thoroughfares of Kobe, Yokohama, Nagasaki, and Osaka.

The booming trade in *Japonisme* thus offered new business and career opportunities for suppliers of curios and antiquities—notably looters, shop owners, and middlemen. Reflecting the cosmopolitan nature of the curio trade, the most commercially successful curio dealers and auction houses (such as Sotheby's and Christie's) catered to a well-heeled and well-traveled clientele based in Paris, London, and Berlin (Takagi Yōko 2002). The book *Plunder and Pleasure: Japanese Art in the West, 1860–1930* translates the personal diaries of two of the most successful art dealers of the day, Phillip Sichel (1840–99) and Raymond Koechlin (1860–1931). The personal stories of these two resourceful businessmen (based in Berlin and Paris, respectively) indicate that, with the easing of travel restrictions, they had ventured as far as Osaka, Kyoto, and Hyōgo. Thus, for the first time in three hundred years, inland cities became the destinations of dealers looking for bargains (Put 2000, 19–30). The chapter titled "Notes of a Parisian Art Dealer in Japan" (Notes d'un bibleoteur au Japon) documents Sichel's brief journey to Japan in 1874 specifically to shop for antiquities at the newly opened ports (Put 2000, 19–31). Sichel's colorful stories recount the joys of making direct contacts with Osaka textile merchants and making deals in out-of-the-way places where all-night bargaining sessions were accompanied by musical entertainment provided by geishas. Sichel bragged that on his return trip to Paris, he took with him more than 450 crates containing more than 5,000 objects (ceramics, textiles, lacquerware, and religious objects; 71). Needless to say, vast fortunes were made, and often lost, overnight. Such business dealings and freewheeling lifestyles, and the spirit of market capitalism crossing three continents are reminiscent of today's international art market, where large sums of currency and illegally traded antiquities still exchange hands in secret locations.

The art world is familiar with the names of collectors such as William Sturgis Bigelow (1850–1926), the scion of a Boston Brahmin family of physicians, zoologist/archaeologist Edward Morse, and art historian Ernest Fenollosa (1853–1908)—all respected members of learned societies and the departments of imperial universities (fig. 2.4). They were some of the more prominent foreigners to be invited to exposition openings and VIP social events attended by members of the imperial family, foreign dignitaries, and art dealers. The trio's personal acquisitions are now part of the storied Japanese collections housed at the Boston Museum of Fine Arts, the Peabody Essex Museum in Salem, and Harvard University's Peabody Museum of Ethnology and Archaeology. Although all three men of science and the arts are hailed as the first generation of scholars who opened the eyes of the world to the beauty of Japanese arts, we cannot ignore the fact that all three were avaricious collectors who amassed personal fortunes while serving as employees of the Education Ministry, which was charged with the ostensible mission of protecting the art and architecture of Japan. Although government laws prohibiting trade in "lost and stolen" antiquities were implemented in 1871, it seems that the Meiji authorities made exceptions for celebrities and foreigners of high status, who were permitted to roam freely about Japan.

Morse's published diaries, *Japan, Day by Day* (1917), have left us vivid accounts of his two-year tenure (1877–79) as an invited professor of zool-

FIG. 2.4. *From left to right*: Sylvestor Morse, Okakura Kakuzō, Ernest Fenollosa and William Sturgis Bigelow, c. 1882. Okakura was serving as an interpreter for the temporary treasures survey commissioned by Itō Hirobumi. Source: Thrasher 1984.

ogy at Tokyo Imperial University, where he spent summer vacations either alone or accompanied by Fenollosa and Bigelow "ransacking curio shops up and down the Kansai regions" (fig. 2.5):

FIG. 2.5. Pottery shops in the Kiyomizu section of Kyoto, where collectors and dealers went curio hunting, c. 1880s. This street, now a popular tourist destination leading to Kiyomizu Temple, is still lined with scores of souvenir shops and vendors hawking everything from green tea ice cream to kimonos, postcards, fans, and food. Photo by Edward Morse. Konishi and Hideo et al., 2005, plate 164.

Japan is a veritable paradise for The Collector of bric-a-brac finds, for wherever he goes he finds second-hand shops or the *furui dōguya* … displayed old objects of every description: pottery, metal and lacquerwork, basketry, swords, and sword furniture, pictures, etc. In the smallest villages through which ones rides, one finds some shop … cannot help recalling the fact that in our country the second hand furniture, second hand books, second hand clothing, and only a few of the larger cities will have shops containing bric-a-brac, etc. Furthermore, it may be observed that in the Japanese shops, the objects with few exceptions being from China and Korea, while in our country the objects are invariably from Europe or Asia, Dutch delft, Italian majolica, German ironwork. It is a significant fact that one looks in vain for any art object worthy preserving in our own country." (Morse 1917, 105)

Suffice it to say, for these three men, Japan was like a candy store. They were also able to get rare glimpses of and chances to negotiate good prices for the most sought-after items because they were adept at massaging the egos of notable local collectors (110). Luckily for the trio, they were not competing with each other, because each had a different obsession (247). Fenollosa went after paintings, Bigelow coveted lacquerware and sword guards (the most desired items among major British collectors of the day), and Morse went mostly for pottery (Earle 1986). Morse's lifelong fascination with Japanese pottery was an extension of his first love, zoology. Morse's vast pottery collections, photographs, and folk crafts are now exhibited at two major museums in Massachusetts: the Peabody Essex Museum in Salem, where he served as curator from 1880 to 1914, and the Boston Museum of Fine Arts, where he was also hired as curator in 1890 to oversee more than 5,000 items of pottery.[15] Last, but not least, despite Morse's self-confessed pillaging activities, we have to credit Morse for his meticulous sketches, descriptions, and photographs of "everyday Japanese things." His photographs and sketches of the architecture and interiors of Japanese homes, farming tools, subsistence practices, and festivals are still consulted by curators when recreating tableaus of authentic "Edo village scenes" at theme parks and folk museum exhibitions (Gluck 1998; Konishi and Oka 2005; Minpaku 1990).

Fenollosa also amassed his own personal fortune while surveying for the temporary treasures survey committee sent by the Education Ministry between 1882 and 1886. He was able to conduct quick surveys because he knew exactly where he was heading, since by the summer of 1878 he had traveled to the Kansai area with Morse and Bigelow for weeks at a time, dashing between Kyoto, Nara, and Wakayama (Murakata 1982, 324). Upon his return to the United States, Fenollosa supported himself with income coming mostly from art sales. His own personal collection was later sold to one of the many scions of the Weld family, Charles Goddard (1857–1911), who later donated his collections to the Boston Museum of Fine Arts in

1911. Goddard's collection at the time numbered 2,072 pieces. That same year Bigelow also donated 14,893 pieces to the museum (Murakata Akiko 1980, 1: n.p., appendix table). Despite the large number of paintings Fenollosa shipped out of Japan, leading authorities on Meiji cultural history give him due credit as the first informed connoisseur (*shikibetsuka*) to authenticate (*kantei*) and catalogue "national masterpieces" (*bijutsu mohan*), a revolutionary concept for the time (Takada 1997; Takagi 1995; Yamaguchi 1982, 14).

Fenollosa also seems to have been well financed during these trips since he could rely on the largesse of three other companions, including John Lowell Gardner (1837–98) and his wife, Isabella Stewart Gardner (1840–1924), Percival Lowell (1855–1916), and John Gardner Coolidge (1863–1936), a prominent collector of Chinese ceramics. The most eccentric of the Boston collectors was Isabella Stewart Gardner, who seems to have been inspired by Okakura Kakuzō's *Book of Tea* (1906) as well as by her trips to teahouses in Japan—to the extent that she built her own teahouse on the extensive grounds of her Green Hill home in Brookline, now a suburb of Boston, after returning from a memorable trip to Japan. According to William Thrasher, author and expert on the Japanese tea ceremony, Gardner had once compared a photograph of her teahouse to the one she had taken of Shūgakuin Rikkyū, the detached villa belonging to the Imperial family located northeast of the city of Kyoto. Although there are no reliable records of Stewart's original building, the construction may have been carried out under Okakura's guidance. Gardner's fascination with the Orient fueled subsequent trips, at which time she made known her desire to collect works of exceptional quality with the express purpose of founding a museum. Needless to say, the exquisite architectural decorations, paintings, and art ripped from old castles, churches, and temples were reassembled for maximum effect in her now-storied Isabella Stewart Gardner Museum, a proud Boston landmark. According to contemporary news sources, guests at Gardner's inaugural garden party at Fenway Court in 1903 were enthralled by the nostalgic atmosphere of her recreated Renaissance-style palazzo courtyard surrounded by flowers, a flowing fountain, and mood lighting emanating from Japanese lanterns.[16] There is no doubt that the collecting tastes of rich patrons from Boston in turn influenced the acquisition agenda of Imperial Museum curators and art specialists, who throughout the Meiji era continued to favor paintings and decorative arts preferred by major collectors of the time (Inoue Yoshihirō 2005; Satō 1999).

On the supply side of the trade in *Japonisme*, the abundance of goods for sale at these secondhand shops reflected the very unstable political, economic, and social conditions of the waning years of the Bakufu regime, when formerly well-to-do samurai households were forced to sell off their estates and heirlooms to make ends meet. The other major suppliers were desperate monks who had also fallen on hard times since the promulgation of the 1868 edict on the separation of Shintō and Buddhist orders (*shinbutsu bunri*).[17] This edict, which essentially gave Shintō priests license to invade Buddhist temples (fig. 2.6) to remove Shintō objects and to strip Buddhist appurtenances from shrines (*haibutsu kishaku*), proved to be a major psychological and economic blow to prominent temple sects, who had shared power with rulers for more than a millennium (Hardacre 1989, 27; Vesey 2004, 54–60).

The authority of temples had for centuries rested on the monks' knowledge of esoteric Buddha relics, which were intricately interwoven with imperial rituals for three reasons: as gifts of the imperial court, Buddha relics were perceived as valuables invoking the authority and person of the giver; as remnants of the historical Buddha, they served as tokens of the authority of the founder and his religion; and as objects believed to have apotropaic powers, the offering of relics ideally conferred the protective power of Buddhism on their recipients (Ruppert 2000, 44). It is no wonder, then, that the monks resisted Fenollosa's demands to open up the inner sanctums of Hōryūji Temple, since they resented the Meiji regime not only for robbing them of their long-held religious and political authority but also for threatening their very existence as the imperially sanctioned caretakers of sacred relics.[18] Therefore, rather than surrender all of their remaining valuable possessions, the financially strapped monks had resorted to concealing the temple's most valuable relics from the authorities, waiting for the opportunity to sell them on the black market or leak them through the secondhand shops lining major tourist destinations such as Kiyomizu Temple in Kyoto (Fenollosa 1909; Matsuyama 1993).

Machida Hisanari (1837–97) is widely cited as the patriot and visionary (see fig. 2.1) who first alerted Meiji officials to the plight of antiquities leaving the country (Tanaka 1982; Tokyo Teishitsu Hakubutsukan 1938,

FIG. 2.6. Temple buildings at Tsurugaoka Hachimangū, Kamakura, Japan, c. 1868. *Top:* Pl. 46: Kagura den (Hall) viewed from a different angle. It appears that the picture was taken at a different time. *Bottom:* Pl. 47: Rotating Sutra Repository (Rinzō) storing Buddhist scriptures located left of Kagura Hall. It was dismantled following the separation of Shintō from Buddhism (*Shinbutsu bunri)* laws. Photo by Felice Beato. Source: Yokohama Kaikōshiryokan [The Port of Yokohama Historical Museum] ed., *F. Beato Bakumatsu Nihon shashinshū* [Catalogue of Felice Beato's photographs dating to the Late Tokugawa Era] (Yokohama: Benridō, 1987).

34; Matsuyama 1993, 199). Like Fukuzawa, Machida, as an experienced mission member, had led nineteen students on a study-abroad program to the South Kensington Museum and the 1867 Paris Universal Exposition (Tanaka 1982, 267; Shiina Noritaka 1988, 35). Upon his return, Machida was appointed to the exalted position of counsel for the Ministry of State (Daijōkan) on April 25, 1871 (Tokyo Kokuritsu Hakubutsa 1976, 2:605–6). On May 23, 1871, Machida's office announced his three-step program to track down illegally trafficked antiquities as well as anticipate those that might get lost or stolen or damaged. First, Machida recommended the formation of a Depository for Antiquities (Shūkokan) whose assigned mission was the authentication and collection of antiquities (*kobutsu*) that would serve as evidence for tracing their origins, development, past trends, systems, and material culture (*bunbutsu*). Second, in lieu of the fact that the government lacked such a facility at that time, due to budget constraints, the government would immediately promulgate preservation laws throughout every prefecture. Third, Machida called for the appointment of specialists capable of drawing illustrations (*zuka*) to compile records and copies (*mosha*) of antiquities for inventorying purposes (Shiina Noritaka 1988, 34; Matsuyama 1993, 179). Machida also drew up detailed instructions on how to make a report if one came into possession of such an item: the citizen must report the discovery—including the location and the item's owner—in detailed writing to the local office (*kan*), usually the police. During his tenure, Machida was highly critical of his fellow officials, whom he accused of "suppressing the old in order to compete for the new" (*atsukyū keishin*) in their relentless pursuit to modernize Japan. In recognition of his efforts, he was appointed the first director of the newly established exposition office on January 1872, when he was set up on the former cathedral grounds in Yūshima (see fig. 2.1) in the neighborhood of Kanda (Yagi Shizuyama 1935, 420).

That same year, Machida was sent on a nationwide survey to draw up an inventory (*mokuroku*) listing potentially valuable treasures (*hōmotsu*) throughout the country (Iwao 1993, 768). During his trips to Kyoto, Osaka, Nara, Shinagawa, Aichi, Wakayama, Gifu, and Shiga, Machida made several reports to the Imperial Household Agency and the Education Ministry implicating temple abbots whom he suspected of stashing away treasures to sell to foreign buyers (Tokyo Kokuritsu Hakubutsukan 1976,

2:607–16). The enduring legacy of Machida's 1873 initiative was his recommendation that the treasures owned by Tōdaiji Temple and the Shōsōin (see fig. 7.1) should be included in the Nara Exposition (Tokyo Kokuritsu Hakubutsukan 1976, 2:614–19). By 1875, the management of three hundred treasures and documents from the Shōsōin and Tōdaiji was transferred to the Imperial Household Agency (Suzuki and Takagi 2002, 6). The Interior Ministry also supported Machida's proposition mandating that the repairs on, the preservation of, and treasures belonging to the two temples should be placed under the direct jurisdiction of the Imperial Household Agency. Since then, Hōryūji Temple (fig. 2.7) has been promoted in catalogues and officially issued tourist postcard sets as the sole guardian of Japan's "grandest collection of curios" (Hōryūji 1907), despite the fact that the Imperial Household Agency remains the sole zealous guardian and curator of Japan's most prestigious cache of national treasures (Matsuoka 1935; Tokyo Kokuritsu Hakubutsukan 1992, 61).

FIG. 2.7. Hōryūji Main Hall (Kondō), c. 1900. Photo by Ogawa Kazumasa (1860–1929) *Shōhon Nihon Bijutsushi* [First draft of the history of Japanese art], 1st ed. (Tokyo: Nōshōmuchō (Ministry of Agriculture and Commerce, 1901).

With the growing recognition of the economic and symbolic value of antiquities on the world stage, nation-building politicians and historians began to turn their attention to the physical remains of tombs, or *kofun,* in search of "sacred relics" attesting to the divine lineage of emperors (*bansei ikkei*) traced back to the supernatural deity, the Sun Goddess.[19] However, despite the Imperial Household Agency's grandiose claims of their own divinity and antiquity, in truth very few buried artifacts from identifiable tombs were excavated (Saitō 1982, 9–10). To add insult to injury, dates of tomb construction and concrete links to dead emperors remains were impossible to verify, since antiquarians and looters over the centuries had made off with the grave goods that had inscriptions.[20] The Imperial House-hold Tomb Office was established in 1871 to prevent the further destruction of imperial remains and looting activities. Three years later, in May 1874, the Education Ministry decreed that "excavations of any tomb, whether known by legends, oral traditions or site resembling *kofun* is strictly prohib-ited" (Saitō 1982, 318). The law also stipulated that the Meiji state dispatch centrally appointed tomb guardians to protect the security of specifically designated imperial tombs, as well as nearby burial mounds, ancient sites, and famous places associated with former emperors, empresses, and consorts. This official promulgation of Japan's first buried properties law explicitly banning unauthorized excavations signaled to the public that any physical relics or material evidence related to imperial history was now under state ownership and management.[21]

The Education Ministry laws for the handling of "lost and stolen antiqui-ties," promulgated in April 1876, defined "buried remains" as archaeologi-cal data with potential value for "academic or art historical research"—such as stone tools, bronzes, iron tools, pottery, pottery figures (*haniwa*), horse bells, mirrors (*magatama*), tubular beads, gold, and rings—as well as simi-lar accessories from which "we could infer the lifeways (*seikatsu*) and level of civilization (*kaika*) of the ancient people (*kodaijin*)" (Tokyo Kokuritsu Hakubutsukan 1976, 2:262). These laws also specified that any buried objects pertaining to ancient lifestyles and history would be sent to Tokyo Imperial University for safekeeping, with the following attached informa-tion: (1) quality (*hinshitsu*); (2) form (*keizō*); (3) the excavated year, month, and date; (4) location; (5) associated oral traditions and legends, and so on; (6) any facts that may serve as proof of antiquity; and (7) attached illustrations (*moshazu*; Tokyo Kokuritsu Hakubutsukan 1976, 2:257–59). On March 28, 1878, supplemental *kofun* laws mandated that all citizens report discovered burial goods to the local police. Once such lost or stolen antiquities were reported to the local police or prefectural office, the state had the authority to confiscate them and the obligation to store them, and to submit to the Interior Ministry detailed reports of the status of these items. These ministry archives, made up of the detailed reports, locations, and illustrations of *kofun* sites, later served as the primary reference materials consulted by preservation committee investigators and museum curators (Teikoku Kosekishū Chōsakai 1900).

The Jimmu mausoleum enshrining the mythical founding emperor was the first major public monument project (fig. 2.8) taken on by the Imperial Household Agency.[22] The tomb's dedication was timed to coincide with the three days of celebrations at Tōdaiji Temple on February 8–11, 1877, before

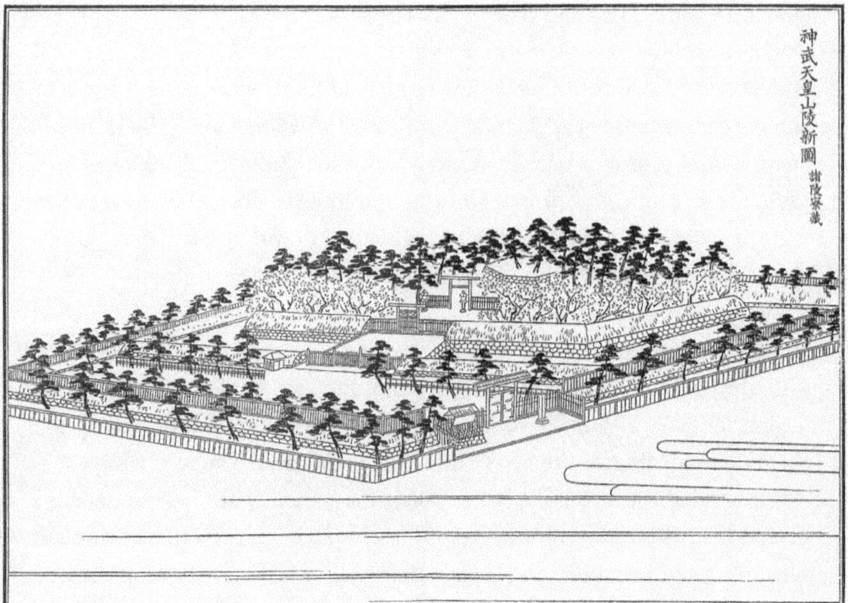

FIG. 2.8. Illustration of Emperor Jimmu's Tomb after an octagonal mound was erected, c. 1898. Source: Jingūshichō, compiled in Kojiruien, Teiōbu (Tokyo: Tsukiji Kappan, 1896). Reproduced from Walter Edwards, *Monument to an Unbroken Line: The Imperial Tombs and the Emergence of Modern Japanese Nationalism* (2003), fig. 4.

the grand opening of the 1877 Nara Exposition.[23] These public celebrations were planned as year-long events that would include elaborate processions, ancestral ceremonies, and prayer rituals staged at various imperial landmarks, including Kasuga Shrine, Hōryūji Temple, and the Shōsōin. As modern-day reenactments of "old customs" (kyūkan) targeting a world audience, the pomp and pageantry signified the coming of age of imperial rituals staged as national theatre and spectacle, featuring the emperor as the principal actor (Geertz 1980; Fujitani 1996). The main political agenda in the fabrication of the unbroken 2,500-year-old lineage of the imperial family was to affirm the Meiji emperor's divine status and his direct kinship ties (tenkei) to the mythical founding ancestor emperor, Jimmu.[24] By erecting massive tombs and monumental shrines, placed strategically at legendary locations where mythical emperors had performed supernatural feats, the Imperial House Agency was thus able to inscribe ever more "must-see landmarks" or famous "scenic places" (meishō) into the imagined national landscape (Suzuki and Takagi 2002, 15).

On November 15, 1880, the Imperial Household Agency ordered all prefectures and counties to file any reports of finds, whether legendary or rumored, and cases of accidental destruction of kofun caused by farming, encroaching forests, and infrastructure construction. In the case of suspected imperial tombs, the identity had to be verified and cross-checked with historical records for proof of authenticity (kōshō). Field excavations were to be carried out only after consultation with the Tokyo University Anthropology Department, whose archaeology students were dispatched to conduct preliminary surveys. The Museum Department and the Home Ministry were jointly responsible for making any final ruling regarding the authenticity of a kofun or its excavated finds before issuing excavation permits, according to the 1908 Home Ministry laws. The following excavation guidelines (promulgated in 1884) mandated that preliminary field investigations and surveys must also include the parameters of ancient sites, in case of accidental damage. To ensure the security of excavated materials from theft and damage, the processing of antiquities throughout all prefectures was streamlined. First, by Home Ministry decree, excavated materials from all provinces were to be delivered to the imperial museums. Second, the materials were to be stored at prefectural offices, with one or two selected items deposited at a local police station. However, if the item was an ancient bronze vessel found inside a *kofun,* it was to be sent to directly to the Imperial Household Ministry. Third, all excavation reports were to be submitted to the Imperial Household Ministry. Fourth, a specialist dispatched from the Imperial Museum was to make the preliminary decisions, verifying an item's relevance to imperial history. Depending on the specialist's recommendation, the object might be purchased for the Imperial Museum, with the cost to be reimbursed from state coffers. Last, but not least, the state would purchase all private lands where any *kofun* or ancient stele were found.

In order to procure as many *kofun* goods as possible, the Imperial Household Agency also made public appeals urging local citizens to get involved in the identification of new burial sites (Suzuki and Takagi 2000, 268). To persuade citizens to turn over their finds to the authorities rather than sell them on the black market, the agency announced that the museum would compensate anyone who turned in a lost or stolen object, with the amount to be negotiated with the museum (Tokyo Kokuritsu Hakubutsukan 1976, 2: 257–58). A museum staff member was given the task of determining the monetary value of the objects in question after careful authentication of the object and consideration of its historical value as a testament of the past. The finder was compensated the full amount, or half that, with funds provided by the Museum Department and the rest by the state treasury.[25] Depending on the wishes of the finder and the nature of the object, items could either be sent to the imperial museums or to Tokyo Imperial University, for the general education of the public, who could study them as reference materials for inferring about the past (*kōgi engeki*).

The Imperial Committee on the Investigation of Ancient Sites (Teikoku Kosekishū Chōsakai, hereafter Teiseki Chōsakai) was formed in 1900 as a consulting body for the execution of these complex laws. The society's nationalist agenda is clearly articulated in their inaugural newsletter, published in December 1900:

> Since the Meiji Restoration, it has come to our attention that our ancient remains are being threatened with imminent destruction by the daily expansion of infrastructure and transportation. The construction of roads, railroads, canals, and factory buildings are cutting down mountains and forests on a daily basis. Henceforth, in order not to lose our precious memories of

the past, we must figure out how best to preserve against further destruction sacred imperial remains that have been passed down for generations. As we know, countries in Europe and America have had more than a century of preservation laws to guide the preservation of ancient remains, and it is now time for us to do the same. Therefore, we must organize our old national records, and authenticate the locations of the remains of our imperial ancestral burials, heroes, filial sons, patriots, and famous clans in order to uphold and show respect for our imperial identity [kokutai]. We want to restore our imperial remains so that we will not be ashamed when foreign tourists come to visit our country. The purpose of this committee is to create and preserve beautiful sites for eternity to promote our great ancestral achievements and their morals embodying filial piety, loyalty, and patriotism. Our preservation efforts will create a sense of national landscape [kokufū] and encourage the moral education of our citizens [fūkyō]. Our duty as citizens is to uphold the imperial lineage [ōtō] embodied in our imperial remains and burials so that the authority of the imperial household that has lasted for ten thousand generations will continue to shine on for eternity. (Teiseki Chōsakai 1900, 1–4)

These propaganda statements insisting that the preservation of imperial remains was for the good of all Japanese citizens caught the attention not only of the imperial family members and aristocrats but also of prefectural governors, who eagerly joined the preservation society.[26] Itō Hirobumi (1841–1909; see fig. 6.6) was the most prominent member of aristocrats based in Tokyo's office, which was staffed with a consulting officer, a vice director, an accountant, and an academic advisor appointed by the society. The Imperial Museum director, Kuki Ryūichi (1852–1931), was also invited to serve as a consultant. The committee members' top priority was first and foremost the protection of imperial remains (ōseki), which were divided into six types, or ryū: (1) sacred sites of the imperial family (ōchō seiseki); (2) imperial palatial remains (gyūseki); (3) imperial family burials; (4) prime ministers and famous officials' (meishi) remains; (5) ancient objects and remains that could serve as materials for academic research; and (6) the remains of old temples and shrines (Teiseki Chōsakai 1900, 2). At the committee members' request, every year the society dispatched a small coterie of state-appointed academics from Tokyo Imperial University—including Tsuboi Shōgorō (1863–1913), Yoshida Tōgo (1864–1918), and

Miyake Yonekichi (1860–1929)—as field specialists to investigate and publish site reports.[27] The final reports were edited by a publication committee and distributed to roughly two thousand subscribing members. Unlike academic reports today, the articles included personal anecdotes as well as travelogues by members who had organized group pilgrimages to tour the final resting places of former imperial dynastic emperors, princes, and war heroes (Teikoku Chōsakai 1900–1903). The most visited place on their itinerary, not surprisingly, was Nikkō, the mausoleum complex of Tokugawa Ieyasu (1543–1616) built in the early seventeenth century (fig. 2.9). Once a year, in April, all committee members met to discuss the previous year's field reports and make recommendations on the authentication process and preservation methods (Teikoku Chōsakai 1900).

Despite the enthusiastic support of the aristocracy and local officials, without any systematic surveys or excavations, many historians dispatched to the field were hard-pressed to produce a complete list of verifiable ancient places connected with emperors documented in the oldest texts, such as the Kojiki, Nihongi, or Engishiki.[28] For example, the first issue of the Society's newsletter listed 159 *kofun* sites investigated by the Imperial Household Agency. However, most of these remains in fact belonged to emperors and historical figures based in the imperial capital of Kyoto (794–1868) before the imperial family's main residence was moved to Tokyo following the Meiji restoration (Teikoku Chōsakai 1900, 40–44). Considering the paucity of verifiable ancient tombs, it is not surprising that the Meiji government decided to cast a far wider net, asking for donations of *kofun* materials and any local legends, oral traditions, and folklore and ordering the construction of new imperial *kofun* (Suzuki and Takagi 2002, 18).

By the turn of the century, prefectural governments and local historical societies were fudging historical records, submitting longer additional lists of colorful local heroes and gods, either real or imaginary, in order to compete for coveted state subsidies and tourists. The name of the Meiji historian Miyake Yonekichi lives on in the annals of Japanese historiography as the one brave dissenting voice who spoke out against such fraudulent practices and abuses of power (Naoki 1980, 3). At the peak of his career, Miyake was a rising star at Tokyo Imperial University and a consultant on the executive board on the Imperial Preservation Society. However, when Miyake returned from a two-year study abroad at the British Museum in London in

FIG. 2.9. Nikkō Tōshōgu Karamon Gate at the mausoleum of Tokugawa Ieyasu and his grandson Iemitsu, Tochigi Prefecture, c. 1900. Initially built in 1617, this is now a registered UNESCO World Heritage site. Photo by Ogawa Kazumasa, *Scenes in Nikkō and Vicinity*, published by Sole Agent Kelly Walsh Limited in Yokohama, Shanghai, Hong Kong, and Singapore (1900).

1888, the academic climate had turned entirely in favor of the ultranationalist historians, who were emboldened by the new imperial constitution that had declared that the emperor's divinity could not be compromised (Teshigawara 1995, 77). Targeted by Shintō scholars and right-wing nationalists, Miyake was forced to abandon his teaching post at Tokyo University in 1893.[29] Several years later, Miyake defended his position in a controversial article in which he criticized government officials for refusing to carry out systematic archaeological investigations of the long waiting list of submitted historical sites. He argued that tomb sites necessitated special considerations, since there was a possibility that there were even more valuable remains buried underneath. Under these circumstances, the usual method of sticking a small sign demarcating the surface area and declaring it off-limits would not ensure long-term protection of the site (fig. 2.10).

Miyake pointed out that the preservation society's standardized guide-

FIG. 2.10. Nationally designated site markers identifying important cultural properties (*Juyō bunkazai*), Kyoto, 2007. The sign on the left bears the logo of the Japan Cultural Affairs Agency (Bunchō) and reads, "Love and protect our important registered temple buildings, in this case at Kōrin-in temple. Constructed in 1520 (Muromachi period). No flammable equipment permitted. Sponsor, Hitachi." The sign on the right provides historical information about the temple. Photo by author.

lines for protection could not be applied to all sites, for a palace site and a battle field required entirely different strategies for protection due to differences in their layouts and physical remains. Establishing a perimeter around a designated site was also utterly inadequate, since different sites had different needs (Teikoku Chōsakai 1903, 2). Third, Miyake raised serious concerns about the veracity of the "scholarly" documents that accompanied annual requests sent to the state asking for protection status, since he could not find any proof that these records actually supported the antiquity of the reported tombs finds. Finally, he blamed the many greedy land owners who were deliberately submitting fake documentations in order to receive state funds so that they could expand their own estate holdings as well as boost local tourism (Miyake 1903, 8–9).

To remedy the chaotic state of affairs and prevent collusion, Miyake advised the committee that, in the case of *kofun* remains, it must adhere to the following rules: an archaeologist should be sent to conduct a comprehensive site survey to determine the structural configurations and confirm that the site's architecture was indeed as old as the local officials claimed, and the archaeologist should make an accurate map to judge the site's spatial configuration. In order to stop the abuse and misuse of state funds, Miyake recommended that the government closely supervise the heads of local preservation organizations as well as private individuals. This inspection at the local level was necessary to monitor restoration and construction costs and to expose forgeries of ancient remains (*kishaku*) for private gain. Miyake also proposed that the maintenance of local graves should be paid out of the local landlord's own pocket, as had been the norm during the preceding Tokugawa era, before the advent of state buried properties laws. Last, but not least, Miyake condemned the national obsession with identifying imperial remains, which had resulted in the wanton destruction of other, lesser sites, such as the graves of former samurai clans, which were fast disappearing without a trace. Despite Miyake's warnings that the reputation of "sacred sites" (*seiseki*) would be tarnished in the eyes of future citizens if the state did not adopt his measures, his recommendations were ignored (Miyake 1903, 8–9). The rise and fall of Miyake's career resonates to this day, since archaeological and historical sites that do not fit neatly into conventionally "valued national assets," either for propaganda purposes or for commercial development as tourist venues, continue to be bulldozed.

In summary, imperial legislation governing buried remains upheld four main administrative goals. First, only state-appointed specialists at three national institutions (the Imperial Museum, the Tokyo University Anthropological Laboratory [Tokyo Jinrui Gakkai Hyobon Shitsu, hereafter TJGK], and the Kyoto Imperial University Museum) were permitted to investigate and handle buried properties. Second, only the latter's students and professors were hired to authenticate, arrange, and catalogue buried remains. With the exception of prehistoric materials sent to the TJGK and historical materials deposited at the Kyoto Imperial University Museum that were deemed not directly related to the imperial heritage (Tokyo Kokuritsu Hakubutsukan 1976, 2:262–65), all *kofun* materials were stored in one of the three imperial museums in Tokyo, Kyoto, and Nara. Third, the Imperial Household Agency could request at any time that university museum curators hand over their collections if they were required for research and commercial purposes, such as planning for expositions. Finally, the Imperial Household Agency and the Interior Ministry issued buried properties laws that were designed to restrict public access to imperial sites, *kofun*, and research collections so that the state could monopolize and utilize all tangible assets in the emperor's myth-making project (Fujitani 1996; Takagi and Suzuki 2002).

In conclusion, the bureaucratic foundations of Japanese state-manufactured categories, authentication processes, and record keeping of portable antiquities and imperial tombs were all established by the mid-Meiji period. For example, Machida's 1871 directives are more or less in operation today. And the legal definition of a state antiquity (*kogibutsu*) as something that can provide "evidence or testament" (*kōko no shōko*) for the study of the ancient past, historical trends, and customs is still in effect today (Shiina N., 1988, 34). Only state-appointed specialists are involved in the verification process, for supporting records are required to authenticate its age, artistic merit, and monetary value. Specialists can also be brought in when processing claims, since an object's projected monetary value determines its pricing and its insurance coverage when printing catalogues and staging exhibitions. Finally, the act of collecting included not only the physical objects themselves but also physical records of their likeness (*mosha*) in the form of illustrations and photographs for inventorying purposes.

The main goal of the Exposition Office, Agriculture, and Commerce

Department, historical societies, and imperial museums was ultimately to build up a large cache of arts and crafts and famous places catering to the export market and tastes of European consumers, collectors, and globe-trotters with deep pockets, such as Bigelow and Stewart Gardiner (Umesao, Lockeyer, and Kenji 2000; Satō 1999). In the process of documentation and authentication for exhibition and commercial purposes, the meaning, function, and monetary value of everyday Japanese objects, old and new, were transformed into "works of national art" to be arranged, catalogued, and exhibited for international buyers, collectors, and judges. The new taxonomies created for the export market eventually relied on museum curators to evaluate the scientific value, national worth, and monetary estimates of popular collectibles of the day, such as lacquerware, swords, sword guards, *netsuke,* and other curios (Baird 2000; Yoshida Kenji 2001). Consequently, the collecting agenda and curatorial goals of museum directors, archaeologists, and ethnologists employed by the oldest research institutions and museums have established standards for authenticity, antiquity, and beauty, and for how the "Other" continues to be presented to a world audience (Karp and Lavine 1991; Yoshida and Mack 1997).

CHAPTER 3

TRACING JAPAN'S LINEAGE

Art, Architecture, and Conquest Dynasties

Balancing the "old and the new," that is, promoting free trade and commerce on the one hand, and enforcing protectionist measures to staunch the outflow of antiquities on the other, posed a major dilemma for Japan's senior statesman, Itō Hirobumi (1841–1909), who served as the first prime minister of the new cabinet (see fig. 6.6) from 1885 to 1888. Having studied in England as a young man, Itō understood that the ancient arts could be used to promote Japan as a cultured and civilized nation with an illustrious past on par with the nations of Europe (Fenollosa 1886). Realizing that he needed expert help in gauging market trends and the ever-evolving tastes of exposition commissioners and museum curators, Itō appointed four young men to carry out his directives for policing Japanese arts at home and abroad: Ernest Fenollosa (1853–1908), Okakura Kakuzō (1863–1913), Kuki Ryūichi (1852–1931), and architect Sekino Tadashi (1868–1935). These four men laid down the classificatory and epochal approaches that formed the disciplinary foundations of art and architectural history in Meiji Japan (see appendix, table 4).

Itō's first appointee was Ernest Fenollosa, who was only twenty-five years old when the Education Ministry hired him to lecture on political economy and philosophy at Tokyo Imperial University on September 10, 1878. Like many of his contemporaries, such as zoologist Edward Morse (1838–1925), who had recommended him to Itō, he was one of the many foreign specialists (*oyatoi gaijin*), that included military advisors, technicians, scientists, medical doctors, engineers, professors, and architects who were contracted to train a new generation of leaders to guide the modernization (*fukoku kyōhei*) of Japan's education, military, and economy (Yamaguchi

1982, 1:2). Fenollosa spent a total of twelve years in the service of the Meiji government, in multiple roles—as professor at Tokyo Imperial University and Tokyo Fine Arts School, and as director of treasures' field surveys.[1] During his lifetime, he counted among his students the likes of Okakura, Kuki, and Itō Chūta (1867–1954), who would graduate to become the first generation of native scholars and specialists in the field of arts, museums, and architecture, respectively. Circulating in the inner circles of power and high society, Fenollosa developed a reputation as a "taste maker" with a discerning eye for collectibles and influenced a new generation of connoisseurs of *Japonisme*, at home and abroad. Unprecedented for a foreigner, he was decorated on four separate occasions by the Meiji emperor, including three of the most prestigious medals, the Order of the Chrysanthemum, the Phoenix, and the Third Order of the Sacred Treasury for his many contributions to Japanese arts and cultural affairs. Fenollosa died suddenly of heart problems on September 21, 1908, at the age of fifty-six, in London, where he was spending a summer abroad collecting slides for his publication. According to his wishes, his ashes were brought from Highgate to be reburied at a secluded mountain temple overlooking Lake Biwa, where he was honored with an elaborate state funeral with full rites.[2] In 1920, more than two hundred government officials and former students again gathered at the dedication of Fenollosa's memorial on the grounds of Ueno Tokyo Fine Arts School, where Fenollosa taught briefly in 1899.

Fenollosa's professional career began in 1882 when the Education Ministry commissioned him to track down all of the items stored in the inner sanctums of the oldest temples in Nara, Kyoto, and Saga prefectures, including Hōryūji, Kinkakuji, Tōdaiji, Tōfukuji, and Enryakuji (fig. 3.1). His 1882–83 survey records are recognized by art historians as constituting the oldest inventory of Japanese cultural properties classified by genres and epochs (Fenollosa 1912; Murakata Akiko 1982b, 1:211–90, appendix).

Fenollosa's aesthetic sensibilities and classificatory approach to the study of Japanese art is best captured in his introduction to his posthumous work *The Epochs of Chinese and Japanese Art*, first published in 1912:

> Art is the power of the imagination to transform materials—to transfigure them—and the history of art should be the history of this power rather than the history of the materials through which it works. At creative periods, all

FIG. 3.1. The original caption reads, "A mass of broken statues and interesting refuse such as was found by Professor Fenollosa in the year 1880, at Shodaiji." Due to the promulgation of the 1868 Meiji laws separating shrines and temples, many temples estates, statuary, and Buddhist paraphernalia were destroyed by Shinto priests (see also fig. 2.6). Source: Fenollosa 1912, 100.

forms of Art will be found to interact. From the building of a great temple to the outline of a bowl which the potter turns upon his wheel, all effort is transfigured with a single style. Thus, classification should be epochal, and in attempting thus to treat it for the first time it becomes possible partially to trace style back to its social and spiritual roots. The former method may be called that of the curio-collector, the latter, of the student of sociology. (Fenollosa 1912, xxvii)

As we can see, for Fenollosa the main purpose of studying art was to trace material and stylistic change through time in order to reveal its cultural sources and spiritual origins. Therefore, it comes as no surprise that Fenollosa also claimed sole credit for convincing officials of the immense "national" artistic and historical value of Hōryūji and the Shōsōin as Japan's oldest repository of "imperial treasures." According to Fenollosa's account, his credentials from the central government enabled him to requisition the opening of the inner temples around 1884, despite the opposition of the monks who remained superstitious about exposing sacred objects with supernatural powers (Fenollosa 1912, 45–72). Of all the many temple treasures he uncovered, Fenollosa sang the most rapturous praises of the "exceptional quality of the three Buddhist artworks—the sculpture of the Kudara Kannon of the central altar of the Kondō Temple (see figs. 2.7 and 3.2), Tamushi shrines, and the standing bodhisattva of Yumedō Pavilion—as the "finest Korean inspired pieces of early sculptures" in all Japan" (48–50). Below is Fenollosa's account of how he was able to gain access to the inner shrines and alert the world to the existence of "a being from a new Buddhist world."

The central space of the octagonal Yumedō was occupied by a great closed shrine, which ascended like a pillar towards the apex. The priests of Hōryūji confessed that traditions ascribed the content of the shrine to Corean [sic] work of the days of Suiko, but that it had not been opened for more than two hundred years. On fire with the prospect of such a unique treasure, we urged the priests to open it by every argument at our command. They resisted long, alleging that in punishment for the sacrilege an earthquake might well destroy the temple. Finally we prevailed, and I shall never forget our feelings as the long-disused key rattled in the rusty lock. Within the shrine

FIG. 3.2. Replica of *Kudara Kannon* [The Paekche Avalokitesvara] at the British Museum, May 14, 2009. This is a replica of the original 210-centimeter-tall sculpture in Nara's Hōryūji Temple, which was registered as Japan's first national treasure in 1897. Photo by author.

appeared a tall mass closely wrapped about in swathing bands of cotton cloth upon which the dust of ages had gathered. It was no light task to unwrap the contents, some 500 yards of cloth having been used, and our eyes and nostrils were in danger of being choked with the pungent dust. But at last the final folds of the veering fell away, and this marvelous statue, unique in the world, came forth to human sight for the first time in centuries. It was a little taller than life, but hollow at the back, carved most carefully from some hard wood which had been covered with gilding, now stained to the yellow-brown of bronze. The head was ornamented with a wonderful crown of Corean open-work gilt bronze, from which hung long streamers of the same material set with jewels (Fenollosa 1912, 50).

For Fenollosa, the main attraction and "aesthetic wonders" of this wonderful piece derived from its Grecian sculptural elements mixed in with Chinese Han and Korean traits:

> From the front, the figure is not quite so noble, but seen in profile it seemed to rise to the height of archaic Greek art with distinctive Greek features such as: The long lines of drapery, sweeping at the two sides from shoulders to feet, were unbroken in single quiet curves approximating straight lines, giving great height and dignity to the figure. The chest was depressed, the abdomen slightly protruding, the action of the hands, holding between them a jewel or casket of medicine, rendered with vigorous modeling. But the finest feature was the profile view of the head, with its sharp Han nose, its straight clear forehead, and its rather large—almost Negroid—lips. On which a quiet mysterious smile played not unlike Da Vinci's Mona Lisa (Fenollosa 1912, 51).

Fenollosa firmly believed that such archaic stylistic elements dating back thousands of years must have derived from the cultural influences of the great empires of Sumer, Babylonia, Persia, Greece, and Rome, which had spread their great art and high culture via India, Han China, and Korea and therefore must have contributed to the creation of early Japanese sculptural style. Despite the fact that Fenollosa had never conducted fieldwork in these places or studied art history in any systemic manner, he subscribed to the then-dominant "diffusionist" paradigm, according to which successive waves of superior races and cultural influences moving from high to low civilizations had marked the three-stage development of the ancient Japanese arts—the Suiko period (Graeco-Buddhist art or Nara period), mystical Buddhist art and the Fujiwara period (Fenollosa 1912, 30–52). He then concluded that the oldest Buddhist arts of Japan represented the consolidation of the two main aesthetic traditions of the oldest Buddhist sculptural traditions transferred from the continent: first, the infiltration of the northern Chinese Sui style, and second, the southern Liang dynastic influence. Fenollosa's hypothesis played a pivotal role in spreading the idea in the West that the "Suiko era" as in Suiko *shiki* (style), named after

Emperor Suiko (592–628 CE), whose name since Fenollosa has become synonymous with the formative period of Japanese arts. Although in historical hindsight it seems obvious why classically trained scholars would reserve their most enthusiastic reviews for the oldest-standing sculptural arts in Nara, it is important to emphasize here that, before the arrival of Fenollosa, antiquarians as well as exposition organizers considered only portable objects—such as seals, documents, paintings, bronzes, and curios—as worthy national assets (Murakata Noriko 2002; Tokyo Teishitsu Hakubutsukan 1901, 12–16).

By 1886–87, Fenollosa had persuaded the Education Ministry to send him on an all-expenses-paid, nine-month "fact-finding mission" to tour art schools, museums, and crafts industries in Italy, Austria, Germany, England, France, Holland, Belgium, Spain, and the United States (Murakata Akiko 1982a; Yamaguchi 1982). On this trip, he was accompanied by Okakura (see fig. 2.4) and Kuki, whom he praised as the only two men in Japan qualified to assist him in his extraordinary mission to salvage the arts. In his own words, the first purpose of the expert commission he had organized to the Western countries was to gather "information by visiting leading art schools and ateliers of the West for Japanese specialists was thus to devise concrete plans, so as to ascertain "methods of art education especially in the space arts of design." The second purpose was to study the administration of European fine art museums, their exhibitions, and their classification systems—"not with the intention of copying outright any such Western Institution, building, organization and arrangements, but of learning as much as possible of what was vital and universal," such as the Western museums' arrangement methods, which were certain to be of practical use in creating the art administration that Japan was contemplating. The third purpose was to address the question of their possible future use and development of Japanese fine arts and architecture.[3] Upon his return to Japan, Fenollosa submitted to Itō his frank assessment regarding commercial trade in Japanese works of fine art, and future plans to boost the production of crafts for export. His sincere recommendation was that Japan needed more than ever to tap into the growing market and demand for decorative arts in the United States, where there was a burgeoning number of ornate mansions that needed furnishings (Fenollosa 1887). Although Fenollosa was ultimately not able to persuade Itō to invest in the building of a permanent museum devoted to fine arts and archaeology during his tenure, his argument that creating museums would lead to the long-term growth of the export industry did not fall on deaf ears, and were later implemented by his student, Okakura.

Outside of his civil service, Fenollosa was the founding member of Japan's first art appreciation society (*kangakai*), a public forum that eventually served as a power base and platform for spreading his ideas on Japanese art. Fenollosa's inaugural lecture to its society members, recorded in the 1885 constitution of the Art Appreciation Society, echoes his epochal approach and preservationist agenda for the study of Japanese arts discussed above: "Art is strictly national, rooted in all that is best and conservative of ancient theory and practice, modified along the lines of natural development only, and carefully 'preserved' from all taint of radically distinct methods derived from foreign sources" (Fenollosa 1885). This opening was followed by Fenollosa's mission for the club: "the regeneration of Japanese art by all appropriate means such as the study [and] criticism of past masterpieces, encouragement, criticism, instruction of living artists, special study of the theory, and possibilities of art in Japan; [and the] commendation to the public as much as possible of the above matters by means of lectures, certificates, exhibitions and publications" (Fenollosa, *History of the Kangwakai*).

From the above statements, we can see that, as an educator, Fenollosa understood that the thorny issue of the transmission of artistic skills and traditions had to be tackled when considering the education and training of future artists and students. He was also keenly aware that the demise of the Tokugawa regime had also hastened the influx of outside threats, including materialism, Western art education, and the power of European design. In his opinion, unstable economic and social conditions had also brought with them the dangers of modern commercial methods, that is, mass production, which were in his opinion effectively killing off the best of Japanese indigenous artistic traditions (Fenollosa 1887). He was especially adamant about getting rid of the old guard, such as the "bad monks" who had let temples be burned, collections scattered, artists die, geniuses starve, and traditions be lost. Like Machida before him, Fenollosa blamed government officials for impoverishing monks and priests, who, in order to survive, had resorted to hiding treasures from the authorities so that they could continue to make private dealings and keep the profits for themselves (Fenollosa 1888, 5; Murakata Akiko 1980, part 1, 3–33).

As we can see, in stark contrast to Fenollosa's rhapsodic reviews of the sublime beauty of Nara's ancient sculptures, he was extremely critical of what he perceived to be the steep decline of Japanese arts in general since medieval times.[4] In a paper titled "The Future of Japanese Art Industries" (1889a), he opined that the deteriorating condition of Japanese arts resulted from centuries of stagnation: "Japanese art at its best stayed the level of about where Italian did at the middle of the fifteenth century; and the real problem of Japan today is how to advance along a similar road of expansion, maintaining its own individuality as did the Italian by clothing it with more powerful and adequate expression, but avoiding the fatal errors of pride, formalism, insincerity and scientific pedantry into which the artists of the following era fell and were destroyed" (Fenollosa 1889a). In several unpublished papers, with titles such as "Can Japanese Art Be Revived?" (1885), "The Prospect of Japanese Art" (1889), and "National Treasures Fast Disappearing (1909)," Fenollosa made dire the prediction that, due to government neglect and the insatiable appetite for curios on the part of foreigners, Japan's unique cultural heritage was on the verge of utter destruction, about to be irretrievably lost. He rightly pointed out that Meiji authorities had funds set aside for temple repairs and regular maintenance, to protect wooden buildings that were under constant threat from natural hazards and from man-made disasters such as fires. Fenollosa warned officials that if such conditions were allowed to persist, Japanese art would continue in the course of steep decline experienced over the past five centuries.

Fenollosa also condemned the negligence of a "self-anointed civilized government" whose weak, ineffectual, and despairing stance toward art was equivalent to "Japan not solving the question of art but ignoring it." He further drove his point home by asking, "What is the use of setting in motion a government educational machinery that confesses that it can do no more to educate than leave existing tendencies to themselves? Has not Japan gone exactly in this way for the last twenty years?" And, with no proper educational art institutions, he was convinced that there would soon be no qualified artisan to replace the craftsmen (Fenollosa 1888, 4; Fenollosa 1895). What little private art education there was at that time, he noted, was completely inadequate, for the "Western schooling of art" had resulted only in hastening the deteriorating conditions. To regenerate the arts, Fenollosa recommended that the Education Ministry appoint the few surviving progressive monks skilled in the arts of painting, sculpture, metal casting, bronze casting, lacquer making, and so on, to instruct the students. He also pushed for a competitive entrance examination for the planned fine arts academy in order to recruit enthusiastic classes of young men so as to hasten the transmittal of the traditions before they should die out forever. In one letter, Fenollosa alerted Itō Hirobumi of the special importance of the appointment of judges for the national art exhibitions, who would be gleaned from the leaders of this movement (Fenollosa 1893, 3). If Fenollosa's complaints to the government are to be taken at face value, the state of arts and architecture in Japan in the 1880s was indeed in crisis, with old schools of design dying out, without any pupils, qualified teachers, or concerned patrons or managers to speak of.[5]

With historical hindsight, it seems highly hypocritical for someone like Fenollosa, who was openly dealing with curio dealers himself, to call attention to arts being smuggled out of the country.[6] However, despite the large number of paintings Fenollosa had shipped out of Japan, art historians still give him due credit as the first informed connoisseur (*shikibetsuka*) to identify and authenticate (*kantei*) "national masterpieces" (*bijutsu mohan*), a revolutionary concept at the time (Takada 1997; Takagi Hiroshi 1995; Yamaguchi 1982, 14). Whatever his faults, art historians agree that Fenollosa introduced the fundamental concepts and tools for devising a comprehensive national arts collection and registration system: systematic surveys; a card-cataloguing system; and a classificatory or "genres" approach, divided into sculptures, documents, paintings, and crafts (Murakata Akiko 1980, 33). Although his ambitious projects to regenerate the Japanese arts with the building of permanent fine arts museum collections and the establishment of a school to nurture, protect, and exhibit the best of the ancient arts were not realized during his lifetime, his former student Okakura Kakuzō took up his mantle when Fenollosa left Japan for good in 1890.

Okakura, the son of a wealthy silk merchant from Yokohama, was all of twenty years old when he accompanied Fenollosa on his Nara survey in 1882. Seven years later, he was appointed professor at Japan's first arts academy, the Tokyo School of Fine Arts, when it opened in 1889. The following year, he was formally promoted to principal of the school. During his tenure as curator of the fine arts division of the museum department, Okakura's major achievement was creating a systematic grading scale for ranking national objects, which he prioritized by age, quality of painting, style of design or manufacture, and state of preservation, as follows: (1) things that can serve as evidence for history or a model (*mohan*) for art, crafts, and architecture; (2) things that ought to serve as evidence for history or a model for art and architecture; (3) things that are useful as historical references for authenticating art, crafts, and architecture; (4) products (*yōhin*) that ought to be consulted for evidence for history or art, crafts, and architecture; (5) things that can be consulted for evidence for history or art, crafts, and architecture; (6) things that may be consulted for historical and registration purposes; and (7) things that can be consulted in order to register treasures (Okakura 1980, 4:512)

The first official treasures inventory list (totaling 215,091 state-owned items registered by Okakura) was disseminated nationwide through government publications as well as daily newspapers from May to August 1888. Reflecting the tastes and influence of his mentor, Fenollosa, Okakura recorded the largest number for paintings (74,731), followed by arts/crafts (57,436), and sculpture (45,550).

By all accounts, Okakura also excelled as a teacher and mentor to artists and university students alike, using teaching methods that were innovative for Japan, encouraging question-and-answer sessions and using visual aids such as lantern slideshows taken from his field surveys of Nara's art and architecture (Okakura 1980, 4:1–8, appendix). His syllabi and class handouts show that he taught a wide range of subjects in all world areas, including ancient Egypt, Assyria, Phoenicia, Rome, Greece, India, and China. His former students fondly remembered that, on weekends, Okakura organized field trips to the imperial museum, pointing out masterpieces— Egyptian mummies, Chinese jades, and pottery, as well as Japanese-style paintings, or *nihonga*. On these field trips, the students report that they were in constant awe of Okakura' sharp eye and attention to detail, which enabled him to pick out the best museum objects in shape, color, and form. They agreed that these hands-on experiences proved invaluable learning tools for judging the artistic value of material culture, but also for understanding the trajectory of Japanese art history in a broad, worldwide context.[7] Last, but not least, his former students were in agreement that his lectures were packed and lively events that attracted a regular following of Tokyo University's faculty members and outside guests, including anthropologist Torii Ryūzō (1870–1953), historian Kuroita Katsumi (1874–1946), and philosopher Watsuji Tetsujirō (1889–1960; Okakura 1980, vol. 4, appendix).

Outside of Japan, Okakura's wide social network included the scions of Boston Brahman society, including Charles Appleton Longfellow (1844–93), the eldest son of the New England poet Henry Wadsworth Longfellow (1807–82), William Sturgis Bigelow, and the aforementioned globe-trotting Isabella Stewart Gardner. Okakura was invited to the Boston Museum of Fine Arts twice, in 1904–5 and then again in 1912–13, to supervise artisans who had been brought in to restore and repair items from his former mentor's vast collections amassed during his field surveys. Although he hobnobbed with the rich and famous inside and outside of Japan, even a cursory review of his publications and personal ruminations indicates that he remained profoundly ambivalent about his own role and status as a cultural ambassador amid the backdrop of a rapidly changing geopolitical environment.[8] According to Fred Notehelfer, the Russo-Japanese War (1904–5) marked a turning point in Okakura's writings, when, like many educated Japanese, he was concerned that his country was the brunt of undeserved negative press, portrayed as a "barbaric" kingdom to be feared as a military and political threat to the fragile balance of power in the Far East (Linhart 2005; Notehelfer 1990).

Okakura's main goal in writing for an English audience was, in his own words, "to rectify the many widespread misconceptions that foreigners had propagated about Japan, its culture and its people." He was even critical of his close friends, that is, the abovementioned wealthy European and American connoisseurs "who were constantly preaching the superiority of their own culture and art to those of the East" (Okakura 1904, 198–99). Here, he is likely attacking the likes of Alcock and Fenollosa, who in their publications had openly denigrated Japanese arts for lacking any knowledge of "high art." Okakura's major English-language publications, which cemented his reputation as a learned man possessing encyclopedic knowledge of the East and the West, boasted grand titles such as *The Ideals of the East with Special Reference to the Art of Japan* (1903), *The Awakening of Japan* (1904), and *The Life and Thought of Japan* (1913). In these works, one of his ways of counteracting such negative publicity and condescension was to assert that Japanese rulers had from ancient times been responsible for the transmission of old customs, arts, rituals, and ceremonies. He also believed that China, hobbled by its present difficulties and uncertain future, was no longer "of benefit of a living art to excite our rivalry on to fresh endeavors" and that therefore it was now up to Japan to be the leader of the arts in Asia (Okakura 1903, 220–44).

In the following passage Okakura explains how the divine imperial household was able to subdue and assimilate a wide array of inferior races that in ancient times had migrated from the continent to form one great homogenous, unified nation:

The "Head House," the Great Ōyake are the ancestors called the imperial family. It thus forms the sole focus of Japanese society whither all the lesser families, great and small, old and new, unanimously send their several tributes of rays, to burn in the common cause of loyalty and patriotism. True, there were rebellious chiefs who opposed the conquering army of the first Emperor. But, they soon learned to feel the irresistible force of the persuasive belief in his super-natural origins, which made them think it wise to sur-render themselves to the descendants of the Sun-Goddess.... And as to those swarms of immigrants from China and Korea, who crossed the sea at various periods in the early days of Japanese history, it did not take many generations before they came to adopt the views of the people with whom it was their interest in every way to get mixed, and thus they lost their own identity.... in this manner, notwithstanding an extensive admixture of foreign elements to our original stock, we find ourselves as a closely unified nation as if we had been perfectly homogenous from the very beginning. One and the same blood is felt to run through our veins characterized by one and the same set of religious and moral ideas. These may perhaps be due to the fact that the three elements of the conquering, the conquered, and the immigrants belonged originally to the same Mongolian race, with very little trace of any mingling of Ainu or Malayan blood.... Anyhow, there exists a strong feeling prevalent among us that we have all sprung from one and the same stem, that we all belong to the same family, with common ancestors, that we are closely related to one another in blood, and that even the humblest of us, we own our origins to the same divine agency as the Emperors, who are so to say our "seniors" and "elders" in the most exalted sense. (Okakura 1913, 48–49)

A similar convoluted argument from another popular publication, *The Awakening of Japan* (1904), emphasizes how the Yamato race was formed from various mixed races and was predestined to move west, subjugating all in its path, and driving out the native Ainu:

The origin of the Yamato race who drove the aboriginal Ainos [*sic*] before them into Yezo and the Kurile islands, in order to establish the Empire of the Rising Sun, is so lost in the sea-mists out of which they sprang. Whether they were a remnant of the Acadians who mingled their blood with that of the Indo-Tartaric nations, in the passage along the coasts and islands of south-eastern Asia; or whether they were a division of the Turkish hordes who found their way through Manchuria and Korea to settle in the Indo-Pacific; or whether they were descendants of the Aryan emigrants who pushed through the Kashmirian passes, to be lost amongst the Turanian tribes from the Thibetans, Nepalese, Siamese, and Burmese, and to bring the added power of Indian symbolism to the children of the Yang-tse Kiang valley, are questions still in the clouds of archaeological conjecture. (Okakura 1903, 14–15)

Okakura's grand racial conquest narrative also advanced the teleological argument that the stone cists graves, stone knives, armor, and *magatama* (comma-shaped jade) beads found in prehistoric sites were deposited by the same "Proto-Japanese" race that arrived from China via Korea (Okakura 1904, 14–15). Once they arrived on the Japanese islands, their rituals of Shintō, or "the path of the gods," somehow miraculously transformed everyone and everything into the unique Yamato, the race of ruling emperors (Okakura 1980, 4:12). Okakura stands out among his contemporaries for having somewhat sheepishly admitted that his opinions were at best "conjecture," since there was no archaeological proof supporting his conquest theory of the Yamato. The lack of material evidence, however, did not deter him or other prominent scholars of his generation from advancing the idea that all of Japan's ancient pictorial arts, sculpture, and architectural elements could be traced back to the Han dynasty (Hamada 1906, 1907). He also suggested that Empress Jingū must have been motivated to brave the seas "for the protection of the tributary kingdoms in Korea, in the face of China, the continental empire," and that she launched a foreign expedition (c. 201 CE?) precisely so that she could bring back these Han inventions to

Japan (Okakura 1903, 20). Therefore, another sea crossing, this time in the opposite direction, served as the catalyst in establishing ancient Korea-Japanese relations and eventually led to an active diplomatic and cultural exchange of monks, artisans, and diplomats who traveled back and forth to between the kingdom of Kudara (or Paekche in Korean). It is beyond the scope of this chapter to delve into the numerous historiographical issues pertaining to the rewriting of Japan's imperial past and state-formation theories.[9] Suffice it to say, after more than a century of controversy, it has still not been resolved as to whether the legendary empress and her expedition to Korea are fact or fiction (Kuno 1967, 1–13). The fact remains that the calculation of such a mythohistorical divine lineage was indispensable to the rewriting of the dynastic record, which had to be brought up to date chronologically and plotted spatially so as to overlap with the newly occupied territories in Manchuria and Korea (Pai 1999a).

In Okakura's emperor-centered universe, all major cultural, religious, and technological shifts resulted from wars, invasions, or transfers of seats of power instigated by conquering dynasties, which in turn influenced his periodization scheme. For Okakura, the formation of a true "Japanese" artistic lineage (*Nihon koyū no tensei*) emerged from a mixture of Han dynasty elements and "Korean" influences via Kyūshū dubbed the "Suiko" period, a term later adopted by Fenollosa and others as a generic name for the "preclassic" period of Japanese art. It was then followed by the classic, or Tenpyō period, equivalent to the late Nara period that ended in 794, when the capital was moved to Nara (Okakura 1980, 4:508–18). During the classic phase, Okakura argued, Buddhist artistic traditions were carried to Japan through western China by later migrations of nomadic races from India during the Northern and Southern Dynasties.[10] As we can see, Okakura's "three-age system" mirrored Fenollosa's diffusionist hypothesis in which successive waves of imperial conquests and the transfer of seats of power across continents and oceans demarcated epochal changes in the arts: antiquity (*kodai*), Middle Age (*chūdai*, spanning the periods from Heian to Fujiwara), and modern (*kindai*, spanning the periods from Ashikaga to Tokugawa) (Takagi Hiroshi 1995). Okakura further subdivided the three ages following the transfer of the seats of power from Nara (700 CE) to Kyoto (800 CE) to Kamakura (1192) to Ashikaga (1338), Hideyoshi (1583) and the Tokugawa (1600).

With his chronology scheme focusing on the eastward migration of the high arts, Okakura tried to convince himself and his readers that Japan's artistic lineage (*tsukei*) was the rightful successor to the great civilizations of the ancient Orient, Greece, and Rome, whose traits resurfaced with the great sculptural Engishiki-style art (901–23 CE; Okakura 1980, 4:5–64; Takagi Hiroshi 1995, 86–87). As the most respected and influential art historian serving on the board of the Imperial Museum office as well as the national treasures committee, and with his loyalist sentiments, imperial tastes, and aesthetic preferences, Okakura left us a lasting legacy of what types of Japanese paintings and art objects have been inventoried and preserved in imperial museums and in the Boston Museum of Fine Arts.

The monumental task of sketching, measuring, and ranking the oldest architectural remains in the capital, Nara, was assigned to Sekino Tadashi (1868–1935), a Tokyo University–trained architect (see fig. 5.1) who is widely recognized as a pioneer in the field of East Asia architecture (Nihon Kenchiku Gakkai 1972). Born into a samurai family from the provinces, Sekino attended Tokyo Imperial University Engineering College in 1892, where he majored in sculptural arts in the predecessor to today's Department of Architecture. In addition to taking classes in the required subjects, such as building construction, structural engineering, freehand drawing, and sketch design, Sekino also took classes in European decorative arts, aesthetics, and the history of Japanese architecture (Fujii et al. 2005, 67–102). Upon graduating, he was briefly hired to design the interiors and the exterior façade of the Bank of Japan. His drafting skills and knowledge of decorative arts led to a part-time lecturer's position at the Tokyo Fine Arts School in 1896. Sekino's career took off in July that same year, when the Home Ministry appointed him chief surveyor of the newly established Commission for the Preservation of Shrines and Temples, the first national organization dedicated to the preservation of architecture (Shiseki Meishō Tennen Kinenbutsu Hozonkai 1942; Hirose 2003, 10). Established five months earlier, in April, this commission was headed by Kuki Ryūichi (1852–1931), then director of the Imperial Museum, and also included Okakura, then principal of the Tokyo School of Fine Arts, and Itō Chūta, Sekino's mentor at his alma mater. The survey team's mission was, in Sekino's own words, "to uncover finds demonstrating superior value as historical evidence or as an example of fine art [*bijutsu kōgeihin*] throughout the nation."[11] This commission introduced a new protected category dubbed "special buildings" (*tokubetsu kenchiku*), to be distinguished from earlier regulations that had covered only objects and sculptures considered as "national treasures" (Sekino Takeshi 1978, 3).

As the first architect to map and document eighty of the oldest-standing temples, including those at Hōryūji, Tōdaiji, Yakushiji, and Kōfukuji, Sekino's Nara field archives (fig. 3.3) are now counted as the "earliest scientific records" documenting the art and architecture of Japan (Fujii et al. 2005, 401–6). Most importantly, Sekino's architectural training distinguished him from his predecessors, Fenollosa and Okakura, since his surveys produced detailed sketches, architectural plans, measurements, and site maps that were later used to outline the state's long-term preservation plans (Hirose 2003).

FIG. 3.3. Sekino Tadashi's sketches of the Yakushiji Buddha of the Nara period, c. 1896. Collections of the University Museum, University of Tokyo. Source: Fujii et al. 2005, plate 13.1.

Following his Nara surveys, Sekino devoted the rest of his career to promoting and preserving the oldest art and architecture of Japan and Korea. Throughout his life, he remained enamored with the temples in Nara, which he praised for their "simplicity, grace, and refinements." Even though they may comparatively lack in "grandeur, power, and magnificence" compared to later buildings, Sekino firmly believed that they represented the continuity of the Japanese architectural lineage since ancient times—for several reasons. First, the religious piety and patronage of citizens—from high princes of the imperial household and nobility to the lowest classes— had contributed to the preservation of Japanese architecture since Nara times. Second, for centuries peacefully coexisting diverse faiths and sects—including Shintō and the various Buddhist sects of Hossō, Kegon, Tendai, and Shingon—had devoted themselves to the maintenance of the oldest Shintō shrines and Buddhist temples, and their treasures. Third, unlike other countries, Japan had been spared the destructive forces of change, such as revolutions and foreign conquests, that had befallen other great civilizations of the world. Fourth, due to peaceful cooperation, the Tokugawa family and the feudal lords had also made an effort to preserve architectural monuments from wars and violence in the previous two and a half centuries. Fifth, the daimyo had also been allowed to build magnificent palaces and castles, while imperial princes living in sumptuous mansions in Kyoto had continued to support the arts. Finally, the samurai families had continued to enrich family treasure rooms by patronizing the arts and by purchasing antiquities and passing them on as heirlooms from generation to generation.

As we can see, Sekino's positive outlook toward the state's architectural preservation efforts was in direct opposition to Fenollosa's very pessimistic view. However, like Fenollosa, he believed that the government should take the initiative "to preserve our precious monuments and heirlooms of the race, representing 1,300 years of 'pure un-altered' Japanese traditions of religious piety and imperial patronage unblemished by foreign influences" (Sekino Tadashi 1929, 3). He also asked the authorities to raise public awareness and to educate citizens on the importance of studying and preserving ancient "imperial landmarks" demonstrating the steady progress of Japanese civilization. As a professionally trained engineer, Sekino was also able to instruct government engineers on how to carry out urgent repairs on the oldest temples, which by the Meiji period had fallen into various stages of disrepair, were "leaning, decaying, or otherwise in unfortunate conditions" (1). He argued that Japan's standing wooden architecture, exposed daily to the dangers of rain, wind, and fire, made vigilance a daily necessity. In addition, he pointed out to the authorities that damage caused by centuries of natural and man-made disasters was further compounded by the country's humid climate and lengthy rainy season, which accelerated unwanted vegetation growth, moss, and rot, contributing to continuous decay and deterioration, and posing formidable challenges for conservators, engineers, and carpenters (1–2).

Based on the strength of Sekino's recommendations, and backed up by a vast body of attractive drawings and field sketches, the government enacted the Ancient Shrines and Temples Act, more commonly known as the National Treasures Act (Kokuhōhō) on June 5, 1897. A permanent Commission for the Preservation of Ancient Shrines and Temples was set up on October 27, 1897, to serve as "as an advisory board given the duty of submitting its opinions on which building would receive future government subsidies to the Home Ministry." As stipulated by the Regulations for the Enforcement of the Preservation Act (enacted December 25, 1897), a shrine or temple receiving a subsidy for the repair of its buildings or of any treasures must itself bear no less than half of the total cost; such a charge, however, was subject to reduction in special circumstances (Sekino Takeshi 1978, 4). The committee was also responsible for coordinating field specialists, investigators, and local police, who worked together in submitting on-site reports and monitoring the storage and transfer of site finds and the progress of construction sites so that valuable treasures were not stolen or damaged. The actual work on the ground was executed under the direction of the Home Ministry and the governors of each prefecture. The minister of education made the final decision on who would receive funding for the annual restoration. As with buried properties legislation, the organizational structure of the commission charged with preserving architecture was again a top-down chain of command dictated by the bureaucrats of the Imperial Household, the Home Ministry, and the Ministry of Education, who supervised the commissions meetings, disbursed funds, and kept track of the status of registered items on the list of "special architecture" (*tokubetsu kenzōbijutsu*). Whether or not an work of art or a building was awarded the much-coveted restoration funds provided by the Home Ministry depended on the status reports submitted by specialists (Xu 2002, 57–58). All of the national treasures registration forms required attached historical documentation, survey maps, photographs, and diagrams to be submitted to the Home Ministry. In order to petition the minister of home affairs (or the minister of education) for a grant-in-aid, one had to include an expert's detailed account of the remains, including the treasure's (1) name, (2) proprietorship and location, (3) origin and history, (4) construction and style, and (5) measurements.

Sekino's architectural commission thus inaugurated Japan's first comprehensive nationwide preservation laws, covering not only antiquities but also standing architecture (Japan Bunkachō 1960, 1988, 1997). Since Sekino's 1896 Nara surveys, the verification of all reported remains and relics have been assigned to university-trained professionals and museum curators, whose main job is to produce the "raw data" made up of historical records, maps, sketches, measurements, and survey photos on inventory cards for the purpose of authentication (kōshō). Subsequent committees have since consulted this vast body of accumulated cultural resource management materials to rank the categories of special buildings prioritized by age, preservation state, and urgency for future repairs (Nara Kokuritsu Bunkazai Kenkyūjo 2006). Therefore, for more than a century, university experts' ranking recommendations, whether high or low, have determined the amount of subsidies set aside for restoration costs. When we look at Sekino's recommended list of buildings to be protected as national monuments, we can clearly detect his preference for the oldest architecture, since more than half of his recommendations were from three regions in Kansai: 194 from Nara, 300 from Kyoto, and 121 from Shiga—out of the more than 1,116 shrines and temples registered by 1929. Of these, Sekino identified twenty-nine wooden buildings in Nara prefecture as "wonderfully high" on his scale of important buildings because of "their remote antiquity" (Sekino Tadashi 1929, 7–9). For example, Sekino's own records show that the state budget for preservation activities jumped fourfold, from 44,944,505 yen to 165,038,850 yen. Sekino estimated that, between the years 1898 and 1904, the average total of annual subsidies hovered between 150,000 and 200,000 yen. The total budget costs for repairs for the thirty years from 1878 to 1928 amounted to a grand sum of 6,296,942 yen (Sekino Tadashi 1929, 12–13).

The disciplinary biases, loyalist sentiments, and career ambitions of Fenollosa, Sekino, and Okakura also had an effect on the new medium of photography, which was being widely adopted as the most important tool for inventorying ancient arts in Japan (Murakata Noriko 2002; J. Oakes 2009). Beginning with Fenollosa's 1882 survey to salvage Japan's ancient sculptural arts for posterity, his companion was Edward Morse, who was an accomplished photographer and sketch artist in his own right (Konishi and Oka et al. 2005). By the mid-1880s, with the spread of commercial photographic studios, photographic technology became rapidly adopted as the "scientific" tool of choice for the next generation of field researchers trained in ethnography, archaeology, and art history.[12] For the 1886–87 and 1888 surveys in Kinai, the official photographer to the Imperial Household Ministry, Ogawa Kazumasa (1860–1929), recorded over four hundred and eight hundred photographs, respectively, of the highest-ranked treasures selected by Fenollosa, Okakura, and Kuki (Murakata Akiko 1980, part 1, 34; J. Oakes 2009, 220). The original glass plates, photographs, catalogues, and historical documentation were subsequently submitted to the Imperial Household Agency and preserved as the primary database for locating the provenance of art-historical remains (Yamaguchi 1982). Later on, Ogawa's studio, known for its high-tech and quality printing machines imported from America, was also recruited as the publisher for the art magazine *Kokka* when it debuted in 1889 (Ōzawa 1994). Ogawa's lavishly produced souvenir photo albums, filled with exotic geisha and picturesque vistas of scenic destinations such as Mount Fuji, Hakone, the Great Buddha or Kamakura, Nikkō, and so on, played an instrumental role in spreading romantic images of "Old Japan" to sailors, travelers, globe-trotters, and tourists.[13]

Relying on this abundance of field records and attractive photographic images, the Ministry of Agriculture and Commerce commissioned the Imperial Museum editorial staff—headed by Okakura, Miyake Yonekichi, and Itō Chūta—to write up an illustrated history of Japanese art and architecture in 1899 to be included in the exhibition catalogue for distribution at the 1900 Paris Exposition Universelle.[14] The editorial committee for the exposition's catalogue deliberately emulated the layout format and genre arrangements featured in the major European museums of the day, hoping to gain much-sought-after recognition and international standing as an emerging art center (Takagi Hiroshi 1995, 290). With this goal in mind, a well-known Paris-based antiquity dealer of Japanese origin, Hayashi Tadamasa (1853–1906), was hired to translate the first French edition, which was titled *Histoire de l'art du Japon* (Baird 2000). This French printing proved to be so popular that a Japanese-language edition, titled *Shōhon Nihon Bijutsushi*, has been reprinted four times, in 1908, 1909, 1913, and, most recently, in 2003 (Tokyo Teishitsu Hakubutsukan 1901).

Tellingly, a special section of these volumes was devoted to showcasing Sekino's fine architectural plans and panoramic views of Nara's temples. Under the genre rubric "architectural division" (*kenchikubu*), Sekino's artwork and photographs were separated from other genres, such as sculpture and decorative arts, which were subsumed under Okakura's period divisions. Identical copies of Sekino's exquisitely executed drawings were later disseminated in hundreds of other publications, including handbooks and manuals issued by the Japan's Cultural Affairs Agency, or Bunkachō, which explained cultural properties. The imperial collections from the temples of Shōsōin and Tōdaiji were also singled out in the same catalogue as the "Treasure House of the East" (*tōyō hōmotsu*) for preserving thousand-year-old masterpieces of art and sculpture inspired by the arts of ancient India, Central Asia, and China.

The frescoes in the Golden Hall of Hōryūiji, for example, were promoted as being identical to the murals of India's Ajanta Caves (c. 2nd century BCE), ignoring the eight-hundred-year time gap as well as the physical distance of thousands of miles. Sculptures at Yakushiji that were sketched by Sekino (see fig. 3.3) were also compared to those of the Longmen Grottoes (near Luoyang in China's Henan Province), which date to the Northern Wei (386–535) and Sui dynasties (581–618). By insisting on these far-flung cultural connections to other famous Buddhist monuments in India and China, the catalogue editors attempted to demonstrate that the "whole history of the wooden art and architecture of Japan was matchless in excellence in the world" (Tokyo Teishitsu Hakubutsukan 1901, 293–325).

Last, but not least, it is important to note here that the inauguration of Japan's oldest and most prestigious art journal, *Kokka*, was timed to coincide with the opening of the 1889 Paris Universelle. On September 20, 1889, the director of the Imperial Museum, Count Kuki Ryūichi, wrote virtually identical essays on the topic "The Essence of Japanese Spirit" for both the

1900 Paris exposition catalogue and the preface to the first volume of the art journal *Kokka* (Kuki 1889, 4–5). Kuki stated that the mission of the imperial museum was "on the one hand to promote the exports industries, but on the other, to promote the authority and prestige of the ancient Meiji imperial house to the world." Kuki noted that the museum had decided to launch publication projects at that time because, "though Japanese art is now well regarded throughout the world, unfortunately there were no existing books on subject of Japanese art history." To prepare for the volume, he went on,

> we organized a countrywide survey commission devoted to preserving the spirit of our treasures. We therefore surveyed and authenticated the artists, dates, [and] forms, and their historical origins. These were all preparations so that we could compile our thousand-year-old art history. At this time, the art history editorial committee has edited this concise history in order to prepare for the opening of the Paris exposition.... Therefore, since the Meiji restoration, we have begun with renewed fervor in rewriting our art history to promote the beauty of our history. (Tokyo Teishitsu Hakubutsukan 1901, 2–3)

Kuki's final statement quoted here is indicative of how much faith the Meiji exposition officials placed on the arts as a vehicle for nation building: "Art is the essence of a civilized [*bunmei*] nation.... Artworks [*bijutsuhin*] are material objects crystallizing the history of one's civilization and thus reflect its citizens' [*kokumin*] religion, thoughts, character [*seikaku*], trends [*keikō*], and skills. Therefore, a study of the history of art epochs [*rekidai*] must provide the materials to build the future fortunes of the nation" (Tokyo Teishitsu Hakubutsukan 1901, 1–2).

The editorial committee also did not forget to appeal to the main target audience of the inaugural volume, that is, connoisseurs and collectors: "The goal of the journal is to cooperate with art connoisseurs as well as businessmen regarding the study, promotion, preservation, and appreciation of Japanese arts from Meiji back to Nara times" (Kuki 1889). In the essay, Kuki also laid out his three future goals for the Imperial Museum: to employ the best scholars and specialists, who as connoisseurs of art would be sent around the country to investigate the secrets of old temples and shrines; to uncover more relics that had been forgotten so that the unique sequence of a hundred generations (*hyakudai*) of ancestral achievements led by heroes and the lords of great aristocratic clans would inspire patriotism and promote the progressive image of Japan (*kokutai*) to the world; and to promote archaeological investigation so as to pinpoint historical sites that would provide objective proof for understanding the geographic locations of East-West contacts (Tokyo Teishitsu Hakubutsukan 1901, 2).

In order to achieve these curatorial, commercial, and research goals articulated in the Paris catalogue and in *Kokka*, Kuki emphasized that the state needed all three departments (the Education Ministry, the Museum Department, and the Ministry of Agriculture and Commerce) to work together so that the government could guide national artists in developing superior and saleable arts abroad. When we read Kuki's impassioned message, it is clear that the writing of art history and the publication of exposition catalogues in Meiji Japan was a marketing vehicle that not only sold Japanese curios but also met the economic and political ends of the Meiji state (Satō 1999).

CHAPTER 4

SEARCHING FOR THE MISSING LINK

Prehistory, Ethnology, and Racial Discourse

"Prehistory," "evolutionary theory," and "the typology of races" were first introduced by European and American scientists who were hired to guide the young men of Japan in catching up with Western science and medicine (Oguma 1995, 3–42). The German doctor Phillip Franze von Siebold (1796–1866) and his son Heinrich (1852–1908), William Gowland (1843–1922), an English chemist who served as a consultant to the Mint (1872–88), and John Milne (1850–1913), an English seismologist and professor of Geology at Tokyo University (1876–94) were scholars who pioneered the fields of ethnography, archaeology, and racial sciences (Saitō 1974; Kudō 1979; Teshigawara 1995; Hudson 1999). The idea of the Ezo (Ainu) as the "indigenous" population of Japan was first proposed by Philipp Franz von Siebold, who in turn may have been inspired by the noted eighteenth-century antiquarian and collector Sekitei Kinouchi (1724–1808), who had first suggested that stone arrowheads were tools made by the Northern peoples (Motomura 1996, 11–12). John Milne was another early racial theorist, who, between 1880 and 1881, proposed that the prehistoric shell middens scattered throughout Japan belonged to the Ainu. Another novel idea attributed to Milne was his identification of a previously unknown population of non-Ainu people called the Koro-pok-guru, whom Milne thought had built the pit dwellings farther north.[1] Milne traced the name of Koro-pok-guru to an Ainu-English dictionary published in 1877 by John Batchelor (1854–1954), a Methodist reverend who had lived among the Ainu for thirty years collecting myths, legends, and customs. Batchelor had inferred from oral Ainu legends that the Koro-pok-guru were a separate race of prehistoric "pit dwellers" who had predated their Ainu's arrival in the North (Milne 1882, 194; Starr 1904).

Edward Morse (1838–1925) is well known as the father of prehistoric archaeology in Japan (see fig. 2.4) because of his sensational discovery of the shell mound of Ōmori, a story that has been retold in many accounts documenting the birth of modern Japanese archaeology.[2] Morse was on his way from Yokohama to Tokyo to take up his new position at Tokyo University as professor of zoology (Teshigawara 1995, 33–38). Upon passing the train station at Ōmori (now part of Tokyo city), he happened to look out the train window. He instantly recognized a large shell mound looming in the horizon. Impressed by the size of the "kitchen midden" (in the terminology of the day), he waited for three months for an excavation permit from the Ministry of Education. The permit came in October 1877 (Saitō 1982, 64). Armed with a letter from the ministry and an introduction from the ōmori train station manager, he began a preliminary survey, accompanied by two of his favorite Tokyo University students, two professors, and six laborers. The three hundred pounds of materials he lugged back to Tokyo University included pottery, artifacts, and seashells, and constituted the first batch of archaeological and zoological collections for the future Tokyo University Museum. For the next two years, Morse devoted himself to the organization and study of the excavated materials, eventually publishing his findings in a report titled "Shell Mounds of Ōmori" (E. Morse 1879). Written in both English and Japanese, the volume inaugurated the prestigious series Memoirs of the Scientific Department of the University of Tokio, the Meiji predecessor to Tokyo University Press (Rosenstone 1988, 54–147).

Morse's two short months digging at Ōmori became a career-defining event for Morse as well as a pivotal turning point in the history of Japanese archaeology, for several reasons. First, it was the first site to be excavated stratigraphically. Second, Morse's excavated finds demonstrated that material remains unearthed from the ground could be used to infer about prehistoric inhabitants and trace changes in their lifestyles. Third, Morse's excavation report, which grouped specimens by their likeness in sketches and photographs, left a lasting legacy for "scientific" documentation methods. This is because his training in comparative zoology at Harvard University, as well as his skills in drafting, sketching, and photography, helped him recognize patterns—both man-made and naturally formed. That same year, Heinrich von Siebold published the first archaeological treatise on "Stone Age" Japan, which was printed in Yokohama in

1879 (Siebold 1879). Siebold's catalogue, which was full of black-and-white photos and sketches, identified two types of stone tools—polished stone tools (*masei sekki*) and chipped stone tools (*tasei sekki*)—has since been recognized as the first attempt to establish a modern typology of the prehistoric stone tools of Japan (Kudō 1979, 43; Teshigawara 1995, 36). Fourth, Morse is also remembered as the first scientist to propose an absolute dating sequence based on excavated materials (Teshigawara 1995, 38). His 1,500- to 2,000-year-old estimates for pottery taken from the deepest layers of shell mounds were cross-dated to ancient flora, fauna, and fossils and proved instrumental in overturning centuries-old myths that had speculated that gods or giants were responsible for transporting the shells from the Eastern Sea of Japan and depositing them in the mountains. In fact, it was Morse who coined the name Jōmon in 1886, to refer to the distinctive "cord-marked designs" on pottery fragments found widely in shell mounds (Kudō 1979, 24). In time, it became accepted as the generic name of a cultural and chronological unit, as in Jōmon period or culture, synonymous with the earliest phase of Japanese prehistory, currently carbon-dated to go as far back as 10,000 BC (Ikawa-Smith 1995). Morse also worked hard to train his students at the university specimens lab in the taxonomic organization of material remains excavated from Ōmori based on their physical attributes, such as form, style, design, and source materials (Saitō 1982, 76–114). Morse's archaeological discoveries also influenced the curators at the Imperial Museum Department, who, in 1879, for the first time included prehistoric pottery (*doki*), stone tools, and bones in the museum exhibition inventory (Tokyo Kokuritsu Hakubutsukan 1976, 2:223).

Last, but not least, Morse was the first scholar to actively work at promoting the field of prehistoric archaeology and the racial sciences to the foreign community. Despite his busy schedule with excavations and teaching, he managed to deliver a lecture on his preliminary findings, "Traces of Early Man in Japan," to the Asiatic Society of Japan in Yokohama on October 13, 1877. The audience, which came mostly from the German, English, and French foreign communities, bore witness to what is now recorded as the first public speech delivered on the topic of prehistoric archaeology of Japan (Saitō 1982, 69–71). At this historical meeting, Morse announced that his excavated Ōmori remains belonged to an extinct population he dubbed "pre-Ainu," a population that was racially distinct from that of modern-day Japanese.[3] He also hypothesized that the "pre-Ainu" may have been of same "primitive" racial makeup as American Indian populations such as the Eskimos and the Northern races residing in Kamchatka and Karafuto (present-day Sakhalin) (Kudō 1979, 54).

Morse's Ōmori excavations thus laid the foundations of the archaeological method and of the ethnohistorical approach to material data, which paved the way for the first generation of young native anthropologists— Tsuboi Shōgorō (1863–1913), a medical student; Miyake Yonekichi (1860– 1929), a historian; and Shirai Mitsutarō (1863–1932), a biologist and former student of Morse's (fig. 4.1)—who formed the Tokyo Anthropological Society (Tokyo Jinrui Gakkai) on October 17, 1884, on the Tokyo University campus (Matsumura 1934; Oba 1935). Emulating Morse, these college students began their careers tramping around the outskirts of Hongō campus looking for their own field sites to dig on weekends and holding informal meetings at their homes comparing notes.[4] Their stratigraphic excavations of shell mounds such as those at Okadaira, Shinji, Nishigawara, Shizuka, and Atamadai in the 1880s enabled the next generation of archaeologists to delineate the prehistoric pottery sequence of Japan's Stone Age, from prehistoric Jōmon pottery to Iron Age (Yayoi) pottery and Kofun (Sueki) pottery (Teshigawara 1995, 55).

The *Journal of the Tokyo Anthropological Society* (Tokyo jinrui gakkai zasshi, hereafter TJGK), launched in 1886, remains the leading scientific publication covering the fields of prehistoric archaeology, biological anthropology, and racial sciences today. The inaugural issues of the journal clearly articulated the academic purpose of the society, which was devoted to revealing the natural laws (*shizen no ri*) of man by encompassing all subjects, including general anthropological topics (*jinruigaku ippan*), physical anthropology, social anthropology, and archaeology, as well as local histories (Pai 2004). The topics advocated by the journal were reminiscent of the "hodgepodge" character of the leading European scientific journals of the day, ranging among human biology, dissection, genetics, psychology, subsistence, old customs, shell mounds, pottery mounds, old vessels, subterranean dwellings, burial mounds, history of writing, linguistic lineages, dialects, music, kinship, village organization, classification of peoples, and the distribution of man (TJGK 1886).

The journal's main criteria for evaluating articles for publication and

人類学教室標本整理係になった頃の鳥居龍蔵
前列右から、下村三四吉、井上喜久治、坪井正五郎、八木奘三郎、後列右から、鳥居龍蔵、若林勝邦、山崎直方。1893（明治26）年撮影。鳥居龍次郎氏提供

FIG. 4.1. Members of the Tokyo Anthropological Specimens Laboratory, 1893. *Back row*: First on the right is Torii Ryūzō, who was put in charge of the laboratory in 1893. *Front row*: Second from the left is Tsuboi Shōgorō. Seated to his right is Yagi Sōzaburō. Photo by Torii Ryūzō. Source: Sasaki Kōmei, ed., *Torii Ryūzō no mita Ajia* ["Asia" Photographed by Torii Ryūzō] (Osaka: Tokushima Kenritsu Hakubutsukan (Tokushima County Museum) / Minpaku (National Museum of Ethnology), 1993, 17.

citation was to prioritize submissions from dispatches sent directly from the field (*tsūshin*). The emphasis on publishing only data collected in the field was a strategy to distance the members from earlier Edo-era antiquarians and "armchair" scholars who had relied mostly on textual sources and portable antiquities for their information. By emphasizing on-site investigations and raw field data, the editorial board members presented themselves as the vanguard of the new "scientifically" trained professionals in the European mode. They also encouraged the submission of measurements, illustrations, and photographs along with the manuscripts. In the second year of the journal's publication, at the twenty-third monthly meeting in June 1888, the members voted to include a list of contents in English. The translated articles' titles demonstrated the members' desire to reach out to other intellectuals in Europe and America. At an executive committee in 1886, the members also voted to change the name of the journal from *Anthropological Journal* (Jinrui gakkai zasshi) to *Tokyo Anthropological Journal*, indicating that the founding members were concerned about distinguishing themselves from other anthropological institutions in Europe with whom they had arranged publication exchange agreements. The members also maintained similar contracts with other learned societies inside Japan in related fields such as geology, anatomy, biology, geography, and history (TJGK 1886, 2). A typical journal issue in the 1880s usually consisted of four or five feature articles relating new discoveries of Stone Age tools, of pottery and relics from shell mounds in Hokkaido or the Ryūkyūs, and racial classification and anthropometric studies of the Ainu by foreign experts such as Heinrich von Siebold. In addition, there were many short research reports from outside Japan—stone tools, pottery analyses, and burial identifications from the Korean peninsula; studies of subterranean dwellings in China; and customs documented from as far away as the New Hebrides, Samoa, and the Solomon Islands (Mokuyō Club 1996). The back section of every issue was devoted to introducing the latest cultural events, such as the openings of new museums in Europe and the latest exciting news from international expositions and from new ethnography publications. By the 1890s, the journal was publishing photos and correspondence sent in by Torii Ryūzō (1870–1953), the man in the field dispatched to Manchuria, Taiwan, China, the Kurile Islands, and Korea (see map 1) who had become a regular contributor to the journal (Pai 2009). Such a broad coverage of subjects, as well as up-to-date news from expeditions to faraway places (from Siberia to the South Pacific) that were just beginning to open up to Japanese exploration, military, and commercial ventures, no doubt contributed to the exponential increase in the number of subscribers curious about foreign lands and peoples. In 1886, the first year of publication, the membership count was 25, made up mostly of Tokyo University students. The number increased tenfold, to 119, the second year, 139 the third year, and by the fourth year, there were 210 members.[5] By 1908, there were 492 subscribers. By the time of the society's fiftieth jubilee celebration in 1934, the society's membership averaged a respectable total of around 350 (Matsumura 1934).

The society's monthly meetings were the main stage on which Tsuboi Shōgorō (1863–1913)—by all accounts a polymath, world traveler, and charismatic leader—instructed his peers on the latest news emanating from cutting-edge field sciences of the day, including geology, biology, archaeology, and ethnography. As a fan of the works of Victorian-era "classical evolutionists" such as John Lubbock (1744–1866), Lewis Henry Morgan (1818–81), and Edward Tylor (1832–1917), Tsuboi was always eager to debate on the theoretical issues of the day, including the validity and application of the "three-age system," degeneration theory, survivalism, and universalism. He was especially keen on applying his knowledge to reveal the racial identity of the inhabitants of Japan in relation to the hierarchy of man (Ikawa-Smith 1982, 300). In 1888, in search of skull measurements, Tsuboi and his colleague in anatomy, Koganei Yoshikiyo (1859–1944), went to Hokkaido for three months to investigate shell mounds, museum collections, and cemeteries. Upon their return, Koganei sided with Morse, arguing that the Jōmon remains belonged to the prehistoric Ainu and not an earlier, now-extinct population of the Koro-pok-guru (Ikawa-Smith 1996, 45–46). He reasoned that the living Ainu, after more than two centuries of Russian contact and colonization, had simply forgotten how to make stone tools and pottery as their ancestors had done. Tsuboi, on the other hand, agreed with Milne's assertions that the earliest prehistoric inhabitants were the Koro-pok-guru, whom he believed were a race that had once occupied Honshū as far back as 30,000 BCE. He gave three reasons for his hypothesis. First, geologically, prehistoric shell-mound sites were found far from the current shoreline. Second, stratigraphically, human artifacts were found in the deepest layers. Third, morphologically, the differences between the ancient mollusks and the present ones were vast (Tsuboi 1889). Once he made up his mind, Tsuboi dedicated the rest of his life to promoting his extinct Koro-pok-guru population, who had once inhabited all of Japan.

When we read Tsuboi's articles on the Koro-pok-guru, the majority of which were published during the three years he was studying in London (1889–92), they show that, in contrast to the first generation of samurai mission members, Tsuboi clearly understood that the purpose of a museum was to collect "primitive rituals, and arts and crafts" from around the world,

and to group them together so as to demonstrate the material and technological progress of man (Tsuboi 1889). As early as 1889, Tsuboi was reported
to have submitted a racial diagram to the Paris Universelle titled "A Pictorial Reference for Understanding Anthropology." Working with a talented
artist, he commissioned a series of ethnographic portraits of the Koro-pok-
guru drawn in the traditional style of *fūdoki* (gazeteer) illustrations (Tsuboi
1895). This collaboration produced fine-lined pen drawings of strikingly
attractive young men and women dressed in embroidered costumes, albeit
in the mode of "the noble savage," imitating the highly romanticized
photographs of American Indians popularized by Tsuboi's contemporary,
Edward Curtis (1868–1952) (Jackson 1992). Tsuboi's series of ethnic tableaus of the Koro-pok-guru people consciously emulated museum dioramas
he had seen in expositions and museums in Europe, which paid meticulous
attention to every detail and texture of clothing, accessory, and hairstyle, as
well as to realistic habitats for subsistence activities such as pottery making, fishing, and hunting expeditions.[6] Women were drawn carrying out
household chores such as making and firing pottery on an open fire. The
pottery they made resembled Jōmon pottery featuring the coiling method.
Their loose garments were also reminiscent of the kimono-like garb adorning prehistoric pottery figurines, or *haniwa*, dating to the Yayoi period.
Commenting on the tattoos that he noticed decorating the mouth, eyes,
and hands of many *haniwa* figurines, Tsuboi referred to his student Torii's
report from the colony of Taiwan, where the latter had identified similar
practices on the part of aborigines (fig. 4.2), a custom that both interpreted
as a universal marker of primitiveness (Pai 2009, 279–80).

In contrast to the well-decked-out and domesticated women, the men
were posed in "masculine" activities: carrying stone axes and adzes, and
using bows and stone arrows for hunting game, catching fish, and building
huts. Some were also depicted wearing huge eye goggles reminiscent of the
bug-eyed *haniwa* figurines, as well as the Eskimo sunglasses Tsuboi had
seen displayed at expositions. Some illustrations were encircled in borders
with exact replicas of stone tools, pottery figurines, and weapons taken
from the Tokyo Anthropological Laboratory collections. The captions for
these hand-drawn artifacts sometimes included Tsuboi's classificatory
names and, in a few cases, when known, the geographic locations of their
finds in Japan (Tsuboi 1895).

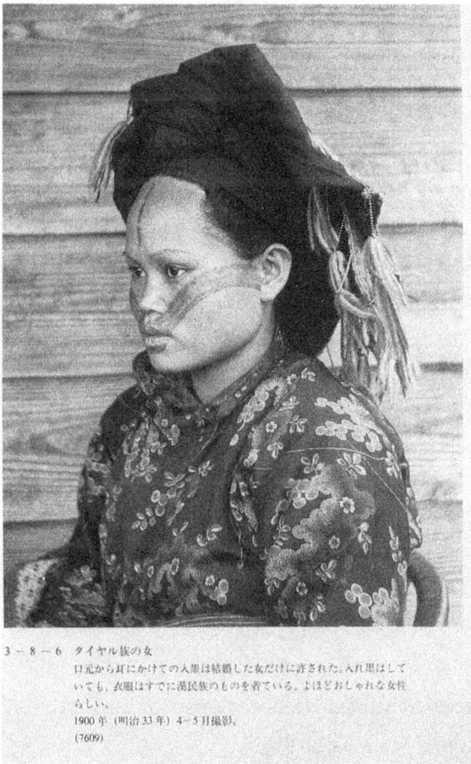

FIG. 4.2. Taiyal woman with tattoo, c. 1900. Only married women were permitted to tattoo their cheeks in this way, from mouth to ear. The woman is wearing a Han Chinese dress. Photo by Torii Ryūzō. Collection of the University Museum, University of Tokyo. Source: Akazawa et al. 1992, p. 52, plate 2.12.

More importantly, Tsuboi's graphic depictions of his imagined "Koro-pok-guru" people were first published in a popular magazine called *Illustrated Customs and Landscapes* (Fūzoku gahō), which was founded by two prominent commercial artists of the late Meiji era (1889–1916). This lavishly illustrated monthly proved to be a big hit at the time because it featured the latest travel news regarding ethnographic customs and foreign correspondence from Taiwan, Sakhalin, Korea, and the Pacific, which had recently been opened to merchants, scholars, and journalists following the Sino-Japanese and Russo-Japanese Wars.

Largely due to Tsuboi's international reputation, the Tokyo Anthropological Laboratory was chosen by the Education Ministry as the sole designated repository for prehistoric stone tools, pottery remains, and other ethnographic specimens acquired not only domestically but also from abroad (Teshigawara 1995, 73–87). Upon his return to Japan from a government-sponsored, three-year study-abroad visit to London in 1893,

Tsuboi started to tackle the organization of his growing lab collections. Inspired by the ethnographic displays he had observed in museums and expositions while traveling in the capitals of Europe, his main project was to arrange artifacts and pottery based "on form, function, and subsistence activities." As early as 1889, Tsuboi had noted that *kofun* pottery, or ritual pottery (*iwaibe doki*), was entirely different from earlier prehistoric finds he had uncovered (Tsuboi 1889, 19–29). He observed that such a dramatic shift in pottery style and design reflected not only a transformation in religious beliefs and cooking and storing methods but also indicated the presence of class differentiation, a revolutionary idea at that time. In a series of seminal articles titled *Lectures on Japanese Archaeology* (Nihon kōkogaku kōza), published between 1889 and the early 1900s, Tsuboi outlined his classificatory scheme (*shubetsu*) for pottery and stone objects accordingly: (1) form (bowls, plates, jars, dishes, bottles, and figurines) and distinctive features in handle shape and rim design; (2) function (eating, serving, cooking, storage, and religious; tools were divided by usage: axes, adzes, spears, and arrowheads); and (3) surface design (*moyō*): cord-marked or geometric hatching. His pottery figurines, or *haniwa*, were also differentiated by the kind of clay, the color, and the types of surface decorations, such as hairstyles, headgear, and body ornaments (such as tattoos).

By 1893, Tsuboi was also advising three very capable lab research assistants—Torii Ryūzō , Yagi Sōzaburō (1866–1942), and Ōno Entarō/Nobutarō (1863–1938)—who, unlike the rest of the community, were in the enviable position of having direct access to a massive database of collections of stone and bone tools, pottery, bronzes, and iron weapons from all over Japan. Embracing their mentor's "ethnological approach," Tsuboi's assiatants set to work organizing and arranging the vast number of prehistoric tools and ethnographic artifacts as "representative stage markers" for delineating man's development from "savagery" to "barbarism" to civilization. The earliest illustrated catalogues of prehistoric artifacts produced at the turn of the century were hand-drawn by Ōno, a talented artist who devised the following criteria for analysis: (1) polished stone tools as evidence of subsistence activities, such as agriculture or hunting (semilunar knives, polished stone knives, and arrowheads); (2) bronzes indicating knowledge of metallurgy (swords, slim daggers, and *dōtaku* or bells); (3) pottery designs, as indicators of advanced thinking and artistic sensibility (for example, Jōmon geometric pottery or "plain" Yayoi pottery); and (4) *kofun* burial styles indicating monumental architecture and beliefs about the afterlife (Yagi Sōzaburō 1894; Ōno 1904; Tsuboi 1903). Under Tsuboi's supervision, his research assistants attempted to come up with a typology of prehistoric clay figurines (*dogu*) and tomb clay figurines (*haniwa*) focusing on the figurines' facial features and designs motifs, or *moyō* (Ōno 1904). Like their mentor, these young and idealistic Tokyo anthropology lab students were eager to address the larger questions pertaining to the nature and origin of primitive man, to distinguish the evolving universal stages of human progress, and to document the spread of prehistoric peoples and cultures. Their main academic mission was to prove to the world the educational value of the fields of Japanese ethnology and archaeology (Tsuboi 1905).

By 1908, the Welcome Society of Japan (Kihinkai; the predecessor to the Japan Tourist Bureau) and the Tokyo Chamber of Commerce were advertising the lab as one of the "must-see destinations" in Tokyo (along with Ueno's Imperial Museum) for diplomats, foreign businessmen and tourists (Welcome Society 1908, viii). With a stream of visiting dignitaries—including Edward Morse, Frederick Starr (1858–1933), and the crown prince of Sweden, Adolf Gustaf VI (1882–1973), an avid amateur archaeologist and founder of the Museum of Far Eastern Antiquities in Stockholm (see fig. 5.9)—the lab became widely recognized as the vanguard of scientific research in Japan at the turn of the century.

Despite such open endorsements and VIP visitors, to the dismay of these budding young archaeologists, by the late 1890s the Imperial Household Agency began to enforce bans on the investigations of tombs, and on buried remains in particular. One of the more interesting anecdotes, which was made public only after Tsuboi's untimely demise in the winter of 1913 during a conference trip to St. Petersburg, tells a cautionary tale of how even this respected man ran afoul of the government censors. His story first appeared in a lengthy obituary published in a special edition of the *Tokyo Anthropological Society Journal* that was dedicated to Tsuboi. The chief editor, Matsumura Ryō (1880–1936), recounted how Tsuboi's repeated requests to the Imperial Household authorities to grant excavation permits for scientific purposes fell on deaf ears. According to Matsumura, the Imperial Household authorities, prompted by the "pressures of conservative forces," had strong-armed Tsuboi into abandoning any future inquiries into the archaeological origins of imperial family (Matsumura 1934). After this fractious run-in with the Imperial Household Agency, Tsuboi, like many others of his generation, decided to practice self-censorship, no doubt to hang on to his social position and professional career (Teshigawara 1995, 77–78). Despite Tsuboi's personal failings, he was nonetheless a revolutionary figure who pioneered the ethnohistorical approach (*dozoku gaku*), which encompassed the three fields of historical archaeology (*ishi*), protohistory (*genshi*), and prehistory (*zenshi*) (Saitō 1971, 132). Tsuboi's firm stance that "ethnology could provide the answer to the central question in Japanese archaeology," that is, "what kind of lifestyles, physical characteristics, knowledge, arts, and crafts can be correlated to the remains that our ancestors have left behind" (Tsuboi 1889, 18), served as the mantra for successive generations of anthropologists produced by the Tokyo University program.

Despite more than two decades of protracted discursive battles and classificatory schemes floated in journal issues and university reports, the major players, Koganei, Tsuboi, and Torii, never reconciled their disagreements on whether it was the Ainu or Koro-pok-guru who were more likely to have been the earliest inhabitants of the islands (Kudō 1979, 93–99). Handicapped by the ban on the excavations of tomb remains and the scrutiny of the Imperial Household Agency, Tsuboi chose to devote the latter part of his career to outreach efforts disseminating his pet Koro-pok-guru theory. Sad to say, Tsuboi's racial theories did not outlive his sudden demise (Motomura 1996). In fact, it was his own protégé, Torii, who was responsible for the death knell of his mentor's pet theory when in 1899 Torii was dispatched by the Ministry of the Navy to the Kurile Islands (see map 1). Citing earlier Russian ethnographers' reports, upon his return Torii announced that the remains of semisubterranean dwellings were built by the ancestors of the present Ainu.[7] Referring to his new collection of stone tools, pottery, and semisubterranean dwellings, he confirmed that the living Ainu in Hokkaido and the Kurile Islands all belonged to one prehistoric population (*shuzoku*).

These heated racial debates (*jinshūron*) reached their peak in the late 1890s and early 1900s, when Japanese military penetration into Taiwan, Manchuria, Korea, and the South Pacific coincided with the ongoing struggle on the part of nation-building intellectuals, academics, and politicians to find their rightful place in the hierarchy of races and world civilizations

(Oguma 1995). Although speculations on the origins, customs, and status of the Ainu had been the source of much controversy as far back as the eighteenth century, Western scientific racism (based on a vulgarized Darwinian evolutionary perspective) was ultimately responsible for denigration of the Ainu as the "Primitive Other" (Morris-Suzuki 1994, 1998a; Hirano 2009). By the 1900s, the majority of foreign scientists, ethnologists, and educators (such as Heinrich von Siebold, Milne, and Morse) had more or less reached a consensus that the Ainu, the obviously biologically inferior "species," had simply lost out in the struggle for survival and been driven into far northern regions by the more "advanced" and superior ancestral Japanese race that had migrated from the continent (Kudō 1979, 53–84). Colonialists, settlers, and developers were also eager to embrace the hypothesis that the Ainu were remnants of a bygone "Stone Age" population so that they could justify their exploitation of Hokkaido's rich land resources, fisheries, and local labor force (*kaitaku*) under the slogan of racial assimilation and cultural enlightenment (Howell 2004).

In summary, by 1899 the Imperial Household Agency reigned over a trio of state-funded cultural resource management institutions: the Education Ministry; the three imperial museums (*teishitsu hakubutsukan*) in Tokyo, Nara, and Kyoto; and the Tokyo Imperial University–based Anthropological Society Laboratory. These national institutions were charged with micromanaging "national properties," from the issuance of excavation permits to registering and monitoring the circulation of antiquities and the construction of imperial palaces, temples, and mausoleums. At all stages, as state-appointed specialists, university academics were responsible for carrying out the complex bureaucratic procedures required to authenticate, inventory, rank, and recommend art and architecture for registration and preservation. Nationalistic scholars and thinkers such as Kuki, Okakura, Torii, and Sekino thus played major roles in resurrecting "Japanese antiquity" from the ground up, with fabricated imperial remains, reenacted rituals, and relics staged for public and for the media (Fujitani 1996; Takagi Hiroshi 1995).

These scholars' periodization schemes (which relied on a fictitious clan of migrating divine emperors who crossed thousands of miles, passing through the Near East, Greece, India, China, and Korea, to pick up much of the "high" artistic and religious traditions) did not deviate from mainstream archaeological discourse. In the late nineteenth and early twentieth century, the "hyperdiffusionists" school was dominated by the likes of Grafton Elliot Smith (1871–1937) and V. Gordon Childe (1892–1957), who argued that all major technological, artistic, cultural, and religious innovations were made but once and then diffused from a common centre, unless there was contradictory archaeological evidence (Trigger 1968, 66–67). Without any empirical proof of conquering emperors or empresses, art historians, architects, and curators who were building imperial collections (such as Kuki and Okakura) and were steeped in the romance of "Graecophilia" relied on art objects in their attempts to situate Japan's racial, artistic, and cultural lineage as being directly descended from great civilizations of the ancient world, on a par with Greece and Rome—and they began with Japan's number-one national treasure, Hōryūiji's Kudara Kannon or the Paekche Avolikitesvara (see fig. 3.2).

Needless to say, the Meiji state monopoly over all aspects of heritage administration—banning excavations of imperial burial mounds and allowing only limited access to archaeological sites and research collections—resulted in a dearth of stratigraphic excavations, severely impeding the progress of the scientific field archaeology in Japan. Consequently, Japanese art historians had no other choice but to rely on hypothetical conquest schemes until they could launch systematic excavations in the colony of Korea in 1916. Okakura's racial narrative, in which the Korean peninsula was a conduit for the transmission of ancient Han dynastic innovations and Buddhist art in ancient times, not only inspired his own students but influenced the continental direction of Japanese archaeological, anthropological, and art surveys, beginning with the Korean peninsula in 1900. Forward-thinking curators such as Kuki also believed that a national museum must collect and exhibit "archaeological evidence" to be accepted as a serious research institution. Thus, when field opportunities opened up following the Sino-Japanese War in 1895, Tokyo University did not waste time dispatching its best students and experts to conduct comprehensive art, archaeological, and ethnographic surveys in Korea, China, Taiwan, and Inner Asia (Xu 2002). Finally, the Meiji intellectuals' and scientists' rejection of the Ainu as being too primitive in appearance and lifestyle to be the direct ancestors of the Japanese race spurred the advancement of Japanese archaeology and ethnography in the colonies (Pai 2004, 2009).

Once scholars reached a consensus that Japan's prehistoric finds and inhabitants were not physically, religious, artistically, or culturally related to the divine Yamato, the search for the missing racial link that would bridge the time divide between the arrival of the Yamato race and earlier "Stone Age inhabitants" turned toward the continent (Oguma 1995; Pai 2004; Saitō 1974; Teshigawara 1995, 92).

By the turn of the century, with tantalizing photographs, correspondence, and survey reports filtering in from Korea, Tokyo University administrators, professors, and learned societies requested financial and logistical support from the Meiji state, the army, and colonial administrators so as to conduct fieldwork in the newly incorporated territories on the Korean peninsula and in Mongolia, Siberia, China, and Taiwan (Pai 2009). The five members of the Tokyo Anthropological Executive Committee headed by Tsuboi discussed sending Torii to the Liaodong Peninsula on June 30, 1895, only two months following the conclusion of the Sino-Japanese War. Their dispatch letter dated July 1 was sent the following day to Torii. The contents of this dispatch letter (*shokutaku fuinsho*) instructed Torii to adopt "a comprehensive approach for investigating the customs of the natives, collect ancient objects [*kobutsu*], and to search for prehistoric remains [*iseki*] and to report back his findings to the society." Four days later, official notifications were sent to the commander-general in Liaodong asking local officers to assist Torii anyway they could, including making provisions for transportation, porters, and guides to haul equipment and coordinate logistics (TJGK 1895, 148).

At the turn of the century, Torii Ryūzō was the only Japanese field researcher to earn an international reputation as a professional anthropologist (Askew 2003; Pai 2009). His academic legacy both inside and outside of Japan can be attributed to the longevity of his eighty-three-year-long life and an academic career that was mostly spent traveling, living, and lecturing outside of Japan. His interdisciplinary and intraregional outlook not only incorporated ethnographic observations, physical anthropological measurements, and archaeological surveys but also included documentation of oral traditions and myths recorded in ancient Chinese textual sources and Russian ethnographies (Torii 1925b). Beginning with his very first expedition to the Liaodong Peninsula in August 1895, Torii's wide-ranging interests took him to remote tribal villages, ancient ruins, library archives, museums, and military outposts (Torii 1953, 1976). As we can see in map 1, he traveled as far north as the Kurile Islands (1899) and the Kamchatka Peninsula (1911); south to Taiwan (1896), the Ryūkyū Islands (1904), and the mountains of Yunnan (1902-3); as far west as Siberia's Lake Baikal (1919); and Manchuria (1895), Mongolia (1906-8), and the Korean Peninsula (1910-11).

As a technically skilled photographer, Torii was also the first to take a camera to the field—to Taiwan in 1896 (see fig. 4.2). Consequently, his ethnographic reports included some of the earliest-known photographic images of "Mongoloid peoples" posed in their native settings depicting "semibarbaric" exotic customs, Shamanistic religions, and nomadic life-styles (Akazawa 1991, 1992). Torii is widely credited with grouping the Paleo-Asiatics, the Tungus, and the Dongyi (Eastern Barbarians) as direct descendents of a common stock of Neolithic/Bronze Age peoples, the most "primitive peoples of Northeast Asia." His racial classificatory studies also attracted a wide following in the European scientific community because his visually striking images of ruins and relics in faraway Asia usually accompanied his reports and articles printed by the Tokyo Anthropological Society (Barclay 2001; Pai 2009; Torii 1925a, b). Torii's position that the indigenous peoples of Northeast Asia had not changed in over two thousand years became widely accepted by prominent racial scientists of the day, including Joseph Deniker (1900), Carleton Coon (1962), and Russian ethnologist S. M. Shirokorogoff (1966), who all referred to his reports written in French.

Yagi Sōzaburō (1866-1942) was the first archaeologist sent to Korea by the Tokyo Anthropological Society in 1900 (see fig. 4.1). His opening statement in a letter sent that same year to his advisor, Professor Tsuboi Shōgorō, is reminiscent of any young graduate student going off to conduct fieldwork for the first time in its mixture of hubris and idealistic research goals: "I humbly want to state my three research goals in Korea as: First, racial makeup [jinshujō], second, its archaeology [kōkogaku], and third, ethnography [dozoku gaku]" (Yagi Sōzaburō 1900). As early as 1894, Yagi had proposed dividing kofun pottery into two types: "pure Japanese style" (junsui Nihon fū) versus "China-Korea style" (Shina Chōsenfū), which represented the intrusion of foreign elements. At that time, since there had not been any fieldwork whatsoever in Korea, Yagi did not have any means of comparing the relative chronology of *kofun* pottery in Korea. He just presumed that "Chōsen-style" pottery (generically referred to as *sueki* style (stoneware) today) was older because it came from Korea. He claimed that the shards he had picked up from surface finds in Korea were identical to the *iwaibe*, or "ritual-style," pottery found in *kofun* burials (Yagi Sōzaburō 1894). For Yagi, the distribution of this pottery concentrated in the southeastern part of Korea (around Pusan, Kimhae, and Kyŏngju; see map 2), the areas closest to Japan (Yagi Sōzaburō 1900, 1902), demonstrated proof of his hypothetical racial links. Yagi's correspondence from Korea dating to 1900–1902 thus marked a turning point in the history of Japanese archaeology on the Korean Peninsula (appendix, table 5).

Tokyo Imperial University also dispatched Sekino Tadashi (1868–1935) to Korea in the summer of 1902 to document art and archaeological remains located in and around the former dynastic capitals of Keishū (Kyŏngju), Kaijō (Kaesŏng), Heijō (P'yŏngyang), and Keijō (Seoul). His field report titled *Investigators' Reports of Korean Architecture* (Kankoku kenchiku chōsa hōkoku), published by the Tokyo University Engineering College in 1904, is recognized as the first accurate account of Korea's art and architectural history (Sekino Tadashi 1904). Sekino's comprehensive two-hundred-and-fifty-page report was filled with detailed descriptions of the locations, measurements, textual sources, and photographs of hundreds of sculptures, temples, gates, and palatial architecture, as well the tombs of Yi dynasty rulers that he had personally surveyed in only three short months. His work also proposed the first schematic periodization of Korea's art into four main dynastic periods: (1) Three Kingdoms, (2) Unified Silla, (3) Koryŏ, (4), and Chosŏn. This 1904 report was also groundbreaking because of Sekino's photographs of ancient temples, pagodas, and tombs, which first alerted the academic world to the existence of thousand-year-old ruins in Korea.

In 1906, Imanishi Ryū (1875–1932), another Tokyo Imperial University-trained history student, made the discovery of a prehistoric shell mound at Kimhae, near Pusan (Imanishi 1907). At his request, the following year the Tokyo Anthropological Society sent another young graduate student, Shibata Jōkei (1877–1954), who made a quick survey that summer. Both researchers agreed that the size and distribution of finds of shells, animal bones, stone tools, and, most importantly, the presence of *iwaibe* pottery, all indicated definite correlations with Yayoi and *kofun* remains in Japan (Shibata 1908). Imanishi thus concluded that the antiquity of Korean civilization was most interesting because of its obvious "prehistoric" origins and because of the "advanced" nature of its culture dating back to the Three Han times (now dated to 0–3rd century CE), which had preceded the Three Kingdoms (Imanishi 1907). When Torii reexamined the stratigraphic sequence of the Kimhae shell mound, his proposal that the "*gen Nihonjin*" (proto-Japanese race) represented a later migration of the "plain-pottery race" (Yayoi) of rice farmers who constructed megalithic tombs (dolmens) and carried iron weapons became widely accepted as fact in prewar archaeological circles (Teshigawara 1997, 91–92; Saitō 1974). By the 1920s, Torii proposed that the "plain pottery" people had evolved into the "Kimhae-style" people equated with the Three Kingdoms period (4th–7th century CE). Consequently, Torii became the first prehistoric archaeologist to propose a working hypothesis for cross-dating prehistoric remains in Manchuria, Korea, and Japan by identifying two separate racial migrations with two distinct types of "Yayoi" or "plain-looking" pottery versus the earlier decorated Jōmon-style (Torii 1922, 1923, 1925a, 1937). Since Torii's proposal, pottery finds from shell mounds in Korea continue to serve as key time-markers for dating not only Japan's protohistorical remains but also the prehistoric chronology of the Neolithic and Bronze Ages in Korea (Torii 1924; Kim Wŏl-lyong 1986; Pai 2000, 77–126).

These initial discovery reports on Korea published by Tokyo University–sponsored field researchers were revolutionary for the times, for they represented the earliest examples of the application of the idea of a "Japanese prehistory" recoverable from the colonies (Pai 1999a, 2004, 2006). These observations by young graduate students during the turn of the century also paved the way for the conceptual development of a common "Japanese/Korean" cultural and racial lineage based on tracing the development of "Japanese" artifacts, art, and architecture on the continent (Kita 1921; Fujita 1948, Torii 1923; Umehara 1923). In terms of architectural resources, the wealth of material evidence from decorative and structural elements (such as roofs; the shape and design of roof tiles, columns, and pillars; interior paintings; and Buddhist sculptural art forms) that Sekino had personally surveyed in Korea, China, and Inner Asia in his lifetime, revolutionized the field of East Asian art, archaeology, and architecture as we know it today

(Fujii et al., 2005). In this preconceived prehistorical trajectory tracing the birth of early Japanese civilization to the continent, "archaeological" data from Korea soon took precedence over traditional dynastic accounts recorded in the ancient records of the *Nihon Shoki* and *Kojiki*. Therefore, even before any excavations were done or concrete dates for establishing an absolute chronology or sequence of remains were set, Tokyo University scholars were convinced that the peninsula's archaeological record would prove invaluable in bridging the time gap or "missing racial link" in the transitional stage between the "proto-historic" or Yayoi period and the full-fledged state formation in the Nara period (710–84). By the time of the annexation of the Korean Peninsula in 1910, the field observations made by Tokyo University students in the colonies were accepted as the primary "scientific" evidence for tracing the continental origins of the Japanese race and civilization (Pai 2004, 2006, 2010a).

CHAPTER 5

EXCAVATING KOREA'S PAST

Colonialists, Archaeologists, and Nostalgic Ruins

The Korean peninsula became the field of choice for Tokyo University graduates due to a variety of intertwined economic, political, and research agendas. First, the banning of most tomb excavations had a crippling effect on the field of scientific archaeology that had once shown so much promise in the early Meiji era (Oba 1935; Yagi Shizuyama 1935). Consequently, ambitious students such as Yagi Shizuyama, Sekino Tadashi, and Torii Ryūzō jumped at the chance to go the colonies in search of "raw" data free of Imperial Household Agency intervention and government censorship (W. Edwards 2003; Naoki 1980). Second, the colonies offered new career opportunities for young men belonging to all class backgrounds, occupations, and education levels due to the unprecedented pace of Japanese colonial industries' advancement into the Korean Peninsula and Manchuria (Park Soon-wŏn 1999). By the 1890s and 1900s, major conglomerates, or *zaibatsu*, such as the the Bank of Chōsen, the Japan Mail Steamship Company (Nippon Yūsen Kaisha), the South Manchuria Railroad Company, and Ōkura and Company (a defense contractor providing ships and ammunition to the army and navy) had all calculated that the export of Korea's agricultural products (rice and cotton) and the import of military supplies and weapons, as well as the mobilization of troops to the new frontier, would prove to be profitable enterprises for investors, contractors, and retail merchants (Duus 1995, 34–168; Young 1998). Soon, all kinds of businesses were racing to broker concession deals, setting up branches in all of the major ports and population centers in Korea and Manchuria (CST Chōsen Ginkō 1919). By the 1905 signing of the Portsmouth Treaty, the Korea branch of the Japan Imperial Railways (Chōsen Sōtokufu, Tetsudō-kyoku, hereafter CSTTK) had opened the Keifu and Jinsen lines (see map 3), which connected population centers in the southern ports of Pusan and Inch'ŏn to the capital Keijō (Seoul).

Third, to meet the growing demand for accurate information about Korea by millions of passengers and potential travelers—including Japanese, Koreans, Chinese, foreign missionaries, soldiers, administrators, businessmen, students, and settlers buying round-trip tickets on steamers and railways—the Japan Imperial Government Railways (hereafter, JIGR) began working closely with Gotō Shimpei (1857–1929), the South Manchuria Railroad Company founding director who had earned his reputation as head of the civilian affairs bureau in Taiwan. For imperialists such as Gotō, the ultimate goal of hiring field experts was to collect reliable data on the customs and habits of a populations so as to facilitate future real-estate development deals, locate the best natural and mineral resources, and exploit cheap labor conditions. It was Gotō's idea to set up a historical research division within the company, hiring the best minds of the day, including graduates from the Tokyo University History Department, such as Naitō Kōnan (né Torajirō, 1866–1934), Shiratori Kurakichi (1865–1942), and Ikeuchi Hiroshi (1878–1952).[1] As the first generation of scholars to pioneer the field of Japan's East Asian studies, these scholars were instrumental in incorporating the language, geography, ethnography, religions, and history of the new colonies of Manchuria and Korea as an integral component of Japan's "Oriental" studies (tōyōgaku) at the turn of the century (Itō Takeo 1980; Mansenshi Chirirekishi 1915–41; Yoshikawa 1976; J. Young 1966). At the same time, once this vast body of field data made up of historical documents, ethnographies, survey maps, photographs, and statistical data were collected and organized under one roof, the Government-General of Chōsen (or Chōsen Sōtokufu, hereafter CST) publication committee was able to use them as educational resources and propaganda tools in the textbooks being prepared for the elementary school system (futsu gakkō) introduced in Korea and Taiwan in 1907 (CST 1929b).

Fourth, as part of the CST's overall long-term strategy to develop Korea's natural, human, and cultural capital for the benefit of the Japanese settler population, the CST and municipal governments began constructing public spaces such as parks, gardens, sports facilities, and museums in the 1900s. The construction of a multipurpose public park modeled after Tokyo's

FIG. 5.1. Sekino Tadashi carrying out his assigned duty as a core member of the CSKCIK, jotting down notes and the measurements of a stone pagoda dating to the Three Kingdoms period, Ch'angnyŏng, Kyŏngnam Province, c. 1916. Source: Chōsen Sōtokufu (Government-General of Korea) *Chōsen Koseki Zufu* [Album of ancient Korean sites and relics], vol. 3 (Tokyo: Keijō: Chōsen Sōtokufu, 1916), plate 1503.

Ueno Park, replete with a botanical garden, a zoo, and the Prince Yi Family Household Museum (Riōke Hakubutsukan) broke ground in November 1909 at Ch'anggyŏng-wŏn, which was chosen for its reputation as the oldest (c. 1405) and "most scenic" of the four Yi dynastic palaces in the capital (Sokei-en annai, n.d.). The first collections of fine art to be displayed in the colonies were purchased using CST subsidies awarded to the de facto puppet government, the Prince Yi royal family household (Riōke Hakubutsukan 1912). In 1909, the same year the Prince Yi Family Household Museum opened, the CST Ministry of the Interior appointed Tokyo University architect Sekino Tadashi (fig. 5.1) to head the archaeological survey team to identify more relics and remains for future museum exhibitions.

Sekino's 1904 Tokyo University report (full of photographs of ruins of Korea's oldest Buddhist temples, pagodas, and ancient tombs, in various states of decay and appearing much older than anything found in Japan proper) not only impressed his peers at his alma mater but also captured the attention of the newly appointed resident-general of Korea (see fig. 6.6), Itō Hirobumi (r. 1905–09), who was by then an avid collector of prized celadonware.[2] In 1909, the CST Home Ministry hired Sekino and two young field assistants from his alma mater, Yatsui Seiichi (1880–1959) and Kuriyama Shun'ichi (1882–?), as the "dream team" that was sent out on a five-year mission to survey all thirteen provinces.[3] This time, in contrast to Sekino's first trip riding on horseback, the team took advantage of the newly opened railway links and of the post offices equipped with telegraphs and telephones, which facilitated instant communication with the CST headquarters in Keijō (Yang 1999). In addition, they could rely on accurate cadastral survey maps provided by the CST's forestry section (Ōta 2000). For example, the team was able to rush to the Kangsŏ region in Hwanghae Province (see map 2) as soon as they received a telegram posted by local school teachers who had come upon a large group of painted tombs in 1912 (see fig. 5.8), later dated to the Koguryŏ period.[4] Consequently, the trio managed to locate hundreds of previously unknown and abandoned ruins of pagodas, temples, and burial sitess in the remote mountain valleys of Korea's hinterlands (Hirose 2003).

The team's preliminary survey report, *Studies in the Art of Korea* (Chōsen geijutsu no kenkyū), was submitted to the newly established architectural division of the CST and published in 1910, the year of the annexation treaty. Sekino's inventory listed 579 remains, identified by rank, province, name, type, and estimated epoch (Sekino 1910, 32–73). Sekino's first rank (*kō*, or "first class") was, in his own words, reserved for remains demonstrating "superior artistic workmanship" (*seisaku yūshū*) and therefore "must be preserved (*hozon beki*)." The second class (*ōtsu*) was assigned to objects reflecting "time-honored traditions and legendary accounts [*yuisho*]" that ought to be "considered for protection." The third class (*hei*) was assigned to remains that could serve as historical evidence, and that should be considered for protection. The lowest tier (*dei*, or "fourth class") was a tentative category that was open to discussion (Sekino Tadashi 1910, 2). In the final analysis, Sekino assigned the highest grade, "must be preserved" (*hozon beki*), to 235 art and architectural monuments made of stone, which made up 40.6 percent of the grand total. His second-ranked category consisted of buildings made of wood, numbering 139 items (24 percent of the total), followed by 80 pieces of sculpture (14.2 percent) and 81 ancient remains (*koseki*) at 13.9 percent of the total (Hirose 2003, 62). As we can see from Sekino's preliminary listings, as a classically trained architect, Sekino recognized that the oldest free-standing pagodas, steles, sculptures, and wooden architectural monuments in Korea were much older that anything preserved in Japan.[5] His recommendation that Korea's ruins must be preserved as the oldest standing relics demonstrating the transfer of Buddhist art and architecture from Korea to Japan convinced the CST to initiate long-range plans to protect the colony's valuable "treasures" that were threatened by looters and developers (Sekino Tadashi 1910, 1).

The year following the publication of Sekino's report, the CST invited Imanishi Ryū (1875–1932) and Torii to launch more comprehensive surveys to identify, collect, and photograph Korea's prehistoric remains, documents, and customs (Hirose 2003, 61; Pai 2006, 2009). In 1911, the CST issued preservation guidelines, beginning with the announcement of the Temples and Shrines Preservation Laws (Jisatsu Rei). Based on Japan's 1897 laws, the legislations mandated that all temple assets were to be placed under the control and management of the CST. The results of the temple surveys, published in two massive volumes as *Records of Temple Investigations by the Chōsen Sōtokufu* (Chōsen Sōtokufu jisatsu chōsa shiryō), listed a detailed inventory of every single temple possession. The volumes also included addresses, descriptions, and measurements of architecture, pagodas, bells, sculptures, sutras, steles, and paintings (CST 1911). From 1911 on, all activities (aside from daily prayers) required prior CST approval—including staffing matters such as the appointment of temple abbots (as well as his duties and obligations), the issuance of permits to hold public religious events, and regulations dictating the use of temple estates, including surrounding forests and harvested natural resources (CST 1924, 191–95). Such detailed information was to be reported directly to the CST on special registration forms that included the quantity, measurements, and preservation quality of temple objects, as well as attached commentaries on the significance of their historical and research value. The enforcement of the 1911 laws and regulations was assigned to the local police and the governor of each province, who now answered directly to the CST. Needless to say, as in Japan, these temple edicts dealt a major blow to the autonomy of the Buddhist clergy, who were required to relinquish control of all of their temple assets and were no longer permitted to sell, remove, dispose of, or change any registered item without the Home Ministry's written permission (Kurata 1991). However, from the colonial administrators' perspective, these 1911 laws governing temples were lauded for their effectiveness in transforming temple estates into the largest and most important repositories of ancient Korean antiquities (CST 1911, 1).

The grand opening of the Chōsen Sōtokufu Museum (Chōsen Sōtokufu Hakubutsukan) in December 1915 was timed to coincide with the first colonial exposition sponsored by the Chōsen Cooperative for the Promotion of Industry, an executive committee made up of both Japanese and local business leaders mainly based in Keijō (Chōsen Kyōsankai 1915). To showcase the most important archaeological collections in the empire, the CST commissioned a British architect, who designed a two-story white marbled structure supported by Greek columns in the "Japanese neo-Renaissance" style of the day (fig. 5.2). Photographs of the museum building as well as of its displays were featured in the pages of numerous photo albums, textbooks, travel magazines, and printed postcards distributed throughout the empire to show off the cultural, scientific, commercial, and architectural achievements of CST-employed scientists, scholars, enterprises, and architects.[6] The museum was soon included in the must-see itinerary of the leading visiting scholars, who wanted to consult with the best, brightest, and most talented graduates of Japan's leading imperial institutions and universities, who had taken up posts at museums in Korea (Koizumi 1985; Kang and Yi 1997; Mokuyō Club 2003).

As we can see in figure 5.2, Kyŏngbok Palace, the former seat of the Yi dynasty royal government, was relandscaped to accommodate the large number of anticipated visitors who expected to see grand spectacles, as well as to ensure security against theft and damage to the exhibits. The tourist space was reorganized and the exhibition grounds were reordered to display the wide range of products submitted by over two hundred local and imperial enterprises based in other colonies, such as the Ryūkyū Islands, Taiwan, Hokkaido, and Manchuria (Ch'oe Sŏk-yŏng 2001; Hachizume 2005).

The establishment of the CST museum was followed by the promulgation of Regulations on the Preservation of Ancient Sites and Relics of Chōsen (Koseki oyobi ibutsu hozon kitei) in 1916. The brains behind the CST laws

FIG. 5.2. Panoramic view of Government-General Museum building and grounds, c. 1915. Note the relandscaped grounds and manicured lawns of Kyŏngbokkung in preparation for the first colonial exposition, planned for December 1915. Source: *Kungnip Chung'ang Pang-mulkwan Sojang Yuri Kŏnban* [Gelatin plates in custody of the National Museum of Korea: The royal palaces of Chosŏn Exhibition Catalogue], (Seoul: Kungnip Chung'ang Pangmulk-wan [National Museum of Korea], 2007), 48–49.

for classifying and inventorying archaeological sites and relics was Kuroita Katsumi (1874–1946), the Tokyo Imperial University professor who had once headed the Meiji Education Ministry board publication committee's series of national history textbooks. Between 1899 and 1901, the Education Ministry sent him on a fully subsidized world educational tour. He visited all of the wonders of the ancient world (in Egypt, Persia, and Italy) as well as major museums in the capitals of Europe. Just as with Fenollosa's team, the assigned mission was to bring back new ideas—including cultural policy initiatives, the latest classification and exhibition schemes, teaching tools, and preservation methods. The ultimate goal was to raise the level of the nation's artistic sensibilities by expanding its knowledge of the applied arts as well as raising the quality of museum and library collections at home and in the colonies (Kurota 1900, 10; Kaneko Atsushi 2001; Satō 1999). Like Fukuzawa Yukichi and Machida Hisanari before him, Kurota returned with a newfound respect for European governments' efforts to protect their national pasts (Kurota Katsumi 1912).

In 1912, Kurota's article "An Opinion Paper on the Preservation of Historic Sites and Remains" (*Shiseki hozon ni kansuru ikensho*) was published in the prestigious historical journal *Shigaku Zasshi* (Kurota 1912). In this groundbreaking paper, Kurota urged the Imperial Household Agency and the Education Ministry to emulate the precedent set by advanced nations such as France, England, and Germany by implementing a more comprehensive nationwide inventory system (*taichō tōroku*) that went beyond antiquities, buried properties, and temples and shrines to encompass all historical sites (*shiseki*) and relics (*ibutsu*; Kurota Katsumi 1912, 507–9). Kurota argued convincingly that Japan's ancestral monuments, like those of the European monarchs, could be used to promote patriotism and solidarity by forging a sense of the citizens' pride in their national landscape and fostering a love of ancient things (*kokumin no fūkyō and kobijutsu aiko*; Kurota Hakushi Kinenkai 1974, 201). As the first step in this direction, Kurota proposed the formation of a special committee to review all of the relevant historical documentations that were needed for research and authentication purposes, many of which were disappearing without a trace and being threatened daily by developers and grave robbers who were smuggling priceless objects out of the country (Yi Sŏng-si 2004). As a pragmatist, Kurota also knew that the Meiji government was strapped for funds, man power, and resources and could not preserve everything. Therefore, he proposed that the Education Ministry come up with a standardized "system of rankings" for evaluating all nationally designated historical sites (*shiseki*), specially protected buildings (*tokubetsu kenzōbutsu*) and national treasures (*kokuhō*). He suggested that it would be most efficient for the Japanese government to adopt the hierarchical ranking system worked out in France, England, Germany, and Italy, where the governments had prioritized edifices belonging to monarchs, local rulers, and the church, followed by significant places commemorating major historical events and the progress of industry, subsistence technology, and commerce, as follows: (1) palace dwellings and burial mounds; (2) religious establishments (Shinto shrines, altars, and temple estates supported by the imperial family); (3) past battles and government institutions (official buildings, fortress walls, beacons, old battlefields, steles, and monuments); (4) industrial and commercial sites (farmers markets and old manufacturing sites, such as kilns, storage buildings, military weapons, mines, and smelting operations); (5) sites of agricultural activities (farms, pastures, and orchards); (6) transportation routes (canals, old roads, bridges, road signs, horse stations, and old gates); (7) educational facilities (schools and commemorative steles); (8) subsistence activities (wells, gardens, and streams); (9) prehistoric remains (shell mounds, semisubterranean dwellings, and stone tool workshops); (10) changes to the natural environment (hot springs, lakes, and beaches); and (11) legendary sites (Kuroita Katsumi 1917, 574–82).

Although Kuroita had vigorously petitioned the Education Ministry to carry out his comprehensive plans in 1912, his ranking system was first tested on the Korean Peninsula in 1916 before its official adoption three years later in Japan proper (appendix, tables 4 and 5). In 1919, the same act, now renamed the Historic Remains, Famous Places, and Natural Monuments Act (Shiseki Meishō Tennen Kinenbutsu) was promulgated simultaneously in Korea and Japan.[7] The most distinguishing feature of this act was that it expanded the scope of state-registered monuments to include geological formations such as mountains, trees, lakes, caves, and indigenous plants and animals. Prior to the decision to include natural monuments, the Committee on Historic Remains, Famous Places, and Natural Monuments Act, formed in 1911, had debated for several years whether it was feasible to develop their own mountain lakes, hot springs, beaches, and waterfalls. They were interested in developing them into destinations modeled after some of the more famous summer resorts and hiking and skiing spots in Switzerland, France, and Germany (Kanda 2003; Kuroita Katsumi 1912).

This act also launched the formation of the first preservation trust in the colonies, the CST Committee on the Investigation of Korean Antiquities (Chōsen koseki chōsa iinkai, hereafter CSKCIK). It was given the charge of overseeing the administration of the 1916 laws covering the investigation of archaeological remains, and of the planning of museum exhibitions, the preservation and reconstruction of monuments, the registration of national remains, and the publication of the CSKCIK's research activities (Pai 2001, 2006). Indicating the importance of its mission, the executive committee members consisted of officials representing the highest echelons in the colonial bureaucracy, including the Central Council (Chūshūin); directors of the departments of public works, construction, treasury, secretariat, archives, education, and forestry; and provincial section chiefs. The advisory board members all had degrees or former affiliations, or were current faculty hailing from the three imperial universities, in Tokyo, Kyoto, and, later, Keijō (founded in 1926). The first task assigned to the CSKCIK executive committee was to carry out five-year excavation plans targeting the cities with the highest number of threatened prehistoric sites, temples, and tombs (see map 2 and table 5)—beginning with capital city of Keijō (Seoul) and its vicinity, including the regions of Kaijō (Kaesŏng), the former seat of the Koryŏ dynasty (c. 9th–14th century), and Heijō (P'yŏngyang), the former capital of the Koguryŏ kingdom (c. 5th–7th century).

Attesting to the breakneck speed of the colonial industrial machine, news of archaeological discoveries reported by construction crews, farmers, and developers involved in large-scale salvage projects were featured in CST-controlled dailies such as the *Mainichi Shinpō* and magazines such as *Chōsen* throughout the Taishō and early Shōwa years (1912–35). Upon arrival at the endangered sites, all investigators were required to meet with the local police chief, to whom they reported their daily activities and findings, for the record. The director of field operations was also responsible for writing a detailed site report and submitting copies to the CSKCIK committee head, as well as to the CST. The artifacts collected from the site were catalogued and their custody turned over to the local police—with the exception of artifacts that were considered likely to be damaged during transportation (CST 1924, 147–49). Due to the usual budget and time constraints, it was up to the committee members in the field to pinpoint remains that were to be considered for further excavation, registration, or demolition (Arimitsu Kyōichi, pers. comm., 2001). According to the first article of the 1916 laws, the sites targeted for future preservation were identified as *koseki* (ancient remains), prehistoric sites containing shell mounds and implements made of stone, bone and horn, as well as subterranean dwellings, ancient tombs, town fortresses, palaces, barricades, barrier gates, station posts, stages for setting signal fires (beacons), sites of government offices, sites of shrines, mausoleums, temples, ruins of ceramic industry (kilns), old battlefields, and other ruins, together with sites associated with historical facts. The category of *ibutsu* (relics) encompassed old pagodas, steles, bells, stone and metal images of Buddha, flag-pole supporters, stone lanterns, and other artifacts that may have historical, artistic, or archaeological value (Sekino Tadashi 1931, 7).

This list of what qualified as a Korean object or site was followed by the second article, which stipulated the mandatory reporting process that an investigator or reporter must observe, such as notifying the local police. The latter then had to fill in all required information on forms submitted for police records. The chief of police of the district was obligated to immediately notify the CST as stipulated by the rules regulating buried objects and lost or stolen antiquities (CST 1924, 233–42). His report must also include the relic's name and location; the name and the address of its owner or manager; its current condition; any associated legends or stories; and, finally, a recommended method for its preservation. In the case that any item on the registration form had to be altered, the investigator had to report it to the CST and the local police, who were required to have all reports on file at all times.

The third article covered mandatory reporting by a person needing to deal with an already-registered *koseki* (CST 1924, 151–52). In the case that someone wanted to change, remove, or repair a monument, he or she had to apply to the CST for permission. For example, according to the regulations governing the preservation of stone and bronze inscriptions, it was stipulated that one needed permission from the CST even to take a rubbing. The CST was concerned that "in recent years, the value of stone and bronze inscriptions have increased due to their value for studying Korean ancient history" (CST 124:156–57). Therefore, it was required that any damage or effacing of steles or inscriptions on stone or bronze be reported to the police. If one wanted to make a rubbing from a monument that was state-owned property, one was also required to ask the permission of the CST. If the monument belonged to a Buddhist temple, one also had to obtain the permission from the CST. The application form also had to include the registration number, name, purpose of removal or repair, methods or plan for repairing or removal, and an outlined budget (ibid., 156–57). The above-mentioned detailed rules and forms were also applicable if one needed to export any registered properties or items outside of Japanese territory. They also had to be inspected by a customs official, who was required to check first to see if any of the items had been reported as stolen (ibid., 160). If they had, the police were to be notified immediately. If there was any suspicion that any of the above processes were not carried out, or if anyone had been found violating *koseki* regulations or temple ordinances, the police were to be notified. Only when the objects were cleared by the CST could they pass through customs and be permitted to leave the country. Finally, there were penal consequences for anyone caught violating any of these rules. The offender would be fined up to two hundred yen or jailed for up to six months. As we can see, the CST had the final authority to issue permits and require exact forms of registration for the reporting, storage, transportation, and trafficking of all antiquities, arts, and crafts throughout the country (CST 1924, 158).

Through this rigorous process of investigation, excavation, authentication, and documentation, in 1924, only eight years following the promulgation of the 1916 laws, the CST published an impressive registry of 193 items that included all of the known information to that date (CST 1924). This initial list recorded ancient remains in sequential numbers, beginning with the monuments located in Kyŏnggi-do, Seoul (Seoul), and then followed by all thirteen provinces. The characteristics of this 1924 registry are illuminating, since the distribution patterns of registered sites have more or less determined the general direction of Korean heritage management governing state properties to this day, as covered in chapters 1 and 2. First of all, the regional distribution of the total number of registered remains was enumerated by province, in descending order, as follows: (1) North Kyŏngsang, 41; (2) Keijō/Kyŏngi-do, 38; (3) Kangwŏn-do, 26; (4) South Ch'ungchŏng, 25; (5) North Ch'ungchŏng, 13; (6) North Chŏlla, 13; (7) North Ch'ungchŏng, 9; (8) North Chŏlla, 8; (9) South P'yŏngan, 7; (10) North P'yŏngan, 4; (11) Hwanghae, 5; (12) South Hamgyŏng, 2; and (13) North Hamgyŏng, 1 (Pai 2001, 83). The province of Kyŏngsang-do topped the list, with the largest number of ancient remains, because the principal investigators—Kuroita, Imanishi, Hamada Kōsaku (1881–1938), and Umehara Sueji (1893–1983), all archaeologists and ancient historians— had concentrated their efforts in the Kyŏngju region, the former capital of the Silla dynasty (c. 1st–9th century CE), where Sekino had identified the largest concentration of temples, pagodas, sculptures, and burial mounds. From the burial mounds in the Kyŏngju region in the 1920s, they unearthed an impressive array of gold crowns, jewelry, and iron swords, which were displayed at the Keishū Museum when it opened in 1926 as a regional branch of the CST museum (Arimitsu 1933). Some of the more prominent national treasures today that were found on the 1924 list were the elegantly carved tomb markers of the Silla kings (*wangnŭngbi*), such as 1924's number 88, the tomb of King Muyŏl (r. 654–61; currently *kukpo* number 25); number 90, Chŏmsŏngdae, considered to be the oldest observatory (currently *kukpo* number 31); and number 92, Sŏkping-go (currently *pomul* number 66), a cold storage facility.[8]

After Kyŏngju, the second-largest number of registered remains were located in the capital Keijō (Seoul), which reflected the region's six-hundred-year history as the capital of the long-lived Yi dynasty (1392–1910). In addition, because the city of Kaesŏng was included under the jurisdiction of the province of Kyŏnggi-do, there was also a large concentration of Koryŏ dynastic ruins (936–1388), such as royal tombs, temples, and palatial ruins (for example, Manwŏldae). Considering the area's combined history of nearly eight hundred years of continuous occupation, it is not surprising that the colonial investigators would have found many standing and relatively intact architectural remains in this region. The first remains to be registered as *koseki* (ancient remains) was the ten-story Wŏn'gaksaji Pagoda (fig. 5.3; currently *kukpo* number 2) dated to the tenth year of King Sejo's reign (1464).[9] Finally, relics—mostly pagodas and steles that were too far removed to be monitored—were moved to the CST's museum grounds at the recommendation of Sekino (*koseki* numbers 14, 20, 38, 67, 102, 136, and 159).

The regions of Puyŏ (the former captial of Paekche Kingdom in South Ch'ungch'ŏng) and Iksan (North Chŏlla) came in third on the list, with the Paekche-period temple site Iksan Mirŭksaji registered as *koseki* number 69, along with Mirŭksaji's Stone Pagoda (*koseki* number 70, currently *kupko* number 11). The records at the time indicate that these had yet to be identified as dating to the Paekche era (3rd to 7th century; CST 1924, 2–7). The oldest inscription found to date in Korea is the inscribed stele of Chŏmche-hyŏn (Chinese Pinyin, Nianti-xian), which was listed as *koseki* number 126. Dating from the era of the Eastern Han dynasty (c. late 1st century), the stele was found at Yonggang-gun Haeun-myŏn Yongjŏng-ni in 1915. The CSKCIK, recognizing the historical significance of the stele (which identified one of the twenty-two counties established by the Han martial emperor

FIG. 5.3. Ancient remains (*koseki*) number 1, Wŏn'gaksaji ten-story pagoda, Pagoda Park, Seoul, c. 1905. This pagoda, constructed in the tenth year of Sejo's reign (1464), is currently listed as *kukpo*, national treasure number 2. Before the promulgation of the 1916 preservation laws, many photographers staged photo shoots with "natives posed as cultural markers" next to decaying ruins to lend more authenticity to souvenir photographs for sale. Once the area was designated a historical park, it was no longer permitted to climb monuments to take photographs. Photographer unknown. International Center for Japanese Studies Library Archives.

Han Wudi, who invaded Korea in 108 BCE), erected a pavilion to protect it from the elements, as was the usual recommendation for a protected monument at that time (CST 1924, 114). The discovery of this dated stele marked a major turning point in the history of Korean archaeology, for it prompted intense surveying of the surrounding areas that revealed more than two thousand tombs (fig. 5.4) belonging to the Han dynasty commandery of Rakurō (Chinese Pinyin, Lelang), centered around T'osŏngni, now located south of the city of P'yŏngyang, across from the Taedong River in Taedong-gun County (Komai 1965). The decade between 1925 and 1935 was when the CSKCIK excavated hundreds of multichambered tombs, unearthing inscribed bricks, roof tiles, seals, bronze mirrors, equestrian equipment,

FIG. 5.4. View of excavations carried out by Sekino and others at Taedong-gun Lelang (J. Rakurō, K. Nangnang) Tomb number 2, located south of P'yŏngyang, c. 1915. The left caption identifies the remains as some sort of altar. On the right is a picture of a large Han dynasty stoneware jar, probably a tomb artifact patched up with strings and glue. Chōsen Sōtokufu (Government-General of Korea), Chōsen Koseki Zufu, vol. 1 (1915), plates 80–83.

and exquisite lacquerware (Pai 2000, 130–33). The related publications and reports, which documented a large cache of luxury goods—jeweled accessories, a gold filigree belt buckle, jade disks [bi], bronze weapons, and iron swords from the tombs of Wang Guang and the Painted Basket—confirmed that the Han officials in the Lelang commandery (c. 108 BCE–3rd century CE) were indeed the richest officials stationed outside of mainland China (CSKCIK 1934, 1935; Hayashi Minao 1976; Komai 1965; Pai 2000, 160–72).

Next to the finds in P'yŏngyang, the 1909 discovery of Pulguksa and Sŏkkuram, the two most iconic destinations in Korea, received the most press coverage during the colonial era, prompting personal visits by successive governor-generals, imperial family members, foreign heads of state, collectors, and organized tour groups (Asakawa 1929; Oda 1922, 1923). Although in premodern times, historical data from the historical records

FIG. 5.5. View of Sŏkkuram Grotto, Kyŏngju T'ohamsan, c. 1912–13. Photo by Tōyōken Studio. Chōsen Sōtokufu (Government-General of Korea), *Chōsen Koseki Zufu*, vol. 4, plate 1836.

of the *Samguk sagi* and Yi dynastic records indicate that monks continued to worship at Sŏkkuram well into the Yi dynasty, it was not mentioned in Sekino's earlier reports (Sekino Tadashi 1904). In 1906, when Imanishi first arrived in Kyŏngju, he had heard rumors of Sŏkkuram but in fact never paid a visit because of its remote mountainous location atop T'ohamsan (fig. 5.5).

Sekino's subsequent research into the two monuments, based on the textual records of the *Samguk yusa* (Tales of the three kingdoms, 13th century) and the *Tongguk yŏjisungram* (Augmented survey of the geography of Korea, 16th century), revealed that Kim Dae-sŏng, a Silla royal family member, was the chief architect who designed the main temple buildings and the sculptures (including the two stone pagodas and the lanterns) and who later on erected two pieces of bronze sculpture. As is evident in the state of destruction of the Sŏkkuram seen in figure 5.5, Sekino was correct in his assessment that the main Buddha was in danger of the rains washing down sand and earth from the mountains and causing the front arch capstones to collapse. Sekino's first impressions of the Pulguksa site appear in his 1910 *A Study of Korean Art* (Chōsen keijutsu no kenkyū), in which he lamented its very precarious state of disrepair, with bridges and wood rafters rotting away and grass growing everywhere.

Sekino's reviews that the thousand-year-old remains of Sŏkkuram and Pulguksa, dating to the time of King Kyŏngdŏk (late 8th century), were better preserved than any similar structure anywhere else in Asia persuaded CST officials to launch the most expensive and extensive restoration project in the colonies so as to preserve them as "standing witnesses to history" (*rekishi shōko*; CST 1938, 1). The Sŏkkuram reconstruction project was carried out in several phases and took a total of sixteen years (1913–28) to complete. During the first phase of the repairs (1913–24), the cave and all of the relief panels and walls surrounding the Buddha were completely dismantled by the CST construction department's team of engineers, who worked with carpenters brought in from Nara. The grotto cave was then rebuilt from the foundation up, with a separate roofed entrance to accommodate tourists' viewing and group pictures (see fig. 6.5).

Pulguksa temple repairs lasted eight years (1918–25) because the base and platform had to be rebuilt from the foundation up. From April to August 1924, the dirt and debris that had buried the east and west ends of the stone foundations was cleared away (fig. 5.6) and the ground was paved with new stones. The engineers from the CST construction department concentrated on preserving the two crumbling bridges, as directed by Sekino, who had insisted that these two structures were to be preserved for their artistic magnificence and detailed elegance reflecting the Silla architects' superior design sense. Following their multiyear restoration (fig. 5.7), the site was registered for the first time in the updated colonial inventory of treasures published in 1934 as follows: Pulguksa Tapot'ap (Stone Pagoda) as Hōmotsu Treasures number 84 (current *kukpo* number 20); Pulguksa Samchŭngt'ap (Three Story Pagoda) as Hōmotsu Treasures number 85 (current *kukpo* number 21); the two Pulguksa stone bridges of Yŏnhwa-gyo and Ch'ŏng'un-gyo (figure 22) as Hōmotsu Treasures numbers 87 and 88 (current *kukpo* numbers 22 and 23); and Sŏkkuram Cave Grotto as Hōmotsu Treasures number 89 (current *kukpo* number 24). Furthermore, the entire temple grounds of Pulguksa were designated as the premier scenic place, or *meishō*, in 1936 and were featured on the cover of many tourist brochures written in Japanese and English (Japan Tourist Bureau n.d., hereafter JTB).

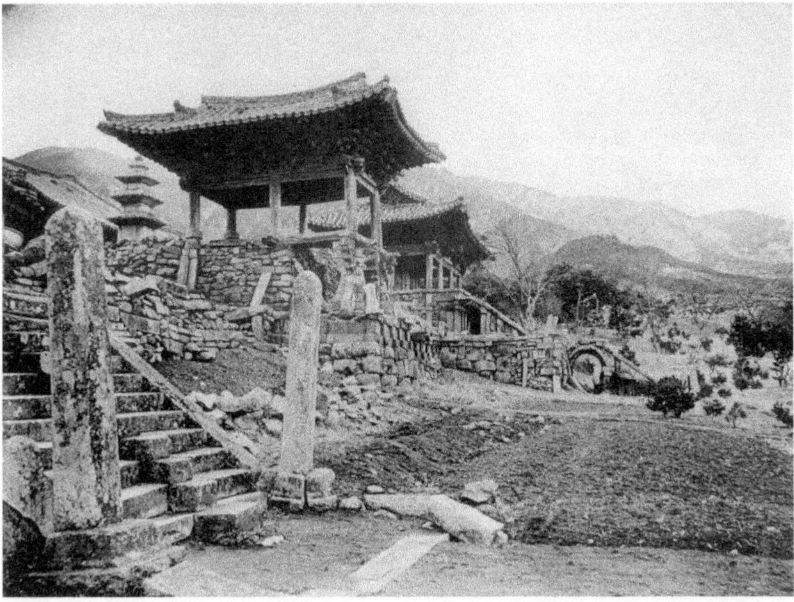

FIG. 5.6. *Top:* Two views of the ruins of Pulguksa Temple from different angles before reconstruction, Kyŏngju, T'ohamsan, c. 1913. Note the crumbling bridges and foundations on both the east and west ends. Source: CST 1938, *Bukkokuji to Sekkutsuan* [Pulguk Temple and Sŏkkuram Cave in Keishū], vol. 1 of *Chōsen hōmotsu koseki zuroku* [Album of Korean treasures and ancient sites] (Kyoto: Bunseidō), plate 7.

FIG. 5.7. Postcard views of Pulguksa from same angles as fig. 5.6 after reconstruction for tourists, Kyŏngju, T'ohamsan, c. 1938. Source: CST 1938, *Bukkokuji to Sekkutsuan* [Pulguk Temple and Sŏkkuram Cave in Keishū], vol. 1 of *Chōsen hōmotsu koseki zuroku* [Album of Korean treasures and ancient sites] (Kyoto: Bunseidō), plate 2.

In order to finance these massive multiyear reconstruction projects, the Kyŏngju Historical Preservation Society (Keishū koseki hozonkai 1922, 1935) was formed in 1911 with donations solicited from local businessmen, the Bank of Chōsen, and provincial officials.[10] The society members also lobbied the CST Interior Ministry to come up with the phenomenal sum of 33,250 yen to subsidize their projects (Kim Hyŏn-suk 2007). The total budget for Pulguksa's restoration eventually ballooned to the astronomical sum of 48,456 yen. Despite the enormous financial burdens, these construction projects were enthusiastically endorsed by provincial officials, businessmen, and local leaders, who wanted to lure tourists to Kyŏngju's many scenic destinations.[11]

The pace of infrastructure development was stepped up throughout the cities in Korea and Manchuria with the establishment of the Japanese puppet state of Manchukuo in 1932, which led to accelerated destruction and looting of the past (L. Young 1998, 251–68). In 1933, a revamped preservation committee, the Chōsen Sōtokufu Committee for the Preservation of Korean Treasures, Ancient Remains, Famous Places, and Natural Monuments (Chōsen Sōtokufu Hōmotsu Koseki Meishō Tennen Kinenbutsu Hozon Iinkai, CSHKMT) was established to monitor the increasing number of illegally trafficked "treasures" circulating among dealers of antiquities, local preservations societies, and rich collectors (CST 1937, 1–5). That same year, the new committee enacted the Treasures, Ancient Sites, Famous Places, and Natural Monuments Act (Hōmotsu Koseki Meishō Kinenbutsu) and introduced a more expanded definition of the most prestigious category of "treasures" (*hōmotsu*) that would include "architecture and artwork that included books, sutras, calligraphy and paintings, crafts, and documents" that demonstrated: (1) ancient origins; (2) superior execution or rarity; (3) a famous figure's work or writing; or (4) artifacts or remains serving as historical evidence (CST 1937, 5–7).

The most important task assigned to the committee members in the late 1930s was drawing up long-term preservation and reconstruction plans, and budget allocations for the development of peninsula-wide tourism, including the building of transportation, inns, hotels, and resorts. Preservation methods included minimal provisions such as the erection of fences and walls, the installation of plumbing and drainage systems, and the posting of guards to ensure that there was no looting (Fujita 1933). All of these plans had to be documented in formal applications submitted on special registration forms that included information such as the categories and locations of the monuments targeted for investigation or reconstruction and the proposed preservation methods and anticipated construction time. Finally, the CSHKMT was also given the task of systematically collecting old books and rare documents to complement archeological research of Korea's ancient remains. With all of these added responsibilities, by 1937 the executive committee numbered over fifty members, including high-ranking bureaucrats of the various CST government branches, the Home Ministry, the Construction Department, and the Education Ministry, as well as the Central Council. At that time, the academic members represented the "who's who" of faculty from Kyoto University, Tokyo University, and Keijō University, such as Kuroita Kutsumi, Ikeuchi Hiroshi, Harada Yoshito, Hamada Kōsaku, and Umehara Sueji, who all commuted from Japan to attend monthly committee meetings chaired by the vice-consul general at the CST headquarters (see fig. 6.3, left photo). Fujita Ryōsaku, a professor at Keijō Imperial University and the director of the CST Museum, was also a member. Oda Fujio, Koizumi Akio (1897–1993), and Arimitsu Kyōichi were then low-ranking museum staff employees who in fact prepared most of the paperwork, lived in the field, and submitted survey documents (Arimitsu Kyōichi, pers. comm., 2003). The only two Korean members were Ch'oe Nam-sŏn (1890–1957) and Yi Nŭng-hwa (1869–1945), both Japanese university–educated rising stars who represented the first generation of native-born literary pioneers and folklorists/anthropologists, respectively (CST 1937, 59–62).

From an archaeologist's perspective, what is most remarkable about Korean archaeology in the 1930s is that the CSHKMT managed to continue digging even though the CST's budget had been drastically curtailed following the Kantō earthquake in 1923 (Mokuyō Club 2003). According to Fujita, the CSHKMT was able to survive only due to the generous subsidies awarded by the Imperial Household Agency (15,000 yen), the Foundation for the Promotion of Japanese Sciences, or Nihon Gakujutsu Shinkōkai (35,000 yen); and the Prince Yi Family Household, which pitched in another 10,000 yen between the years 1931 and 1935 (Fujita 1933). It addition, other contributors included several aristocratic donors and rich business-men interested in gaining the name recognition, prestige, and bragging rights associated with being part of the greatest discoveries in East Asian archaeology (CSKCIK 1934, 1935, 1938). Such private funding sources also enabled the CST and the CSHKMT to continue hiring the most talented artists, architects, and engineers, and employing the latest photographic and printing technologies to produce excavation reports and museum catalogues—and paying for security guards to patrol Korea's archaeological sites and remains to scare off potential grave looters.[12]

The CSHKMT members were heavily involved in advertising "Korea's thousand-year-old ruins" (CST 1915–35, vol. 1), and wrote for a wide variety of publication outlets, including CST newsletters such as *Chōsen*, museum catalogues, and excavation and restoration reports (CST 1915–35, 1918–41, 1919–30, 1938). The fifteen-volume series *Album of Ancient Korean Sites and Relics*, inaugurated by the CST in 1915, marked a milestone in the history of colonial archaeology of East Asia (CST 1915–35). The volumes were divided into periods, from the oldest to the most recent: Han dynasty Rakurō (vol. 1); Koguryŏ (vol. 2); Three Kingdoms (vol. 3: Paekche, Imna, and Silla); Unified Silla (vol. 4: temple sites, stone lanterns, pagodas, steles, and bells; vol. 5: Buddhist sculpture, roof tiles, and pottery); Koryŏ remains (vol. 6: fortresses, temples, and stone sculpture; vol. 7: Buddhist relics and sculpture, burials; vol. 8: pottery and ceramics; vol. 9: decorative arts); Yi dynasty (vol. 10: palace architecture; vol. 11: fortresses, shrines, pavilions, burials, and other architecture; vol. 12: temple architecture; vol. 13: sculpture; vol. 14: paintings and decorative arts (*kōgei*); vol. 15: ceramics).

For the series, chief editor Sekino chose as his illustrator Oba Tsune-kichi (1878–1958), a graduate of the Tokyo School of Fine Arts and a nearly thirty-year veteran of his field survey team (1912–43). Oba's fine oil paintings were recognized for his skill at reproduction techniques (*mosaku*) that captured the fragile wall paintings for posterity and for students of art history.[13] According to Arimitsu, Sekino's trusted illustrator solved the logistical dilemma of lighting the tomb interior by coming up with the idea of using large mirrors placed at strategic angles at the entrance of tomb so as to refract the sunlight into the inner shaft of the corridor (Mokuyō Club 2003). During the same tomb surveys, Sekino also instructed the two Kyoto University professors, Hamada Kōsaku and Umehara Sueji, on plane-table surveying methods for measuring the topographic layout of architectural remains above and below ground. The two later reintroduced Sekino's pioneering mapping techniques and the technical skills that were developed at Korean sites back into Japan.

The life-size illustrated copies of the spectacular murals produced by CSHKMT members were later exhibited to much acclaim at Tokyo University. Figure 5.8 is a photograph of a miniaturized Koguryŏ tomb model dating from the period, preserved in pristine condition at the Kyoto University Museum.[14] It shows a cross-section of the tomb mural, featuring Oba's renditions of Koguryŏ tomb interiors and frescoes—in this case, depicting two of the four mythical creatures on the walls of Sashin Tomb in Kangsŏ (c. 5th century CE) outside of P'yŏngyang City. According to the university museum catalogue published in 1922, a Kyoto-based company was commissioned by Hamada Kōsaku to craft minimodels of Korean relics as teaching aids for his classes on Korean archaeology at the Kyoto Imperial University Department of Archaeology (Kyōdai Hakubutsukan 1923).

For the printing of thousands of survey pictures, Sekino adopted the same collotype printing process adopted by Ogawa Kazumasa for the mag-

FIG. 5.8. Miniaturized reproductions of Oba Tsunekichi's sketches of the Koguryŏ tomb chambers' interior murals depicting two of the four mythical creatures on the walls of Sashin Tomb in Kangsŏ (c. 5th century CE), 2005. Collection of the Kyoto University Museum. Photo by author.

azine *Kokka*. As we have seen in the examples of figures 5.1 and 5.4 through 5.7 above, the high-quality reproductions of Sekino's and Oba's original survey sketches, black-and-white photographs, and colored drawings were able to capture in vivid detail and texture many excavated artifacts and examples of architecture, from standing dolmens to painted Koguryŏ tombs frescoes. At the time, these major technical and artistic innovations surpassed any other scientific publications available for Japanese archaeological reports. In 1917, Sekino was awarded a prestigious prize for the series Le Prix Stanislas Julien (named after the famous French sinologist and epigrapher Stanilas Aignan Julien, 1797?–1873) by the Académie des Inscriptions et Belles-Lettres, one of the five institutions belonging to the learned society of the Institut de France founded in 1663 (Nihon Kenchiku Gakkai 1972; Sekino Takeshi 1978).

The colonial-era researchers' main academic goal for documenting archaeological remains in Korea in such lavish volumes was clearly stated in the preface to the monumental first volume of the *Album of Ancient Korean Sites and Relics* was to "reveal historical proof [*rekishi shōko*] and artistic models [*bijutsu mohan*] hidden amongst the mysteries of the past." Although it is never mentioned explicitly whose past they are referring to in the series, the authors begin the preface with a declaration of how the 1910 annexation of Korea as part of the Japanese empire became the catalyst for launching the first systematic surveys of the peninsula (CST 1915–1935, 1:1). By the end of the colonial period in 1943 (the last year the registry was updated), the CST registry had expanded to include an impressive 591 items, divided into five separate categories: (1) 340 treasures (*hōmotsu*); (2) 101 ancient remains (*koseki*); (3) two ancient remains/famous places (*koseki/meishō*); (4) one famous place (*meishō*); and (5) 146 natural monuments (*tennen kinenbutsu*) KSMKG 1997). Consequently, Korea's archaeological remains, excavated stratigraphically and preserved in situ, were embraced by colonial administrators, scholars, and educators as the most authentic and scientific evidence for understanding Japan's long-lost imperial past on the continent (Pai 2006).

Unfortunately, in contrast to the technological advancements in excavating, preserving, dating, and publishing Korea's buried past, colonial archaeologists' interpretations of the origins of Korean and Japanese civilizations remained bogged down in nineteenth-century paradigms focused on conquests, invasions, migrations, and diffusions to explain culture change (Rouse 1986). When we look at the major anthropological and art-historical synthesis penned by the most prolific scholars of the day—Torii (1925a, 1925b, 1937); Sekino Tadashi (1932); Shiratori (1986); Hamada (1953); and Fujita (1948, 1963)—the most important catalyst for cultural, artistic, and racial change in the Korean peninsula was a series of invasions from the continent in the following sequence: (1) invasion by northern nomadic "Tungus," who were equated with the Tōi (Chinese Pinyin, Donghu) and the Yemaek beginning in late prehistory (7th–5th centuries BCE); (2) arrival of the Wiman dynasty in 195–194 BCE; (3) the Han Commamdery of Lelang (J. Rakurō) (108 BCE–4th century CE) and the imposition of "Yemaek-related" dynastic states such as Puyŏ, Koguryŏ, and Paekche during the Three Kingdoms period (1st–5th century CE); (4) Empress Jingū (3rd–5th century); (5) the Tang Chinese (7th century); (6) the Mongols (13th century); (7) Toyotomi Hideyoshi (16th century); and (8) the Manchu invasions (17th century).

The master racial narrative deployed by CST officials was that the Koreans, or Chōsenjin, after a more than two thousand years of subordination under "superior" races, had degenerated into a weak and ineffectual people by the time of the late Yi dynasty (Yamamichi 1910). The main reason for the decline was Koreans' innate flaw of serving their larger neighbors (K., *sadae* / J., *jidai*), which had bred a mentality of "dependency" (J., *taritsusei*) on foreign superpowers such as China, Russia, and Europe (Yi Man-yŏl 1976, 79). Consequently, Korean civilization had stagnated (*teitairon*) since its artistic and creative peak during the Three Kingdoms period (Sekino Tadashi 1932; Pai 1994, 41–43). In this preconceived unilinear historical trajectory, the major turning points occurred early on, during the first occupation of Korea under the Chinese Han commandery of Lelang. For colonial archaeologists, the site of Rakurō, in addition to having great potential as a treasure trove of Han grave goods, affirmed the much-debated "invasion" hypothesis (Kuroita Katsumi 1916; Pai 2000, 127–236).

This century-old search for the continental origins of the Japanese conquest state and its civilization profoundly affected the formation of East Asian/Oriental archaeology as a field that was enthusiastically supported at imperial universities throughout the Taishō and Shōwa periods (Yoshikawa 1976; Yoshimura 1999). One of the leading thinkers of the day, Hamada

Kōsaku, the founder of the Kyoto University Museum and department of archaeology. He was the first professor to offer classes on the archaeology of the ancient world, in 1910, well before Tokyo University faculty offered similar courses (Hamada 1922; Yoshii Hideo pers. comm., 2001). In fact, Hamada's undergraduate thesis at Tokyo University's history department was titled *The Eastern Movement of Greek Art* (Hamada 1906, 1907). Like Tsuboi, Hamada had studied at University College London with the noted Egyptologist Sir William Flinders Petrie (1853–1942), who was known for his seriation methods for dating and classifying prehistoric tomb complexes relying on pottery sequences. In Hamada's preface to his widely read textbook introducing European archaeological method and theory, *Tsūron kōkogaku* (Introduction to archaeology), he confessed that his book was largely based on Petries's 1904 work, *Methods and Aims in Archaeology* (Hamada 1922, 2). Hamada was also responsible for introducing the work of Swedish archaeologist and museum curator Oscar Montelius (1843–1921), with his translation of Montelius's magnum opus, *Die alteren kultur-perioden im Orient und in Europa* (1903). Translated as *Methods of Research in Archaeology* (Kōkogaku kenkyū hōhō; Hamada 1932), this book is regarded as the first Japanese work explaining the relative chronological dating methods used to trace the cultural roots of early European Bronze Age artifacts' designs and motifs to ancient Greece and Rome.[15] By 1934, Kyoto Imperial University's course offerings encompassed all of the known civilizations of the East and the West, ranging from Chinese bronzes and Han dynasty Lelang tombs to Silla roof tiles, Hōryūji's architecture, and Stone Age Japan (Hamada 1969, 29).

Hamada also carried on an active academic exchange with the leading Swedish archaeologists of the day, including J. G. Andersson (1874–1960) and Crown Prince Adolf Gustaf VI (1882–1973). The close relationship of the three began when Hamada and Andersson first served as personal tour guides to the crown prince in 1926 and 1932 (Hamada Kōsaku and J. G. Andersson 1932), when his entourage visited archaeological sites and museums in Japan and Korea (fig. 5.9). Hamada's association with Andersson allowed the earliest prehistoric materials of the Far East to be taken to the Museum of Far Eastern Antiquities, which was founded in Stockholm in 1926 (Schnell 1932).

FIG. 5.9. Crown prince Adolf Gustaf VI of Sweden, with Hamada Kōsaku and J. G. Andersson, excavating a Silla tomb in Kyŏngju, c. 1926. The tomb was given the name Tomb of the Prince of Sweden (Sŏbongch'ong) in honor of his visit. Collection of the National Museum of Korea, Seoul.

Outside of archaeological and museum circles, Japanese "Graecophilia" also determined the westward direction of archaeological expeditions into the far corners of Asia at the turn of the century, beginning with CElebrated explorer Count Ōtani Kōzui (1876–1948), a rich abbott who was able to finance his own expeditions to the Tarim Basin and the oasis of Kashgar in the 1900s. The "Silk Road expeditions of Ōtani" were controversial at the time, since Ōtani was funded by the Nishi Honganji, a Buddhist sect that had gained a reputation as the richest sect due to its aggressive expansion into the colonies (Shirazu 2002).

In summary, nation- and empire-building curators, art historians, archaeologists, and collectors, such as Fenollosa, Kuki, Hamada, Okakura, Ōtani, and Sekino, all played an important role in the creation process of a shared body of Japanese-Korean "national treasures" (*kokuhō*), inspired by the ancient Orient that traced back to Sumer, Babylonia, Persia, Greece, and Rome. It was then only a small step to reach the inevitable political conclusion that Japan, as the rightful heir to the glories of the past and to the great archaeological and artistic achievements of the ancient world, was now called upon to rule all of the Far East (Hamada 1906; Inoue Shōichi 1994, 199; Suzuki Hiroyuki 2003).

CHAPTER 6

REDISCOVERING THE HOMELANDS

Travel Myths, Images, and the Narrative of Return

The peninsula's geographic proximity to and strategic location at the cross-roads of three empires, China, Russia and Japan, made Korea an early target for the emerging Japanese tourist industry in the early twentieth century (see table 6). By the 1890s, ships from Japan's oldest international shipping company, the Nippon Yūsen Kaisha (NYK), were already delivering mail, freight, soldiers, and passengers, connecting Shimonoseki to the ports of Inch'ŏn, Wŏnsan, Pusan, and Dairen (Dalian) in the Liaodong Peninsula (Nihon Yūsen Kabushiki Kaisha; hereafter NYK) 1896). In 1904, with the completion of the Seoul-Pusan line (Keifu-sen) and Seoul-Inch'ŏn line (Keigisen), the Chōsen Government Railway (Chōsen Sōtokufu Tetsudo-kyoku; hereafter CSTTK) was carrying passengers to all of the major cities and ports on the Korean Peninsula, such as Taegu (Taikyū), Seoul (Keijō), Inch'ŏn (Jinsen), Kaesŏng (Kaijō), P'yŏngyang (Heijō), and the terminus at Shinŭiju (Shingishū) on the mouth of the Yalu River (see map 3). In 1905, Korea's postal system, which had been floundering under mismanagement in the latter days of the Yi government, was incorporated into the Japan Postal System. The colonial post office branches facilitated the efficient delivery of army mail, correspondence, postcards, and printed materials to all corners of the expanding Japanese empire. They also provided telegrams, telephones, and speedy money transfers, catering to many Japanese companies (such as Mitsubishi Mining and Banking Company), department stores (Mitsukoshi and Takashimaya), purveyors of jewels and pearls (K. Mikimoto), Shiseido Chemists and Druggists, Miyako and Fujiya hotel chains, and the Osaka Brewing Company (Asahi beer) that had opened shops in the colonies (NYK 1894, 1896; Welcome Society 1908).

The business goal of Japan's oldest *zaibatsu* (conglomerates) entrepreneurs who had ventured into Korea and Manchuria was the same as that of the transportation companies such as the South Manchuria Railroad Company (hereafter referred to as SMR) and the Chōsen branch of the Japan Imperial Government Railways (hereafter referred to as CSTTK): to attract as many customers as possible so that they could recoup their enormous financial investments in infrastructure (such as ports, dams, roads, buildings, and waterworks) to facilitate the movement of people, goods, and services throughout the empire. With the arrival of financial companies, retail businesses, and industrial colonial capital, hundreds of thousands of Japanese settlers eager to make their fortune in the frontier boomtowns started purchasing second- and third-class cabin tickets for steamers and railway cars bound for Korea or Manchuria (Uchida Jun 2005). Soon shipping companies, government railways, hotel chains, and *zaibatsu* branches keen on attracting rich foreign tourists as well as a loyal customer base in the colonies began printing passenger manuals, postcards, and travel guidebooks in order to advertise new destinations in the empire (Haraguchi 2002; Kwŏn Hyŏk-hŭi 2005; Tomita 2003, 2005). Therefore, by the time of the annexation in 1910, the Korean peninsula was no longer the "hermit kingdom" in terms of transportation and communications links but in fact was situated in the center of the East-West axis linking the Japanese islands to the Chinese continent (Yang 1999).

The Japan Tourist Bureau (JTB), Japan's oldest travel agency, played the most important role in advertising Japan's travel destinations to a world audience. Popular editions of guidebooks to Chōsen (*Chōsen annaisho*) issued by the SMR and the CSTTK published in the 1920s and 1930s, are significant for our study because the diversity of tourist literature and printed materials on travel to Korea (train schedules, postcards, and tourist brochures advertising historical destinations) far surpassed those of any other colony in quality and quantity. This is because the transportation companies could rely on the vast body of accumulated data supplied by the CST, including visual, historical, and ethnographic records that had already been meticulously documented and arranged in glossy photo albums, museum catalogues, and excavation reports (Pai 2010b). Therefore, even by today's standards, guidebooks on Korea published in the early twentieth century were superior in terms of the kinds of detailed tourist and practical information available for all kinds of travel budgets, from student tour groups to the globe-trotting leisure tourist. Photographic depictions of Korea's many "quaint" customs and manners featured in guidebooks and postcards contributed to the production of the highly romanticized images of Korea as a "timeless" ancient land dotted with pagodas and dancing courtesans, or *kisaeng* (see fig. 6.4).

Much like the staging of international expositions, the structural foundations of Japan's modern tourist industry began as a state-coordinated enterprise attempting to engage in direct commerce with the West. The Welcome Society of Japan was Japan's first tourism board, founded in 1893. Sanctioned by the Imperial Household, its board members included high-ranking diplomats, including foreign ambassadors, dignitaries, aristocrats, and leading entrepreneurs of the day. The society operated from the Tokyo Chamber of Commerce, located inside the landmark Marunouchi Building. The preface of their *Guidebook for Tourists* stated that the aim of the society was

> bringing within reach of tourists the means of accurately observing the features of the country, and the characteristics of the people; aiding them to visit places of scenic beauty; enabling them to view objects of art and enter into social or commercial relations with the people; in short, affording them all facilities and conveniences toward the accomplishment of their several aims, their indirectly promoting, in however small a degree, the cause of international intercourse and trade. (Welcome Society 1908, n. p)

The JTB was founded in 1912 by the Japan Imperial Government Railways (JIGR) corporate office at Tokyo Station. The official chronicle of the JTB states that the JIGR board of directors, while on a business trip to participate in the eighth Exposition of Railways in Bern, Switzerland, had been very impressed by the free-spending leisure classes wining and dining at the grand hotels (Japan Tourist Bureau, Japan Nihon Kōtsu Kōsha [hereafter JTB] 1982, 8–13). When they returned, the board members called a meeting and invited shipping magnates (such as the NYK and the OSK, Osaka Shōsen Kaisha), department store chains (Mitsukoshi and Takashiyama), and the Tokyo Imperial Hotel management to name some of the original *zaibatsu*. They were asked to join in a new venture to transform Japan into "the Paradise of the Orient" (JTB 1982, 16; JTB 1926). The immediate financial objective of this JIGR-launched tourist directive was to attract foreign revenue to replenish government coffers that had been severely drained by the expensive military campaigns in Korea and Manchuria during the Russo-Japanese War.

The other mission was more diplomatic in nature, for the JTB was charged with devising ways to promote a more "civilized and modern" national image, which had been much tarnished in the foreign press by the numerous demeaning caricatures of the Japanese as a warmongering people as depicted in postcards circulating at that time (JTB 1982, 13–14; Linhart 2005). The JTB also joined forces with the Japan Hotel Association to construct a chain of JIGR-managed station hotels providing the kinds of customer service found in the grand hotels of Europe and America. The Japan Hot Springs Association also initiated the development of seaside hotels, hot springs, and mountain resorts for escaping the hot summers (JIGR 1922, 1926). The JTB opened outposts in Taiwan, Manchuria, and Korea in 1912 (fig. 6.1), the same year it was founded in Tokyo. Once the JIGR began a regular schedule for trains departing for the ports of Yokohama, Nagasaki, and Kobe, JTB offices started selling all-inclusive tours to Korea and Manchuria with discounted steamship passage tickets, railway pass coupons, and hotels (with the choice of American and European meal plans for foreign passengers; JTB 1914, 1926). The mission of the JTB branches in the colonies was to coordinate these excursion tour packages and connect major colonial destinations by maximizing inter- and intra-empire traffic networks (Tamura 1990). The JIGR, SMR, CSTTK, and Taiwan Railways were soon working together with shipping companies such as NYK and OSK to develop railways, trams, and roads linking tourist facilities (hotels, spas, and mountain resorts) so visitors could access historical cities, famous places, and natural monuments from Harbin to the South Pacific (JTB 1982). By 1914, branches of the JTB were distributing 3,000 English maps featuring not only Japan but also its colonies, including maps of Keijō, Dalian, and Taipei. The peak year for the number of inbound visitors was 1918, when Japan's hotels reported sold-out conditions due to the sudden rush of Russian aristocrat émigrés escaping the Russian Revolution; the years 1917 and 1918 recorded 7,780 and 8,165 Russians, respectively—triple the numbers from previous years (JTB 1982, 30).

FIG. 6.1. Japanese tourists being helped by a smiling JTB agent in Korea, c. 1939. The original caption reads, "Japan Tourist Bureau Inquiry Office." Note guidebooks and postcard sets for sale in the glass cages below the counter. Japanese Tourist Bureau (JTB) 1939b.

Following the end of World War I and runaway inflation in Europe, the JTB experienced some tough financial times when foreign demand for travel coupons declined steeply. In 1918, as an alternate business plan, the JTB started selling packaged tours to the colonies for the domestic consumer (JTB 1982, 32). In order to advertise the latest colonial destinations to the increasing number of outbound travelers perusing the discounted circular and round-trip travel coupons, the JTB started publishing Japanese-language tour guidebooks in 1919. Even many homebound Japanese were curious to learn about conditions in the colonies, since the media and the government were promoting the new frontier as the greatest hope for Japan's economic future. The new territories were advertised by corporations and colonial administrators as being abundant in farmlands and natural and mineral resources waiting to be claimed by enterprising Japanese citizens (CST Chōsen Ginkō 1919). The rise in the sale of domestic tickets heading for the colonies also persuaded the JTB to open offices inside major department store chains, such as Mitsukoshi, Daimaru, and Takashimaya. The years 1925 to 1935 represented the peak decade for outbound tourists, who by then represented a wide range of classes and occupations, including teachers, student groups, soldiers, and businessmen. The educated masses, who were hungry for news of the latest tourist destinations and leisure trends, near and far, spawned the publication of travel magazines such as *Tourist* (1913–42), a bilingual (English/Japanese) periodical, and *Tabi* ("Trip," 1924–present), the first travel magazine designed for Japanese readers (JTB 1924–present). The success of the JTB's worldwide advertising efforts could be felt not only in the wide range of services they offered but also in national financial coffers. By the mid-Shōwa era, tourism had become Japan's fourth-most-important source of foreign revenue, behind cotton, raw silk, and silk products. By 1936, the number of inbound tourists reached 42,586 annually, and these spent a total of 107,688,000 yen (JTB 1982, 50). Although this represented only a small fraction (4 percent) of Japan's overall trade (including exports and imports), the amount exceeded Japan's persistent trade deficit (94,000,000 yen; Leheney 1998, 125).

The *Handbook of Information for Passengers and Shippers*, printed for first-class NYK steamship passengers, represented the earliest form of pocket-sized travel manual introducing the country of Japan to the world traveler (NYK 1894). Subsequent editions of the NYK featured handbooks that included not only weekly steamship and railway arrival and departure schedules but also essential travel information on baggage, customs and passports, currency, weights and measures, postage and parcels, tariffs, prohibited or dangerous goods, and detailed cabin regulations (NYK 1896, 1–2). The year following the Sino-Japanese War, in 1896, NYK began issuing excursion passes called "through tickets" during the summer months, with ships departing weekly from Kobe, Yokohama, and Nagasaki destined for Inch'ŏn, Shanghai, Manila, Singapore, Honolulu, Seattle, Adelaide, Antwerp, London, New York, and Vladivostok (NYK 1896, 71). Ship passengers were also encouraged to take side tours to scenic places in interior Japan, such as Nikkō (see fig. 2.9), the Great Buddha at Kamakura, Hōryūji Temple in Nara (see fig. 2.7), and hot-spring resorts such as Atami and Hakone—all of which were only a day's train ride from the ports of Yokohama, Osaka, and Kobe (NYK 1894). For the more adventurously inclined, the handbooks recommended passages to Hokkaido, the "land of the Ezo," where one could see the Ainu in their original habitat (Murray 1894). Many firms also bought advertising space to announce the grand openings of their latest foreign branches, located from Shanghai to Harbin, with ads pushing Japanese-made consumer products and services, including the latest state-of-the-art cruise ships, hotel accommodations, guns for protection, photographic studios, and sundry items such as soap, drugs, and custom-made travel clothes (NYK 1894, 1896; Welcome Society 1908).

The 1896 edition of the NYK guidebook was the first Japanese guidebook written for foreigners that recommended excursions to destinations in the Liaodong and in Korea. On NYK's new steamer line, the *Higomaru* left every four weeks and on the way also called on Shimonoseki, Tsushima, Pusan, Inch'ŏn, Chefoo, and Taku, an outpost of Tientsin (see map 3). Ships bound for Pusan from Shimonoseki departed twice a day, one in the morning and one late in the evening, a relative easy passage of only ten hours, since the straits measured a total distance of only 122 miles (NYK 1896). The guidebook also recommended a sight-seeing tour of the newly opened ports in Korea with the caveat that one should try it only "if one had an extra three weeks or thereabouts, to complete a round voyage leaving from either Shimonoseki or Nagasaki" (73–74). The first documented tour group made up of private Japanese citizens that visited the new frontier in Korea and Manchuria set sail in 1906, the year following Japan's much-celebrated victory over Russia and the establishment of a protectorate under the residency-general (Ariyama 2002). The tour was organized by Japan's leading daily, the *Asahi* newspaper company, which came up with its own plan to capitalize on the consumer craze for Russo-Japanese War memorabilia. With an eye to selling more newspaper subscriptions, the *Asahi* ran advertisements for a cruise to the frontier that would revisit the great "battle sites" of the Sino-Japanese and Russo-Japanese Wars in Korea and Manchuria that were featured in the best-selling photographs, silk prints (*nishikie*), and postcards (Keene 1976; Kōgō 2003; Itō Mamiko 2003; Morse et al. 2004, 17–18). Three days following the first announcement recruiting passengers for the "Cruise Touring Manchuria and Korea" (*Man-kan junyū sen*) in *Asahi*'s June 22, 1906, edition, all three classes of cabin ticket were sold out when eighty people signed up. This was indeed an auspicious start for a first-time commercial pitch to market Manchuria and Korea as "the new world [*shintenchi*]," where one could see for oneself the farthest edge of the emperor's authority and domain (Ariyama 2002, 33). Following the media success of the 1906 tour, subsequent discounted tours began to sell out in large numbers, thus giving birth to the packaged educational tour (*shūgaku ryokō*) as we know it today in Japan and Korea (see fig. 6.7).

In 1909, the most celebrated literary figure of the day, Natsume Sōseki (1867–1916), was persuaded by his school chum, Nakamura Zekō (president of the SMR, 1867–1927), and the *Asahi* newspaper to tour Manchuria and Korea on an all-expenses-paid junket.[1] By the late 1910s, the transportation companies NYK, CSTTK, and SMR had joined forces with the JTB to distribute large numbers of detailed guidebooks, maps, and train schedules, as well as picture postcards capturing the scenic destinations, peoples, and customs (*fūzoku*) of Korea at ticket offices at major piers, railway stations, and department store branches from Tokyo to Keijō, from Keelung (Jilong) to Formosa.

Despite the wide variety of businesses and publishers engaged in the production of tourist information in the colonies, the overall organization, content, and layout of photos, maps, and advertisements were remarkably uniform, irrespective of destination. This is because guidebooks for the Japanese colonies were all modeled after an earlier generation of Victorian-era handbooks on Japan penned by foreign advisors and educators hired by the Meiji government and published by commercial presses. The authors included former Tokyo University professors, diplomats, and soldiers, such as Ernest Satow and A. G. S. Hawkes (Satow and Hawkes 1881), David Murray (Murray 1894), Basil Hall Chamberlain (Chamberlain and Mason 1907, 1913), and commercial publishers such as Frederic De Garis. The beginning of any guidebook covered what was deemed "essential travel information," such as customs and passports, as well as the locations of JTB offices, hotels, transportation links and fares, and post offices from which one could send telegrams or get banking services.[2]

The introduction also included an "overview of the land," including topography, population, and history. Korea's climate was always promoted as the "most pleasant and agreeable in the empire," making it an ideal location for summer retreats. A fold-out map sometimes included schedules for ships and trains, and transfer information. For the "through-traffic" passengers who rode the Pusan-Seoul line (Keifusen), the terminus was Shingishū (Shinŭiju) Station, where one transferred to the SMR lines departing the Antung Station, heading northeast toward Manchuria's new cities. Since most of the passengers who arrived by ship from Osaka, Kobe, or Shimonoseki docked at Pusan, the first place in the recommended itinerary, followed by Taegu and other stops along the Keifu line (see map 3). At the JTB offices on Pusan's pier, Shinŭiju, Ch'ŏngjin, and Najin stations, the SMR and CSTTK distributed train schedules and timelines so travelers could calculate itineraries and budgets for reaching major terminals along the Keifu line. The main section of each guide covered the major scenic, cultural, and business destinations along the main arteries of the CSTTK lines, as well as side trips to seaside and hot-spring resorts linked by private trams, buses, or shuttle services. the costs of transportation, admission to museums and zoos, food, and recommended hotels, inns, and restaurants (with the choice of Western, Chinese, Korean, and Japanese cuisines) were also included, for the budget-conscious consumer.

The guidebooks offered different tours, side excursions, and group itineraries, depending on one's purpose for visiting Korea, be it educational or business. The recommended routes linked major cities, with side trips to famous places and resorts that connected to the main arteries of the CSTTK via private trams, buses, or shuttle service. For major cities like Seoul, Kaesŏng, and P'yŏngyang, there were options such as historical and city tours, tours of mountain resorts and hot springs, and even tours of industries (such as commercial museums, factories, and ginseng farms). Finally, the appendix section of the guidebooks included a thick section of advertisements placed by local businesses (tram and taxi companies, inns, hotels, tailors, pharmacies, and department stores) whose ad fees subsidized the publications. Other local merchants catering to tourists (such as curio dealers, ginseng shops, photographic studios, and restaurants specializing in different cuisines—Chinese, Japanese, and Korean) also bought advertising space. By the late 1930s, the JTB had established operations inside the largest department store chains. Minakai boasted seven outlets

FIG. 6.2. Tourist photograph of reconstructed South Gate (Namdaemun), c. late 1920s. The gate, often referred to in colonial sources as the doorstep (*kenkan*) to Keijō, dates to 1398, during the seventh year of King T'aejo's reign, and represents the oldest standing wooden structure in Seoul. The GGC registered it as Korea's number one national landmark on August 27, 1934. Photo in author's collection.

in the cities of Seoul, Pusan, Taegu, Taejŏn, P'yŏngyang, Hamhŭng, and Wŏnsan. Mitsukoshi (now Shinsegye) was also centrally positioned at the intersection of Namdaemun (South Gate) Street (fig. 6.2, photo on right), the main traffic hub connecting all of the city's the major thoroughfares to financial centers, military barracks, and CST administrative offices.[3] The move to department stores was a strategic one, since that was where the urban upper class, both Korean and Japanese, congregated to shop and socialize at cafes in the 1930s.

In Seoul, the city tour buses and trams left from Namdaemun, where the through-ticket passengers disembarked for rest or for sightseeing on the way to China or Manchuria. City tours were planned as half-day itineraries to visit Chōsen Jingū (the main Shintō shrine on the slope of Namsan), Namdaemun (South Gate), the Botanical Garden and Zoo (Ch'anggyŏng-

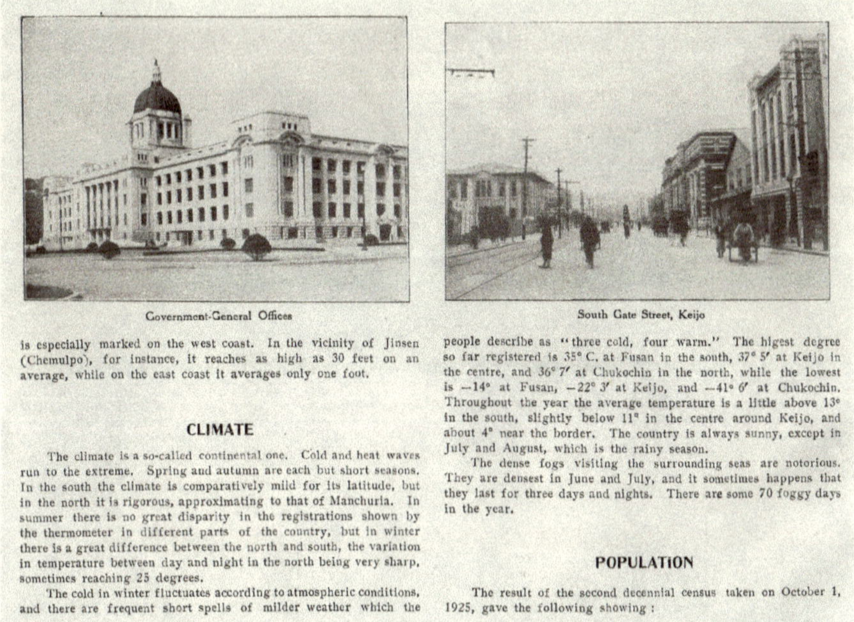

Government-General Offices

South Gate Street, Keijo

is especially marked on the west coast. In the vicinity of Jinsen (Chemulpo), for instance, it reaches as high as 30 feet on an average, while on the east coast it averages only one foot.

CLIMATE

The climate is a so-called continental one. Cold and heat waves run to the extreme. Spring and autumn are each but short seasons. In the south the climate is comparatively mild for its latitude, but in the north it is rigorous, approximating to that of Manchuria. In summer there is no great disparity in the registrations shown by the thermometer in different parts of the country, but in winter there is a great difference between the north and south, the variation in temperature between day and night in the north being very sharp, sometimes reaching 25 degrees.

The cold in winter fluctuates according to atmospheric conditions, and there are frequent short spells of milder weather which the

people describe as "three cold, four warm." The higest degree so far registered is 35° C. at Fusan in the south, 37° 5′ at Keijo in the centre, and 36° 7′ at Chukochin in the north, while the lowest is −14° at Fusan, −22° 3′ at Keijo, and −41° 6′ at Chukochin. Throughout the year the average temperature is a little above 13° in the south, slightly below 11° in the centre around Keijo, and about 4° near the border. The country is always sunny, except in July and August, which is the rainy season.

The dense fogs visiting the surrounding seas are notorious. They are densest in June and July, and it sometimes happens that they last for three days and nights. There are some 70 foggy days in the year.

POPULATION

The result of the second decennial census taken on October 1, 1925, gave the following showing :

FIG. 6.3. Typical postcard views of a modern Keijō cityscape featured in propaganda photo albums. *Left*: Chōsen Sōtokufu headquarters building. *Right*: Namdaemun Street, c. 1929. Chōsen Sōtokufu (Government-General of Korea) 1929a, p. 2.

wŏn), the CST headquarters building (fig. 6.3), the CST museum located at Kyŏngbok Palace (see fig. 5.2), and the fine arts museum at Tŏksu Palace (CSTTK 1938). Palace grounds became the locus for GGC-sponsored events, such as the staging of the 1915 Chōsen expositions, and royal cultural events targeting both locals and imperial subjects. The Seoul city tours also recommended side excursions to the beach resort of Wŏlmido in Inchŏn, as well as to the fortress of Suigen (Suwŏnsŏng, see fig.1.1), after which one could head northwest to the Heijō region cities (P'yŏngyang, Kaesŏng, and Chinnampo). For nightlife in the cities, one could hire Korean *kisaeng* (courtesans) or Japanese geisha to dance and sing.

The 1926 *Guidebook to Japan* explains "geisha dances" as "popular and universal forms of entertainment at banquets and other functions in Japan. Geisha may be hired at any time, anywhere, the charge of the dance depending upon the reputation and number of dances" (Japanese Tourist Bureau

FIG. 6.4. Originally captioned "Keisang, Korean Dancing Girls," this image of "Chōsen beauties" in full costume remains the most iconic image representing "local color " (*Chōsen fūzoku*) found across the spectrum of colonial print media, including postcards, advertisements for CGR hotels, magazines covers, the guide book covers, newspapers, and consumer products, from cigarette boxes to record covers. Japan Tourist Bureau 1939b.

1926, 16). The demand for young, attractive, and accomplished female entertainers to accompany male customers partying at high-class Korean restaurants led to the establishment of a school for *kisaeng* in P'yŏngyang. The school offered a curriculum of intensive training in musical accompaniment, dance, and popular songs of the day to be performed on stage in both Japanese and Korean language (Japanese Tourist Bureau 1939).

Of the many scenic historical cities excavated by archaeologists, seasoned travelers and curio collectors, such as Asakawa Hakkyō, Osaka Rokuson, and Oda Kanjirō, promoted the Kyŏngju area as being well worth taking a few extra days' detour (CSTTK 1936; Keishū Koseki Hozonkai 1922, 1935; Japanese Tourist Bureau 1939, n.d.; Oda 1922, 1923). Takimoto Jirō, a former SMR officer and author of *Guidebook to Japan, Manchuria, Korea,*

FIG. 6.5. Imperial family members (Kanin-no-miya Tenka Haruhito and wife) and entourage posing in front of the restored Sŏkkuram during their tour of Korea, October 1, 1935. Keishū Koseki Hozonkai 1937.

and China, observed that Silla's remains reminded him of his "pristine homeland" of Nara because of the presence of ancient tombs belonging to the House of Jimmu (Takimoto 1928, 102–3). When the Gold Crown Tomb (Kinkantsuka) dating back to the Old Silla Kingdom (c. 5th century CE) was excavated in 1921, it was widely hailed in the Japanese media as the greatest archaeological discovery of the century. The other tourist sites recommended included the three Silla kings' tombs, such as Kwenŭng, Hwangnamni, Kim Yu-shin Tomb (8th century CE), and Punhwang-sa Pagoda (see fig. 6.7).

By the 1930s, the beautifully restored Sŏkkuram and Pulguksa, and the Keishū museum, located at the center of the largest concentration of Silla royal burial mounds, became the favorite settings for photo ops by touring imperial family members (fig. 6.5), as well as European royalty such as the crown prince Adolf Gustaf VI of Sweden (see fig. 5.9), the amateur archaeologist and collector who founded the Museum of Far Eastern Antiquities in Stockholm (Hamada Kōsaku and Andersson 1932). The popularity of Kyŏngju as Korea's must-see heritage destination thus originated with the Keishū tourist boom of the 1930s (CSTTK 1936; Kim Hyŏn-suk 2006; Keishū Koseki Hozonkkai 1922, 1935, 1955).

The northeast corridor represented by P'yŏngyang and Kaesŏng were also popular destinations, with the tomb of Kija, the legendary founder of the ancient state of Kochosŏn; Manwŏldae (the Koryŏ dynastic palace remains); the Han Lelang and Rakurō Tombs; and the Koguryŏ painted tombs (c. 5th c. CE). The restored tombs of the Han dynasty commandery of Lelang were promoted in guidebooks and travel literature as the earliest "scientifically" excavated Han tombs in Asia (see fig. 5.4), since at that time no intact tombs dating from the Han dynasty (c. 2nd century BCE–3rd century CE) had been identified in China (*Nippon* 1939a; Pai 2000, 127–236). The regions of Puyŏ and Kongju (c. 4th–7th century), where archaeologists had identified tombs, pagodas, and temples belonging to the kingdom of Paekche, also drew the interest of local developers. The Puyŏ Preservation Society (Fuyo Koseki Hozonkai) was formed in 1929 by local officials of Puyŏ County. They teamed up with prominent art collectors and the major newspaper *Tonga Ilbo* to raise funds for the restoration of the ruins of Mirŭksa Temple and to create tourist accommodations such as inns, roads, bus stations, and taxi services. Because of the kingdom's well-documented close diplomatic and cultural relations with Japanese monarchs in ancient times, Puyŏ was promoted in Japanese tourist brochures as the sacred place where Koreans and Japanese had coexisted peacefully in ancient times (*Naissen ittai*). The colonial tourist industry was thus responsible for promoting Puyŏ's current profile as the artistic source of Asuka art and the inspiration for Nara's many artistic treasures. Tourism received an extra boost with the building of a Shintō shrine in 1939 to commemorate the 2,600th anniversary of the Empress Jingū's apocryphal conquest of Korea (Ch'oe Sŏk-yŏng 2003; Ruoff 2010, 106–28).

The majestic vistas of the Diamond Mountains of Kŭmkangsan (Kongōsan), advertised as "the most spectacular natural beauty under the heavens," was the only tourist region far from these commercial centers and historical cities. Photos of the two thousand spiky peaks of Outer Kŭmkang were featured in many CSTTK posters and magazines, from the *Tourist* to *Nippon*, a heavily illustrated glossy magazine written in German and English targeting hikers accustomed to the Swiss alpine resorts (CSTTK 1932; Weisenfeld 2000). In the 1930s, the most widely promoted sports and leisure activity was mountain climbing, which was adopted as a way of training the minds and bodies of Japanese, who were taught early on at school that mountains symbolized the quintessential Japanese national landscape (*fūto*). An empire-wide national park system introduced in 1930 was instrumental in the development of Diamond Mountain tours for mountaineers (Chŏng Chin-guk 1999), and Taiwan's Arisan high mountain areas, where tourists could visit "mountain savages" (Kanda 2003; Matsuda 2005). The CSTTK built two mountain resorts, one at Onjŏng-ni Station (1915) and one at Changan-sa Temple (1924) deep in the mountains, as a hunting lodge-cum-hot springs hotels. The hotels were accessible from two different directions, either riding on the Keigen line (Seoul-Wŏnsan) or coming up the east coast by car, driving north from Onjŏngi Station (see map 3). The goal of the CSTTK operators was to emulate the high-class ski resorts and spa hotels they had visited in the resorts of Switzerland, France, and Germany, where they had witnessed many rich tourists enjoying leisure and sport activities (Zimmer 1998). The CSTTK thus advertised heavily in newspapers and magazines to recruit hikers interested in joining their backpacking group during the summer months. Other scenic high mountains in Korea that were recommended for climbers included Paektusan and Chirisan. These mountainous regions were also recommended for the rugged adventurer types who wanted to hunt large game (unavailable in Japan), such as tigers, bears, wild boar, and birds (Bergman 1938).

Finally, since, in an ever-changing world, guidebooks are only as good as their last entry, then, as now, the CSTTK and JTB's guidebooks all went through several editions listing the latest tourist improvements, such as the introduction of a taxi service by the Kyŏngju Preservation Corporation, or on-site photographic studios taking commemorative photos, as well as new kinds of nightlife spots, such as cafes, movie houses, and dance halls. JTB travel club agents were regularly dispatched on junkets to check guidebooks for accuracy. One of the most comprehensive guidebooks on colonial Korea was CSTTK's two-hundred-page 1923 edition (CSTTK 1923). Although pocket-sized, it included detailed information, including statistical breakdowns of the populations of each city and province, divided by ethnicity (Koreans, foreigners, or Japanese); historical information, including the dates of dynasties, kings, major events, invasions, and monuments; educational facilities and universities; public works; and main industries.[4] The minutiae also included the latest statistical figures on exports, land holdings, and market conditions (such as annual rice production, the fish harvest, and ginseng monopolies). This kind of guidebook may have been written to impress visiting government officials, colonial administrators, and potential investors, and to show off the successes of the Japanese-controlled tourist economy. Reflecting the tastes, hobbies, and expectations of wealthy foreigners, these colonial corporate print media were thus responsible for mapping the itinerary of "must-see" cultural, commercial, and leisure destinations in Korea.

From the early days of the Meiji regime, photography had been appropriated as a tool of nationalistic propaganda and used to promote a new image of Japan as a rising imperial power to a world audience (Kinoshita 2003; Nihon Shashin Gyōkai 1971). By the turn of the century, dozens of Japanese-owned commercial photographic studios located in Nagasaki, Yokohama, Pusan, Inch'ŏn, and Seoul were being commissioned to record official events, field surveys, and even mountain expeditions; they were drawn to the "irresistible" pull of the romance of ruins and the unknown throughout the empire.[5] It has been well documented that the most successful commercial photographers, such as Felice Beato (1825–1904) and Baron Raimund von Stillfried (1839–1911), were businessmen first and artists second; they understood that visually striking and aesthetically appealing settings, such as natives on the verge of extinction, reenacted battle scenes, "natural" landscapes, and cityscapes manufactured in the studio sold prints and postcards (Banta 1988; Yokohama Kaikō Shiryokan 1987). Some of the more famous shots, initially taken in studio settings, were then massproduced in guidebooks, postcards, and souvenir photo albums (Chōsen Sōtokufu, Chōsen Ginkō 1919; CST 1935).

To commemorate the annexation of Korea in 1910 as a historical union between the imperial family and the royal Prince Yi family, the CST commissioned an official photo album titled *Commemorative Photo Album of the Annexation of Chōsen* (Heigō kinen Chōsen shashinjō; Sugi 1910). For example, figure 6.6 shows the crown prince Yoshihito of Japan (the future Taishō emperor, r. 1912–26) standing side by side with the handpicked heir

FIG. 6.6. Itō Hirobumi, the newly installed resident-general, posing with the crown princes of Japan (the future Taishō emperor Yoshihito, r. 1911–25) and Korea (prince Yi Un as a young boy) at Kyŏnghoeru Pavilion, Kyŏngbokkung, c. 1907. They are flanked by admiral Tōgō Heihachirō, major general Katsura Tarō, and Yi Wan-yong (one of the Yi dynasty royals who brokered the annexation agreement). The original caption reads, "Photograph taken on the occasion of the Visit of Korea of the Crown Prince." Sugi 1910.

to the Korean throne, Yi Un (also known as Prince Yŏngch'in, 1897–1960), as a young boy. Next to them stands the imposing senior statesman Itō Hirobumi, flexing his muscle as the newly installed resident-general, flanked by admirals Tōgō Heihachirō (1848–1934) and major general Katsura Tarō (1848–1913), both war heroes of the Sino-Japanese Wars. More importantly, they are posed in front of Kyŏnghoeru, the banquet hall of the Yi dynasty's last seat of power, Kyŏngbok Palace. Although this photo was published in 1910, it was probably taken three years earlier, in 1907, the year that the eleven-year-old prince was taken to Japan by Itō, ostensibly to further his education and be groomed as a member of Japanese royalty.

Another photo in the same album shows Itō and his staff leading King Sunjong (1874–1926), who are depicted strolling across the moss-covered ruins of the Koryŏ dynasty's last palace of Manwŏldae (c. 12th century) in

P'yŏngyang. In these photos, we can see that the decaying ruins most identified with Korea's fallen dynasties were chosen for their symbolic power
and convey the inevitable decline of the Koreans, who had lost out in the
struggle for survival against the new imperial power of Japan.

The medium of photography also played a critical role in circulating
tourist images of the "manners and customs" (fūzoku shashin) of the
Korean people in the form of picture postcards and print advertising
distributed throughout the empire.[6] A typical photo spread in most travel
guidebooks juxtaposed images of "Old Korea" (mukashi) with Korea "now"
(ima). The former usually depicted grainy black-and-white photos of "rustic Korea" dominated by peasant women engaged in everyday chores and
subsistence activities, such as washing clothes by the river, ironing at home,
and carrying jars on their heads and children on their backs. Korean men
were rarely portrayed in tourist images, unless they were street vendors ply-
ing their wares, rickshaw drivers, or nonthreatening old yangban (gentry
class of officials) relaxing or smoking in their distinctive black hats (Kwŏn
Hyŏk-hŭi 2003, 2005). To lend more authenticity and an air of antiquity
to their photographs, local photographers working in Korea also hired
attractive young women—mostly kisaeng, because as skilled performers
and entertainers, they instinctively knew how to pose seductively in front of
cameras (see fig. 6.4)—adding a more exotic atmosphere to famous places.
Scholars of colonial print media have pointed out that the kisaeng's low
social status and availability as potential sex-partners-for-hire made them
very desirable marketing tools.[7] Throughout the colonial period, images
of kisaeng appeared in a wide range of advertising for Japanese-made
consumer products, from cigarette boxes, record albums, and cosmetics to
travel ads, restaurant signss, and postcards. Such commodified images of
"exotic Korean beauties" were designed to be consumed both literally and
figuratively by the male gaze, Japanese and Korean (Kwŏn Haeng-ga 2001).

In contrast to the rustic landscape of "Old Korea," the representative
images of modern Korea featured towering edifices of Japan's colonial
modernity in the form of monumental public works and imposing architectural structures, such as the CST headquarters (see fig. 6.3, left), banks,
post offices, museums, shiny steel bridges, train stations, dams, schools,
and hospitals. The most attractive photographs of newly built modern
infrastructures and cityscapes taken by professional photographers also

found their way into the pages of guidebooks and company handbooks, persuading both Japanese citizens and the English-speaking world of the economic, cultural, and political successes of their modernizing projects (CST Chōsen Ginko 1919; CST 1929a,b, 1935, 1972). By the 1920s, tourist photographs of "picturesque" scenes and the "quaint" customs of Korea appeared in a wide range of print media, business almanacs, and travel magazines issued by major colonial enterprises, such as the Bank of Chōsen and the South Manchuria Railroad Company.

In contrast to the "rustic" view of Namdaemun (South Gate), which was depicted with archetypical figures of the "backward" Chōsenjin represented by white-robed *yangban*, *chigekkun* (porters), and disheveled children (see fig. 6.2), the CST headquarters and cityscapes are depicted as imposing monuments to Japanese modernity and urbanity (see fig. 6.3). This visual technique—juxtaposing the "Old" versus the "New"—was widely deployed not only in guidebooks but also in CST-controlled media, from daily newspapers to school textbooks and corporate reports. In many colonial publications, these images contrasting "modern Japan" and "backward Korea" were also complemented by a historical narrative explaining the inseparable ties between Korea and Japan since time immemorial (*mukashi kara*). A typical passage, taken from a brochure titled *The Story of Chōsen* (Chōsen no hanashi), printed by the CSTTK in the 1930s, reads,

From the time of Empress Jingū's conquest (c. 3rd century CE) of the Three Han [Sankan], Chōsen is the country that has had the closest relationship with our nation, a tie that can never be severed. On a clear day, one can see the mountains of Pusan in the country of Chōsen across the sea from Japan. It is now only an eight-hour trip on a boat leaving morning and night from Shimonoseki. From there, one can transfer to a train. In olden times, Kankoku [Korea] was formerly an independent nation, but in August 1910, it was incorporated into the empire. Since then, the Chōsenjin have become our brethren for all time to come, and because our races have merged again, just like ancient times, the future prosperity and happiness of our mutual countries depends on forging very close ties, just like in olden times [*mukashi*] when Mimana was our colony. It is a historical fact that the ancient Three Kingdoms of Silla, Koguryŏ, and Paekche in olden times paid tribute to our emperors. It is also true that we have continuously exchanged items of material culture [*bunbutsu*] for hundreds of years. During Yi dynastic times, however, due to the inept and corrupt administration, the land was no longer productive and the people were living in dire poverty. Consequently, some factions in the palace plotted a coup and the government was overthrown. When it became clear that the Yi government was not fit to suppress the violent Tonghak uprising (the Qing dynasty's troops were equally helpless), our country came to the rescue of our allies to protect them from its previous subordinate status as a tributary state of China. We decided then to assist the Korean republic to revolutionize its political system when China and Russia intervened. Following the Sino-Japanese and Russo-Japanese Wars, our nation signed peace treaties and we acquired the peninsula as well as Ryōjun [Port Arthur] and Dairen situated in the Liaodong. Because of the patriotism and superior morale of our troops, we won the Russo-Japanese War, after which we decided for our own national defenses to take over Manchuria by force so as to avoid future instability. For the eternal peace of the Far East, we decided to annex Korea. Since then the industries of Korea, including rice exports and fishing, and agricultural exports, including fruit, ginseng, and silk, have expanded many times over. The population has also increased in all of the major cities. We have also brought new transportation and infrastructure, such as ports, railways, roads, trams, and cars, as well as new educational improvements. Now anyone can travel in Korea and experience the same beauty and level of efficient and convenient service as we do in Japan proper [*naichi*], since there is now no difference between Korea and Japan. This is the way it should be, since we are now one with many of our citizens. For students joining group tours, we wanted them to see in one glance what a warm and peaceful nation the land and people of Chōsen are. Although there has been some misunderstanding in the past, in fact we are now one and the same people, as proven by the many research investigations that have been carried out by our scholars. Our nation is very concerned about the future destiny of the Chōsen people, and we believe that the development of Chōsen will also contribute to our happiness. So our great mission is to bring future happiness to Chōsen and eternal prosperity to the whole empire. (CSTTK n.d., n.p.)

As we can see in the final paragraph, the CSTTK's and the JTB's propaganda was specifically aimed at students (fig. 6.7) and tour groups, empha-

FIG. 6.7. Ewha Girls School students in front of Punhwangsa Pagoda, on an educational group field trip to Kyŏngju, c. October 1934. Photo in author's collection.

sizing that the act of visiting Korea affirmed a spiritual journey by evoking memories of conquest emperors and their continental expeditions (Kuno 1967). In the colonial period, Korea's excavated remains and beautifully restored temples and tombs from the Three Kingdoms were touted as the most tangible body of evidence for tracking Japan's conquest lineage to the continent (Pai 2006; Pai 2010b). Consequently, with the Japanese ethnological, archaeological, and art historical "rediscovery" of Japan's antiquity in the early twentieth century, the ancient history of the Korean Peninsula became seamlessly integrated into discourse on Japanese racial identity, state formation, and empire building (Yi Sŏng-si 2004; Pai 2006).

In conclusion, the CST, the CSTTK, and the colonial tourist industry promoted the idea that the "objective" acts of excavating and reconstructing Korea's ancient buried remains enabled the reification of mythical founding emperors, whose conquests were projected two thousand years later into the colonial present (Pai 2006; Ruoff 2010; Yi Sŏng-si 2002, 2004). The travel industry and print media played a pivotal role in disseminating a "nostalgic" image of the Chōsenjin as Japan's long-lost poor country cousins who had been salvaged from the Dark Ages by the timely return of the superior Japanese and their "enlightened" government (Pai 2000, 35–43). The photographic images and the meanings of Korea's archaeological discoveries were also manipulated as powerful propaganda tools, not only to justify the annexation of Korea as a predestined reunion of the of Japanese and Korean racess (*Nissen dōsoron*) but also to show off the successes of Japan's "civilizing mission" in the colonies (Kita 1921; CST Chōsen Ginko 1919; CST 1929a, b; Yamamichi 1910). Although the recurring theme of the imagined "imperialist nostalgia" that romanticized the conquered "Other" in time and space is not unique to Korea and Manchuria, it had a lasting effect on how Korea and its people are promoted to this day both inside and outside of Japan (Pai 2010b).

CONTESTED OWNERSHIP

The Plunder and the Return of Cultural Treasures

To recapitulate, we have seen that in the past century the evolution of the concepts and categories "local," "national," and "global heritage" have paralleled the search for antiquity, authenticity, and identity by Japanese empire-building politicians, exposition organizers, collectors, scholars, businessmen, and leisure tourists. These aesthetic tastes and preferences, and ideological, commercial, and disciplinary agendas have thus reinscribed the spatial, cultural, and geographic boundaries of Korean/ Japanese things, peoples, and destinations presented to a world audience as follows.

First, the collecting agenda and curatorial goals of archaeologists, art historians, and ethnologists employed by the oldest established research institutions and museums in Japan and in their former colonies continue to have an effect on how the "Other" is presented to museum visitors and tourists today (Karp and Lavine 1991; Yoshida and Mack 1997). For example, Torii Ryūzō's six decades in the field and his research career spent mostly abroad, living and teaching in Korea, Manchuria, and China, resulted in the accumulation of tens of thousands of archaeological and ethnographic items, as well as illustrations, maps, books, and thousands of glass-plate photographs (Akazawa et al. 1991, 1992; Sasaki 1993; Pai 2009). In August 1975, over six thousand items formerly housed at the Tokyo Anthropological Laboratory were transferred to the National Museum of Ethnology (Minpaku), established the previous year at Senri Expo Park, built for the 1970 Osaka World Expo.[1] The museum has since grown into one of the world's leading centers for field research, exhibitions, and the publication of ethnographic works.

According to Yoshida Kenji, professor and director of the Research Center for Cultural Resources at the Osaka Museum of Ethnology, the donations from Tokyo University constituted a significant portion of the museum's early collections. The geographic distribution of Torii's items demonstrates the territorial reach of Japan's colonial ethnographic surveys (in descending order): Taiwan governor-general (1,223), Micronesia (826), Hokkaido Ainu (501), Ryūkyū (334), Korea (295), China (269), and so on (Yoshida Kenji 2001). Torii's visual legacy as the first Japanese anthropologist to record portraits of indigenous peoples in Asia at the turn of the century was featured in a major retrospective sponsored by three different museums (Tokyo University, Minpaku National Museum of Ethnology, and Torii's hometown's Tokushima County Museum), which have inherited his photographic collections. At the same time, curators from research libraries and museums in former colonial metropoles in Shenyang, Changchun, Dalian, Taipei, and Seoul have also been engaged in an international collaborative effort to identify, catalogue, and preserve Torii's photographic collections under their stewardship. Today, Torii's favorite subjects of the late nineteenth century—including the Ainu, the mountain tribes of Taiwan (see fig. 4.2), and natives of Yunnan—are still exhibited at the Minpaku; the Yunnan Museum of Nationalities, Taiwan; and Hokkaido's ethnic theme parks as "timeless people" without history (Hiwasaki 2000; Hsieh 1999; Kendall 1992; Kirshenblatt-Gimblett 1991; Niessen 1994; Pai 2009).

Second, many contemporary works on race, history, and ethnicity produced in Korea and Japan—regardless of whether they were written by administrators, journalists, scholars, or museum staff—frequently do not distinguish between concepts such as "race," "tribe," "clan," "ethnic group," and "ethnic state." Terms such as *shuzoku, minzoku,* and *minzoku kokka* are applied interchangeably, just as in the colonial era (Doak 1998, 2001; Morris-Suzuki 1998a, 1998b). It is also common practice for authors to project their nationalistic concept of the isomorphism "race = ethnicity = culture = history = language = nation" upon their descriptions of other peoples in Northeast Asia.

Third, as to who and what constituted the "ethnic" or "racial" groups, Japanese scholars at the turn of the century for the most part refined racial classifications that had been proposed earlier by Russian anthropologists. Shiratori Kurakichi and Torii agreed with their Russian colleagues

(Leopold von Schrenck, E. G. Ravenstein, and S. M. Shirokogoroff, to name but a few) that the area covering Manchuria, Korea, and the Russian Maritime Province was the central prehistoric meeting place, where all "Far Eastern" races, including the Paleo-Asiatics, Tungus, Manchus, and Koreans, had evolved together (Shiratori 1986; Torii 1925b, 1976). The Russians' racial classification scheme rested on the basic assumption that the indigenous inhabitants of the regions of the Sungari, Yalu, and Amur River valleys (*Manshū genjūmin*) and the Ainu in the northern portions of the Japanese archipelago had remained culturally unchanged since prehistoric times. The assumption was based on the belief that a large number of ethnic groups continued to practice "primitive" nomadic or seminomadic lifestyles involving fishing, hunting, and gathering well into the early twentieth century (Shiratori 1934, 1986; Shirokorogoff 1966). Adding a Sinological dimension to the efforts of their Russian colleagues, early twentieth-century Japanese scholars also insisted on the incorporation of Chinese historical records on ancient Northeast Asian peoples, such as the Eastern Yi (Korean: Tongi/C. Dongyi), Sushen, Yilou, Xiongnu, Yemaek (Chinese: Weimo or Huimai), and Chōsen (Chinese: Chaoxian), into the ethnographic and historical accounts of the racial lineage of the Japanese, Koreans, Mongols, and Manchus (Torii 1925b, 1937; Shiratori 1986; Wada 1938; Pai 1999a).

Fourth, the idea that Manchuria was a special place, to be distinguished from China proper, was later adapted as a political tool for legitimizing the Japanese occupation of Manchuria and North China (Dubois 2006; Hirano Ken'ichiro 1986, 50). As a result, "racial harmony" (J. *minzoku kyōwa*) became the most popular slogan propagated in official channels prior to and following the state-building activities (J. *kenkoku*) of the Japanese puppet state of Manchukuo in 1931–32 (Amino 1992). By the 1930s, with the expansion of the Pacific War front, Japanese anthropologists were sent to remote islands of Southeast Asia and the South Pacific to search for more tangible physical and material evidence to confirm their theories of racial superiority and their manifest destiny to rule over poorer and weaker minorities (Bremen and Shimizu 1999; Oguma 1995; Sakazume 1997). Historians of Japanese imperialism and anthropology, such as Paul Barclay, Robert Eskildsen, Kevin Doak, David Howell, and Tessa Morris-Suzuki, have reached similar conclusions that the military men, colonial administrators, businessmen, and anthropologists dispatched to the colonies in Hokkaido, Ryūkyū, and Taiwan were convinced that Japan's racial superiority and its civilizing mission (*bunmei kaika*) justified the enforced settlement, assimilation, and economic exploitation of "subjugated minorities" as far back as the 1870s (Barclay 2001; Doak 1998, 2001; Eskildsen 2002; Howell 2004).

As we have seen, imperial "Japanese origins" theories, rather than being truly "scientific" in nature, were based on a widely scattered, highly selective sample of artifacts, archaeological sites, and racist postcard images that were more or less arbitrarily identified as "proto-Japanese" (Pai 2009, 287). This relentless search for "Japanese" racial markers in prehistory and protohistory has for the most part disregarded rigorous archaeological criteria (such as absolute dating, stratigraphy, cultural assemblage, and settlement/subsistence data) that are minimally needed to give proofs of migrations, invasions, and foreign conquests, to say nothing of warrior races, marauding tribes, or clans of horse-riding nomads (Egami 1964; Ledyard 1975, 1986). But such niceties have been of no concern to the historians and archaeologists on both sides of the Straits of Japan who, from colonial times until the present day, have insisted on a vaguely defined "Korean-Continental" and "Korean-Japanese" cultural exchange (Kurihara 1978; Pai 1999a).

Furthermore, the anachronistic idea of the immutable nature of the "Japanese" cultural and artistic lineage, descended in spirit and form from millennia-old caches of Silk Road–inspired imperial treasures, is widely circulated in textbooks and guidebooks. Proving the enduring romance with the "Ancient Orient," Silk Road–related events (such as novels, movies, documentaries, and musical scores performed by Kitarō and cellist-turned-world-music-director Yo-Yo Ma's Silk Road Ensemble) continue to captivate the minds, hearts, and pocketbooks of millions of tourists who trek to remote Buddhist destinations such as Dunhuang, Longmen, Yunkang, Turfan, and Khotan. The sponsors and donors who have funded exhibitions, field surveys, excavations, and restoration projects to Turkey, Mongolia, China, and Inner Asia, and as far south as Vietnam, Cambodia, and Laos, include the Ministry of Education, the Japan Society for the Promotion of Sciences, the Toyota Foundation, NHK Broadcasting Company, Asahi News Corporation, and other travel and news cable channels keen on attracting viewers, tourists, and advertisers.

Despite more than a century of exploration by Japanese amateurs and specialists alike, no archaeologist or art historian has convincingly produced any proof, archaeological or otherwise, that would explain the thousand-year time gap or thousands of miles separating the Greek islands and Japan, and make plausible a Greek influence on the emergence of Nara art in the late seventh century (Inoue Shōichi 1994, 54–62; Takagi Hiroshi 1995, 83–84). It is also highly unlikely that a breakthrough will happen anytime soon, since the Imperial Household Agency still restricts access to "sacred" tombs, imperial archives, and imperial objects, with rare exceptions made for VIP visitors to Shōsōin (Matsuoka 1935). Ueno's Tokyo National Museum and Nara National Museum also continue to monopolize the management of Shōsōin treasures (fig. 7.1), which are displayed for brief annual exhibitions, adding to the aura of secrecy and the mystery of the unknown.[2]

FIG. 7.1. Crowds attending the Fifty-Ninth Annual Shōsōin Treasures Exhibition held at the Nara Museum, October 27–November 12, 2007. Despite the thousands of visitors who showed up that day, November 7, the lines moved smoothly, due to the experienced museum staff, who expertly guided the crowds through the exhibition venue. Photo by author.

The idea that Hōryūji's architecture (see fig. 2.7) reflects the classical proportions and perfect spatial symmetry of ancient Greek temples was propagated by architects such as Itō Chūta and Sekino Tadashi, who, along with Ernest Fenollosa, believed that Greek and Roman engineering techniques contributed to the shape, or "entasis," of the shaft of Hōryūji's columns (Kurosawa 1890a). The myth of the Grecian origins of Hōryūji's columns still endures, despite the fact that specialists working at the Nara Institute of Cultural Properties, relying on scientific excavations and tree-ring dating sequences, have revealed that the original columns could not have been much older than the seventh century. Therefore, "Graecophilia"—tracing Japan's Buddhist arts to imagined cultural roots in ancient glories of Greece and Rome—was and still is an integral part of the search for a Japanese version of a "trans-Asian" essence (Kuki 1889; Yamaguchi 1982, 5). As shown by busloads of tourists (both foreign and domestic student groups on packaged educational trips destined for Nara's many World Heritage sites), the success of joint educational and national tourist policies in promoting ancient Buddhist temples as the spiritual source of Japanese identity has been a resounding success for more than a century.[3]

Today, even after thirty years of archaeological reeducation emphasizing Japanese racial homogeniety and cultural descent from a simple and peaceful community of Jōmon hunter-gatherers and agriculturalists who evolved into Yayoi rice farmers, the fascination with invasion scenarios still lives on in the popular imagination (W. Edwards 1991; Fawcett and Habu 1989; Ikawa-Smith 1995). The century-old self-inflicted Japanese identity dilemma thus reflects a continuation of prewar obsessions with reclaiming a unique racial identity, heritage, and cultural standing in the Far East (Befu 1994; Nanta 2008; Yoshino 1992; Oguma 1995, 1998; Weiner 1987).

Finally, in the postwar era, Japan's Agency of Cultural Affairs (Bunkachō) has evolved into a massive hierarchichal organization divided into a dozen directly administered units, as well as independent administrative insitutions. The agency currently oversees a network of national museums (the Tokyo National Museum, the Nara Museum, the Osaka Museum of Ethnology, and so on), excavations, research and conservation units (such as Nabunken, the Nara Institute of Cultural Properties, and Tōbunken, the Tokyo Research Institute of Cultural Properties), and the National Theater (devoted to reviving traditional performing arts, such as Noh, Kabuki,

Bunraku, and so on). Together these state agencies employ thousands of staff members, anthropologists, archaeologists, art historians, academics, curators, and conservators trained as specialists in the management and conservation of lacquer, bronze, and wood. Nationally designated artisans and craftsmen, listed as "living national treasures" (*ningen kokuhō*), are awarded monthly stipends so that they can attract disciples who will transmit to the next generation the skills and knowledge of the many vanishing traditional arts (Siegenthaler 1999). Among all of the caretakers of the national treasures, the Cultural Properties Department, as the oldest and most influential division of the Bunkachō, still commands the most respect and funding, as in prewar times. Japan's national museums, art galleries, and research institutions (such as Nabunken and Tōbunken) are also home to conservation labs equipped with the latest Nikon and Olympus digital imaging computers and cameras developed by specialists and engineers to scan and measure artifacts for authentication, documentation, and dating purposes (Mitsutani Takumi, pers. comm., 2001). Such advanced technical know-how is the envy of conservation labs the world over, who regularly dispatch their own curators and experts to train under Japan's leading conservators based in Nara and Tokyo.

Despite Japan's leadership role in funding and directing conservation projects around the world, the majority of its curators, archaeologists, and practitioners, many of whom are engaged daily in cultural administration, remain mostly unaware of this pioneering fieldwork and of the existence of the vast colonial archives in their own library stacks. This general ignorance on the part of many museum curators, bureaucrats, and faculty reflects the broader social and political climate of postwar Japan characterized by self-induced "selective amnesia" concerning its imperial past. For more than five decades, it has been well documented that nationalistic politicians and educators have deliberately censored not only the content of exhibitions at national war memorials (from Yasukuni Shrine to the Hiroshima Bomb Museum) but also school textbooks. The suppression of public discourse continues to be directed at erasing memories of wartime atrocities perpertrated on innocent civilians living in China, Manchuria, Korea, Okinawa, and the Phillipines so as to propagate the master narrative of Japanese people as collective victims and not the militant aggressors of the Pacific War (Amino 1992; Breen 2008; Kal 2008).

However, in the postwar era, citizens in Japan's former colonies in China, the two Koreas, and Taiwan also continue to identify with the old platitudes concerning the indigenous, prehistoric origins of distinct races, which they have incorporated into their new nationalistic narratives to explain the ethnic foundations of their respective modern ethnic states (Askew 2003; Harrell 1995; Mori 1997; Pai 1999a, 2000). These ethnic regeneration phenomena are highly ironic in view of the widespread anti-Japanese rhetoric on the part of postwar politicians and citizens, who proudly embrace and celebrate their respective racial origins, unique cultural traditions, and prehistoric customs reenacted at folk villages, religious festivals, and theme parks, without realizing that they are buying into "demeaning" nineteenth-century colonial racial and ethnic stereotypes.

In the case of the Republic of Korea, the most contentious topic—next to unresolved issues stemming from the Pacific War, such as the territorial disputes over the island of Tokdo and the compensation of comfort women, soldiers, and laborers—concerns the "return of cultural treasures," which has cast a long shadow over bilateral diplomatic relations since the issue was first put on the table at the 1965 Korea-Japan normalization treaty negotiations (Hatada 1965; Yi Hong-jik 1964). According to mimeographed copies of the original 1965 treaty documents submitted by the delegates, the official list of items suspected to have been smuggled out of Korea contained 489 items belonging to one Yangsan Pubuch'ong, and a Silla tomb excavated in 1920, all of which are now part of Tokyo National Museum's collections.[4]

To add insult to injury, in 1965, president Park Chung-hee opted to accept monetary reparation in lieu of objects so that he could raise much-needed cash to finance his ambitious infrastructure projects, such as the construction of the Seoul-Pusan highway system and steel mills. Therefore, from the Japanese government perspective, the 1965 treaty put an end to any claims against Japan. According to Donald MacIntyre, the former correspondent for *Time Asia*, nearly sixty years after Japan's surrender, only a paltry 1,326 items (852 books and 438 pieces of pottery) had been returned to the Korean government (MacIntyre 2002). Echoing the more publicized case of "contested ownership" involving the Elgin Marbles waged between the British Museum and the Greek government to this day, the official position on the part of the Japanese government is that it is not responsible for the vast numbers of treasures plundered and purchased by individual citizens that have ended up in private art galleries and national and metropolitan museums.[5] For example, the Tokyo National Museum is currently home to miscellaneous collections from Korea—mainly ceramics, pottery, and stoneware that was collected as far back as 1885. These artifacts, ranging from Neolithic-period comb-patterned wares and Rakurō bronzes to pottery and lacquerware, did not become part of the CST Museum because they had been deposited by private individuals such as archaeologists Fujita Ryōsaku and Oba Tsunekichi. The committee for the preservation of Ogura's Takenosuke collections also donated more than a thousand objects. The Museum of Oriental Ceramics Osaka possesses the largest collection of Korean ceramics courtesy of the descendents of Sumitomo and the Ōkura Mining Company, conglomerates that were active in Korea at the turn of the century.

The negligible results of official negotiations have resulted in much heated anti-Japanese rhetoric, voiced by the Korea (South) Munhwajae Kwalliguk staff and heritage specialists who have collectively condemned imperial Japanese colonial archaeologists for engaging in an imperialistic conspiracy to plunder Korea (Yi Hong-jik 1964; Kim Yŏng-sŏp 1966, 1973; KSMKG 1996a; Yi Ku-yŏl 1996; Yi Man-yŏl 1976). Professor Hwang Su-yŏng (1917–2010), who served as one of the two cultural properties delegates sent to the normalization talks, was the first prominent art historian and former national museum director to raise public awareness of the question "Who is to blame for the plunder of Korea?" In the preface to a 307-page report titled "References on the Japanese Destruction of Korean Cultural Relics," published by the Art Historical Society of Korea in 1973, Hwang expressed his profound disappointment with what he perceived as an unacceptable, humiliating outcome (Hwang 1973, 2). Yi Ku-yŏl, the journalist and author of the 1966 work *The Tortuous History of Korea's Cultural Relics* (Han'guk munhwajae sunansa) and its revised edition, *The Secret History of Korea's Cultural Relics* (Han'guk munhwajae pihwa), was also instrumental in sensationalizing the details of Hwang's catalogue (Yi K.Y. 1996). Despite the provocative titles of Hwang's and Yi's publications, their proof of a litany of Japanese misdeeds consisted of anecdotal evidence taken directly from museum curators' meeting minutes, CST newsletters, correspondence, and site reports submitted to the CST by Sekino, Imanishi

Ryū, Hamada Kōsaku, Fujita Ryōsaku, and Koizumi Akio (1897–1993), the former director of the Kyŏngju Museum. Although both publications failed to make a convincing case for the neglect, mismanagement, corruption, and trafficking in stolen antiquities on the part of archaeologists that would hold up in an international court of law, the duo's publications have often been referred to as the "smoking gun" implicating the CST in utilizing knowledgeable specialists' research publications to more efficiently loot Korea.

What has been critically omitted in the vehement anti-Japanese rhetoric is that, in contrast to postwar Europe, where the Allies had mounted concerted efforts to track down the hundreds and thousands of masterworks, paintings, and other treasures seized by the Nazis, it seems that there were no such initiatives adopted by General Douglas MacArthur (1880–1964), the Supreme Commander of the Allied Powers (SCAP), who was headquartered in Tokyo from 1945 to 1951. Moreover, the general was reported to have opposed restitution; he was far more concerned with pressing US political goals for containing the spread of communism (MacIntyre 2002). Furthermore, unlike the case of Europe, where the authorities were familiar with the inadequacies and failings of modern treaties and conventions, dating back to Hague Conventions following the looting and destruction after World Wars I and II, SCAP did not adopt any official position regarding the return of treasures taken by Japan from its former colonies (US Department of State 1949, 821–71). To further complicate matters, on August 15, 1945, with Japan's sudden surrender, the US Army Military Government in Korea (hereafter USAMGIK), was thrust into the role of reluctant steward of Korea's cultural treasures and museums.

The actual transfer of museum collections and directorship of the CST Museum involved three key figures representing three overlapping governments: Eugene Knez (1916–2010), Kim Chae-wŏn (1909–90), and Arimitsu Kyōichi (1907–2011). Knez (1949–53), a young American captain who had been assigned to Korea and Japan following the end of the Pacific War, was put in charge of USAMGIK's Bureau of Culture and the National Department of Education in Seoul, with the specific mission of restoring cultural and religious activities, including museums.[6] According to Knez's private papers, he was given this important duty because he majored in American Indian anthropology and worked briefly as a park ranger and historian for the National Park Service in Arizona (Knez Papers 1984, 213). Kim Chae-wŏn (r. 1945–70), the incoming director of the National Museum of Korea, was chosen as the new director because his PhD from the University of Munich distinguished him from other Korean elites whose advanced degrees were from Japanese schools (Kim Ri-na, pers. comm.). Arimitsu Kyōichi, the last Japanese museum director (1941–45), had arrived fifteen years earlier to work for the CSHKMT. Like many of his colleagues, including Saitō Tadashi (1908–) and Kayamoto Kamejirō (1901–70), Arimitsu opted to go to Korea after graduating from Kyoto University's department of archaeology because there were no entry-level positions for archaeologists in Japan (Arimitsu Kyōichi, pers. comm., 2001).

According to Kim Chae-wŏn's autobiographies, the three first met on Liberation Day (August 15, 1945), when Kim was greeted warmly by Arimitsu and two other remaining museum staff members, Kayamoto and Sawa Shun'ichi (1891–1965), the longtime staff photographer (Kim Chae-wŏn 1991, 1992). Accounts of the same historical meeting also appear in Knez's private correspondence to his family. Although Knez was at first concerned about major language barriers, he was much relieved that Arimitsu's "broken English proved to be sufficient" (Knez 1984, 217). Fifty-six years later, when I questioned Professor Arimitsu about this eventful day, to my surprise he could recall in vivid detail his first meeting with Knez. He said that Knez had made quite an impression on him because the latter had marched into the museum building brandishing an article written by Edwin O. Reischauer (1910–90), the celebrated Harvard University professor who had also served as an expert on Japanese affairs for the US Army intelligence service during World War II (Mokuyō Club 2003, 25). Knez had demanded to know if the man in front of him was indeed the same Arimitsu whom Reischauer had praised in his article "Japanese Archaeological Work on the Asiatic Continent," which had been published in the *Harvard Journal of Asiatic Studies* in 1939 (Reischauer 1939). In no time, the three were engaged in stimulating conversations on the many urgent matters and preparations required to reopen their museums the following year (Knez Papers 1984).

Knez had also requested that Arimitsu remain in Seoul with them so that he could train the first generation of young Korean graduates of Seoul National University (formerly Keijō Imperial University) to resume the excavations that had been abandoned with the outbreak of the Pacific War in 1941. At the time, Arimitsu confessed that he had misgivings about accepting this offer, being anxious about his family heading for Japan without him. However, he also told me that he felt a strong sense of professional duty and pride as the only qualified archaeologist who could direct tomb excavations tombs in Kyŏngju (Mokuyō Club 2003; Knez Papers 1984, 245). Despite Arimitsu's bravado, it is also important to note here that the main reason that there were no qualified native-born archaeologists to run field sites was because the 1916 laws stipulated that only Japanese staff were permitted to conduct surveys and excavations (Pai 2001). Such discriminatory hiring practices were in fact widespread institutionalized phenomena among the upper echelons of the CST administration and Japanese-owned companies throughout the colonies, causing much resentment among the second generation of imperial university graduates.

In his personal correspondence, Knez also brags that his "fast-talking" skills had persuaded his commanders that Arimitsu was politically harmless but "scientifically" valuable.[7] He was soon able to acquire the necessary permits to retain Arimitsu for an extended six-month stay (Knez Papers 1984, 222). The following year, in May 1946, Kim, Knez, and Arimitsu headed for Kyŏngju to dig at the Silver Bell Tomb, the first tomb to be excavated by Korean hands (Kim Chae-wŏn 1948). Finally, Arimitsu vehemently denied the widely circulated postwar rumors that the CST had planned to evacuate Korea's museum collections to Japan. His reply was an emphatic "No way!" (tondemonai). He made it perfectly clear to me that the CST museum staff were painfully aware of the eventuality of allied bombings and so had agreed that it would be much safer to leave their imperial treasures on the peninsula. In conclusion, my research into the trio's intertwined lives at a critical juncture in the history of the National Museum of Korea reveal that, because of Arimitsu, Knez, and Kim, the most celebrated, reported, and exhibited museum artifacts were inherited mostly intact by the National Museum of Korea on Liberation Day.[8]

In contrast to the safe handover of museum treasures on August 15, 1945, what happened during the panicked retreats from Seoul during the Korean War is an entirely different story. The second retreat from Seoul, in December 1951, was especially rushed, since Knez and Kim were the only two responsible individuals charged with the coordination of evacuation plans to salvage the contents of three museums: the Kaesŏng Municipal Museum, the Prince Yi Family Household Museum, and the National Museum (Pai 2000, 237–43). On a chilly winter night, Kim supervised the wrapping and packing of artifacts onto trucks bound for Seoul Railroad Station. The freight cars commandeered by Knez were deliberately labeled as "hardware" so as to avoid theft and suspicion (Knez 1984, 342). Three days later, Kim, who rode on the same train as the boxes, wired Knez reporting their safe arrival in Pusan, where the boxes stayed for the duration of the Korean War. By all accounts, this feat, only one step ahead of the invading North Korean army, is worthy of the plot of a Hollywood thriller and would not have been possible had it not been for Kim's and Knez's foresight and speedy execution (Kim Chae-wŏn 1992, 122–29). Knez was awarded the Order of Cultural Merit (Gold Medal) by the Republic of Korea in 1995 for his contributions to protecting Korea's museum relics.

Despite the timely rescue of thousands of the GGC museums' treasures, not all of the reported objects survived the war; the Ministry of Culture and Information records show that 6,580 items were reported missing between 1950 and 1951 (Korea [South] Munhwa Kongbobu 1979, 315–27). The 20,000 items accounted for in the KSMKG archives, in fact, represented only half of a grand total of 50,902 items that had been in the GGC museum's possession in August 1945. One unpublished catalogue that I was able to track down in Langdon Warner's archives at Harvard University's Rubel Library indicates that the Pusan museum staff accounted for 10,021 items taken from the National Museum of Korea and the Kaesŏng Municipal Museum in December 1951 (KS Pangmulkwan 1951). Harvard art historian Langdon Warner (1881–1955) may have procured this catalogue during his time on staff with the SCAP, when he oversaw the Monuments, Fine Arts, and Archives sections for the US Army (Warner 1941). Even though many brave soldiers and curators undoubtedly risked their lives to protect Korea's national museum treasures in wartime, it is also true that we will never know how many other museums' artifacts, documents, displays, storage buildings, and historical sites were destroyed, burned, dismantled, and smuggled out of the country as war loot during the chaos of not only the fall of Japan and the bloody Korean War (1950–53) but also the innumerable large-scale invasions dating as far back as the Mongols (13th century) and Toyotomi Hideyoshi (1592–97).[9]

Most experts agree that the largest outflow of Korean objects in the modern era dates to the decade between the 1890s and the 1900s, right after the Sino-Japanese and Russo-Japanese wars, when porous borders and general lawlessness in the northern regions of Korea created ideal conditions for smuggling (KSMKG 1996a). Fueled by the increased demand for novelties and war trophies among Japanese soldiers, businessmen, and exhibition organizers working for commercial museums, many secondhand shops had opened in Wŏnsan, Pusan, Shinŭiji, P'yŏngyang, and Seoul, where the heaviest concentration of Japanese army staff and settlers could be found (Han Yŏng-dae 1997). The clients who frequented these secondhand shops were mostly foreign diplomats, visitors, and connoisseurs of the arts seeking bronze vessels, Koryŏ celadonware (c. 13th–14th centuries), and Yi dynasty porcelain (c. 17th–19th centuries). By the early 1900s, it is estimated that there were close to a thousand individuals involved in a peninsula-wide network linked by professional tomb raiders, middlemen, and corrupt police who supplied most of the celadon used for bribes and gifts to curry favor with high-ranking officials and rich entrepreneurs (KSMKG 1996a, 45–63; Han Yŏng-dae 1997, 26–96). A famous anecdote dating to 1907 relates the story of the arrogant and ignorant King Kojong (r. 1864–1907), who, when shown a celadon piece by Itō Hirobumi, asked, "Which country is it from?" (KSMKG 1996a, 57). By the time Itō was assassinated in 1909 by An Chung-gŭn (1879–1910) at the SMR train station in Harbin, Itō was reported to have amassed well over 1,000 pieces of celadon (MacIntyre 2002). His successor, the third resident-general and first governor-general, Terauchi Masatake (r. 1910–15), also managed to take back to Japan 1,855 works of calligraphy, 432 books, and 2,000 pieces of celadon, mirrors, and other artifacts. His collections, of which a small fraction was returned to Korea, are now part of Yamaguchi's Women's University. Ironically, Terauchi was the same governor who was responsible for the 1916 promulgation of the empire's first set of preservations laws governing archaeological remains.

On the supply side of the antiquities trade in the colonies, reference guides to Keijō show that by the 1920s and 1930s in Seoul alone there were over a hundred registered secondhand shops catering to the lower-ranking colonial government employees and school teachers who were emulating the tastes of the rich and famous. The best known were the brothers Asakawa Noritaka né Hakkyo (1884–1964) and Asakawa Takumi

(1891–1931) and a close friend, Yanagi Muneyoshi/Sōetsu (also known as Yanagi Sōetsu, 1889–1961). The trio are recognized by art historians and *mingei* (arts and crafts) scholars today for their comprehensive approach to the study and collecting of Korean ceramic and folk arts (Brandt 2000, 2007). According to their biographies penned by Takasaki Sōji (1944–), a professor and researcher of Korean ceramics at the Museum of Oriental Ceramics, Asakawa, a native of Yamanishi prefecture west of Tokyo, was the first to move to Korea in 1913 as an employee of the CST Ministry of Agriculture (Takasaki 2001, 2002). He eventually found a permanent teaching job at an elementary school situated in the financial district of South Gate. Takahashi writes that Sekino's 1904 report on the art and architecture of Korea published by Tokyo University (Sekino 1904) influenced Asakawa's decision to set sail for Seoul in 1913. Asakawa was most eager to visit the Prince Yi Family Household Museum in the Ch'anggyŏng-wŏn Palace grounds, which was opened for public viewing in 1909 (Takahashi 2003, 11–12). The fact that the CST museum collections appealed to the tastes of educated young men like Asakawa is not surprising, since the objects and paintings had been purchased by donations from the Prince Yi Household Agency with Ito's blessing (CST 1911; Riōke 1912). Once he set foot in Korea, Asakawa devoted the rest of his life to accumulating a vast trove of ceramics and pottery for study and display. At every opportunity he sent his purchases back to Japan, where they were exhibited in his home. In less than a decade, his extensively researched treatises on the development of the ceramic arts of Korea were appearing in not only CST official publications and newsletters such as *Chōsen* but also in the prestigious journal *Shirakaba* (White Birch), which was widely read by the literati and art lovers of Japan in the Taishō era. Asakawa's approach to Korean pottery not only focused on understanding the genre as an art form but also included historical facts related to the manufacturing process (including technological innovations in kiln construction, clay sourcing, and potters' signatures). His treatises also commented on ceramics as a valuable commodity to be bought and traded. When we read his essays, it is clear that Asakawa's main goal was to integrate his Japanese and Korean pottery research into the broader framework of tracing the evolution of Korean and Japanese civilizations and artistic traditions (Asakawa 1935).

Noritaka's passion for Korean pottery influenced Takumi, who followed in his older brother's footsteps, departing for Korea in 1914. Like his brother, Takumi was employed by the Agriculture and Forestry Division, an excellent place for a budding collector, since the office kept the most detailed cadastral surveys maps of mineral, forestry, and water resources—all key for pinpointing ideal kiln locations in the peninsula. Takumi is also much admired by ethnographers and folklorists because, like Edward Morse, his sketches represented the earliest attempts to work out a classification scheme for ethnographic objects identified by "Korean" names and uses (Asakawa 1929, 1935). He not only refined Noritaka's typology of ceramic styles by adding regional variations but also widened his collecting agenda to include decorative furniture and housewares such as small tables, lamp holders, and kettles. Takumi's work also appeared in the influential magazine *Kōgei* (published 1931–51). Takumi's name eventually surpassed that of his brother as a notable connoisseur of Korean arts in Japan. By the 1930s, Yanagi had teamed up with the two brothers to form the Society for the Study of Korean Arts and Crafts (Chōsen kōgei kenkyū kai), which became famous for organizing a series of annual decorative arts exhibitions at major department stores in Korea and Tokyo (Brandt 2007, 184). The society also published seven lavishly printed and bound exhibition catalogues containing both black-and-white photos and color plates, all designed to showcase the latest acquisitions from Korea for buyers and collectors (Chōsen Kōgei Kenkyū Kai 1934–41). For example, the inventory from a Tokyo exhibition catalogue held in Takashimaya in 1941 listed more than two thousand objects supplied by Bunmeidō, a major antiquities dealer with branches in both Seoul and Tokyo.[10]

What is interesting in looking at the wide range of looted Han artifacts, Three Kingdoms' tomb accessories, and Buddhist sculptures offered for sale and appreciation in the 1930s, is that the tastes of the well-to-do citizens of the empire were evolving along with the latest archaeological discoveries in Korea. The society's collecting and promotional events in the 1930s not only established new parameters for standards of beauty for ancient Korean curios but would go on to revolutionize the *mingei*, or "arts and crafts," movement in Japan and in the West (Brandt 2007, 39–232; Takasaki 2001, 6; Yanagi 1982).

The large number of looted tomb objects listed for sale in these sumptuous catalogues constitutes irrefutable proof that the Asakawa brothers and Yanagi had ventured deep into the hinterlands of Korea to carry out private excavations (*shigutsu*). Although they bragged that they had made their own discoveries, it is more likely that they were assisted by local grave robbers who were familiar with the locations of abandoned tombs and kilns in Kyeryongsan and Kangjin that dated back several hundred years to the Koryŏ and early Chosŏn periods (Takasaki 2001, 6–29). It is also evident that the CST turned a blind eye to their illegal activities because the staff wanted to learn from these young and energetic collectors' research in order to revive the royal pottery manufacturing techniques for the export and tourist market.[11] Despite the fact that the trio's foraging activities contributed to the smuggling of Korean antiquities, their achievements have been openly admired in postwar Korea (Shim 1996). Their public image as collectors of folk art (*mingei*), rather than prized museum-worthy antiquities and celadon, is probably the main reason that, unlike the much-maligned archaeologists, their scholarly reputations have remained intact. For example, when Takumi died in 1964, his body was buried in Manguri, a cemetery on the outskirts of Seoul. His grave marker, in the shape of a white jar reminiscent of Yi dynasty ware, is conspicuously the only non-Korean burial marker (Takasaki 2001, 22–23). Yanagi was the recipient of a posthumous Gold-Crown Medal (Munhwa Hunjang), a prestigious award given by the government for his contribution to introducing Korean culture to the world (Takasaki 2001, 10).

The rapacious appetites of the wealthiest Japanese collectors can be gauged by an anecdote from one of Knez's personal letters, dated December 1945, five months after Japan's surrender, when Knez had managed to stop the shipping of two large vaults of art treasures from Pusan: "I found jade, gold, silver, bronze items; old precious glass, superb ceramic ware, beautifully painted scrolls, exquisite lacquer work inlaid with a mother of pearl, skillfully fashioned woodwork, and so on. It was an art collection worth millions of yen" (Knez 1984, 219–20). Knez eventually had to round up four military policemen to escort five truckloads back to the Kyŏngju museum, a hundred miles north. Although Knez never identified the owners of these hoards by name, he speculated that one was a wealthy physician and another was the president of the South Korea Electric Company. (224). The latter figure was probably the notorious Ogura Takenosuke who had absconded with more than 1,100 artifacts, some of which are now part of the Tokyo National Museum collections. A recent special exhibition held at the National Museum of Korea in 2008 titled "Echoes of Life: The Enduring Traditions of Unified Silla Sculpture" featured nineteen national treasures and seventeen registered cultural properties from collections loaned by the Tokyo National Museum and the Nara National Museum.

Knez himself cannot be absolved of blame for the plunder, for his personal correspondence shows that he was also engaged in buying and trading "genuine" Korean art. In a letter dated February 8, 1946, he asks his mother to "take particularly good care of the two care packages because the bronzes from the Silla dynasty were approximately 1,000 to 1, 200 years old, and therefore she should not underestimate its value" (Knez 1984, 232). Gregory Henderson (1922–88), the American attaché to the US embassy during the Korean War, was recognized in the West as one of the foremost scholars of Korean ceramic arts (Gompertz 1963, 1977; Henderson 1962). However, in Korea, his reputation is closer to that of a latter-day Itō Hirobumi—a power-hungry bureaucrat who used his position and influence to loot tombs in Kaesŏng and Kyŏngju during the chaos of the Korean War. A small portion of Henderson's extensive collections of Silla pottery and Koryŏ celadonware is now part of the Sackler Museum at Harvard University.

In summary, even though there were greedy individuals and private excavations of Korean ancient sites, it is certain that most excavated artifacts reported by the CSHKMT were inherited by the National Museum of Korea in the postwar period (Pai 2000, 237–43). Contrary to the former claims of many Korean scholars and lawyers, at present scant evidence exists that the CST-employed specialists were the culprits (ŏyong hakja) who were motivated to dig only for personal gain, fame, and profit.[12] The situation in the field was much more complex and nuanced, since it was not in the interest of CST policy makers and employees to loot Korea, because the colonial tourist industry was heavily invested in restoring tombs, temples, and palaces with the long-term goal of developing them as leisure travel destinations.

Contested claims of cultural ownership constitute an ongoing dilemma for museum curators, preservation trusts, and former imperial institutions that have inherited colonial-era collections from around the world (Messenger 1989; Gill and Chippindale 2005). Although for more than a century, most nations around the world have implemented export prohibitions to prevent the theft and smuggling of antiquities, the most desired and rare items continue to be smuggled out of the poorest countries to meet the perennial demand for antiquities from the spectacular ruins of ancient civilizations such as Greece, Rome, Egypt, Sumer, India, China, Cambodia, and Mexico (O'Keefe 1999; Prott 2005). Currently, this lucrative trade in antiquities is also big business on Internet auction sites such as eBay as well as at storied auction houses such as Sotheby's and Christie's. Ten years ago, the world media and archaeological community unanimously condemned US invasion forces for the neglect and ignorance that resulted in the plunder of the Iraq National Museum during the chaotic fall of Baghdad in April 2003. This sensational news is just one glaring recent example of how war, violence, and poverty contribute to illicit trafficking in antiquities around the world today. The most recent case of government accusations of illicit trafficking has embroiled the government of the People's Republic of China (PRC) and the auction house Christie's, which was commissioned by the former partner of deceased fashion designer Yves Saint Laurent (1936–2008) to auction off the couple's entire collection of antiquities that had once decorated their world-renowned Paris apartment. The PRC has requested that the sellers to return a pair of large bronze animal heads, claiming that they were plundered from the Summer Palace by British soldiers in 1860 (Hevia 2003, 74–88).

In the postcolonial era, native scholars from former colonies whose antiquities continue to be the target of looters have been the most vocal in denouncing their colonial-era predecessors for their biased interpretations and misrepresentations of the colony's past that deliberately portrayed their "backwardness" by highlighting the "prehistoric and primitive" nature of their art and ethnographic collections. This inseparable link between imperialism, collecting, and the production of knowledge have resulted in the three most contested issues in cultural heritage circles today: repatriation, reparation, and ownership (Dirks 2001; Messenger 1989). Instigated by the former owners, individual artisans, leaders of tribal groups, and national governments, who have claimed ownership of or indigenous rights to sacred places, ancestors' skeletons, natural and mineral resources, archaeological remains, and religious artwork, as well as documents and photographs taken without their permission or knowledge decades or centuries ago (Clifford 1988). In lieu of reclaiming the actual material objects, these disparate forces are all attempting to recover some sort of perceived just compensation in the form of monetary reimbursements, copyright permissions, or usage fees for the lost treasures that were illegally smuggled, plundered, or exploited for commercial gain by their former colonial overlords (Brown 2003).

The smuggling of antiquities is condemned by all sovereign nations as well as by UNESCO officials, since it poses a major threat to the development of any national tourist heritage industry. The goal of architectural restoration is to preserve "monuments in situ," lending a sense of place and public memory for all to see and learn (Stone and Molyneaux 1994). Although UNESCO national representatives and local politicians and bureaucrats have called on local and international media support to raise citizens' awareness of their endangered cultural assets, in reality the pace of bulldozers has only accelerated with the increase of massive industrialization and urbanization projects as many more countries join the ranks of developing nations. Not only have architectural monuments, historical sites, and natural landscapes been obliterated in the past two centuries but countless millions of people have been forced to abandon farmlands, forests, and pastures to make way for railroads, freeways, bridges, and urban sprawl, resulting in the demise of tribal communities around the world. Today, in many underdeveloped regions of Asia, Africa, and South America, tourism has again been hyped as the best way to save endangered habitats, animal species, and local cultures (Brown 2003). However, with tourism emerging in the last decade as the world's largest industry (according to the World Tourism Organization [UNWTO]), global capital, spearheaded by luxury hotel chains and real-estate developers collaborating with government agencies, now dictates the day-to-day management of the most famous World Heritage sites, from Mexico's large pyramid complexes to Cambodia's Angkor Wat. Many experts have also pointed out that the arrival of mass tourism and the invasion of multinational corporations have also resulted in the loss of jobs and income for local agriculture and small businesses because of the resulting pollution and environmental degradation. Consequently, many indigenous peoples have again lost control over their own destinies, as well as revenue, since they cannot afford the exorbitant concession rents and vendor permits at famous heritage sites catering to planeloads of foreign tourists (Rowan and Baram 2004).

Japanese citizens still comprise the largest package tour groups visiting their former colonies, due to the geographic proximity and the bargain prices. At the peak of tourism in 2007, Japan's Ministry of Tourism and Culture's official website recorded around fifteen million outbound as opposed to eight million inbound tourists.[13] The huge discrepancy between the number of outbound and inbound visitors has been the source of much consternation for the government since the 1970s, when the rise of the purchasing power of the yen drove Japan's tourists abroad for leisure. South Korea's tourism board has also kept detailed statistics for four decades, covering Japanese preferences and their spending behavior at restaurants, spas, golf resorts, duty-free shops, and souvenir outlets. The main strategy is to keep prices competitive so as to undercut not only their rival Asian neighbors but also compete with Japanese domestic tourist businesses such as golf and spa resorts. South Korea's close monitoring strategy has been a spectacular success, since Japanese and recently PRC make up the largest nationalities arriving at Korean airports. Therefore, despite the postwar rhetoric denouncing Japanese wartime atrocities, national tourist policies have always accommodated changing tourist demographics (Hanjin Kwan'gwang 1996): GI's seeking "R & R" in the 1960s; middle-class Japanese salarymen on notorious *kisaeng kwan'gwang* (a common euphemism for sex tours) in the 1970s; shoppers buying counterfeit luxury brands in the 1980s; educational packaged tours in the 1990s; and, most recently, *este* (spa tourism) and medical tourism, including the rise in the popularity of Kangnam as a destination for plastic surgery (Moon 2009).

In 2012, with the rise of the "Korean Wave" (the unprecedented popularity of Korean TV dramas, movies, and idols spreading far and wide to encompass China, Taiwan, and Southeast Asia) the total number of foreign visitors rose to its highest inbound number of eleven million, composed largely of young and middle-aged female fans addicted to Korean soaps, pop singers, and film stars, many whom booked packaged tours. A typical three- to four-day itinerary highlights "fictional" destinations such as recreated historical drama production sets and behind-the-scenes movie sets designed to evoke a sense of history, romance, and nostalgia—the main themes of the most popular Korean soaps, *Chumong*, *Taejangǔm*, *Winter Sonata*, and *The Princess Diaries* (*Kung*). However, this time it is the Korean Tourism Organization, the Korean Film Council, local tourism boards, and travel agencies, such as Lotte-Hana Tours, which is in alliance with the JAL/JTB, as well as major media conglomerates such as CJ Entertainment, who have hired TV actors, actresses, and pop idols as official and unofficial ambassadors of desire, display, and consumption (Cho Hae-jŏng 2005; Hayashi and Lee 2007). The latest planned joint tourism resort–theme park venture, dubbed "Hallyu-Wood" in homage to the infinitely more glamorous Hollywood, was green-lighted by the Seoul Metropolitan Government and the Seoul Grand Park in June 2009. Slated to open in 2017, the park will showcase recreated movie and television sets as well as theme rides so that fans can relive their favorite drama moments and characters (*Korea Times*, June 18, 2009).

The proliferation of mega theme parks located next to the largest urban centers (from Shenzhen's Splendid China to Seoul's Everland to Disneylands in Tokyo and Hong Kong to Osaka's Universal Studios) epitomizes the most potent force of cultural and economic change in twenty-first-century East Asia. Together these theme parks attract hundreds of millions of domestic and international visitors with their miniaturized worlds, luxury brand-name-only shopping complexes, upscale hotels and resort casino, and food courts. The most popular attractions are the thrill rides designed so that the whole family can experience the nonstop adrenaline rush of Hollywood blockbusters such as *Indiana Jones*, *The Mummy*, *Pirates of the Caribbean*, and *Jurassic Park*. The potent mixture of an engaging narrative featuring swashbuckling heroes, hostile natives and wild creatures, set amid gigantic IMAX screen images of crumbling ruins, echoes the themes of travel, danger, and the discovery of the unknown. The global reach of popular cable channels such as National Geographic, the History Channel, Animal Planet, and the Discovery Channel have also contributed to the increasing homogenization of tourist destinations, where entertainment has replaced "authenticity" in creating a sense of place and historicity (Hendry 2000a, 2000b). Today, the joint forces of tourism development and the commodification of ethnicity have transformed once-functioning villages, mausoleums, shrines, and temples into "tourist spaces" of consumption and commerce. However, we cannot deny that "the irony of these times is that as actual places and localities become ever more blurred and indeterminate, *ideas of* culturally and ethnically distinct places have become perhaps even more salient" (Gupta and Ferguson 2001, 390).

TABLES

TABLE 1. Registry of cultural properties, by category, according to the Ministry of Cultural Heritage Administration (2001–11)*

National Registry Inventory Years	2001	2002	2003	2004	2005	2006	2007	2008	2009	2010	2011
Cultural Properties Categories											
1. National Treasures	303	304	305	306	307	307	309	313	313	313	314
2. Treasures	1,315	1,337	1,371	1,401	1,420	1,482	1,513	1,573	1,588	1,667	1,710
3. Historic Sites	423	428	439	445	453	462	479	478	490	491	479
4. Historic Sites/Scenic Sites	9	9	9	9	9	9	10	10	delisted	0	0
5. Scenic Sites	7	7	10	12	15	19	30	51	67	72	82
6. Natural Monuments	329	329	330	337	358	367	381	389	404	407	422
7. Important Intangible Cultural Properties	108	108	108	109	110	112	113	114	114	114	114
8. Important Folklore Materials	237	239	240	240	241	242	253	254	261	262	264
Totals	2,731	2,761	2,812	2,859	2,913	3,002	3,088	3,178	3,237	3,326	3,385

*Category 4, "Historic Sites/Scenic Sites," was delisted after 2008 and merged with Category 5, "Scenic Sites."

TABLE 2. Registered tourist facilities, by type, according to the Ministry of Cultural Heritage Administration (2005–10)

REGISTRY YEARS	2005	2006	2007	2008	2009	2010
Types of Tourist Facilities						
Religious	32	42	50	51	51	53
Adminstration	47	56	60	65	67	67
Education	28	31	38	41	41	41
Accomodation	26	32	33	35	35	36
War Monument	7	19	20	25	25	25
Cultural	10	10	10	7	7	7
Medical	11	11	11	12	12	12
Industrial	13	17	24	25	25	25
Public	37	57	60	64	64	65
Famous Figures	14	18	21	21	22	22
Commercial	2	3	6	6	5	5
Movable properties	0	9	16	52	80	91
Other	0	14	17	18	18	17
Total	227	319	366	422	452	466

TABLE 3. Excavations, by category, according to the National Research Institute of Cultural Properties (1991–2006)

Years	Purely Academic	For Reconstruction	Rescue Excavation	Totals
1991	31	46	30	107
1992	29	26	31	86
1993	27	21	47	95
1994	11	28	63	102
1995	14	34	97	145
1996	14	41	137	192
1997	19	40	180	239
1998	10	53	191	254
1999	14	71	246	331
2000	47	31	241	319
2001	21	82	366	469
2002	14	91	493	598
2003	27	76	602	705
2004	30	102	867	999
2005	12	104	1,036	1,152
2006	23	70	1,207	93
2007	37	74	1,148	1,259
2008	30	99	1,250	1,382
2009	41	90	1,574	1,705
2010	32	116	1,479	1,627
2011	52	98	1, 108	1,258

TABLE 4. Chronology of Meiji field surveys and heritage management (1871–1911)

1862	Rutherford Alcock organizes official submissions at the Great London Exhibition
1868	Meiji government edict on the separation of Shintō and Buddhist orders (Shinbutsu bunri)
May 1871	The Promulgation of the Preservation Laws Governing Antiquities and Relics (Koki kyūbutsu hozon) by the Minister of Education; establishment of the Imperial Household Agency (Kunaichō) Tomb Office
September 1871	Establishment of the Department of Museums (Hakubutsukyoku)
March 1872	First domestic exposition held in Yūshima in Tokyo, May Vienna Japan Pavilion opening
May 1874	Banning of excavations of legendary "burial mounds" (kofun) and sacred sites
March 1875	Museum Department moves to Interior Ministry
April 1876	Lost and Stolen Antiquities Laws and buried properties (maizō butsu)
September 1876	First Home Ministry Laws on investigation, reporting, and documentation of kofun announced by Machida Hisanari, director of the Museum Department
September–October 1877	Edward Morse excavates at the Ōmori shell mound
October 1877	Home Ministry decrees that all excavated materials from the provinces must be delivered to the museum for preservation
1878	Construction of the Tomb of Emperor Jimmu in Nara (see fig. 2.8)
October 1879	Buried properties from burial mounds (kofun) will be excavated only under the direction of the Imperial Tomb Office
1881	Museum Department moved to the newly established Agriculture and Commerce Office
1884	The establishment of the Tokyo Anthropological Society at Tokyo University (prehistoric archaeology specimens deposited)
1886	Tokyo Anthropological Society Journal begins publication (Tokyo jinrui gakkai zasshi)
1886	Museum Department incorporated into Imperial Household Agency
1886–87	Ernest Fenollosa sent on fact-finding mission to Europe by the Education Ministry to survey museums, art schools and industries; reports to Itō Hirobumi
1887	Beginning of Japan's racial origins debate: Ainu vs. prehistoric Koro-pok-guru (pre-Ainu?)
1888	Imperial Office sets up Office of Preliminary Survey of Treasures (Rinji zenkoku Hōmotsu Saicho kyoku)

TABLE 4. *(continued)*

1887	Tokyo Fine Arts School established in Ueno Park
1889	Okakura Kakuzō launches first art history journal, Kokka
1893	Tokyo Imperial University Anthropological Society Specimens Laboratory headed by Torii Ryūzō (see fig. 4.1)
1895	Archaeological Society of Japan founded; begins publication of Kōkogaku zasshi in December
April 1895	Nara Imperial Museum opens; Temples and Shrines Department established at the Interior Ministry
1896	Sekino Tadashi, Tokyo University architect, sent to survey Nara; Torii sent on first survey of Taiwan and Manchuria after Sino-Japanese War (see map 1)
1897	Promulgation of preservation laws governing temples and shrines; government takes over the management and preservation of nationally registered art, artifacts, and documents belonging to temples and shrines (beginnings of national treasures system); Kyoto Imperial Museum opening
1899	Sekino Tadashi conducts first systematic art historical survey of the ruins of Heijō in Nara; Torii begins ethnological survey of the Kurile Islands
1899	Prehistoric remains deposited at Tokyo Imperial University anthropological lab; kofun-related materials under the primary jurisdiction of Imperial Household Agency
1900	Japan participates in Paris World Expo; Imperial Committee on the Investigation of Ancient Sites (Kosekishū Chōsakai); Itō Chūta takes first survey trip to Qing capital Beijing
1902	Sekino Tadashi conducts first survey of art and architecture in Korea
1902–3	Torii sent to southwest China (Sichuan, Yunnan, Hunan, and Hubei; see map 1)
1904	Russo-Japanese War; Tōrii sent to the Ryūkyū Islands
1906	Heijō Palace remains at Nara is registered as a protected site; Tōrii's wife takes a teaching position in Mongolia; Tōrii researches Mongolia
1911	Tōrii conducts first systematic survey of archaeological remains throughout the Korean Peninsula; establishment of the Historic Sites, Famous Places, and Natural Monuments Protection Committee (Shiseki Meisho Tennen kinenbutsu Hozonkai) in Japan
1911	Kyoto Imperial University authorized as excavation unit for historical-era remains

TABLE 5. Chronology of Colonial Archaeological Heritage Management Activities in Korea (1900–1961)

1900	Tokyo Anthropological Society sends Yagi Sōzaburō to Korea
1902	Sekino Tadashi sent by Tokyo University to conduct general survey of shrines, temples, palaces, and burial mounds in North and South Kyŏngsang and Kyŏnggi-do
1905	First Koguryŏ fortress identified by Torii Ryūzō in T'unggou Jian, Manchuria (see map 2)
1906	Imanishi Ryū surveys tombs in Kyŏngju, North Kyŏngsang province (see map 2)
1907	Imanishi discovers Kimhae shell mound in Pusan City
1908	Prince Yi Family Museum opens in Ch'anggyŏngwŏn Palace gardens (Keijō)
1909	Sekino Tadashi, Yatsui Seiichi, and Kuriyama Shun'ichi conducts the first systematic field investigations of old art, architecture, and tombs in all of the provinces; the trio are commissioned by the colonial resident-general Itō Hirobumi and dispatched by the Interior Ministry
1910	Annexation of Korea; the CST (Governor-General Office of Chōsen, or Chōsen Sōtokufu) coordinates all archaeological, historical, and publication projects; Torii is dispatched by the CST to collect archaeological, ethnographic, and historical data from all of the provinces to compile school textbooks; Promulgation of Temples and Shrines Laws (Jisatsu rei)
1912	Koguryŏ painted tombs at Kangsŏ are investigated (see map 2); Sekino Tadashi supervises reconstruction of Sŏkkuram, carried out by the CST Construction Department; Imanishi investigates Han dynasty commandery site Rakurō (Lelang), the Han dynasty commandery earth fortress at T'osŏngni, and the Nianti-xian stele in South P'yŏngan Province; Taifang (Taebang) earth fortress and inscribed bricks from the Lelang period (c. 2nd c. BCE–2nd c. CE) confirmed in Hwanghae Province
1913	Imanishi begins systematic collection of historical documents; first excavations of Koguryŏ tombs in Jian, China
1915	Establishment of the CST Museum at Kyŏngbok Palace grounds in Keijō; Paekche Nungsanni tombs in Puyŏ investigated.
1916	Committee on Korean Antiquities (CSKCIK) formed to coordinate systematic surveys, excavations, and preservation activities; Kuroita Katsumi investigates Hwangnyongsaji and Sach'ŏngwangsa temple remains in Kyŏngju and Songgwangsa Temple in Chŏlla Province; excavations of Koguryŏ tombs in Jian; beginnings of Rakurō (Lelang) tomb excavations in P'yŏngyang; Paekche-era Sŏkch'ondong tombs investigated in Keijō (Seoul)
1918	Reconstruction of Pulguksa begins (taking eight years); Kuroita and Harada Yoshito excavate tombs in Kyŏngju; Mimana (Imna) tombs excavated in Koryŏng, Ch'angnyŏng, and Kimhae
1919	Historic Remains, Famous Places and Natural Monuments Act (Shiseki Meishō Tennen Kinenbutsu) promulgated in Japan
1920	Yangsan Pubu tomb excavations in Kyŏngju; Kimhae shell mound excavations; Ipsilli bronzes discovered

TABLE 5. *(continued)*

1921	Tomb of the Gold Crown (Kŭmkwan-ch'ong) excavations by Hamada Kōsaku and Umehara Sueji; Kyŏngju Museum established
1923	Great Kanto earthquake in Japan results in budget cuts for the CST
1924	Tomb of the Gold Bells (Kŭmnyŏng-ch'ong) in Kyŏngju excavated; Han dynasty tomb of Sŏkkam-dong burials excavated
1926	Sŏbongch'ong excavations in Kyŏngju
1931	Tomb of the Painted Basket (Lelang Ch'aehyŏpch'ong) excavations in P'yŏngyang
1933	Treasures, Ancient Remains, Famous Places, and Natural Monuments (Hōmotsu, koseki, meishō, tennen kinnenbutsu) preservation laws promulgated in Japan and Korea; Kongju Songsanni Paekche burial excavations
1934	Kimhae excavations of stone cists graves and jar burials lead to designation of "Kimhae style" pottery
1938	Naju Pannam-myŏn jar burials of the Paekche period excavated
1939	Puyŏ Museum branch opened
1940	Kongju Museum branch opened; Tomb of the Dancers (Koguryŏ Muyongch'ong) excavations in Jian
1943	The last year the colonial registry of treasures and remains is updated
1961	Establishment of the Office of Cultural Properties (Munhwajae Kwalliguk); colonial inventory inherited by Republic of Korea Office of Cultural Properties totalled 591 items, which were divided into the following five categories: 340 treasures; 101 ancient remains; 3 ancient remains/famous places; 1 famous place; and 146 natural monuments

Source: Fujita 1933, 1027–47.

TABLE 6. Chronology of the Colonial Tourist Industry and the Japan Tourist Bureau (1863–1943)

1893	Founding of Welcome Society of Japan (Kihinkai), a nonprofit organization providing free travel services (information, maps, guidebooks, etc.) for foreigners touring Japan
1895	Sino-Japanese War; the Japan Mail Steamship Company launches its American line and opens shipping lanes to the Liaodong
1904	Completion of Chōsen Government Railways (CGR); opening of Keifu-sen (Keijō-Pusan) line
1912	March 3: the Japan Tourist Bureau (JTB) is established at Tokyo Railway Station; first Bureau-issued pamphlet is printed in English (2,000 copies) and French (3,000 copies); March 3: Chōsen Mail Steamship Company established; November 12: JTB branches established in colonial cities Dalian (South Manchuria Railroad Company, SMR), Taipei (Taiwan Government Railways Station Hotel), and CSTTK Office (Keijō Station)
June 10, 1913	Magazine *Tourist* published as a bimonthly with bilingual (English/Japanese) articles; August 8: establishment of New York Agent of the JTB managed by the Japan Society
January 1914	Publication of English maps of Keijō, Dalian, and Formosa (3,000 copies distributed)
February 1914	JTB agents/branches are set up in thirty locations around the world
March 3–July 1, 1914	JTB sets up temporary headquarters at the Ueno Taishō Exposition; JTB established Yamato Hotel, a chain of railway hotels opens in Dalian, Fengtian, Changch'un, and Port Arthur
October 1914	Keijō Chōsen Hotel opens and is managed by the CSTTK
February 1915	Japan Imperial Government Railways (JIR) "through pass," linking ship and rail services between Manchuria and Chōsen, are sold at Tokyo Train Station (tickets discounted up to 30 percent and valid for six months)
August 1915	Kŭmkangsan Station Hotel opens in Onjŏngni in the Diamond Mountains
April 1915	Guidebooks on Japan printed in Russian
December 20, 1916	JTB sells Osaka Steamship Company steamer tickets
December 1916	JTB travel posters printed
June 1917	JTB sells steamer tickets to Shanghai, Tianjin, Keelung, Dalian, and Qingdao
December 1917	Exponential increase in foreigners coming to Japan due to influx of immigrants fleeing Russian revolution
January 1, 1918	JTB ticket agency established in Harbin on the South Manchuria Railroad line (SMR station)
March 1, 1918	JTB sets up ticket agency in Beijing Wangfujing district
July 1, 1918	Kŭmkangsan Station Hotel opens in Changansa in Diamond Mountains

TABLE 6. *(continued)*

November 1919	JTB sells Shandong Railways tickets
July 15, 1920	Foundation of the Nihon Travel Club, affiliate of the JTB
March 13, 1921	Japanese Emperor Taishō's family departs for around-the-world tour
January 1922	JTB sells ticket coupons for lines bound for Europe and America
1925	JTB and CSTTK open offices in department stores, including Mitsukoshi branches in Tokyo Nihonbashi and Osaka
1926	CSTTK/SMR joint office sets up in Tokyo Shinjuku and Shimonoseki, and stations; Keijō tram service begins; SMR operates twenty-four hours a day; JTB opens branch inside Mitsukoshi Department Store in Keijō
1932	Formation of Chōsen Hotel Company to run former CSTTK hotels located in Keijō Chōsen, Pusan Station, Shinŭiju Station, Kŭmkangsan Onjŏngni, Changanri, Keijō station restaurant, and train restaurants; JTB P'yŏngyang branch opens in Minakai department store
1943	JTB shuts down branches due to the expansion of the Pacific War

Source: Japanese Tourist Bureau (JTB) 1982

NOTES

NOTES TO PREFACE

1   The term "heritage" was first institutionalized in England in 1975, when the old land
    fund was renamed the National Heritage Fund. In 1989, it was used to create the friendly
    sounding name of the Historic Buildings and the Monuments Commission (HBMC), also
    known as English Heritage. The latter is "a body established under the National Heritage
    Act of 1983 with responsibility for the protection and the promotion of public enjoyment
    and understanding of the historic and archaeological heritage" (Walsh 1992, 78). As a
    quasi-autonomous nongovernmental body (quango), the organization receives most of
    its financial support from the government, while, in theory, it is free to run its affairs
    without direct government influence (79). See the *Archaeological Review from Cambridge*
    in their special issue, "Archaeology and the Heritage Industry," for a succinct overview of
    the origins of the heritage industry in England (Baker 1988).

2   The complete text of the convention document adopted by the General Conference of
    the United Nations Educational, Scientific, and Cultural Organization at its seventeenth
    session in Paris on Novermber 16, 1972, can be accessed on the home page of the World
    Heritage Centre under the menu link "About World Heritage," http://whc.unesco.org/en/
    convention text. The document can be downloaded in eight different languages: Arabic,
    Chinese, English, French, Hebrew, Portuguese, Russian, and Spanish. Due to the limited
    scope of this book, we will not be addressing the topic of natural heritage.

3   For an overview of World Heritage Centre's mission, global strategy, list of participat-
    ing countries, listing criteria, activities, and publications, along with an interactive map,
    see the home page of the UNESCO World Heritage Centre. At present, there are listed
    745 cultural monuments, 188 natural, and 29 mixed properties, with many more on the
    nomination list pending approval. The close working relationship between the World
    Heritage Centre and the global tourist industry is made patently evident by the button
    link to TripAdvisor, a popular Internet travel agency featured on the World Heritage
    Centre home page. The travel agency is described in the right sidebar of the center's home
    page as "working in partnership with UNESCO World Heritage Centre to help protect
    and preserve the world's greatest landmarks" (World Heritage Centre,
    http://whc.unesco.org/en/list, accessed December 6, 2012).

4   For information on the National Commission for UNESCO's relations role in the
    designation of World Heritage sites in Korea, I recommend the following publications:
    *UNESCO Regional Workshop for the Preparation of Periodic Reports on the State of
    Conservation of World Cultural Heritage Sites in Asia, July 11–13, 2001* (Kyŏngju, Republic
    of Korea: UNESCO); *Sustainable Development of Traditional Historic Villages, November
    11, 2002,* ICOMOS Symposium Korea, sponsored by the Office of Cultural Properties
    Administration (Seoul: KS Korean National Committee for UNESCO 2001); and Lee
    Kyŏng-hui, 1997, *World Heritage in Korea* (Seoul: Organizing Committee of the Year
    of Cultural Heritage 1997 / Samsung Foundation of Culture). To read about current
    educational, cultural, humanitarian activities and publication programs sponsored by the
    Korean National Commission for UNESCO, see the commission's home page at http://
    www.unesco.or.kr/eng/front/main/, accessed July 24, 2011. This office also publishes the
    long-running *Korea Journal,* which celebrated its fiftieth anniversary in 2011. See http://
    www.ekoreajournal.net/main/index.htm, accessed July 25, 2011.

5   In theory, a registered World Heritage site is subject to annual comprehensive inspections
    in order to receive World Heritage Fund subsidies for conservation. However, in reality,
    according to several knowledgeable members of ICOMOS whom I have consulted, for
    most sites, the funds are too meager to adequately address any of the pressing problems,
    such as structural maintenance or security upgrades, on a comprehensive level (Yi In-
    suk, pers. comm., 2010).

6   For a comprehensive survey of the political, commercial, and colonialist goals of world
    fairs in the nineteenth century, see Peter H. Hoffenberg, *An Empire on Display: English,
    Indian, and Australian Exhibitions from the Crystal Palace to the Great War* (2001). Mak-
    ing extensive use of a wide range of contemporary media sources, pundits, and literary
    luminaries, from journalists to literary authors and government officials, Hoffenberg
    traces the web of complex power and economic relationships linking the many different
    kinds of players—imperial commissioners, greedy merchants, scholars, auction houses,
    advertisers, and arrogant bureaucrats—who were involved in staging, managing, and
    promoting the international spectacles of the day.

7   I want to take this opportunity to thank Professor Takagi Hiroshi for agreeing to par-
    ticipate as a discussant when I presented my paper on the history and politics of heritage
    management in colonial Korea in 2001 at the International Center for Japanese Studies,
    Kyoto.

8   At the same time, ruins as the most visible iconic landmarks have been manipulated by
    politicians, religious leaders, and the media to provide irridescent views of one landmark
    as opposed to another. Not surprisingly, world-famous tourist landmarks such as the
    Buddhist Caves of Bamiyan, Angkor Wat, the Luxor Temple, and the Great Pyramid of
    Giza have been stategically targeted by fanatical religious groups such as the Taliban and
    the Khmer Rouge as sites for violent insurrections, calculated destruction, and hostage
    taking in order to grab media headlines and bring attention to their causes.

9   Although, ideally, the history of heritage management in both countries should be
    addressed in any discussion of nationalism and archaeology, it is at best impractical to

consider the case of the Democratic People's Republic of Korea (DPRK) at this junc-ture. This is because, due to the xenophobic and authoritarian nature of North Korean government, society, and academia, it has been impossible for me to get access to any reliable sources that would give a glimpse into the inner workings of the DPRK's heritage management policies and practices.

10 The fifteen-volume series *Album of Ancient Korean Sites and Relics* published by the Government General of Korea (CST 1915–35) and edited by Tokyo University professor Sekino Tadashi (1868–1935) are still being consulted today by heritage specialists because the series contains the oldest survey records, illustrations, and photographs of architec-tural remains (see figs. 5.1, 5.4, 5.5, and 5.6) before they were moved, taken apart, or rebuilt as tourist destinations (Kang Hyŏn 2006; Yoshii 2007).

11 Murakata and Yamaguchi have also supplemented Fenollosa's archives with annotations cross-referenced to contemporary Meiji records, including imperial museum newsletters, newspaper articles, and art publications, as well as Imperial Household and Education Ministry archives. Finally, Yamaguchi's account also follows Fenollosa's career after his Tokyo departure in 1890, when he departed for America with many boxes of artwork he had amassed on the side. His collections were eventually sold to the Boston Museum of Fine Arts (Murakata 1982b; Yamaguchi 1982).

CHAPTER 1

1 The Ministry of Culture, Sports, and Tourism (http://www.mcst.go.kr) was founded in 1998, the same year the new presidency of Kim Dae-jung was inaugurated. It was formerly called the Ministry of Culture and Sports. The Tourism Office (http://www.visitkorea.or.kr/intro.html) was transferred from the Ministry of Transportation four years earlier.

2 See http://english.cha.go.kr.

3 For example, in a typical year in the 1990s, CHA committee divisions (a division can range from seven to eleven members) made decisions on over 910 different items, includ-ing submissions for the designation of additional national treasures, the recognition of nineteen new public and private museums, and the issuing of permits for the excavation of buried remains (KSMKG 1998b).

4 In the case of pieces newly acquired by national museums that have been unearthed, purchased, or donated, the estimated market prices of archaeological and art objects such as Bronze Age swords, paintings, and ceramics are also recorded in a computer database inventory system.

5 For the latest statistics, news, and information on the Ministry of Culture Heritage Administration (CHA), see their home page at http//cha.go.kr/English. There are special options for researchers, who can conduct either a basic search or a more advance search by province, area, historical period, or category—such as by world heritage or by clas-sificatory genre (painting, document, national treasure, tomb, etc.). For tourist informa-tion, see the "Visit Korea" site operated by the Korean Tourism Organization, or KTO, at http://english.visitkorea.or.kr/enu/index.kto.

6 Yi's educational background and work experience typifies the extremely closed, exclusive circle of culture brokers linked by region, class, kinship, and alumni connections—not unlike their colonial predecessors trained at Japanese imperial universities. Ch'oe Sun-u (1974–84), Han Pyŏng-sam (1985–92), Chŏng Yang-mo (1993–99), Chi Kŏn-gil (2000–2006), and Yi Kŏn-mu were the other prominent museum directors who were also alumni of the Seoul National University Department of Art and Archaeology (KS Pangmulkwan 2009).

7 The 6.5 m tall eight-ton statue of Yi Sun-shin was erected on April 27 1968. Forty years later, around the time the statue was undergoing extensive restorations (December 2010 and February 2011), it again became the source of much debate because the sculptor, who was a former professor at Ewha University named Kim Kyŏng-sŭng (1915–92), was implicated by a committee who has taken upon themselves to root out "Pro-Japanese" collaborators. In several newspaper articles and blogs, journalists pointed out that as a graduate of the prestigious Tokyo Fine Arts School, Kim had been a much celebrated artist in prewar times. When experts were called in to reevaluate the historical and artistic worth of the statue, they found the following aspects of the statue's features as highly "suspicious" (ŭihok) reflecting Kim's pro-Japanese agenda: (1) Admiral Yi is holding the wrong kind of sword, that is of Japanese make, (2) His pose holding the sword in his right hand implies that he is surrendering, (3) His armor resembles more "Chinese" style suit, (4) His facial expression does not resemble other portraits of the admiral. In June 2011, the National Assembly was swept into this debate when they were forced to discuss whether to tear the statue down or replace it with some other version by a different artist (DT News24, www. dtnews24.com, accessed April 1, 2011; *Segye Ilbo*, http://segye.com, accessed December 23, 2010).

8 My account of the arson fire relies on the front-page article of the *Chosŏn Ilbo,* one of Korea's largest circulating dailies (dated February 12, 2008). This detailed ten-page expose reconstructed the timeline of the progress of the fire and the stunned reactions of the citizens the morning after. The journalists conducted interviews with Seoulites, local merchants from Namdaemun Market; the minister of culture, Yu Hong-jun; the president, Yi Myŏng-bak; emergency-response firefighters; and KT Telecom, the telecommunications company that had first reported the to the authorities about ten minutes after it broke out. Journalists also interviewed art and architectural historians on the prospects of reconstruction and about insurance coverage.

9 The CHA offered these reasons for the change: national treasures numbers one and three were changed to their original (*koyu*) names. The colonial-era names for national treasures numbers two and four were found to be clerical errors in the colonial records and missing complete inscriptions. In this list of KSMKG recommendations, the Depository Building of the Haeinsa Tablets was the only item for which the committee found «definite proof» that the Japanese had distorted its historical value (*kach'i waegok*), by referring to its building as *ko* (Japanese *kura* indicating some sort of storage facility). The CHA surmised that the Japanese scholars had overlooked the historical significance of printing eighty thousand wooden sutra blocks as an act of anti-Mongol resistance in

the early thirteenth century. The KSMKG's final recommendation was to remove the reference to "storage" and rename the tablets "Great Sutra Tablets" (Changgyŏng P'anjŏn, KSMKG 1997a, 13–14).

10 At the same time, the rarest of artifacts and remains unearthed in the provinces are often whisked away to the National Museum in Seoul to be exhibited as objects of national pride. Such predatory practices on the part of the National Museum reflect habits left over from the colonial era that still cause much friction and resentment on the part of provincial museum curators, who are left with replicas filling their museum cases at their home institutions.

11 According to Yi Paek-kyu (head of the Yŏngnam Archaeological Society), programs in archaeology and related fields produce more than five hundred graduates annually. However, less than 1 percent find employment in any public or private museum or university position where their skills can be put to use (KS-NCRIP 1997, 135).

12 For example, Pae Ki-dong pointed out that in 1997, only 0.6 percent of the total budget of the KSMKG, the sum of 664,000,000 won, was allocated for the excavations budget. Calculated at the current exchange rate (US$1.00 = 1,100 won), the amount is only about US$500,000 (KS-NRICP 1997, 147).

13 For a personal observer's account of the current conditions and challenges facing archaeologists working on major dam projects in southeast Korea, see Martin Bale's "Archaeological Heritage Management in South Korea." Bale (as a graduate student participating in dam excavations during the late 1990s) writes that Kyŏngnam provincial officials were faced with many construction delays due to public anger directed against designating heritage protection sites for the dam area, an extension of Chinyang Lake. Villagers and farmers who owned land in the inundation zone had delayed land preparation with their protests against government land expropriation because of inadequate compensation schemes (Bale 2008).

14 The numbers were taken from the National Research Institute of Cultural Properties' web archives, where excavations records have been compiled in five-year installments dating from 1946. The total number of digs in the past decade (1996–2005) set a historical record of 3,701. This sum was more than double the grand total of 1,561 excavations accumulated in the five decades between 1946– and 1995. For a complete list of excavated sites since 1946 (listed by year, institution, period, and location), see the KS-NRICP website link menu item, Haksul charyo (http://nricp.go.kr/kr/data/submain03.jsp). A separate list of prewar excavations by date, name, period, and location can also be found on the left-side menu bar.

15 The two most sensational stories of hurried excavations in the postwar era concern the Paekche Tomb of King Munyŏng and the Silla Tomb of the Flying Horse Ch'ŏnmach'ong. These discoveries were unusual in that they were the only tombs in the postwar period found relatively intact, and containing gold jewelry, lacquerware, armor, housewares, and, in the case of the latter, a famous etched leather bridle with a white flying horse. Furthermore, the grave goods and architectural elements of the Paekche tomb (such as glazed bricks, detailed incisions, and reliefs) were remarkably well preserved despite their

age (c. 5–6 centuries). In the case of the Paekche tomb, we will never really know why Kim Wŏl-lyong ordered his underlings to rush excavations of King Munyŏng, which occurred overnight and without proper documentation or any mapping to speak of (Cho Yu-jŏn 1996, 81). Although over the years, archaeologists have speculated that Kim's well-known disdain for the media (and especially for TV reporters) may have incited this folly, this missed opportunity to document the one and only intact Paekche tomb remains one of the more open secrets in the history of Korean archaeology.

16 For a general overview of the small handful of modern-era architectural monuments still standing in the city of Seoul in various states of preservation and reconstruction, see Chŏng Un-hyŏn, *A Survey of Japanese Colonial Remains in Seoul City* (Seoul sinae Ilche yusan tapsagi) (Seoul: Hanul Press, 1995).

17 For an in-depth and incisive ethnographic study on the latest MCST campaign to renovate the architecture of temples (including heating, modern toilets, showers, etc.) to accommodate foreign tourists' tastes and comfort levels, see Uri Kaplan, "Simulations of Monasticism: Temple Stay Program and the Re-Branding of Korean Buddhist Temples" (master's thesis, Graduate School of International Studies, Yonsei University, 2007).

CHAPTER 2

1 The architecture and arrangement of exposition pavilions have historically reflected the economic power, technological prowess, and marketing ingenuity of nations and empires. For example, at the 1887 Adelaide Jubilee International Exhibition, the most popular items were so-called Eastern goods, which included Japanese earthenware, various Indian crafts, vanilla, and *coco de mer* from the Seychelles. The organizers particularly noted that the manager of the profitable Japanese village provided the host commission with a percentage of receipts as his fee (Hoffenberg 2001, 81).

2 Fukuzawa Yukichi's autobiography recounts the following anecdote about Alcock's arrogance and disdain for his hosts. In one of the many offenses against the state, Alcock had rendered an unpardonable insult to the Japanese by riding his horse through the imperial sacred grounds of Shiba (Fukuzawa 1934, 138). Fukuzawa was made aware of this incident while he was in London when he received a copy of a bill sent by a certain member of Parliament who had condemned Alcock for at times acting "as if Japan were a country conquered by military force." The Shiba Park (Shiba-kōen) is now a beloved Tokyo public park, with a prominent temple and mausoleums dedicated to the Tokugawa shoguns.

3 According to the 1934 English edition of Fukuzawa's biography, the group members of 1862 mission toured six different countries—France, England, Holland, Prussia, Russia, and Portugal. They also attended the 1862 Great London Exposition at the Crystal Palace. The mission was made up of forty men, including three envoys; various secretaries, doctors, and interpreters; and the personal attendants of the ambassadors, such as cooks and general servants. As one of the interpreters, Fukuzawa's rank was on par with the officials. He considered himself as one of the lowest of the diplomatic ranks, however, since he was a member of outside feudal clans and not one of the direct retainers of the shogun

(Fukuzawa 1934, 135). The translator of this biography was Eiichi Kiyooka, who was the fifth child of Fukuzawa's third daughter and her husband, Kuninosuke Kiyooka.

4   The dates of Meiji-era cultural events, museums, and world fairs cited in this work have relied on the chronology (see appendix, table 4) included in *Visual Records of the Hundred and Twenty Years of the Tokyo National Museum* (Me de miru hyakunijūnen), published in 1992, that commemorated the one-hundred-and-twenty-year anniversary of the Tokyo National Museum (Tokyo Kokuritsu Hakubutsukan 1992, 107–11).

5   Wish-fulfilling jewels were believed to have the power to regenerate, enrich, and subjugate, and were therefore prized by the imperial family, beginning with the powerful Fujiwara clans of the eighth century (Ruppert 2000, 168).

6   The Vienna International Exhibition staged along the shores of the Danube lasted six months, from May 1 to November 2, and recorded a total number of 7,222,500 visitors (Tokyo Kokuritsu Hakubutsukan 1992, 14–22).

7   The founders A. H. L. F. Pitt-Rivers (1827–1900), and George Peabody (1795–1869) and Frederick Ward Putnam (1839–1915), respectively, were self-made men who were able to amass substantial collections due to a potent combination of high social status, military connections, and deep pockets (Chapman 1988; Hinsley 1988). The tendency in academia then was to hire the donors as museum directors, since their expert knowledge of foreign cultures, languages, customs, and suppliers' networks qualified them to be on the boards of preservations trusts, learned societies, and research institutes (Reid 2002; Stocking 1985, 1988, 1991).

8   Von Siebold's stature as a doctor and scientist is now memorialized at the Von Siebold Dutch Studies (Dejima Rankan) Museum located inside the Dutch-themed Huis Ten Bosch park in Nagasaki. See http://english.huistenbosch.co.jp.

9   Vos concludes that von Siebold in fact did not quite succeed in his classificatory goal, since the structural framework governing his collection in Leiden was in his mind, arranged for comparative purposes only since he was not a supporter of the idea of evolutionism, which was just coming into vogue at the time. Therefore he included only a small number of non-Japanese (Ainu, Ryūkyū, and Korean) objects to his collections (Vos 2001, 47).

10 A stele was erected in 1913 marking the most likely location of the ancient country (*kuni*) of Chikuzen. The gold seal was registered as a national treasure in 1954. It is not an exageration to state that the historical debates surrounding the origins and territorial extent of the Yamato state have preoccupied the imagination of both scholars and laymen for over two centuries (Barnes 1988, 4–15; Farris 1998). For a summary of the circumstances of the discovery, see *Excavating Japan* (Nihon no hakkutsu; Saitō 1982, 32–58). For a comprehensive discussion documenting the archaeological evidence of the controversies surrounding the legendary Queen Himiko as the possible recipient of the seal, see *Himiko and Japan's Elusive Chiefdom in Yamatai: Archaeology, Myth, and History* (Kidder 2007).

11 The use of the word "zenpō-kōen" is attributed to Gamō Kumpei (1708–1813) to describe a keyholed burial shaped mounds, the largest burial types, which peaked during the Kofun period (300–600 ce). The term he coined has survived to the present and has been incor-

porated into the archaeological vocabulary (Ikawa-Smith 1982, 291). These tomb remains were also the most likely places to dig up desirable objects ranging from jade beads (*magatama*), bronze weapons, mirrors, and in some cases, pottery figurines (*haniwa*).

12 These catalogues sometimes referred to their comprehensive assemblages as "Ten Kinds of Antiquities," or *Shukō jisshū,* which were classified into bell inscriptions, tombs inscriptions, weapons, copperware, musical instruments, framed pictures, writing materials, seals, books, and paintings (Kinoshita 2001, 130). Many of Arai's eighteenth-century classificatory schemes can still be found in art-historical terms used for portraits, stationary, masterpieces (*meika*), paper, stele inscriptions, seals, bronze bells (*dōtaku*), bronze weapons, armor, horse equipment, bows, banners, swords, musical instruments, and old roof tiles.

13 The particular fascination with the various forms, functions, inscriptions, and designs of bronze ritual vessels has been well documented in archaeological and textual records (e.g., oracle bones and bronze inscriptions) as early as the second millennium ce and reached its peak during early Song dynastic times in thirteenth-century China. Throughout, across China, Korea, and Japan, catalogues were published featuring artifacts from both imperial and individual collections. Inscriptions were especially prized and scrutinized if they could reveal genealogical information so as to date the objects in a collection and trace the collection's origins. Edo antiquarians also combined profile drawings of an artifact, facsimiles of any inscriptions, and written descriptions of an object's physical appearance and dimensions (Uchida Yoshiaki 2004). Despite the Song scholars' contributions and Edo-period antiquarians' efforts to classify Chinese Bronze Age ritual vessels, Harvard professor and archaeologist Chang Kwang-chih (1931–2000) has emphasized that the main intellectual pursuit of these antiquarians was to "fill in the lacunae in the classics and commentaries and to correct the errors of classical scholars of the past," and hence cannot be regarded as archaeological in nature in the modern sense of the word (Chang 1980, 8–9).

14 Although much has been written about *Japonisme* in the late nineteenth century, we also have to bear in mind here that it was only one fad among the many Victorian collecting crazes following the fair fever that took hold of consumers in the capitals of Europe between the 1860s and the 1890s (Briggs 1989). For example, records of the holdings of the best-known Parisian collectors between 1860–1925 indicate that, in virtually all cases, Japanese objects formed only one part of the collections (Put 2000, 15). By the early twentieth century, the sheer outflow of material coming from China—both looted and traded curios—meant that Chinese objects would eventually come to dominate the collections of prominent Asian art dealers in the United States, such as that of the Yamanaka Brothers, who boasted branches in New York and Boston (American Art Association 1921 US Government Alien Property Custodian 1943). The trend continues today, reflecting the four-hundred-year-old Western fascination with chinoiserie and imagined visions of mystical Cathay (Honour 1961).

15 See the Boston Museum of Fine Arts' home page link to their permanent collections, at (http://www.mfa.org/collections/).

16 According to contemporary newspaper sources, the music of Bach, Mozart, Chausson, and Schumann was provided by the Boston Symphony Orchestra, accompanied by singers from the Boston Cecilia Company. As the highlight of the social events attended by the cream of Boston High Society, the opening created quite a sensation in Gardner's time (Thrasher 1984, 12–7). To this day, the chamber music concert tradition lives on for subscribing members and tourists (see http://www.gardnermuseum.org).

17 According to Japanese historian Helen Hardacre, at the time of Meiji restoration in 1868, it has been estimated that there were 74,642 shrines and 87,558 temples in Japan (Hardacre 1989, 14). Hardacre has also observed that, following the 1868 edict, the Shintō priesthood targeted the Buddhist establishment in "a ferocious, vindictive destruction of Buddhist priests who were defrocked, lands confiscated, statuary and ritual implements melted down for cannons" (28).

18 As in Christian Europe, relics were objects of patronage and contention for millennia. According to Japanese historian Brian Ruppert, the dominant motif in medieval Buddhist tales is that of the elaborate gift giving of the Buddha during his previous lives as a bodhisattva, or being striving toward full enlightenment. Two features of the tales originating mainly from ancient India and China are integrally related to the cult of relics. One is the theme of the extreme, often corporeal nature of the gifts of the bodhisattva to sentient beings. The other is the fact that in many tales the giver is an incarnation of the Buddha, a ruler or prince who enters the bodhisattva path and proceeds to make elaborate offerings on behalf of other sentient beings (Ruppert 2000, 17–18). Ruppert argues that in the mid-Heian period, clerics, aristocrats, and the imperial family believed that worshipping and enclaving Buddhist relics would generate the body of the emperor as well as enrich the state and realm. This belief was reflected in the development of the practice of inventorying relics, which crystallized the transformation of relics into treasures (103).

19 The broad outline of the Japanese foundation myth taught in school textbooks emphasized that, racially, all Japanese, by virtue of their blood ties, belonged to one large extended unified family and thus belonged to the same imperial blood lineage (kettō; Skya 1994, 55–64). It is beyond the scope of this book to go into the vast literature and philosophical ramifications of the meaning of kokutai, translated over the years variously as "national polity," "national essence," and "body politic." Refer to Walter Skya's dissertation, "Emperor Ideology: The Debate over State and Sovereignty in Modern Japan" regarding the complex constitutional legal debates waged among Meiji thinkers in the 1880s and 1890s.

20 According to Walter Edwards of the Nara National Research Institute of Cultural Properties), the majority of archaeologists working today dispute the veracity of this myth and claim that none of the "imperial tombs" from the three generations prior to Emperor Jimmu can be considered real tombs on archaeological grounds, since they more resemble natural features consisting of two mountain tops and a cave (Edwards 2005, 41).

21 Meiji-era edicts mentioned in the text are listed in the appendix section of the second volume of A Hundred-Year History of the Tokyo National Museum (Tokyo Kokuritsu Hakubutsukan 1976, 2, 257–69).

22 The current Jimmu tomb dates to 1863, when the late Tokugawa government initiated repairs at Misanzai at Nara ken Kashihara shi Ōkubo machi (Suzuki and Takagi 2002). For information provided by the Imperial Household Ministry, see website at http://www.kunaicho.go.jp/ryobo/guide/001/index.html (accessed December 16, 2012). jnto.go.jp/eng/location/rtg/pdf/pg-507.pdf, accessed January 16, 2008.

23 Please see Hiroshi Takagi's book, *A Study of Modern Japanese Imperial Cultural Policies* (Kindai tennōsei no bunkashiteki kenkyū), table 10, for a complete list of the 1877 itinerary of the imperial pilgrimage in Kyoto and Nara (Takagi Hiroshi 2000, 262).

24 For a comprehensive look at the more elaborately choreographed 2,600th anniversary celebrations of the founding of the Japanese nation engineered by government institutions, the media, and, by then, an empire-wide travel industry in the 1940s, see Ken Ruoff's book, *Imperial Japan at Its Zenith: The Wartime Celebration of the Emperor's 2,600th Anniversary* (Ruoff 2010).

25 The compensation system is usually referred today as a "finder's fee." The laws stipulated that jades or coins excavated from temples, shrines, and *kofun*, or any object with legendary or oral traditions associated with the find, must be returned to the local office or to its original owner. The local official was entrusted with deciding the object's historical relevance, its monetary worth, and the level of craftsmanship; it was then required to be turned over to the museum staff (Tokyo Kokuritsu Hakubutsukan 1976, 2:257).

26 A lifelong subscription cost for regular members was five yen (a large sum at that time)—returned upon death or dropped membership. A single report cost five *sen* when subscribed by mail. The committee also accepted donations from the honorary members. One had to include one's clan genealogy when applying for membership (Teikoku Kosekishū Chōsakai 1902, 5–6). Despite these daunting caveats, which are unimaginable by today's standards, many were eager to sign on as members of this illustrious "learned society," which recruited two thousand members in a very short time.

27 The society also accepted manuscript submissions and reports related to burials, stele inscriptions, old fortresses, and battle sites. All reports were to be accompanied by drawings, site measurements, or old illustrations and photographs (Teikoku Kosekishū Chōsakai 1903, 68).

28 The reports had to include supporting photographs and illustrations (*mosha*), submitted to the head office of the society and the Imperial Household Agency, as stated in buried properties laws. In the case of famous officials, a memorial stele was to be erected to ward off destruction, in consultation with the local officials. If there were living descendents of the dead official in question, they were required to ask for state permission to carry out repairs or erect wooden signposts (Teikoku Kosekishū Chōsakai 1900, 2)

29 In the 1880s, Miyake, who was an early convert to Darwinian evolutionism (Miyake 1890), was the pioneering leader of the new school of empirical historical research. Consequently, he advocated that legends and myths must be strictly separated from objectively deduced facts based on material proof in the writing of the nation's past (Naoki 1980, 8; Teshigawara 1995, 73–87). Although he himself served as a hired specialist for the committee, he was the only one who spoke out against the corrupt bureaucratic practices in

the disbursment process of state historic preservation funds, which inevitably favored well-connected politicians and prominent clan leaders (Miyake 1903). After Miyake was forced to leave Tokyo University, he taught at Waseda University. For a compilation of Miyake's more influential articles on Japanese prehistory, see volume 1 of *Anthology of Japanese Archaeology,* edited by Saitō Tadashi (Saitō 1974).

CHAPTER 3

1 My discussion here relies on the archives of Ernest F. Fenollosa, now part of his alma mater, Harvard University's Houghton Library collections. See http://oasis.lib.harvard. edu/oasis/deliver/advancedsearch?_collection=oasis. The most recently boxed materials date to 1978, the year Ōtsu City celebrated Fenollosa's centennial with full Buddhist memorial rites at his burial site in Miitera Temple. Dates for Fenollosa are taken from Seichii Yamaguchi's annotated translations from his anthology, *Ernest Fenollosa: A Life Devoted to the Advocacy of Japanese Culture* (Yamaguchi 1982).

2 Fenollosa's grave is now marked by a small pagoda, flanked to the left by two smaller graves belonging to his closest friends: William Sturgis Bigelow (1850–1926), who accompanied him on several of his Kinai surveys in the early 1880s, and James Woods (1844–1935), another scion of an old Boston family who taught Greek philosophy and was one of the earliest researchers to pioneer the study of Indian yoga philosophy in America. According to the information sheet provided at the temple entrance when I visited there in September 2004, these three friends requested to be buried at the same temple, where they had all converted to Buddhism (Miitera Temple or Hōmyoin, n.d.).

3 For more discussion on the many problems of importing Western technology, architectural design, construction methods, and tools to Meiji Japan, please see William Coaldrake, "Western Technology Transfer and the Japanese Architectural Heritage in the Late Nineteenth Century" (Coaldrake 1994).

4 Fenollosa, like many of his contemporaries, could not escape his own feelings of superiority or his cultural biases as a Western-educated intellectual who viewed Japan as a backward and declining civilization. I will cite only one comment denigrating Japan and its people that can be found in many of his notes to the lectures he delivered in America. His 1891 article, "My Position in America," written May 1, 1891, reads, "I must remember that, however much I sympathize with the civilization of the East, I am in this incarnation a man of Western Races, and bound to my development of Western Civilization. . . . I must cast my desire to compete with European authorities, as a great scholar in the history of Japanese arts. . . . But, in my mission as a prophet and reformer, I must keep clear of politics and parties and rely on reason. I must utilize my power of grasping a subject philosophically. To be truly American, I must learn to seize the peculiar elements of excellence which lie in the American character and intellect, I ought to be the leader of the people. . . . But it is [in] the direction of Fine Art that my most important practical work must be done—I ought to make myself the writer on Fine Art in modern times. I must always be more of a writer than a practitioner or an actual

educator. In practical matters, my function should be that of a critic" (Fenollosa 1891).

5   As his impassioned arguments show, Fenollosa took great advantage of his position as an outsider and hired gun at Tokyo University, for he was quite bold in insisting that the acceleration of the decay and destruction of artistic traditions was partly due to the short-sighted government officials, who, lacking any grand vision for the future long-term viability of the arts, were keen only on staging expositions for quick profit-making schemes.

6   The mere fact that his 1912 book, *Epochs*, remains in print a century later demonstrates that Fenollosa, who knew how to exploit the power of the media, was a savvy self-promoter, for he always made sure to contact local newspapers in advance of his comings and goings. As early as 1881, major city dailies—from Osaka's *Asahi Shinbun* to Tokyo's *Jiji Shinbun* and *Nichinichi Shinpō* to Kyoto's *Shūkai Tenbō*—were carrying news of Fenollosa (Yamaguchi 1982, 1:2–3). Of course, as his name and celebrity status as art consultant to the rich and famous spread, Fenollosa was being introduced to more collectors and dealers.

7   My discussion here relies on the eight-volume anthology titled *Okakura zenshū*, a monumental series celebrating his colorful life, wide ranging interests, and towering status as the father of Japanese art history. The volumes reprinted the vast body of his publications, lecture notes, interviews, diaries, unpublished manuscripts, miscellaneous essays, and correspondences. The publication committee also made an effort to include his personal letters, course syllabi and original class handouts retrieved by his former students (Okakura 1980).

8   Christine Guth and Fred Notehelfer have noted that Okakura, conscious of his standing as a media darling (not unlike many celebrities today), was actively engaged in self-promotion and image branding (Guth 2000; Notehelfer 1990). For example, he would deliberately pose for photographers wearing custom-made long flowing Chinese robes and commute to campus on horseback as part of a carefully cultivated public persona. Guth writes that his style of "cross-cultural" dressing was a sartorial attempt to project himself as an enlightened modern sage who was born to lead the new generation of young minds to modernity. She concludes that such self-mythologizing stunts indicate that Okakura had already understood the potential of photography as an instrument of self-fashioning (Guth 2000, 607–10).

9   Prewar Japanese historians calculated the dates of the conquest genealogy of Japan's imperial lineage based on the legendary records of the eighth-century text of the *Chronicles of Japan* (Nihon Shoki). From this text, they inferred that a legendary empress named Jingū established the colony of Mimana, or Nihonfu, in the southern part of Korea around 201 ce. For a review of century-old debates, competing periodization schemes, and prewar identity politics surrounding the location of the conquest colony, see Saeki Arikiyo, *King Kwanggaet'o Stele* (Kōkakaido ōhi); Takeda Yukio, "Studies on the King Kwanggae-t'o Inscription and Their Basis"; and Boleslaw Szczesniak, "Some Revisions of the Ancient Japanese Chronology Ōjin Tennō Period." After more than a century of exhaustive studies, to this day, the exact nature and extent of the Wa's territorial empire,

spanning Japan, Korea and Manchuria, remain highly controversial, since the veracity of its conquest campaigns rely heavily on the authenticity of a handful of characters taken from faded rubbings of the stele (dated 414 ce) discovered by a Japanese soldier in Jian in 1883 (see map 2).

10 The dates for the introduction of Confucianism and Buddhism are from Okakura's chronology chart, published in the appendix of *The Awakening of Japan* (Okakura 1945, 224–25). For a complete list of emperors' era names and dates, of more recent vintage, see Yamasaki Shigehisa, *Chronological Table of Japanese Art* (1981, 870–85). Archaeologists and historians affiliated with the Nara Institute of Cultural Properties are constantly recalibrating established chronologies based on newly excavated wooden strips (*mokkan*) as well as tree-dating sequences from architectural foundations unearthed in reports of ongoing excavations of palaces, temples, and other physical remains. For the latest statistics and information, see the home page of the Nara Institute of Cultural Properties at http://www.nabunken.go.jp/research/maibun01.html.

11 For an account of Sekino's 1896 Nara surveys, written by an architect, see the article "The Development of Japan's Architecture" (Nihon kenchiku engeki kaisetsu), reprinted in the appendix in Fujii et al. (2005, 401–6). The article was originally published in the Nara prefectural journal *Naraken kyōiku zasshi*, vol. 33, on December 31, 1897. The bulk of these original architectural survey records are now housed at Sekino's alma mater, the Architecture Department of the University of Tokyo. Professors Fujii Keisuke and Saotome Masahirō, an architectural historian and a Korean historian, respectively, have collaborated for more than a decade on arranging the vast archives of Sekino. They also received donations from Sekino's son, Takeshi Sekino (1915–2003), who was an esteemed professor of Chinese archaeology and ancient history at the same university.

12 According to Suzanne Marchand, the adoption of mechanical reproduction by Adolf Michaelis (1835–1910) and Adolf Furtwängler (1853–1907), the two German pioneers in the fields of archaeology and art history, allowed the sort of "objective" comparison of details upon which formalist studies rested. Following their lead, by 1908, the camera came to substitute the draftsmen pen, and modern archaeology took a decisive turn toward stylistic analysis and evolution (Marchand 1996, 107).

13 The souvenir photography trade was pioneered by well-traveled photographers such as Felice Beato (1825–1904) and Baron von Stillfried (1839–1911), who inherited Beato's original archives by buying out Beato's studio in the port of Yokohama in the 1860s. Both are now remembered in the annals of early Japanese photography for their many picturesque views of Japan's landscapes, from Mount Fuji to the temples in Kamakura and Nagasaki (Banta and Taylor 1988; Yokohama Kaikō Shiryokan 1987).

14 Itō Chūta was a pioneering architectural historian, professor of engineering, and mentor to Sekino at Tokyo Imperial University. In 1942, the editorial board of the Committee on Historical Sites, Famous Places, and Natural Monuments published a lengthy interview with Itō, which was included in a special issue commemorating the fifty-year anniversary of the promulgation of the national treasures laws of 1897 (Shiseki Meishō Tennen Kinenbutsu Hozonkai 1942).

CHAPTER 4

1 In addition to the Koro-pok-guru, foreign racial scientists speculated on a wide variety and
   improbable list of populations, gleaned from historical records as well as living ones, including Malays, Polynesians, Mongols, Manchus, Indonesians, Hittites, Aryans, Babylonians,
   Silla, and Han Chinese (Kudō 1979).

2 Two commemorative stones dedicated to Edward Morse's achievements were erected
   by Tokyo University students at the site of Ōmori in the 1930s. Ōmori was designated a
   national historical remain (*shiseki*) in 1950 (Saitō 1982, 60).

3 Morse based on his observations of bone fragments recovered from ōmori made the shock-
   ing observation that the pre-Ainu inhabitants may have been cannibals (Ikawa-Smith 1995,
   46). Although his assertion caused a major sensation at that time, it has since been discred-
   ited (Kudō 1979, 61; Hudson 1999).

4 The team of close friends first made news in 1884 when they uncovered a large intact
   Yayoi jar literally in their backyard in Bunkyō Ward. Yayoi was named after the residential
   neighborhood situated between the Imperial Tokyo University Hongō campus and the Ueno
   Imperial Museum, which was then still under construction. Unfortunately, the period of academic freedom for field archaeologists was to last only fifteen years, from around 1884 to the
   late 1890s, before buried properties laws were enforced by the Imperial Household Agency
   in the late 1890s (Saitō 1982, 89–113; Teshigawara 1995, 55–72). Consequently, the Yayoi
   discoveries made by the Tokyo University students occupy a landmark status in the annals
   of Japanese archaeology. When I visited the Bunkyō Ward Historical Museum in February
   2004, Tsuboi and his teammates were featured prominently in the exhibition commemorating the hundred and twenty years since the discovery of Yayoi Japan.

5 The membership monthly dues were 15 sen, 30 sen, and 50 sen, depending on the type of
   subscription and whether you received the journal or not. The members' meetings were held
   every second Sunday morning in the Geology department starting at 8 am with discussions
   starting at 9 am. The subscription dues were sent to their office at the Tokyo University
   campus. Unlike the contemporary Preservation Committee on Ancient Remains (*Kosekishū
   Chōsa Iinkai*), the very aristocratic preservation society mentioned earlier, this society
   emphasized that it was "open to all men of science and forward looking fields" including
   professors, students, medical students, high school and trade schools' teachers, military officers, merchants, *Gakushūin* university administrators, monks, and middle-school students
   (Matsumura 1934, 422).

6 By the mid-nineteenth century, aboriginal displays at museums and world fairs were
   designed for educational as well as decorative purposes, to enlighten visitors eager to see
   and be entertained by newly discovered peoples as "marvelous attractions" (Maxwell 1999).
   The most popular among the public proved to be dioramas and live exhibits of noble savages, which played a role in instilling a newfound sense of "travel and adventure." The commissioners' main goal in staging these ethnographic tableaus was profit making—getting the
   public interested in buying and tasting exotic products from around the world. The secondary purpose was to lure wealthy businessmen to invest in colonial enterprises (Hoffenberger
   2001, 146–47).

7   The biographies of Torii all mention how his linguistic skills, lab and museum training, and years of living among his field subjects gave him the broad "cultural comparative" perspective necessary to cross-reference earlier Russian ethnographic sources with the newly discovered archaeological materials (Torii 1953, 1976; Shiratori and Yawata 1978; Sasaki 1993).

CHAPTER 5

1   The vast body of archaeological data including rubbings, site maps, lists of scenic resources, historical documents, and ethnographic reports from Korea, Manchuria and Siberia are housed at several former imperial research institutions and universities in Japan. The most comprehensive collections are at the Tōyō Bunko (http://www.toyo-bunko.or.jp), the Oriental Institute at the Tokyo University (http://www.ioc.u-Tokyo.ac.jp/~library/index_e.html), and Kyoto University Archaeology Department Library. Short treatises of major works by the founding historians of the field of *Mansenshi* (Manchuria-Korean) penned by Shiratori Kurakichi (1970, 1986), Ikeuchi Hiroshi (1951), etc., were excerpted in the journal series, *Memoirs of the Research Department of the Tōyō Bunko*. Please see John Young, *The Research Activities of the South Manchuria Railroad Company (1907–1945): A History and Bibliography"* for a history of the SMR as a research institute.

2   According to journalist Yi Ku-yŏl's book *The Tortuous History of Korea's Cultural Relics*, (Hanguk munhwajae sunansa), Itō supposedly instructed his underlings to hire grave looters in Kaesŏng to dig up the royal tombs of Koryŏ rulers. Yi believed that other colonialists stationed in Korea began to buy up celadon pieces because they made valuable gifts and bribes for the CST and the Imperial Household Agency (Yi Ku-yŏl 1996, 64–65).

3   The title "dream team" (composed of an architect, an artist, and an engineer, respectively) was coined by Arimitsu Kyōichi (1907–2011), the last director of the GGC Chōsen Sōtokufu Museum and a former professor at Kyoto University (Mokuyō Club 2003, 3–30).

4   The first Koguryŏ find to cause a major sensation in the media began when rubbings of the Kwanggaet'o Wang stele, found near Ji'an in Jilin, China, were taken by a soldier and brought back to Japan in 1884 (see map 2). The inscriptions, which were considered to be the earliest authenticated textual records describing the exploits of the ancient Japanese Wa kingdom's conquests, marked a major turning point in Japanese historiography in the late nineteenth and early twentieth century (Saeki 1974). Beginning with scholars Shiratori Kurakichi and Ikeuchi Hiroshi, the stele's present location bordering Korea and China was interpreted as affirming that the Japanese military victories in the Russo-Japanese War fought in the same regions meant that they were predestined to return to their long-lost homelands in Manchuria (Shiratori 1986, 453–54; Pai 2000, 27). See map 2 and tables 4 and 5 for the locations and chronology of major Japanese archaeological discoveries.

5   For example, in figure 5.1, Sekino is shown sketching and recording the measurements (such as height, width, and preservation state) of his find—in this case, of the Three King-

dom–era Ch'angnyŏngs Pagoda in the region which is now part of Kyŏngnam Province (Ch'angnyŏng ŭp Naemyŏng).

6 The removal of Kwanghwa-mun Gate to make room for the building of a colossal new GGC headquarters on the former Yi dynasty Kyŏngbok Palace grounds was the source of much controversy among preservationists and connoisseurs, such as Yanagi Sōetsu (1889–1961), who was living in Korea at the time. In 1922, Yanagi made an urgent plea to the CST to refrain from the "senseless" destruction of one of Korea's oldest pieces of architecture (Yanagi 1922, 552). For a discussion of colonial power relations and the politics of urban planning in the transformation of the Yi dynasty capital of Hwangsŏng (Old Seoul) into a modern colonial metropole, see Todd Henry, "Sanitizing Empire: Japanese Articulations of Korean Otherness and the Construction of Early Colonial Seoul, 1905–19" and "Re-spatializing Chosŏn's Royal Capital: The Politics of Japanese Urban Reforms in Early Colonial Seoul, 1905–1919" (Henry 2005, 2008). For postcolonial debates surrounding the demolition of the CST building by former president Kim Yŏng-sam in March 1995, see Kim Yong-sam (no relation to the president), (*Though the Building Is Gone, History Remains* (Kŏnmul ŭn sarajyŏdo yŏksa nŭn namnŭnda, 1995); Jin Jŏng-hŏn, "Demolishing Colony: The Demolition of the Old Government-General Building of Chosŏn" (2008); and Hyung Il Pai, *Constructing "Korean Origins,"* 237–45.

7 For insights into the relationships between colonialism, historiography, and Kuroita's preservation agenda, see Kuroita Hakushi Kinenkai, *The Study and Preservation of Ancient Culture* (Kobunka to hozon to kenkyū, 1953), and Yi Sŏng-si's *Manufactured Antiquity* (Mandurŏjin kodae, 2002) and *Colonialism and Modern Japanese Historiography* (Koroniarizumu to kindai rekishigaku, 2004).

8 Notations in parentheses following colonial listings are ranking numbers according to the 1996 Registry of National Properties (KSMKG 1996a).

9 It was reregistered as South Korea's national treasure (*Kukpo*) no. 2 on December 20, 1962. The significance of this monument today is that its location has given its name to Pagoda Park (T'apkol Kongwŏn, fig. 5.3), the site of the reading of the Declaration of Independence that sparked the largest anti-Japanese uprising on March 1, 1919. The most recognizable Yi dynasty relic on this list would be Koseki no. 3 (Pomul No. 2), the Posin'gak Bell, dated to the thirteenth year of King Sejo's reign (1467). The ringing of this bell by the mayor of Seoul ushering the New Year is broadcasted live and is a popular tourist destination on New Year's Eve.

10 The substantial monetary investments lavished on the two ruins demonstrate the significance of Kyŏngju as the closest cultural destination for Japanese tourists arriving from the port of Pusan. At the time, the funds spent on restoring the two monuments were on par with the restoration budgets for Nara's Tōdaiji Temple (Kang Hyŏn 2006; Kim Hyŏnsuk 2007). Here, I want to thank professor Yoshii Hideo of Kyoto University and Shimizu Shigeatsu of the Nara Institute of Cultural Properties for alerting me to the transfer to Korea of preservation technologies and conservation methods that were carried out by seasoned carpenters dispatched from Nara (Nabunken 2006; Shimizu 2003; Yoshii 2007). The original glass-plate photographs taken of the reconstruction project that were once

owned by Fujita Ryōsaku, the former director of the Sōtokufu Museum, were featured in a 2007 exhibition at the Sŏngyunkwan University Museum. See Kim T'ae-sik et al., *Exhibition Catalogue of the Glass-Plate Photographic Archives of Silla Remains in Kyŏngju* (Kyŏngju Silla yujŏk ŭi ŏche wa onŭl: Sŏkkuram, Pulguksa, Namsan).

11   In addition, the CST also awarded substantial funds for the restorations of other temples, including Pusŏksa (1916–28), Kŭmsansa (1919–28), Chŏndŭngsa (1914–15), and Changansa (1926–30; Fujita 1933).

12   The majority of tombs from the Han dynasty, the Three Kingdoms, and Koryŏ times that were identified by Sekino and the CSKCIK all showed signs of break-ins and extensive looting, since by 1910, burial pottery, especially celadon, were being trafficked to Japan.

13   In 1918, due to their media exposure, Oba's life-size reproductions of Koguryŏ's spectacular tomb frescoes were commissioned for an art exhibition held at Tokyo University, where the originals are now part of the Architecture department collections (Fujii et al. 2005, 239). Oba, because of his many artistic and technological breakthroughs documenting more than three decades of *kofun* excavations in the Korean peninsula, was eventually hired as a professor at the Tokyo School of Fine Arts. In 1949, he was awarded a prize from the Japan Art Academy (Nihon Geijutsu In) for his lifetime achievements (Takahashi 2003).

14   I want to thank the curatorial staff and Professor Yoshii Hideo for allowing me to photograph their collections at the Kyoto University Museum in 2005.

15   Hamada's edition went through several reprints well into the 1960s. One of my informants was Professor Uno Takao, a graduate of Kyoto University's prestigious archaeology program, one of Japan's leading specialists of Kofun archaeology, and a faculty member at the International Center for Japanese Studies. He told me that, as late as the 1970s, when he was an undergraduate, his professors were still assigning Hamada's fifty-year-old publications as class readings (Uno Takao pers. comm., 2001).

CHAPTER 6

1   His travel diary was serialized in the *Asahi*. The English edition of his travelogue, which was titled *Travels in Manchuria and Korea* (Mankan tokoro dokoro), translated and annotated by Inger Sigrun Brodey and Sammy I. Tsunematsu, is titled, "Rediscovering Natsume Sōseki: Celebrating the Centenary of Sōseki's Arrival in England, 1900–02" (Sōseki 2000).

2   This overview of the land was a long-established formula for empire guide books, which were designed so that the would-be colonialist arriving on the shores of the empire would be able to read in one glance the living conditions and judge the level of civilization as favorable or not.

3   By 1929, there were three private electric tramway companies operating thirty miles of rail in Seoul (CST 1929a, 43). For the through passengers bound for Manchuria and China, one could transfer from the CSTTK to the SMR lines bound for Mukden (now Shenyang) via the northern Yalu border town of Antung. From there, one could go

straight on to Vladivostok, where one could catch the Trans-Siberian railways bound for Moscow and Paris. If one wanted to go west to China, one could transfer to the Peking line operated by the East China Railways (see map 3).

4 For example, for the year 1922, the total population of Korea is given as 17,626,761. Japanese numbered 386,493, and Koreans 17,288,319. Foreigners (including Chinese) totaled 32,219 (CSTTK 1923, 1).

5 By the turn of the century, many commercial photographic studios located near railroad stations, ports, and city centers in Pusan, Inch'ŏn, and Seoul were vying to record commemorative events, wars, and archaeological ruins in order to sell postcards for the tourist trade (Ch'oe In-jin 1999; Chŏng Chin-guk 1999).

6 Despite the hundreds and thousands of train schedules, pamphlets, and guide books estimated to have been distributed at major piers, train stations, and department stores throughout the empire, only a minute fraction survive today. This is because, by its nature, tourist literature is a disposable consumer item and in most cases was thrown out after the trip. Consequently, the items most likely to have been preserved at research libraries, personal collections, and museum archives tend to be sturdy pocket-sized guidebooks or caches of attractive postcards printed by advertisers and sponsors that were collected as souvenirs of trips and on shopping ventures, as well as favorite name-brand products (Hayashi Hiroki 2004a, 2004b).

7 For a comprehensive overview of CST regulations governing the sex trade—including red-light district zoning laws, the registration of prostitutes by type and business category (*kisaeng* houses, licensed brothels, restaurants, bars, streetwalkers, etc.), and the monitoring of STD infection rates—see Kang Chŏng-suk, "The Sex Industry and the State Registration of Prostitutes during the End of the Taehan Empire and Early Colonial Era" (Taehan Cheguk, Ilche ch'ogi Seoul ui maech'unŏp kwa kongch'ang chedo ŭi toip, 1998).

CONCLUSION

1 A total of 372 items out of the 6,181 objects that were donated by the Tokyo Anthropological Laboratory originated with Torii's original collections (*Torii Ryūzō shū hyobon*). Their numbers by geographic area (in descending order) are as follows: Taiwan (94), Amur (69), Kuriles (68), Sakhalin (58), northeast China and Mongolia (57), southwest China (25), and the Korean Peninsula (1). There is only one item from Korea, since Torii's collections were left behind at the CST museum established in 1915. See Sasaki 1993, 71–111.

2 In 1997, to commemorate the centennial anniversary of the Preservation of Ancient Shrines and Temples Laws enacted in 1897, the Kudara Kannon statue (see fig. 3.2) was sent to the Louvre. Cosponsored by the Japan-France Exchange of Artistic Treasures Exhibition and the *Asahi* newspaper, this unprecedented event was preceded by the costliest high-tech restoration project in the history of art conservation (Takada 1997).

3 The remaking of Nara as a "national cultural destination" in the popular imagination is often attributed to the writer Watsuji Tetsujirō (1889–1960). His best-selling travelogue, "My Pilgrimage to Old Temples" (Koji Junrei), first published in 1919, has since inspired

millions of Japanese to trek to Nara. The discourse on Japanese origins and civilization (*bunmeiron*) therefore owes much to the late Taishō-era romantism, orientalism, and philhellenism advocated by intelligentsia and artists who wanted to relive the spiritual essence of ancient Japan by retracing the footsteps of their nomadic ancestors.

4 The Korea (South) Munhwajae Kwalliguk (KSMKG) records accounted for the following: (1) 250 individual beads from necklaces and jewelry; (2) 322 pieces of Buddhist parapher- nalia and metal objects, mostly looted from Koryŏ period tombs in the Kaesŏng region; (3) 544 artifacts, including gold bracelets and necklaces taken from the Nosŏri and Hwangori in the Kyŏngju- and Han-period tombs of Rakurō; (4) 97 Koryŏ celadon pieces that were sent by Itō Hirobumi as gifts to the Meiji emperor; and (5) 1,581 items belong- ing to private collections, including that of Ogura Takenosuke (1870–1964). The final requested inventory for return was whittled down to 1,431 Japanese state-owned objects made up of 544 antiquities (*kogo misulp'um*) and 852 books (KSMKG 1965a, 103–11).

5 According to mimeographed copies of the original documents prepared by the KSMKG for the treaty talks in August 1965, a total of 106 items were received in 1958, including: (1) 215 tomb artifacts from Kyŏngju Nosŏri; (2) 16 tomb artifacts from Hwangori; (3) unspecified number of artifacts from Kyŏngnam Ch'angnyŏng–dong tombs in Kyŏngnam; (4) 854 books that had been taken to the Imperial Household Agency; and (5) 97 items from Itō Hirobumi's collections at the Tokyo National Museum. The latter items are presumed to have been taken to Japan at the end of the Yi dynasty (c. 1900s), before the promulgation of the 1916 laws banning the export of relics (KSMKG 1965a, 103–5).

6 One can read the original copies of correspondence and telegrams between specialists assigned the task of custodianship of museums collections and cultural properties and the supreme command of the Allied forces between 1945–51. These formerly classified documents that have been released by the Department of State are included in pages 514–46 of the second volume of *One Hundred Years of Korean Museums* (KS Pangmulk- wan 2009). I have yet to analyze these documents, since I was not aware of their existence when this manuscript went to press.

7 Alan Bain, former head archivist at the Smithsonian Archives Division, was instrumental in introducing me to Knez's archives. The manuscripts were donated by Knez follow- ing the end of his two-decade tenure as associate curator of Asian anthropology at the Smithsonian (1959–78). A small portion of Knez's personnel effects and books are also at the Center for Korean Studies at University of Hawai'i, because Knez and his wife retired in Honolulu. Knez died in Honolulu on June 5, 2010, of a heart ailment.

8 For a detailed chronology based on oral interviews with former museum directors regarding the chaotic conditions at the end of Korean War and the early years of the establishment of the National Museum of Korea, see *One Hundred Years of Korean Muse- ums*, vol. 2: 320–512.

9 The most popular items were Mishima (K. Punch'ŏng) or early Yi dynasty–style tea bowls that had been collected for four centuries by tea enthusiasts engaged in *sadō* (the way of tea). Its *Sadō*'s popularity is said to have originated with the respected tea master

Sen no Rikyū (1522–91), an early trendsetter who was known to have used tea bowls made by master potters. Since Rikyū is known to have served under the warlord Hideyoshi in his later life, around the time of the invasions of the peninsula (1592–98), there is no doubt that Rikyū influenced his master's tastes in Korean pottery and the potters' crafts (Han Yŏng-dae 1997, 97–121).

10 The oldest relic in this volume was a tiny bronze bird sitting on a swing, most likely looted from a Lelang/Rakurō tomb in P'yŏngyang. The caption reads, "A key reference item [sankōhin] signifying the origins of decorative arts in Asia" (Chōsen Kōgei Kenkyū Kai 1941, plate 1).

11 The once-thriving Yi dynasty kiln industry known as the "Punwŏn system" had experienced a steep decline due to the depletion of resources such as firewood, fresh water, and clay, as well as the introduction of Western wares. By the eighteenth century, hereditary potters were leaving their jobs en masse due to the horrible working conditions and low social status of their profession (Henderson 1962; Mori Yuzaburō 1916).

12 For a general treatment of the handful of successful cases of books recording royal rituals of the Yi dynasty (or ŭigwe) being returned from France by an international lawyer involved in the process, see The Search for Our Lost Treasures (Irŏbŏrin uri munhwajae rŭl ch'ajasŏ; Cho Pu-gŭn 2004). Cho's book also provides an introductory survey regarding various diplomatic negotiations, international conventions, and laws governing ongoing repatriation efforts targeting the tens of thousands of Korean artifacts, books, maps, and ethnographic collections scattered throughout the world.

13 In 2007, travelers to South Korea made up roughly a quarter of the total number of outbound Japanese with 2,600,800. The number represented a 22.8 percent increase over the previous year. Taiwan came in a distant second coming in at 1,385,255. There has been a precipitous drop in tourism due to the world financial collapse in the third quarter of 2008 and into 2009. For the latest trends in Japanese tourism statistics by country and region, please see Japan's National Tourist Organization (JNTO) website at http://www.jnto.go.jp/eng/ttp/sta/index.html. The main reason most governments and municipalities around the world court the Japanese tourist and, increasingly, Chinese visitors, is that they are well known as large tour groups who spend the most money on luxury accomodation, spa treatments, gourmet food and DFS purchases such as designer bags, clothes, shoes, etc.

GLOSSARY

atsukyū keishin (J.) 壓舊競新. Meiji slogan meaning suppressing the old in order to compete for the new, a clarion call for the modernization of its institutions.

bijutsu mohan (J.) 美術模範. Meiji term meaning a work of art that can be upheld as a model of national masterpieces—usually referring to museum-worthy collections.

chibang chijŏng munhwajae (K.) 地方指定文化財. Registered cultural properties listed by provincial committees of the Cultural Heritage Administration (CHA) of the Republic of Korea.

chijŏng nunhwajae (K.) 指定文化財. Registered cultural properties designated by the Cultural Heritage Administration (CHA) of the Republic of Korea.

chinbutsu (J.) 珍物. Meiji term for authentic or genuine curios that have been authenticated.

ch'ŏnnyŏn (K.) *kinyŏmmul* (K.) 天然記念物 (J. *tennen kinen butsu*). Natural monuments designated by the Cultural Heritage Administration (CHA) of the Republic of Korea.

Chōsen Sōtokufu Hōmotsu Koseki Meishō Tennen Kinenbutsu Hozon Iinkai (J.) 朝鮮総督府宝物古蹟名勝天然記念物保存委員会. Government-General of Chōsen Committee for the Preservation of Korean Treasures, Ancient Remains, Famous Places, and Natural Monuments.

chungyo minsok charyo (K.) 主要民俗資料. Important folklore materials designated by the Cultural Heritage Administration (CHA) of the Republic of Korea.

Chūshūen (J.) 中秋園 (K. Chungch'uwŏn). Government-general of the Korean Central Council, an advisory body of ruling elites, academics, and bureaucrats.

daichō tōroku (J.) 台帳登録. Card cataloguing or inventory system for registered cultural properties.

fukoku kyōhei (J.) 富国強兵 (K. puguk kangbyŏng). Meiji word meaning "rich nation and strong/powerful army," a government slogan pushing for the modernization of Japanese education, military, and economic sectors modeled after the West.

furui dōguya (J.) 古い道具や. Meiji word for secondhand shops or antique dealers.

hakubutsukan (J.) 博物館 (K. *pangmulgwan*). Generic word for museums.

Hakurankai (J.) 博覧会. Exposition or exposition organization committee.

hōko 宝庫 or *hōzō* (J.) 宝蔵. Premodern word for treasure house or treasures registry.

kach'i waegok (K.) 価値歪曲. Distorted values.

kaimei (J.) 開明. Meiji slogan for government-endorsed enlightenment efforts or civilizing missions.

kami jidai (J.) 神時代. Age of the Gods, or prehistoric times.

kamiseki (J.) 神石. "Stones of the gods," or term for prehistoric stone tools in premodern Japan.

kantei (J.) 鑑定. To authenticate artwork, paintings, and so on

kenmon (J.) 見聞. Fact-finding observation tours and missions—usually study-abroad tours.

kinsekimon (J.) 金石紋. Inscriptions on bronzes, jades, and stone objects.

kobutsu (J.) 古物. Antiquities.

kōchō seiseki (J.) 皇朝聖蹟. Sacred sites of the imperial family.

kokibutsu (J.) 古器物. Old vessels or bronzes.

kokibutsu shūkan (J.) 古器舊物　集館. Buildings for the storage of antiquities before the establishment of Meiji museums.

kokufū (J.) 国風. A sense of national landscape.

kokuhō (J.) kukpo, K. 国宝. National treasures.

kokutai (J.) 国体. Imperial identity, body, or nation.

Kōtō (J.) 皇統. Imperial Lineage of Japan.

maejang munhwajae (K.) 埋蔵文化財 (J. *maizō bunkazai*). Buried cultural remains or properties.

meishe (J.) 名勝 (K. *myŏngsŭng*). Scenic sites; also often referred to as *myŏngso* 名所 (famous places).

Munhwajae Mongnok (K.) 文化財目録. Inventory of Cultural Treasures.

muhyŏng munhwajae (K.) 無形文化財. Intangible cultural properties.

Munhwajae Pohobŏp (K.) 文化財保護法. K. Cultural Properties Preservation Act.

munhwajae taejang (K.) 文化財台帳. Certificate of authenticity for registered cultural properties.

munhwajae tŭnggŭp (K.) 文化財等級. Rankings of cultural properties.

Munhwajae Wiwŏnhoe (Punkwa Wiwŏnhoe; K.) 文化財委員会 (分課

委員会). Cultural Property Committee (Subcommittee) of CHA-appointed specialists who meet monthly to deliberate the rankings of cultural properties.

Munhwajae-ch'ŏng (K.) 文化財聴 (J. 文化庁). Cultural Heritage Administration Ministry of the Republic of Korea, 1998–present), formerly known as the Office of Cultural Properties (Munhwajae Kwalliguk, 1961-98).

oyatoi gaijin (J.) お雇い外人. Foreign specialists—including military advisors, technicians, scientists, medical doctors, engineers, professors, and architects—who were contracted to train a new generation of leaders to guide the modernization of Japan in the Meiji era.

pomul (K.) hōmotsu (takaramono) J. 宝物. Treasures.

posanggŭm (K.) 補償金. "Reward" or finder's fee for turning in discovered or recovered stolen cultural properties to the government.

poyuja (K.) 保有者. Possessors of traditional arts and crafts (living nationally designated artisans or craftsmen).

sadae (K.) 事大 (J. jidai). Subservience or serving bigger neighbors.

sajŏk (K.) 史蹟. (J. shiseki) Term for nationally designated historic sites in Japan and the Republic of Korea.

seiseki (J.) 聖蹟. Sacred sites belonging to imperial royalty.

shikibetsuka (J.) 識別家. Informed connoisseur of the arts.

Shūkokan (J.) 集古館. Depository for antiquities before the advent of museums in the Meiji era.

taritsusei (J.) 他律性 (K. tayulsŏng). The mentality of dependency on more powerful foreign regimes.

teitairon (J.) 停滞論. The stagnation of civilization.

tenjijō (J.) 展示場. Display grounds or exposition grounds during the Meiji period.

tokubetsu kenzōbutsu (J.) 特別建造物. Specially protected buildings under state management.

tongsan munhwajae (K.) 動産文化財. Transportable or movable cultural properties, such as museum objects.

tsūshin (J.) 通信. Dispatches or reports sent from the field.

yuhyŏng munhwajae (K.) 有形文化財. Tangible cultural properties.

zenpō-kōen kofun (J.) 前方後円古墳. Key-hole-shaped burial mounds of the Kofun period.

BIBLIOGRAPHY

Abu El-Haj, Nadia. 2001. *Facts on the Ground: Archaeological Practice and Territorial Self-fashioning in Israeli Society*. Chicago: University of Chicago Press.

Akazawa Takeru et al., eds. 1991. *Kanbanni kizamaretta sekai: Torii Ryūzō no mita Ajia* [Lost worlds on a dry plate: Torii Ryūzō's "Asia"]. The University Museum, Tokyo: University of Tokyo Press.

———. 1992. *The "Other" Visualized-Depictions of Mongoloid Peoples*. Tokyo: University of Tokyo Press.

Alcock, Rutherford. 1878. *Art and Art Industries in Japan*. London: Virtue.

Alexander, Edward P. 1983. *Museum Masters: Their Museums and Their Influence*. Nashville, TN: American Association for State and Local History.

American Art Association. 1921. *The Notable Yamanaka Collection of Artistic Oriental Objects and Decorative Art*. New York: American Art Association.

Amino Yoshihiko. 1992. "Deconstructing 'Japan.'" Translated by Gavan McCormack. *East Asian History* 3:121–42.

Anderson, Benedict. 1992. *Imagined Communities*. Revised edition. London: Verso.

Appadurai, Arjun, ed. 1986. *The Social Life of Things: Commodities in Cultural Perspective*. London: Cambridge University Press.

Arimitsu Kyōichi. 1933. "Keishū no hakubutsukan" [The museum in Kyŏngju]. *Dorumen* 13:44–49.

Ariyama Teruo. 2002. *Kaigai kankō ryokō no danjō* [The birth of foreign travel]. Tokyo: Yoshikawa Kōbunkan.

Asakawa Takumi. 1929. *Chōsen no zen* [Tables of Chōsen]. Tokyo: Kōseikai Shuppanbu.

———. 1935. *Chōsen tōjimei kō* [Nomenclature of the pottery of Chōsen]. Tokyo: Chōsen Kōgei Kankōkai.

Asami Noboru. 1924. "The Japanese Colonial Government." PhD diss., Columbia University.

Askew, David. 2003. "Torii Ryūzō and Early Japanese Anthropology." *Japanese Review of Cultural Anthropology* 4:133–54

Aston, W. G. 1985. *Nihongi*. 7th ed. Tokyo: Charles E. Tuttle.

Atkins, E. Taylor. 2007. "The Dual Career of 'Arirang': The Korean Resistance Anthem that Became a Japanese Pop Hit." *Journal of Asian Studies* 66 (3): 645–81.

219

Baird, Christine. 2000. "Japan and Liverpool, James Lord Bowes and His Legacy." *Journal of the History of Collections* 12 (1): 127–37.

Baker, Frederick. 1988. "Archaeology and the Heritage Industry." *Archaeological Review from Cambridge* 7 (2): 141–46.

Bale, Martin. 2008. "Archaeological Heritage Management in South Korea: The Nam River Dam Project." In *Early Korea,* vol. 1, *Reconsidering Early Korean History through Archaeology,* edited by Early Korea Institute, 213–31. Cambridge, MA: Harvard University, Early Korea Institute.

Banta, Melissa, and Susan Taylor, eds. 1988. *A Timely Encounter, Nineteenth-century Photographs of Japan.* Exhibition at Peabody Museum, Harvard University, and Wellesley College Museum. Cambridge, MA: Peabody Museum Press.

Banton, Michael. 1987. *Racial Theories.* Cambridge: Cambridge University Press.

Barclay, Paul D. 2001 "An Historian among the Anthropologist: The Ino Kanori Revival and the Legacy of Japanese Colonial Ethnography in Taiwan." *Journal of Japanese Studies* 21 (2): 117–36

———. 2003. "Gaining Confidence and Friendship in Aborigine Country: Diplomacy, Drinking, and Debauchery on Japan's Southern Frontier." *Social Science Japan Journal* 6 (1): 77–96: Tokyo: University of Tokyo, Institute of Social Science.

———. 2010. "Peddling Postcards and Selling Empire: Image-Making in Taiwan under Japanese Colonial Rule." *Journal of Japanese Studies* 30 (1): 83–112.

Barnes, Gina. 1988. *Proto-historic Yamato: Archaeology of the First Japanese State.* Ann Arbor: University of Michigan Center for Japanese Studies and the Museum of Anthropology, University of Michigan.

Barringer, Tim, and Tom Flynn. 1998. *Colonialism and the Object.* London: Routledge.

Beaulieu, Jill, and Mary Roberts, eds. 2002. *Orientalism's Interlocutors: Painting, Architecture, Photography.* Durham, NC: Duke University Press.

Befu, Harumi. 1994. "Nationalism and Nihonjinron." In *Cultural Nationalism in East Asia: Representation and Identity.* 107–38. Berkeley: University of California, Berkeley, Institute of East Asian Studies.

Bennett, John. 1995. *The Birth of the Museum: History, Theory, Politics.* London: Routledge.

Bergman, Sten. 1938. *In Korean Wilds and Villages.* Translated by Frederick Whyte. London: John Gifford.

Bhaba Homi. 1994. *Nations and Narration.* London: Routledge.

Bourdieu, Pierre. 1984. *Distinction: A Social Critique of the Judgement of Taste.* Translated by Richard Nice. Cambridge, MA: Harvard University Press.

Boyer, M. Christine. 2003. "'La Mission Héliographique': Architectural Photography, Collective Memory, and the Patrimony of France, 1851." In *Picturing Place: Photography and the Geographical Imagination,* edited by Joan Schwartz and James Ryan, 35–54. London: I. B. Tauris.

Brandt, Kim. 2000. "Objects of Desire: Japanese Collectors and Colonial Korea." *Positions* 8 (3): 712–46.

———. 2007. *Kingdom of Beauty: Mingei and the Politics of Beauty in Imperial Japan.* Durham, NC: Duke University Press.

Breen, John, ed. 2008. *Yasukuni, the War Dead, and the Struggle for Japan's Past*. New York: Columbia University Press.

Bremen, Jans van, and Akitoshi Shimizu. 1999. *Anthropology and Colonialism in Asia and Oceania*. Richmond, Surrey: Curzon.

Briggs, Asa. 1989. *Victorian Things*. Chicago, IL: University of Chicago Press.

Brown, Michael. 2003. *Who Owns Native Culture?* Cambridge, MA: Harvard University Press.

Caprio, Mark, E. 2011. "Marketing Assimilation: The Press and the Formation of the Japanese-Korean Colonial Relationship." *Journal of Korean Studies* 16 (1): 1–26.

Chamberlain, Basil Hall, and W. B. Mason. 1907. *Handbook for Travelers in Japan, Including the Whole Empire from Saghalien to Formosa*. Revised 8th ed. London: John Murray. Distributed in Yokohama, Shanghai, Hong Kong, and Singapore by Kelly Walsh.

———. 1913. *Handbook for Travelers in Japan, including Formosa*. Revised 9th ed. London: John Murray. Distributed in Yokohama, Shanghai, Hong Kong, and Singapore by Kelly Walsh.

Chang Kwang-chih. 1980. *Shang Civilization*, New Haven, CT: Yale University Press.

———. 1983. *Art, Myth, and Ritual*. New Haven, CT: Yale University Press.

Chapman, William Ryan. 1988. "Arranging Ethnology: A. H. L. F. Pitt Rivers and the Typological Tradition." In *Objects and Others: Essays on Museums and Material Culture*, vol. 3 of *History of Anthropology*, edited by George W. Stocking, 15–48. Madison: University of Wisconsin Press.

Chatterjee, Partha. 1993. *The Nation and Its Fragment: Colonial and Post-colonial Histories*. Princeton, NJ: Princeton University Press.

Ching Leo T. S. 2001. *Becoming "Japanese": Colonial Taiwan and the Politics of Identity Formation*. Berkeley: University of California Press.

Cho Hae-Jŏng. 2005. "Reading the Korean Wave as a Sign of Global Shift." *Korea Journal* 45 (5): 147–82.

Cho Pu-gŭn. 2004. *Irŏbŏrin uri munhwajae rŭl chajasŏ* [The search for our lost treasures]. Seoul: Minsogwŏn.

Cho Yu-jŏn. 1996. *Palgul iyagi* [Exavation stories]. Seoul: Taewŏnsa.

Ch'oe In-jin. 1999. *Han'guk sajinsa, 1631–1945* [A history of Korean photography, 1631–1945]. Seoul: Nunbit Publishing.

Ch'oe Sŏk-yŏng. 1997. *Ilche ŭi tonghwa ideollogi ŭi ch'angch'ul* [The invention of the ideology of assimilation during the colonial occupation]. Seoul: Sŏgyŏng Munhwasa.

———. 1999. *Ilcheha musongron kwa singminji kwŏllyŏk* [Theories of shamanism and colonial power under Japanese occupation]. Seoul: Tan'gyŏng Munhwasa.

———. 2001. *Hanguk kŭndae ŭi pangnamhoe, pangmulgwan* [Expositions and museums in modern Korea]. Seoul: Sŏgyŏng Munhwasa.

———. 2003. "Ilche singminchi sanghwang eso ŭi Puyŏ kojŏk e taehan chae haesŏk kwan'gwang myŏngsohwa" [A reinterpretation of the transformation of Puyŏ as a tourist site during the Japanese colonial era]. *Pigyo munhwa yŏn'gu* 9 (1): 109–37.

Chŏn Kyŏng-su. 1999. "Kankoku hakubutsukanshi ni okeru hyōshō no seiji jinruigaku shokuminchishūgi toshite no gurōbalizumu" [Representing colonialism and nationalism in the Korean Museum]. *Bulletin of the National Museum of Ethnology* 24 (2): 247–90.

Chŏng Chae-hun. 1969. "Munhwajae kwalli haengjŏng ŭi kibon panghyang: Hyŏn munhwajae kwalli chŏngch'aek ŭl chungsim ŭro" [The fundamental methods of cultural properties management focusing on present practices by the office of cultural properties]. *Munhwajae* 4:86–122.

Chŏng Chin-guk. 1999. "Ilche Chosŏn Ch'ongdok-pu ŭi Kŭmgangsan t'amsa sajin" [Photographic surveys of diamond mountains by the governor-general of Korea]. In *Arŭmdaun Kŭmgangsan yuri wŏnp'an sajinjŏn* [Special exhibition of glass plates photos of beauteous diamond mountains], edited by Kungnip Chungang Pangmulgwan, 228–35. Seoul: National Museum of Korea.

Chŏng, Un-hyŏn 1995. *Seoul sinae Ilche yusan tapsagi* [A survey of Japanese colonial remains in Seoul City]. Seoul: Hanul.

Chōsen Kōgei Kenkyū Kai. 1934–41. *Chōsen kōgei tenrankai zuroku* [Exhibition catalogue of the Chōsen arts and crafts society]. 7 vols. Tokyo: Bunmei Shoten.

Chōsen Kyōsankai [Chosŏn Cooperative for the Promotion of Industry]. 1915. *Chōsen Kyōsankai jimuhōkoku Heiwa kinnen* [Report on the administration of the 1915 industrial exposition commemorating the peace treaty]. Tokyo: Chōsen Kyōsankai.

———. 1922. *Chōsen Kyōsankai jimu hōkoku-Heiwa kinnen* [Report on the administration of the 1922 industrial exposition commemorating the peace treaty]. Tokyo: Tōa Shūppan.

Chōsen no hanashi [Stories of Chosŏn]. N.d., n.p. Distributed by the Chōsen Sōtokufu Tetsudo-kyoku branches at Tokyo, Osaka, Shimonoseki, and Seoul.

Chōsen Sōtokufu (CST) [Government-General of Korea]. 1911. *Chōsen Sōtokufu jisatsu chōsa shiryō* [Records of temple investigations by the Chōsen Sōtokufu]. 2 vols. Edited by Sekino Tadashi. Keijō: Chōsen Sōtokufu.

———. 1915–20. *Chōsen ihō* [Chōsen Sōtokufu monthly newsletter]. Vols. 1–65 Keijō: Chōsen Sōtokufu.

———. 1915–35. *Chōsen koseki zufu* [Album of ancient Korean sites and relics]. 15 vols. Keijō: Chōsen Sōtokufu.

———. 1918–41. *Hakubutsukan shinretsuhin zukan* [Museum exhibitions catalogues]. 17 vols. Seoul: Keijō.

———. 1919–30. *Koseki chōsa tokubetsu hōkoku* [Special reports of the investigations of ancient sites]. 6 vols. Tokyo: Chōsen Sōtokufu.

———. 1920–44. *Chōsen* [Chōsen Sōtokufu monthly newsletter]. Continuation of *Chōsen ihō*.

———. 1924. *Koseki oyobi ibutsu tōroku taichō shōroku* [Preliminary records of registration documents of ancient sites and relics]. Seoul: Chikazawa Insatsu.

———. 1929a. *Chōsen of Today: Illustrated*. Compiled in commemoration of the vicennial of the government-general of Chōsen, October 1929. In English. Keijō: Chōsen Sōtokufu.

———. 1929b. *Kokusei kyōkasho ni araharedaru Chōsen shiryo shashin mokuroku* [A catalogue of photograph resources of Chosŏn from textbooks issued by the CST department of education]. Edited by Chōsen Kyōikukai. Keijō: Chōsen Sōtokufu.

———. 1935. *Thriving Chōsen: A Survey of Twenty-five Years of Administration by the Government-General of Chōsen*. Keijō: Taishō Shashin Kōgeisho.

———. 1937. *Chōsen hōmotsu, koseki, meishō, tennen kinenbutsu yōran* [Korean treasures, ancient remains, famous places, and natural wonders]. Keijō: Chōsen Sōtokufu.

——. 1938. *Bukkokuji to Sekkutsuan* [Pulguk temple and Sŏkkuram cave]. Vol. 1 of *Chōsen hōmotsu koseki zuroku* [Album of Korean treasures and ancient sites]. Kyoto: Bunseidō.

——. 1972. *Chōsen Sōtokufu shisei sanjūnen shi* [Thirty years of Japanese administration in Korea]. Edited by Chōsen Sōtokufu. Reprint of 1940 edition. Tokyo: Meishō Shūppan.

Chōsen Sōtokufu, Chōsen Ginkō (Bank of Chōsen). 1919. *Pictorial Chōsen and Manchuria.* Compiled in commemoration of the decennial of the Bank of Chōsen. Keijō: Chōsen Ginkō.

Chōsen Sōtokufu, Chōsenshi Henshūkai [Government-General of Korea, Korean History Compilation Society]. 1939. *Chōsenshi henshū jigyō kaiyō* [A summary of the activities of the compilation comittee on Chōsen history]. Keijō: Chōsen Sōtokufu.

Chōsen Sōtokufu, Koseki Chōsa Iinkai/Kenkyūkai (CSKCIK) [Government-General of Korea, Committee on the Investigation of Korean Antiquities]. 1918–1937. *Koseki chōsa hōkoku* [Ancient sites investigations reports]. 16 Vols. Keijō: Chōsen Sōtokufu.

——. 1934. *Rakurō Saikyōzuka: Koseki chōsa hōkoku 1* [Tomb of the painted basket: Excavation report]. Vol. 1. Edited by Akio Koizumi and Sawa Shūnichi. Keijō: Chōsen Sōtokufu.

——. 1935. *Rakurō ōkobo: Koseki chōsa hōkoku* [Tomb of Wang Guang of Lelang: Excavation report]. Vol. 2. Edited by CSHKMT, Keijō: Chōsen Sōtokufu Hōmotsu Koseki Meishō Tennen Kinenbtsu Hozon Kai.

——. 1938. *Shōwa jūninendo koseki chōsa hōkoku* [Shōwa 12 (1937) excavation report]. Tokyo: Chōsen Sōtokufu.

Chōsen Sōtokufu, Tetsudo-kyoku (CSTTK) [Government-General of Korea, Chōsen Government Railways]. 1923. *Chōsen tetsudō ryokō henran* [Guidebook to Chōsen railways]. Keijō: CSTTK.

——. 1932. *Chōsen Kongōsan* [Kŭmgangsan in Chosŏn]. Keijō: CSTTK.

——. 1936. *Keishū* [Kyŏngju]. Keijō: CSTTK.

——. 1938. *Keijō, Jinsen, Suigen, Kaijō* [Seoul, Inchŏn, Suwŏn, Kaesŏng]. Distributed by Senman Annaisho (Chōsen, Manchuria Travel Office) and Japan Tourist Bureau offices. Keijō: CSTTK.

——. 1939. *Heijō* [P'yŏngyang]. *Hotels in Chōsen (Railways Stations Hotels in Chosŏn).* N.p. Distributed by Senman Annaisho and Japan Tourist Bureau offices.

Christ, Carol Ann. 2000. "The Sole Guardians of the Art Inheritance of Asia: Japan and China at the 1904 St. Louis World's Fair." *Positions* 8 (3): 675–709.

Cleere, Henry F., ed. 1989. *Archaeological Heritage Management in the Modern World.* London: Unwin Hyman.

Clifford, James. 1988. *The Predicament of Culture: Twentieth-century Ethnography, Literature, and Art.* Cambridge, MA: Harvard University Press.

Clifford, James, and George Marcus. 1986. *Writing Culture: The Poetics and Politics of Ethnography.* Berkeley: University of California Press.

Coaldrake, William H. 1994. "Western Technology Transfer and the Japanese Architectural Heritage in the Late Nineteenth Century." *Fabrications* 5:21–57.

Cohn, Bernard. 1997. *Colonialism and Its Forms of Knowledge: The British in India.* Delhi: Oxford University Press.

Cook, Thomas, and Son. 1938. *Japan Information for Visitors.* London: Thomas.

——. 1998. *Letters from the Sea and from the Foreign Lands, Descriptive of a Tour Round the*

World. Vol. 3 of *The History of Tourism*. London: Routldege/Thoemmes Press.

Coombes, Annie E. 1994. *Reinventing Africa: Museums, Material Culture, and Popular Imagination in Late Victorian and Edwardian England*. New Haven, CT: Yale University Press.

Coon, Carleton S. 1962. *The Origin of Races*. New York: Knopf.

Darby, Wendy J. 2000. *Landscape and Identity: Geographies of Nation and Class in England*. Oxford: Berg.

Deniker, Joseph. 1900. *The Races of Man: An Outline of Anthropology and Ethnography*. London: Walter Scott Publishing.

Desmond, Jane. 1999. "Picturing Hawai'i: The 'Ideal' Native and the Origins of Tourism, 1880–1915." *Positions* 7 (2): 495–501.

Deuchler, Martina. 1992. *The Confucian Transformation of Korea: A Study in Society and Ideology*. Cambridge, MA: Harvard University Press, Council on East Asian Studies.

Dikötter, Frank. 1992. *The Discourse of Race in Modern China*. Stanford: Stanford University Press.

Dirks, Nicholas. 2001. *Castes of Mind: Colonialism and the Making of Modern India*. Princeton, NJ: Princeton University Press.

Doak, Kevin M. 1998. "Culture, Ethnicity, and the State in Twentieth Century Japan." *Japan's Competing Modernities*, ed. Sharon A. Minichiello, 181–205. Honolulu: University of Hawai'i Press.

——. 2001. "Building National Identity through Ethnicity: Ethnology in Wartime Japan and After." *Journal of Japanese Studies* 27 (1): 1–39.

Duara, Prasenjit. 1995. *Rescuing History from the Nation: Questioning Narratives of Modern China*. Chicago: University of Chicago Press.

Dubois, Thomas D. 2006. "Local Religion and the Imperial Imaginary: The Development of Japanese Ethnography in Occupied Manchuria." *American Historical Review* 111:52–74

Duus, Peter. 1995. *The Abacus and the Sword*. Berkeley: University of California Press.

Earle, Joe. 1986. "The Taxonomic Obsession: British Collectors and Japanese Objects, 1852–1986." *Burlington Magazine* 128 (1005): 864–74.

Edensor, Tim. 1998. *Tourists at the Taj: Performance and Meaning at a Symbolic Site*. London: Routledge.

Edo Rekishi Hakubutsukan. 2005. *Utsukushi Nihon Taishō Shōwa no ryō* [Beautiful Japan tourism in the 1910s–1930s]. Exhibition catalogue for the Tokyo-Edo Historical Museum. Tokyo: Edo Rekishi Hakubutsukan.

Edwards, Elizabeth. 1992. *Anthropology and Photography, 1860–1920*. New Haven, CT: Yale University Press.

——. 1996. "Greetings from Another World." In *The Tourist Image: Myths and Mythmaking in Tourism*, edited by Tom Selwyn, 197–222. Chichester, UK: John Wiley and Sons.

Edwards, Walter. 1991. "Buried Discourse: The Toro Archaeological Site and Japanese National Identity in the Early Post-War Period." *Journal of Japanese Studies* 17 (1): 1–23.

——. 2000. "Contested Access: The Imperial Tombs in Post-War Japan." *Journal of Japanese Studies* 26 (2): 371–92.

——. 2003. "Monuments to an Unbroken Line: The Imperial Tombs and the Emergence of

Modern Japanese Nationalism." In *The Politics of Archaeology and Identity in a Global Context*, edited by Susan Kane, 11–30. Boston: Archaeological Institute of America.

———. 2005. "Japanese Archaeology and Cultural Properties Management: Pre-War Ideology and Postwar Legacies." In *Companion to the Anthropology of Japan*, edited by Jennifer Robertson, 36–49. Oxford: Blackwell Publishing.

Egami Namio. 1964. "The Formation of the People and the Origin of the State in Japan." *Memoirs of the Research Department of the Tōyō Bunkō* 23:35–70.

Eskildsen, Robert. 2002. "Of Civilization and Savages: The Mimetic Imperialism of Japan's 1874 Expedition to Taiwan." *American Historical Review* 107 (2): 388–418.

Farris, Wayne, W. 1998. *Sacred Texts and Buried Treasures: Issues in the Historical Archaeology of Ancient Japan*. Honolulu: University of Hawai'i Press.

Fawcett, Clare, and Junko Habu. 1989. "Education and Archaeology in Japan." In *The Excluded Past- Archaeology in Education*, edited by P. Stone and R. Mackenzie, 218–30. London: Unwin Hyman.

Fenollosa, Ernest F. Papers. 1853–1908. Microfilm copy. 1881–1952 (inclusive), 1881–1909 (bulk). Houghton Library, Harvard University Libraries.

———. 1885. "Can Japanese Art Be Revived?" TS. Carbon copy.N.p., ca.1885. 20 sheets. 20 pages. Incomplete copy.

———. 1887. *Comments on Unfinished Report of 1886*. N.p., December 2. 3s. 5p.

———. 1888. *Proposals for the New Fine Arts School*. 4s. 11p.

———. 1889a. "The Future of Japanese Art Industries." N.p. 8s. 27p.

———. 1889b. "The Prospect of Japanese Art." N.p. 2s. 8p.

———. 1891. *My Position in America*. N.p., May 1. 2s. 4p.

———. 1893. *Contemporary Japanese Art*. N.p., n.d. 2s. 3p. Published in *Century* magazine, August issue.

———. 1895. *Address Normal Art School*. N.p. June 27. 6s. 6p.

———. 1896. *Benefit of Commerce in Art Industry for Japan*. October 26. 7s. 7p.

———. 1909. "National Treasures Fast Disappearing." N.p., n.d. 2s. 8p.

———. N.d. *The Future of Japanese Art*. N.p. 2s. 5p.

———. N.d. *History of Kangwakai*. N.p.]3s. 4p.

———. N.d. *The Fine Arts Expedition to the Kinai*. N.p. 3s. 8p.

———. 1912. *Epochs of Chinese and Japanese Art: An Outline of East Asiatic Design*. Heinemann, NY: Frederick A. Stokes.

Foucalt, Michel. 1970. *The Order of Things: An Archaelogy of the Human Sciences*. London: Tavistock Publications.

Fujii Keisuke, et al., eds. 2005. *Sekino Tadashi Ajia tōsa* [Sekino Tadashi's surveys in Asia]. Vol. 20 of Tokyo University Museum Publications. Tokyo: Tōkyō Daigaku Sōgō Hakubutsukan.

Fujita Ryōsaku. 1933. "Chōsen no koseki chōsa to hozon no enkaku" [The process of the preservation and research of Korean ancient monuments]. In *Chōsen sōran* [Korean almanac], 1027–47. Keijō: Chōsen Sōtokufu.

———. 1948. *Chōsen kōkogaku kenkyū* [Study on Korean archaeology]. Kyoto: Takagirishoin.

———. 1963. *Chōsengaku ronkō* [Essays on Korean studies]. Nara: Fujita Ryōsaku Kinnen Jigyōkai.

Fujitani Takashi. 1996. *Splendid Monarchy: Power and Pageantry in Modern Japan.* Berkeley: University of California Press.

Fukuzawa Yukichi. 1934. *The Autobiography of Fukuzawa Yukichi.* Translated by Eichii Kiyooka. Authorized edition. Tokyo: Hokuseidō Press.

Gathercole, Peter, and David Lowenthal. 1990. *Politics of the Past.* One World Archaeology. London: Unwin Hyman.

Geary, Christraud M., and Virginia-Lee Webb. 1998. *Delivering Views: Distant Cultures in Early Postcards.* Washington, DC: Smithsonian Institute Press.

Geertz, Clifford. 1980. *Negara: The Theatre State in Nineteenth-Century Bali.* Princeton, NJ: Princeton University Press.

Gellner, Ernest. 1983. *Nations and Nationalism.* Oxford: Basil Blackwell.

Gill, David, and Christopher Chippindale. 2005. "From Boston to Rome: Reflections on Returning Antiquities." *International Journal of Cultural Property* 13 (3): 311–31.

Gluck, Carol. 1985. *Japan's Modern Myths.* Princeton, NJ: Princeton University Press.

———. 1998. "Edo Village." In *Mirror of Modernity: Invented Traditions of Modern Japan,* edited by Stephen Vlastos, 263–84. Berkeley: University of California Press.

Gompertz, G. St. G. M. 1963. *Korean Celadon and Other Wares of the Koryŏ Period.* London: Faber and Faber.

———. 1977. "The Appeal of Korean Celadon." *The Korea Branch of the Royal Asiatic Society* 52:45–55.

Greenfield, Jennifer, ed. 1996. *The Return of Cultural Treasures.* London: Cambridge University Press.

Guha, Rauajit, and Gayatri Chakravorty Spivak, eds. 1988. *Selected Subaltern Studies.* New York: Oxford University Press.

Gupta, Akhil, and James Ferguson, eds. 2001. *Culture, Power, and Place.* Durham, NC: Duke University Press.

Guth, Christine. 2000. "Charles Longfellow and Okakura Kakuzō: Cultural Cross-Dressing in the Colonial Context." *Positions* 8 (3): 605–36.

Hachizume Shinya, ed. 2005. *Nihon no Hakurankai: Terashita shoshi korekushyon* [Japan's expositions: The Terashita collections]. Tokyo: Heibonsha.

Hamada Kōsaku. 1906. "Suiko jidai no chōkoku." [Sculptures of the Suiko period]. In *Hamada Kōsaku chōsakushū* [Anthology of Hamada Kōsaku], vol. 2, edited by Hamada Kōsaku Chōsakushū Kanko Iinkai, 39–45. Kyoto: Dōhōsha Shūppan.

———. 1907. "Girishia to Nihon" [Greece and Japan]. In *Hamada Kōsaku chōsakushū* [Anthology of Hamada Kōsaku], vol. 2, edited by Hamada Kōsaku Chōsakushū Kanko Iinkai, 39–45. Kyoto: Dōhōsha Shūppan.

———. 1913. "Petori-kata ni shite" [On professor Petrie]. In *Hamada Kōsaku chōsakushū* [Anthology of Hamada Kōsaku], vol. 7, edited by Hamada Kōsaku Chōsakushū Kanko Iinkai, 183. Kyoto: Dōhōsha shūppan.

———. 1914. "Sutain no Chūa hakkutsu butsu" [Stein and his excavations in central Asia]. *Hamada Kōsaku chōsakushū* [Anthology of Hamada Kōsaku], vol. 7, edited by Hamada Kōsaku chōsakushū kanko Iinkai, 183. Kyoto: Dōhōsha Shūppan.

———. 1922. *Tsuron kōkogaku* [An introduction to archaeology]. Tokyo: Taitō Press.

———. 1932. *Kōkogaku kenkyūhōhō* [Methods of research in archaeology]. Trans. "Die Älteren Kultureperioden im Orient und in Europa," by Oscar Montelius (1903). Tokyo: Ōkasho.

———. 1932. *Keishū kingan tsuka* [Tomb of the gold crown]. Tokyo: Keishū Koseki Hozonkai.

———. 1969. *Kodai bunka ronkō: Hamada Kōsaku sensei tsuioku* [Essays on ancient culture: Remembrances of professor Hamada Kōsaku]. Edited by Kōkogaku Gyōkai. Kyoto: Kōkogaku Gyōkai.

Hamada Kōsaku, and J. G. Andersson. 1932. "The Far East." *Museum of Far Eastern Antiquities* 4:9–14.

Han Pŏm-su, and Kim Tŏk-kyu. 1994. *Yŏksa munhwa kwan'gwang k'osŭ ŭi kaebal pangan* [Recommendations for the development of cultural/historical tourism]. Seoul: Kyot'ong Kaebal Yŏn'guwŏn.

Han Yŏng-dae. 1997. *Chosŏnmi ŭi t'amgujadŭl* [Investigators of Korean beauty]. Translated by Pak Kyŏng-hŭi. Seoul: Hakkoje.

Handelman, Don, and Lea Shamgar Handelman. 1990. "Shaping Time: The Choice of the National Emblem of Israel." In *Culture through Time: Anthropological Approaches*, edited by E. Ohnuki-Tierney, 193–226. Stanford: Stanford University Press.

Handler, Richard. 1985. "On Having a Culture: Nationalism and the Preservation of Quebec's Patrimoine." In *Objects and Others: Essays on Museums and Material Cultures*, edited by G. Stocking, 192–217. Madison: University of Wisconsin Press.

———. 1988. *Nationalism and the Politics of Culture in Quebec*. Madison: University of Wisconsin Press.

Han'guk Kogohakhoe [Korean Archaeological Society], ed. 1997. *Maejang munhwajae palgul chŏnmun kigwan yuksŏng pang'an yŏn'gu kyŏlkwa pogosŏ* [A report on the final recommendations for the development of organizations specializing in archaeological excavations]. Seoul: Han'guk Kogohakhoe.

Hanjin Kwangwang. 1996. *21 seki no kokusaijin no tameni Kangoku shūgaku ryokō* [Korean educational group tours for the twenty-first-century international tourist]. Seoul: Hanjin Kwangwang.

Hara Kakuten. 1979–83. "Mantetsu chōsabu no rekishi to Ajia kenkyū" [The history of the research department of the South Manchuria Railroad and the study of Asia]. *Ajia Keizai*, nos. 20–24.

Haraguchi Takayuki. 2002. *Ehagakini mieru kōtsufūzokushi* [The history of transportation in picture postcards]. Tokyo: Nihon Gōtsu Kaisha.

Hardacre, Helen. 1984. *Shinto and the State, 1868–1988*. Princeton, NJ: Princeton University Press.

Harrell, Steven. 1995. *Ethnic Frontiers*. Seattle: University of Washington Press.

Harrison, Henrietta. 2003. "Clothing and Power on the Periphery of Empire: The Costumes of the Indigenous People of Taiwan." *Positions* 11 (2): 331–59.

Hatada Takahashi. 1965. "Nikkan chōyaku to Chōsen bunkazai henkan mondai" [Japanese-Korean treaty and the problem of the return of Korean cultural properties]. *Rekishigaku Kenkyū* 304:65–69.

Hayashi Hiroki. 2004a. *Kōkoehagaki: Meiji, Taishō, Shōwa no ryokō miru* [Postcard advertisements in vogue during the Meiji, Taishō, and Showa eras]. Tokyo: Satobun Shūppan.

———. 2004b. *Nippon no ro-man ehagaki: Taishō ro-man no sekai* [The romantic world of Taishō postcards]. Tokyo: Graphic Publications.

Hayashi Kaori and Eun-jeung Lee. 2007. "The Potential of Fandom and the Limits of Soft-Power: Media Representations on the Popularity of Korean Drama in Japan." *Social Sciences Journal* 10 (2): 197–216.

Hayashi Minao. 1976. *Kandai no bunbutsu* [Han dynasty artifacts]. Kyoto: Meibunsha.

Henderson, Gregory. 1962. "Pottery Production in the Earliest Yi Period." *Transactions of the Royal Asiatic Society* 39:5–22.

Hendry, Joy. 2000a. "Foreign Country Theme Parks: A New Theme or an Old Japanese Pattern." *Institute of Social Science Japan Journal* 3 (2): 207–20.

———. 2000b. *The Orient Strikes Back: A Global View of Cultural Display.* Oxford: Berg.

Henry, Todd A. 2005. "Sanitizing Empire: Japanese Articulations of Korean Otherness and the Construction of Early Colonial Seoul, 1905–1919." *Journal of Asian Studies* 64 (3): 639–75.

———. 2008. "Respatializing Chosŏn's Royal Capital: The Politics of Japanese Urban Reforms in Early Colonial Seoul, 1905–1919." In *Sitings: Cultural Approaches to Korean Geography*, edited by Timothy R. Tangherlini and Sallie Yea, 15–38. Honolulu: University of Hawaiʻi Press.

Hevia, James L. 2001. "World Heritage, National Culture, and the Restoration of Chengde." *Positions* 9 (1): 219–43.

———. 2003. *English Lessons: The Pedagogy of Imperialism in Nineteenth-Century China.* Durham, NC: Duke University Press / Hong Kong: Hong Kong University Press.

Hinsley, Curtis. 1988. "From Shell-Heaps to Stelae: Early Anthropology at the Peabody Museum." In *Objects and Others-Essays on Museums and Material Culture*, edited by George W. Stocking, 49–74. Madison: University of Wisconsin Press.

Hirano Katsuya. 2009. "The Politics of Colonial Translation: On the Narrative of the Ainu as a 'Vanishing Ethnicity.'" *Japan Focus* 3:1–20.

Hirano Ken'ichiro. 1986. "State-Forging and Nation Destroying: The Case of the Concordia Association of Manchu-kuo." *East Asian Cultural Studies* 25 (1–4): 37–57.

Hirose Shigeaki. 2003. "Chōsen no kenchiku, koseki to sono atono 'bunkazai' hogo" [Japanese investigations into archaeological and architectural sites in the Korean peninsula and cultural properties management since the 1910s]. *Nihon kōkogakushi kenkyū* 10:57–106.

Hiwasaki, Lisa. 2000. "Ethnic Tourism in Hokkaido and the Shaping of Ainu Identity." *Pacific Affairs* 73 (3): 393–412.

Hobsbawm, Eric, and Terence Ranger. 1996. *The Invention of Tradition.* London: Cambridge University Press.

Hodder, Ian, et al., eds. 1995. *Interpreting Archaeology.* London: Routledge.

Hoffenberg, Peter H. 2001. *An Empire on Display: English, Indian, and Australian Exhibitions from the Crystal Palace to the Great War.* Berkeley: University of California Press.

Hong Ki-mun. 1949. "Chosŏn i kogohak e taehan ilche ŏyonghaksŏl ŭi kŏmt'o" [A review of Japanese colonial theories on Korean archaeology]. *Yŏksa munje* 13/14:53–101.

Honour, Hugh. 1961. *Chinoiserie: The Vision of Cathay.* London: J. Murray.

Hooper-Greenhill, Eileen. 1992. *Museums and the Shaping of Knowledge.* London: Routledge.

Hōryūji Temple. 1907. *Hōryūji ehagaki (Grandest Collection of Curios in Japan).* Thirty-six picture postcards of Hōryūji Temple. 3 Vols. Kyoto: Benridō.

Howell, David. 2004. "Making 'Useful Citizens' of the Ainu Subjects in Early Twentieth-Century Japan." *Journal of Asian Studies* 63 (1): 5–30.

Hsieh Shih-chung. 1999. "Representing Aborigines: Modelling Taiwan's 'Mountain Culture.'" In *Consuming Ethnicity and Nationalism: Asian Experiences,* edited by Kosaku Yoshino, 89–110. Honolulu: University of Hawai'i Press.

Hudson, Mark. 1999. *The Ruins of Japanese Identity: Ethnogenesis in the Japanese Islands.* Honolulu: University of Hawai'i Press.

Hwang Su-yŏng. 1973. "Ilchegi munhwajae p'ihae charyo" [The destruction of cultural relics under Japanese rule]. *Kogo Misul.* Vol. 22. Seoul: Han'guk Misulsa Hakhoe.

———. 1989. *Sŏkkuram.* Seoul: Yŏrhwadang.

Ikawa-Smith Fumiko. 1982. "Co-Traditions in Japanese Archaeology." *World Archaeology* 13 (3): 269–309.

———. 1995. "The Jōmon, the Ainu, and the Okinawans: The Changing Politics of Ethnic Identity in Japanese Archaeology." In *Communicating with Japan: Images Past, Present, and Future,* edited by Dennis J. Dicks, 43–56. Montreal: Concordia University.

Ikeuchi Hiroshi. 1941. "Rakurōgunkō" [A study on Lelang commandery]. *Mansen chiri rekishi kenkyūkai hōkoku* 16:1–77.

———. 1951. *Mansenshi kenkyū* [A study on Manchurian-Korean history]. Vol. 1. Kyoto: Sokokusha.

Imamura, Tomō. 1914. *Chōsen fūzokushū* [An anthology of Korean mManners and customs]. Seoul: Shidō-kan.

Imanishi Ryū. 1907. "Chōsen nide hakkenseru kaizuka ni tsuite" [On the discovery of a shellmound in Korea]. *Tokyo jinrui gakkai zasshi* 23 (259): 6–13.

———.1911. "Shiragi kyūto Keishū no chisei oyobi sono iseki ibutsu" [The geography and archaeology of sites and remains in the old capital of Silla]. *Tōyō gakuho* 1 (1): 57–94.

Inoue Hideo. 1974. *Higashiajia minzokushi* [A racial history of the far east]. Tokyo: Heibonsha.

Inoue Shōichi. 1994. *Hōryūji no seishinshi* [An intellectual history of Hōryūji]. Tokyo: Kōbundō.

Inoue Yoshihirō. 2005. "Bijutsu to kōgyō no hazama: Naigoku kengyo hakurankai e no kōgei shūppin kubun o meguru" [An ambiguous domain between the fine art and applied arts in Japan: On the classifications principles of decorative art objects for the national industrial exhibitions]. In *Nihon kokusai hakurankai kaisai kinen ten, seki no saiden Hakurankai no bijutsu* [Commemorating the 2005 Aichi World Exposition, Aichi, Japan, arts of East and West from world expositions], edited by Tokyo National Museum et al., 154–61. 1855–1900, Paris, Vienna, and Chicago. Tokyo: Toppan Shūppan.

Itō Mamiko. 2003. "1904 nen sentoruisu bankoku hakurankai to nichirōsenshi kaigo" [War and diplomacy: Japan at the 1904 St. Louis world's fair]. *Shigaku zasshi* 112 (9): 67–86.

Itō Takeo. 1980. *Life along the Manchuria Railroad* [Mantetsu ni ikite]. Translated by Joshua Fogel. Armonk NY: M. E. Sharpe.

Jackson, Peter. 1992. "Constructions of Culture, Representations of Race: Edward Curtis's Way of Seeing." In *Inventing Places*, edited by Kay Anderson and Fay Gale, 89–106. Melbourne: Longman Cheshire.

Jaeger, Sheila. M. 1999. "Manhood, the State, and the Yongsan War Memorial." *Museum Anthropology* 21 (3): 33–39.

Janelli, Roger L., and Dawnhee Yim Janelli. 1981. *Ancestor Worship and Korean Society*. Stanford: Stanford University.

Jansen, Marius B., ed. 1995. *The Emergence of Modern Japan*. Cambridge: Cambridge University Press.

Japan Association for the World Exposition. 2005. *The Making of Expo 2005*. Tokyo: Takeda Printing.

Japan-British Exhibition. 1911. *Official Report of the Japan-British Exhibition 1910*. Great White City, Shepherd's Bush. London: Unwin Brothers.

Japan Bunkachō [Agency of Cultural Affairs]. 1960. *Bunkazai hogo no ayumi* [The development of the protection of cultural properties]. Edited by Bunkazai Hogo Iinkai. Tokyo: Taishōsho Insatsukyoku.

———. 1988. *Waga kuni no bunka to bunka gyōsei* [Our country's culture and its cultural policies]. Tokyo: Gyōsei.

JIGR (Japan Imperial Government Railways). 1913. *An Official Guide to Eastern Asia: Transcontinental Connections between Europe and Asia, Vol. 1, Manchuria and Chōsen*. Tokyo.

———. 1997. "Bunkazai hogo kankei hōryo shū sanko" [Reference section of the anthology of preservation laws of cultural properties]. In *Bunkazai hogo kankei hōrei shū* [Anthology of cultural properties preservations laws], edited by Bunkachō Bunkazai Hogobu, 195–215. Tokyo: Gyōsei.

Japan Tourist Bureau (JTB) [Nihon Kōtsu Kōsha]. 1913–1942. *Tsu-risto* [The tourist]. Tokyo: Nihon Kōtsu Kōsha.

———. 1924–. *Tabi* [Trip].

———. 1926. Guide to Japan. Pamphlet.

———. 1934. "Keishū mawari" [Touring Kyŏngju]. *Tabi* 1:106–10

———. 1913–1942. Tourist Library Series. 41 vols.

———. 1936. *Hot Springs in Japan*. Tourist Library Series 10.

———. 1939a. *Heizyo* [P'yŏngyang English guide]. *Nihon Kōtsu Kōsha Chōsen Shikyoku* [Tyosen branch of the Japan Tourist Bureau].

———. 1939b. *Keizyo* [Keijō English Guide]. *Nihon Kōtsu Kōsha Chōsen Shikyoku* [Tyosen Branch of the Japan Tourist Bureau].

———. N.d. *How to See Keishū*. Keijō: Chōsen Toppan.

———. 1982. *Nihon kotsu kōsha nanajūnenshi* [Seventy years of the Japan Tourist Bureau]. Tokyo: Nihon Kōtsu Kōsha.

Jin Jŏng-hŏn. 2008. "Demolishing Colony: The Demolition of the Old Government-General Building of Chosŏn." In *Sitings: Cultural Approaches to Korean Geography*, edited by Timothy R. Tangherlini and Sallie Yea, 39–58. Honolulu: University of Hawai'i Press.

Kal Hong. 2008. "Commemoration and the Construction of Nationalism: War Memorial Museums in Korea and Japan." *Japan Focus.* http://japanfocus.org. Posted September 6, 2008. Accessed November 11, 2011.

Kanda Koji. 2003. "Landscapes of National Parks in Taiwan during the Japanese Colonial Period." In *Representing Local Places and Raising Voices from Below,* edited by Toshio Mizuuchi, 112–19. Osaka: Osaka City University Department of Geography, Urban Cultural Center.

Kaneko Atsushi. 2001. *Hakubutsukan no seijigaku* [The politics of museum building]. Tokyo: Seikyūsha.

Kaneko Cho. 1887. "Nihon oyobi Chōsen no hongoku" [The homeland of the Japanese and Koreans]. *Tokyo jinrui gakkai zasshi* 2 (12): 99–108.

Kang Chae-ŏn and Yi Chin-hee, eds. 1997. *Chōsengaku koto shihajime* [The beginnings of Korean studies]. Tokyo: Seikyū Bunkasha.

Kang Chŏng-suk. 1998. "Taehan cheguk, Ilche ch'ogi Seoul ŭi maech'unŏp kwa kongch'ang chedo ŭi toip" [The sex industry and the state registration of prostitutes during the end of the Taehan empire and early colonial era]. *Sŏurhak yŏngu* 11:197–238.

Kang Hyŏn. 2006. "Kankoku kenchiku bunkazaishūri no shōki dankai-Nihonjin ni yoru shūri" [The earliest phases of Japanese repairs of Korean architectural cultural properties]. In *Nikkan ni okeru bunkazai kenzōbutsu hozon no kōryu to tenkai* [The preservation of architectural cultural properties in Japan and Korea], edited by Nikkan Bunkazai Kenzōbutsu Hozon Gyōroku Kyōkai [The joint committee for the preservation of Japanese and Korean architecture]. Sponsored by Japan's Ministry of Cultural Properties, and the Office of Cultural Properties of the Republic of Korea. Unpublished conference paper, 2–12. Nara: National Institute of Cultural Properties.

Kaplan, Uri. 2007. *Simulations of Monasticism: Temple Stay Program and the Re-branding of Korean Buddhist Temples.* PhD diss., Yonsei University Graduate School of International Studies.

Karp, Ivan, and Lavine Steven. 1991. *Exhibiting Cultures: The Poetics and Policy of Museum Display.* Washington, DC: Smithsonian Institute Press.

Kedourie, Elie, ed. 1970. *Nationalism in Asia and Africa.* New York: World Publishing.

Keene, Donald. 1976. "The Sino-Japanese War of 1894–95 and Its Cultural Effects in Japan." In *Tradition and Modernization in Japanese Culture,* edited by D. H. Shively, 121–79. Princeton, NJ: Princeton University Press.

Keishū Koseki Hozonkai [Kyŏngju Preservation Corporation]. 1922. *Shiragi Kyūto Keishū koseki annai* [A guide to ancient remains in Kyŏngju]. Tokyo: Tokyo Zusatsu.

———. 1935. *Shiragi Kyūto Keishū koseki annai* [A guide to ancient remains in Kyŏngju]. Tokyo: Tokyo Zusatsu.

Kendall, Laurel. 1999. "People Under Glass: A Tale of Two Museums." In *Consuming Ethnicity and Nationalism: Asian Experiences,* edited by Kosaku Yoshino, 111–32. Honolulu: University of Hawai'i Press.

Kidder, Edward. 2007. *Himiko and Japan's Elusive Chiefdom in Yamatai: Archaeology, Myth, and History.* Honolulu: University of Hawai'i.

Kim Chae-wŏn. 1948. *Two of the Old Silla Tombs and Silver Bell Tomb: Report of the Research of Antiquities of the National Museum of Korea.* Vol. 1. Seoul: Ŭlyu Publishing.

———. 1991. *Kyŏngbokkung yahwa: Ch'odae pangmulgwanjang hoego* [Back stories of Kyŏngbok palace: Memoirs of the first director of the national museum]. Seoul: T'amgudang.

———. 1992. *Pangmulgwan kwa hanp'yŏngsaeng* [My life with the national museum]. Seoul: T'amgudang.

Kim Chŏng-bae. 1987. "Formation of Ethnic Nation and Coming of Its Ancient Kingdom States." *Korea Journal* 27 (4): 33–39.

Kim Hong-un. 1995. *Han'guk kwan'gwang chiri* [The geography of Korean tourism]. Seoul: Hyŏngsŏl Ch'ulp'ansa.

Kim Hyŏn-suk. 2006. "Kŭndae sigak munhwa sok ŭi Silla Sŏkkuram ŭl chungsimŭro" [Understanding Sŏkkuram from a modern visual cultural perspective]. *Hanguk Kŭndae Misul Sahak* 17 (Dec.): 173–203.

———. 2007. "Ilche Kangchŏmgi Kyŏngju kojŏk pojonhoe ŭi palch'ok kwa hwaltong" [The founding and activities of the Kyŏngju Preservation Society during the Japanese occupation period]. In *Sigak munhwa ŭi chŏnt'ong kwa haesŏk* [A reinterpretation of visual cultural traditions], edited by Kim Ri-na Retirement Commemoration Volume Compilation Committee, 561–83. Seoul.

Kim Kwang-ŏn et al., eds. 2004. *Han'guk munhwa Yong-ŏ sajŏn* [Dictionary of Korean art and archaeology]. Seoul: Hallim Ch'ulp'ansa.

Kim T'ae-sik et al., eds. 2007. *Kyŏngju Silla yujŏk ŭi ŏje wa onŭl: Sŏkkuram, Pulguksa, Namsan* [Exhibition catalogue of the glass-plate photographic archives of Silla remains in Kyŏngju]. Seoul: Sŏngyungwan University Museum.

Kim Wŏl-lyong. 1986. *Han'guk kogohak kasŏl* [Introduction to Korean archaeology]. 3rd. ed. Seoul: Ilchisa.

Kim Yŏng-sam. 1995. *Kŏnmul ŭn sarajyŏdo yŏksa nŭn namnŭnda* [Though the building is gone, history remains]. Seoul: Umjiginŭn Ch'aek.

Kim Yŏng-sŏp. 1966. "Ilbon Han'guk e issŏsŏŭi Han'guksa sŏsul" [Historical writings about Korea in Korea and Japan]. *Yŏksa hakbo* 31:128–47.

———. 1973. "Ilche kwanhakchadŭl ŭi Han'guk sagwan" [Japanese government-scholars' view of Korean history]. In *Han'guksa ŭi pansŏng* [Reflections on Korean history], edited by Yŏksa hakhoe, 29–39. Seoul.

Kinoshita Naoyuki. 2001. "From Weapons to Work of Art: Sword Hunts." In *Japanese Civilization in the Modern World: Collection and Representation,* edited by Tadao Umesao, Augus Lockeyer, and Kenji Yoshida, 119–36. Senri Ethnological Series 16. Osaka: National Museum of Ethnology.

———. 2003. "The Early Years of Japanese Photography." In *The History of Japanese Photography,* edited by Anne Tucker et al., 14–99. New Haven, CT: Yale University Press, in association with the Houston Museum of Fine Arts.

Kirshenblatt-Gimblett, Barbara. 1991. "Objects of Ethnography." In *Exhibiting Cultures: The Poetics and Policy of Museum Display,* edited by Ivan Karp and Steven Lavine, 386–443. Washington, DC: Smithsonian Institute Press.

Kita Sadakichi. 1921. "Nissen ryōminzoku tōgenron" [The common origins of the two races— Japanese and Koreans]. *Chōsen* 6:3–69.

Knez, Eugene I. Papers. 1920s–2000. With information dating back to 1481. National Anthropological Archives, Smithsonian Institution, Washington, DC. Available online at http://www. nmnh.si.edu/naa/fa/knez1.htm. Accessed November 21, 2012.

———. 1984. "The War Years with the U.S. Army and Embassy, 1941–1953." Personal letters, supplementary notes, and related papers. National Anthropological Archives, Smithsonian Institution Archives, Washington, DC.

Kōgō Eriko. 2003. "Teishinshō hatsukō nichirōseneki kinen hagaki sho: So no jitsujō to ii" [The 1900s Ministry of Communications series of commemorative postcards of the Russo-Japanese War: The series background and significance]. *Bijutsushi kenkyū* 41:103–24.

Kohl, Philip L., and Clare Fawcett. 1995. *Nationalism, Politics, and the Practice of Archaeology.* Cambridge: University of Cambridge Press.

Koizumi Akio. 1975. "Rakurō kofun no hakkutsu to Harada sensei" [Excavation of Lelang tombs and Dr. Harada]. *Kogaku Zasshi* 60 (4): 90–92.

———. 1985. *Chōsen kodai iseki no henreki: Hakkutsu chōsa sanjunen no kaisō* [My travels to ancient archaeological sites in the Korean peninsula: Memoirs of thirty years of excavations]. Tokyo: Rokkō Shūppan.

Komai Kazuchika. 1965. *Rakurō-gun chishi* [The site of the seat of local government of Lelang in Korea]. *Kōkogaku kenkyū.* Vol. 2. Tokyo: Tokyo Daigaku kōkogaku kenkyū shitsu.

Konishi Shirō, and Hideo Ōka et al., eds. 2005. *Hyakunen mae no Nihon* [Japan a hundred years ago]. E. S. Morse Collection/Photography at the Peabody Museum of Salem. Tokyo: Shōgaku-kan Press.

Korea (South: KS) Pangmulkwan Kungnip Chungang Pangmulgwan National Museum of Korea (KS). 1951. *Sogaepum Mongnok* [List of Korean collections evacuated from Seoul and Kaesŏng areas]. Unpublished manuscript previously published, Pusan. Mimeograph copy. Professor Langdon Warner Collections, Harvard Rubel Asiatic Library.

———. 1973–. *Pangmulkwan sinmun* [Museum news monthly]. Seoul: National Museum of Korea.

———. 2009. *Kungnip Pangmulgwan 100 nyŏnsa 1909–2009* [One hundred years of Korean national museums]. Seoul: Yŏngshinsa.

Korea (South; KS) Munhwa Kongbobu. 1979. *Munhwa kongbo samsim-nyŏn* [Thirty-year history of the ministry of culture and information]. Ministry of Culture and Information. Seoul: Koryŏ sŏjŏk.

Korea (South; KSMKG) Munhwajae Kwalliguk Kungnip Munhwajae Yŏn'guso [Office of Cultural Property Management]. 1965a. *Hanil hoedam munhwajae kwangye ch'amkojip* [References on cultural properties related articles in the Korea-Japan Treaty]. August. Seoul: Munhwajae Kwalliguk.

———. 1965b. *Munhwajae.* Journal of the Office of Cultural Properties vol. 1, no. 1.

———. 1967. *Munhwajae kwalli kaesŏn ŭl wihan chosa pokosŏ* [An investigative report on improving cultural heritage management]. Seoul: Munhwajae Kwalliguk.

———. 1988. *Munhwajae posu kisul kyojae* [Manual for the restoration of cultural properties]. Seoul: Munhwajae Kwalliguk.

———. 1992. *Munhwajae Yŏn'guso isibo-nyŏn sa* [A twenty-five-year history of the National Research Institute of Cultural Properties].

———. 1996a. "Ilcheǔi munhwajae chŏngch'aek p'yŏngga semina [A seminar report on the reevaluation of Japanese colonial cultural policies]. Seoul: Kungnip Minsok Pangmulkwan [National Folk Museum].

———. 1996b. *1996 Chijŏng munhwajae mongnok* [1996 registry of cultural properties]. Seoul: Munhwajae Kwalliguk.

———. 1997a. *Ilche chijŏng munhwajae chaep'yŏngga kyŏlkwa pogo* [Report on the reevaluation of cultural properties designated during the Japanese colonial era]. Seoul: Munhwajae Kwalliguk.

———. 1997b. *Korean Intangible Cultural Properties.* Vol. 1. Seoul: Samhŭngsa.

———. 1997c. *Maejang munhwajae palgul pansegi* [Fifty years of excavating buried cultural properties]. Conference proceedings. Seoul: Munhwajae Kwalliguk.

———. 1997d. *Munhwajae haengjŏng ŭi silch'e* [The true facts of cultural properties management]. Seoul: Munhwajae Kwalliguk.

———. 1998a. *Munhwajae kwalli nyŏnbo* [Annual report of the office of cultural properties]. Seoul: Munhwajae Kwalliguk.

———. 1998b. *Munhwajae wiwŏnhoe hoeǔirok* [Meeting minutes of the committee of cultural properties]. Seoul: Munhwajae Kwalliguk.

———.1992. *Munhwajae Yŏn'guso isibo-nyŏn sa* [A twenty-five-year history of the National Research Institute of Cultural Properties]. Seoul: NRICP.

———. 1997 *Maejang munhwajae palgul pansegi* [Fifty years of excavating buried cultural properties]. Conference Proceedings. Seoul: NRICP.

———. 2001. *Han'guk kogohak sajŏn* [Dictionary of Korean archaeology].

Korean National Committee for UNESCO. 2001. *UNESCO Regional Workshop for the Preparation of Periodic Reports on the State of Conservation of World Cultural Heritage Sites in Asia.* Sponsored by the Office of Cultural Properties Administration. July 11–13. Kyŏngju, Republic of Korea.

———. 2002. *Sustainable Development of Traditional Historic Villages.* November 11. ICOMOS Symposium Korea. Sponsored by the Office of Cultural Properties Administration. Seoul.

Kosaku Yoshino, ed. 1999. *Consuming Ethnicity and Nationalism.* Honolulu: University of Hawai'i Press.

Kudō Masayūki. 1979. *Nihon jinshūron* [A study on the racial theories of the Japanese]. Tokyo: Yoshikawa Kōbunkan.

Kuki Ryūichi. 1889. "Kokka no hat suda ni tsuite" [Foreword to inauguration publication of Kokka]. *Kokka* 1:1–5.

Kuklick Henrika. 1991. *The Savage Within: The Social History of British Anthropology, 1885–1945.* Cambridge: Cambridge University Press.

Kuno Yoshio. 1967. *Japanese Expansion in the Japanese Continent.* 2 vols. Washington, NY: Kennikat Press.

Kurata Masahiko. 1991. "Tennosei kokka no Chōsen shokuminchi shihai to shūgyo seisaku" [Emperor worship and religious policy during the colonial period]. *Chōsenshi kenkyūkai ronbunshū* 29:60–74.

Kurihara Tomonobu. 1978. *Jōdai Nihon taigaikankei no kenkyū* [Studies on the external relations of ancient Japan]. Tokyo: Yoshikawa Kōbunkan.

Kuroita Hakushi Kinenkai, ed. 1953. *Kobunka to hozon to kenkyū* [The study and preservation of ancient culture]. Professor Kuroita Commemoration Committee. Tokyo: Kuroita Hakushi Kinenkai.

Kuroita Katsumi. 1900. *Meiji Ōbei kenbunroku shūsei* [An anthology of fact-finding observation tours to Europe and America]. Vols. 14 and 15. Tokyo: Yumani Shobō.

———. 1912. "Shiseki hozon ni kansuru ikensho" [An opinion paper on the preservation of historical sites and remains]. *Shigaku Zasshi* 23 (5): 568–611.

———. 1916. "Taidōkō fukin no shiseki" [Historical sites near the Taedong river]. *Chōsen ihō* 11:2–11.

———. 1917. *Tokubetsu hogo kenzōbutsu kokuhō mokuroku* [The national registry of special buildings and national treasures under protection]. Tokyo: Bunkaidō Shoten.

Kurosawa Saneyori. 1890a. "Hōryūji kensetsu setsu" [A theory of the construction of Hōryūji]. *Kokka* 9:1–15.

———. 1890b. "Tōdaiji Shōsō-in no hanashi" [A tale of Todaiji Shōsō-in]. *Kokka* 2:18–19.

Kwŏn Haeng-ga. 2001. "Ilche sidae up'yŏn yŏpsŏ e nat'anan kisaeng imiji" [The image of Kisaeng "Korean dancer" in postcards printed in colonial Korea]. *Misulsa nondan* 12:83–103.

Kwŏn Hyŏk-hŭi. 2003. "Ilche sidae sajin yŏpsŏ e nat'anan chaehyŏn chŏngch'ihak" [The politics of representation in Japanese colonial era picture postcards]. *Hanguk munhwa illyuhak* 36–11:187–217

———. 2005. *Chosŏn esŏ on sajin yŏpsŏ* [Postcards from Korea]. Seoul: Minŭmsa.

Kyōdai Hakubutsukan [Kyōto Imperial University Letters and Sciences Division]. 1923. *Kyōto Teikoku Daigaku Bungakubu shinretsukan kōko zuroku* [Exhibition catalogue of Kyōto University letters and sciences museum]. Edited by Hamada Kosaku. Kyoto: Bunseidō.

Ledyard, Gari. 1975. "Galloping along with the Horse-Riders: Looking for the Founders of Japan." *Journal of Japanese Studies* 1 (2): 217–54.

Lee Kyong-hŭi. 1997. *World Heritage in Korea*. Seoul: Organizing Committee of the Year of Cultural Heritage 1997 / Samsung Foundation of Culture.

Leheny, David. 1998. "Tours of Duty: The Evolution of Japan's Outbound Tourism." PhD diss., Cornell University.

Lewis, Bernard. 1975. *History Remembered, Recovered, Invented*. Princeton, NJ: Princeton University Press.

Li Liu. 1999. "Who Were the Ancestors? The Origins of Chinese Ancestral Cult and Racial Myths." *Antiquity* 73 (281): 602–12.

Lim Shao Bin. 2004. *Images of Singapore from the Japanese Perspectives, 1891–1941*. Singapore: The Japanese Cultural Society.

Linhart, Sepp. 2005. *"Niedliche Japaner" Oder Gelbe Gefahr? Westliche Kriegspostkarten 1900–1945* [Dainty Japanese or yellow peril? Western war-postcards, 1900–1945]. Wien: Lit Verlag.

Lofgren, Orvar. 1999. *On Holiday: History of Vacationing*. California Studies on Critical Human Geography. Berkeley: University of California Press.

Lubbock, John. 1873. *The Origin of Civilization and the Primitive Condition of Man*. New York: D. Appleton.

Lutz, Catherine A., and Jane L. Collins. 1993. *Reading National Geographic*. Chicago: University of Chicago Press.

MacCannell, D. 1999 (1976). *The Tourist*. Berkeley: University of California Press.

MacIntyre, Donald. 2002. "A Legacy Lost." *Time Asia*, January 28.

Mansen chiri rekishi kenkyū hōkoku [Reports on Manchuria-Korea geography and history research]. 16 vols. Edited by Tokyo Teikoku Daigaku Bungakubu. Tokyo: Tokyo University.

Marchand, Suzanne L. 1996. *Down from Olympus: Archaeology and Philhellenism in Germany, 1750–1970*. Princeton, NJ: Princeton University Press.

Marcus, George E., and Michael M. Fischer. 1986. *Anthropology as Cultural Critique*. Chicago: University of Chicago Press.

Matsuda Kyōko. 2005. "Sengyū hyaku sanjūnendai no Taiwan genjūmin o meguru tochishijitsu-sen to hyōjyōsenryaku" [Colonial administrative strategies and the representation of Taiwan aborigines in 1930s Taiwan]. *Nihonshi kenkyū* 520:152–80.

Matsumura Ryō. 1934. "Tokyo jinrui gakkai gojūnenshi" [The fifty-year history of the Tokyo Anthropological Society]. *Tokyo jinrui gakkai zasshi* 49 (11): 419–70.

Matsuoka Asako. 1935. *Sacred Treasures of Nara in "Shōsō-in" and "Kasuga Shrine."* Tokyo: Hokuseido Press.

Matsuyama Iwao. 1993. "Kokuhō to iyū monogatari" [What is a national treasure?]. *Kokuhō* [National treasures], ed. Geijutsushinchō Henshūpu, 177–92. Tokyo: Shinchōsa.

Maxwell, Anne. 1999. *Colonial Photography and Exhibitions: Representations of the "Native" and the Making of European Identities*. London: Leicester University Press.

Messenger, Phyllias M., ed. 1989. *The Ethics of Collecting*. Albuquerque: University of New Mexico Press.

Miitera Temple (Hōmyoin). N.d. *Pamphlet-Guide to Hōmyoin Temple*. ōtsu City.

Milne, J. 1882. "Notes on the Koro-pok-guru or Pit-dwellers of Yezo and the Kurile Islands." *Asiatic Society of Japan* 10:187–219.

Minichiello, Sharon A., ed. 1998. *Japan's Competing Modernities*. Honolulu: University of Hawai'i Press.

Minpaku Minzoku Kokuritsu Hakubutsukan. 1990. *Mo-su Korekushion* [The E. S. Morse Collection]. Exhibition catalogue of *Meiji Crafts from Across the Sea*. Sponsored by the National Museum of Ethnology Osaka (Kokuritsu Minzoku Hakubutsukan), Tokyo Rennaissance Committee and Peabody Museum in Salem.

Miyake Yōnekichi. 1890. "Kobutsu gaku no shinbo" [The rise and progress of prehistoric archaeology in Europe]. *Tokyo jinrui gakkai zasshi* 5 (53): 347–53.

———. 1903. "Koseki no chōsa hozon ni tsuite ikentaiyo" [A survey of opinions on the preservation and investigations of ancient remains]. *Koseki shū chōsa hozonkai kaihō* 3:2–8.

———. 1970. "Miyake Yōnekichi shū" [Miyake Yōnekichi anthology]. In *Nihon kōkogaku senshū* [Anthology of Japanese archaeology] vol. 1, edited by Saitō Tadashi. Tokyo: Tsukiji Shokan.

Mokuyō Club, ed. 1996. "Jinruigaku zasshi saisai no shūi chieki kanren bunken moku-roku—1910 made" [A catalogue of articles relating to Japan's surrounding countries selected from the Tokyo anthropological journal before 1910]. *Nihon kōkogakushi kenkyū* 6:3–20.

———. 2001. "Chōsen kankei bunken mokuroku (kōkogaku, jinruigaku, kenchikushi moku-roku)" [A catalogue of Korea related articles on archaeology, anthropology, and architectural history]. *Nihon kōkogakushi kenkyū* 9:4–20.

———. 2003. "Arimitsu-shi intabyū" [An interview with professor Arimitsu]. *Nihon kōkogaku shi kenkyū* 10:3–30.

Moon Ok-pyo. 2009. "Japanese Tourists in Korea: Colonial and Post-Colonial Encounters." In *Japanese Tourism and Travel Culture*, edited by Sylvie Guichard-Anguis and Okpyo Moon, 147–71. London: Routledge.

Mori Masao. 1997. "Nihon minzoku gaku to kindai Nihon no tasha ishiki" [Ethnology in Japan and Japanese perception of "Others" in the modern period]. *Minzokugaku kenkyū* 62 (1): 66–85.

Mori Yuzaburō. 1916. "Yōgyō ni tsuite" [The pottery manufacturing industry]. *Chōsen ihō* 10:39–44.

Morris-Suzuki, Tessa. 1994. "Creating the Frontier: Border, Identity, and History in Japan's Far North." *East Asian History* 7:1–24.

———. 1998a. "Becoming Japanese: Imperial Expansion and Identity Crisis in Early Twentieth-Century Japan." In *Competing Modernities in Twentieth-Century Japan,* edited by Sharon A. Minichiello, 157–80. Honolulu: University of Hawai'i Press.

———. 1998b. *Time, Space, and Nation.* Armonk, NY: M. E. Sharpe.

Morse, Anne, et al., eds. 2004. *Art of the Japanese Postcard: The Leonard A. Lauder Collection. at the Museum of Fine Arts.* Boston: MFA Publications.

Morse, Edward S. 1879. "Shell Mounds of ōmori." Memoirs of the Science Department of the University of Tokyo 1. Tokyo: Tokyo University.

———. 1917. *Japan Day by Day: 1877, 1878–79, 1882–83.* 2 vols. Boston: Houghton Mifflin.

Motomura Mitsuyasu. 1996. "Ainu, Koro-pok-guru ronso ni kansuru Tsuboi jinruigaku" [Role of Tsuboi Shōgorō's anthropological study on the debate over the origins of Ainu and non-Ainu Japanese]. *Nihon kōkogakushi kenkyū* 6:11–22.

Murakata Akiko, ed. 1980. "Ernest Fenollosa shiryo" [Ernest Fenollosa archives]. Ernest Fenollosa Manuscripts at Houghton Library: Harvard University Fenollosa on the Art Administration of Japan. Part 1. *Museum* 356:30–46. Tokyo: Tokyo National Museum.

———. 1982a. "Ernest Fenollosa shiryo." Ernest Fenollosa Manuscripts at Houghton Library, Harvard University: Fenollosa on the Art Administration of Japan. Part 2. *Museum* 357:26–40.

———. 1982b. Ernest Fenollosa Harvard Manuscripts. 3 vols. Translated by Akiko Murakata. Tokyo: Museum Press.

Murakata Noriko. 2002. "Meijiki no bijutsu shashin" [Art photography in Meiji Japan]. *Bijutsu-shi* 153 (1): 146–65.

Murray, David. 1894. *Japan.* 5th ed.. London: T. Fisher Unwin.

Nakajima Heijirō. 1931. "Yamataikoku oyobi Nukoku ni tsuide" [On Yamato-koku and Nukoku referred to in ancient Chinese records]. *Nihon kōkogaku zasshi* 21 (5): 311–36.

Nakajima Minao. 1996. "Tsuboi Shōgorō no jinruigaku to kōkogaku" [Tsūboi Shōgorō on the relationship between anthropology and archaeology]. *Nihon kōkogakushi kenkyū* 6:3–10.

Namigata Shoichi, et al., eds. 2004. *Tōa ryokōsha Manshū chibu jūnenshi* [Ten years of the Manchuria branch of the Tōa travel agency]. *Shashide miru Nihon keizaishi shokuminchi hen dai 31 hen* [The economic history of Japan series: Colonial era]. Vol. 31. Tokyo: Yumani Shobō.

Nanta Arnaud. 2008. "Physical Anthropology and the Reconstruction of Japanese Identity in Postcolonial Japan." *Social Science Research Journal* 11(1):29–47.

Naoki Kojirō. 1980. "Nihon kodaishi no kenkyū to gakumon no jiyū" [Academic freedom and the study of ancient Japanese history]. *Rekishi hyōron* 7 (363): 3–16.

Nara Kokuritsu Bunkazai Kenkyūjo [Nara Institute of Cultural Properties]. 2006. *Nikkan ni okeru bunkazai kenzōbutsu hozon no kōryu to tenkai* [The preservation of architectural cultural properties in Japan and Korea]. Nikkan Bunkazai Kenzōbutsu Hozon Gyōroku Kyōkai [The Joint Committee for the Preservation of Japanese and Korean Architecture]. Sponsored by Japan's Ministry of Cultural Properties and the Office of Cultural Properties of the Republic of Korea, Third Joint Symposium conference volume. Photocopy.

Niessen, Sandra A. 1994. "The Ainu in Minpaku: A Representation of Japan's Indigenous People at the National Museum of Ethnology." *Museum Anthropology* 18 (3): 18–25.

Nihon Kenchiku Gakkai [Japanese Architecture Society]. 1972. *Kindai Nihon kenchikugaku hattatsushi* [A history of the development of modern Japanese architecture]. 2nd ed. Tokyo: Maruzen.

Nihon Shashin Gyōkai, ed. 1971. *Nihon shashin shi* [A history of Japanese photography 1840–1945]. Tokyo: Heibonsha.

Nippon Yūsen Kabushiki Kaisha (NYK). 1894. *Handbook of Information for Passengers and Shippers.* Tokyo: N. Y. K. Line.

———. 1896. *Handbook of Information for Passengers and Shippers.* Tokyo: N. Y. K. Line.

Nippon Magazine. 1939a. *Chōsen Travel Guide Nippon Special Issue,* no.18. Tokyo: Nippon Kōbo [Japan Studio].

———. 1939b. *Manchukuo, Nippon Special Issue,* no. 19. Tokyo: Nippon Kōbo [Japan Studio].

Nippon Ryokō Kai. 1930. *Dai ni Senman shisatsudan kinen* [Second commemorative report on the fact-finding observation tour to Korea and Manchuria]. Tokyo: Nippon Ryokō Kai.

Nishikawa Hiroshi. 1970. "Nihon teikoku shūgika ni okeru Chōsen kōkogaku no keisei" [The establishment of Korean archeology during the era of Japanese imperialism]. *Chōsen gakuhō* 7 (6): 94–114.

Nobu Shinjutsu. 1923. *Chōsenjin no kenkyū* [A study on the Chōsenjin]. Tokyo: Sekaishijō Kenkyūkai.

Notehelfer, Fred G. 1990. "On Idealism and Realism in the Thought of Okakura Tenshin." *Journal of Japanese Studies* 16 (2): 309–55.

O Se-t'ak. 1996. "Ilche ŭi munhwajae chŏngch'aek" [Japanese policies on cultural properties]. In *Ilche ŭi munhwajae chŏngch'aek p'yŏngga semina* [A seminar report on the reevaluation of Japanese colonial cultural policies], edited by Munhwajae Kwalliguk, 15–44. Seoul: Munhwajae Kwalliguk.

Oakes, Julie C. 2009. "Japan's National Treasure System and the Commodification of Art." In *Looking Modern: East Asian Visual Culture from Treaty Ports to World War II,* edited by Jennifer Purtle and Hans Bjarne Thomsen, 220–21. Symposium volume. Chicago: Center for the Art of East Asia and Art Media Resources.

Oakes, Timothy. 1997. "Ethnic Tourism in Rural Guizhou: Sense of Place and the Commerce of Ethnicity." In *Tourism, Ethnicity, and the State in Asian and Pacific Societies,* edited by Michel Picard and Robert E. Wood, 35–70. Honolulu: University of Hawai'i Press.

———. 1998. *Tourism and Modernity in China*. New York: Routledge.

Oba Iwao. 1935. "Nihon sekijidai kenkyū shōshi" [A short history of prehistorical studies in Japan]. *Dō-rumen* 4 (5): 411–17.

Oda Kanjirō. 1922. "Keishū no nipaku" [Two days in Kyŏngju]. Part 1. *Chōsen* 93 (12): 48–53.

———. 1923. "Keishū no nipaku" [Two days in Kyŏngju]. Part 2. *Chōsen* 94 (1): 108–16.

Oguma Eiji. 1995. *Tan'itsu minzoku shinwa no kigen* [The origins of the myth of the homogenous nation]. Tokyo: Shinyōsha.

———. 1998. *"Nihonjin" no kyōkai* [The boundaries of the Japanese]. Tokyo: Shinyōsha.

Ohnuki-Tierney Emiko, ed. 1990. *Culture through Time: Anthropological Approaches*. Stanford: Stanford University Press.

Ōka Masao, et al. 1948. "Nihon minzoku bunkano genryū to Nihon kokka no keisei" [The origins of civilization and the formation of the Japanese state]. *Minzokugaku kenkyū* 13 (3): 207–77.

Okakura Kakuzō [Tenshin, Yoshishaburō]. 1903. *The Ideals of the East with Special Reference to the Art of Japan*. 1st ed. London: J. Murray.

———. 1904. *The Awakening of Japan*. New York: Century.

———. 1913. *The Life and Thought of Japan*. London: J. M. Dent and Sons.

———. 1980. *Okakura Kakuzō zenshū* [The complete works of Ōkakura Kakuzō]. *Ōkakura Kakuzō zenshū henshūpu*. 8 vols. Tokyo: Heibonsha.

ōkauchi Mitsuzane. 1986. "Mounded Tombs in East Asia from the 3rd to the 7th centuries ad." In *Windows on the Japanese Past: Studies in Archaeology and Prehistory*, edited by Richard Pearson, Gina Barnes, and Karl Hutterrer, 127–48. Ann Arbor: University of Michigan, Center for Japanese Studies.

O'Keefe, Patrick. 1999. *Trade in Antiquities: Reducing Destruction and Theft*. Paris: UNESCO Publishing.

Ōno Entarō. 1904. *Senshi kōkozufu* [Illustrated album of prehistoric archaeological objects]. Tokyo: Takayama gaku.

Oppenheim, Robert. 2008. *Kyŏngju Things: Assembling Place*. Ann Arbor: University of Michigan Press.

Ōta Hideharu. 2000. "Chōsen wajō shitsu shakuzu" [The survey maps of Japanese fortresses]. *Kangoku Bunka* 25.

Ōsaka Rokuson. 1931. *Shūmi no Keishū* [Kyŏngju as a hobby]. Tokyo: Keishū Koseki Hozonkai [Kyŏngju Preservation Corporation].

Ōsawa Kyoshi. 1994. *Shashinkai no senkaku Ogawa Kazumasa no shōgai* [The life of pioneering photographer Ogawa Kazumasa]. Tokyo: Kindai Bungeisha.

Pai Hyung Il. 1994. "The Politics of Korea's Past: The Legacy of Japanese Colonial Archaeology in the Korean Peninsula." *East Asian History* 7:25–48.

———. 1999a. "Japanese Anthropology and the Discovery of "Prehistoric Korea." *Journal of East Asian Archaeology* 1:353–82.

———. 1999b. "Nationalism and Preserving Korea's Buried Past: The Office of Cultural Properties and Archaeological Heritage Management in South Korea." *Antiquity* 73 (281): 619–25.

———. 2000. *Constructing "Korean Origins": Archaeology, Historiography, and Racial Myth*. Cambridge, MA: Harvard University Asia Center.

———. 2001. "The Creation of National Treasures and Monuments: The 1916 Japanese Laws on the Preservation of Korean Remains and Relics and Their Colonial Legacies." *Korean Studies* 25 (1): 72–95.

———. 2004. "Collecting Japan's Antiquity in Colonial Korea: The Tokyo Anthropological Society and the Cultural Comparative Perspective." *Moving Objects: Time, Space, and Context*. 26th International Symposium on the Preservation of Cultural Property Series, 87–107. Tokyo: National Research Institute of Cultural Properties.

———. 2006. "Sinhwasŏk koťo pogwŏn ŭl wihan yujŏk ťamsaek" [Reclaiming the ruins of imagined imperial terrains: Meiji archaeology and art historical surveys in the Korean peninsula, 1900–1916]. In *Ilbon ŭi palmyŏng kwa kŭndae* [The discovery of "Japan" and modernity], edited by Yoon Sang-in and Park Kyu-ťae, 247–84. Seoul: Yeesan.

———. 2009. "Capturing Visions of Japan's Prehistoric Past: Torii Ryūzō's Field Photographs of 'Primitive' Races and Lost Civilizations (1896–1915)". In *Looking Modern: East Asian Visual Culture from Treaty Ports to World War II*, edited by Jennifer Purtle and Hans Bjarne Thomsen, 258–86. Chicago: Center for the Art of East Asia and Art Media Resources.

———. 2010a. "Re-surrecting the Ruins of Japan's Mythical Homelands: Colonial Archaeological Surveys in the Korean peninsula and Heritage Tourism." In *The Handbook of Post-Colonialism and Archaeology*, edited by Jane Lydon and Uzma Rizvi, 93–112. World Archaeological Congress Research Handbook Series. Walnut Creek, CA: Left Coast Press.

———. 2010b. "Travel Guides to the Empire: The Production of Tourist Images in Colonial Korea." In *Consuming Korean Tradition in Early and Late Modernity*, edited by Laurel Kendall, 67–87. Honolulu: University of Hawai'i Press.

———. 2011. "Tracing Japan's Antiquity: Photography, Archaeology, and Representations of Kyŏngju." In *Oriental Aesthetics and Thinking: Conflicting Visions of "Asia" under the Colonial Empires*, edited by Inaga Shigemi, 289–316. Kyoto: International Center for Japanese Studies.

Pak Min-chŏl, et al., eds. *Kŏnch'ukŭn ŏpta?* [Is there no architecture?]. Seoul: Kan'hyang Midia.

Park Saeyoung. 2010. "National Heroes and Monuments in South Korea: Patriotism, Modernization, and Park Chung-Hee's Remaking of Yi Sun-sin's Shrine." *Asia-Pacific Journal* 24-3-10, March 3, n.p.

Park Sang-mi. 2010. "The Paradox of Postcolonial Korean Nationalism: State Sponsored Cultural Policy in South Korea, 1965–Present." *Journal of Korean Studies* 15:67–94.

Park Soon-wŏn. 1999. *Colonial Industrialization and Labor in Korea*. Cambridge, MA: Harvard University Asia Center.

Park Yŏng-mu. 1971. "Chijŏng munhwajae mojop'um saengsan saŏp ŭi poho yuksŏng ŭl wihan sogo" [A recommendation for the protection and development of registered cultural properties' reproduction industries]. *Munhwajae* 5:122–26.

Pearce, Susan, ed. 1991. *Museum Studies in Material Culture*. Washington, DC: Smithsonian Institution Press.

———. 1992. *Museums, Objects, and Collections*. Washington, DC: Smithsonian Institute Press.

Peattie, Mark R. 1984. "Japanese Attitudes towards Colonialism." In *The Japanese Colonial Empire*, edited by Ramon H. Myers and Mark R. Peattie, 8–127. Princeton, NJ: Princeton University Press.

Pelizzari, Maria A., ed. 2003. *Traces of India: Photography, Architecture, and the Politics of Representation, 1850–1900*. Exhibition catalogue. Montreal: Canadian Centre for Architecture.

Pemberton, John. 1994. *On the Subject of "JAVA."* Ithaca: Cornell University Press.

Picard, Michel, and Robert E. Wood. 1997. *Tourism, Ethnicity, and the State in Asian and Pacific Societies*. Honolulu: University of Hawai'i Press.

Prakash, Gyan. 1995. *After Colonialism: Imperial Histories and Post-Colonial Displacements*. Princeton, NJ: Princeton University Press.

Pratt, Mary L. 1992. *Imperial Eyes: Travel Writing and Transculturation*. London, Routledge.

Prott, Lyndel V. 2005. "The International Movement of Cultural Objects." *International Journal of Cultural Properties* 12 (2): 225–48.

Put, Max. 2000. *Plunder and Pleasure: Japanese Art in the West, 1860–1930*. Leiden: Hotei Publishing.

Reid, Donald M. 2002. *Whose Pharaohs: Archaeology, Museums, and Egyptian National Identity from Napoleon to World War I*. Berkeley: University of California Press.

Reischauer, Edwin O. 1939. "Japanese Archaeological Work on the Asiatic Continent." *Harvard Journal of Asiatic Studies* 4 (1): 87–98.

Riōke Hakubutsukan. 1912. *Riōke Hakubutsukan shozōhin Shashinchō* [Catalogue of the Prince Yi Household Museum]. Seoul: Keijō Insatsu.

Rosenstone, Robert. 1988. *Mirror in the Shrine: American Encounters with Meiji Japan*. Cambridge, MA: Harvard University Press.

Roth, Michael S., Claire Lyons, and Charles Merriwether. 1997. *Irresistible Decay: Ruins Reclaimed*. Los Angeles: Getty Research Institute for the History of Humanities.

Rouse, Irving. 1986. *Migrations in Prehistory*. New Haven, CT: Yale University Press.

Rowan, Yorke, and Uzi Baram. 2004. *Marketing Heritage: Archaeology and the Consumption of the Past*. Walnut Creek: Altamira Press.

Rowlands, Michael. 1994. "The Politics of Identity in Archaeology." In *Social Construction of the Past*, edited by George Bond and Angela Gilliam, 129–43. London: Routledge.

Ruoff, Kenneth. 2001. *The People's Emperor: Democracy and the Japanese Monarchy, 1945–1995*. Cambridge, MA: Harvard University Asia Center.

———. 2010. *Imperial Japan at Its Zenith: The Wartime Celebration of the Emperor's 2,600th Anniversary*. Ithaca: Cornell University Press.

Ruppert, Brian D. 2000. *Jewel in the Ashes: Buddha Relics and Power in Early Medieval Japan*. Cambridge, MA: Harvard University Asia Center.

Ryan, James. 1997. *Picturing Empire: Photography and the Visualization of the British Empire*. Chicago: University of Chicago Press.

Saeki Arikiyo. 1974. *Kōkaidoōhi* [King Kwanggaet'o stele]. Tokyo: Yoshikawa Kōbunkan.

Said, Edward. 1979. *Orientalism*. New York: Vintage Books, Random House.

———. 1993. *Culture and Imperialism*. New York: Alfred A. Knopf.

———. 1995. "Secular Interpretations, the Geographical, and the Methodology of Imperialism." In *After Colonialism*, edited by Gyan Prakash, 21–39. Princeton, NJ: Princeton University Press.

Saitō Tadashi, ed. 1971. "Tsuboi Shōgorō shū." In *Nihon kōkogaku senshū* [Anthology of Japanese archaeology], vol. 2, 320–27. Tokyo: Tsukichi Shokan.

————. 1972. "Tsuboi Shōgorō-ryaku nenpyo" [Tsūboi Shōgorō chronology]. In *Nihon kōkogaku senshū* [Anthology of Japanese archaeology], vol. 3, 302–34. Tokyo: Tsukichi Shokan.

————. 1974. "Torii Ryūzō shū." In *Nihon kōkogaku senshū* [Anthology of Japanese archaeology], vol. 7. Tokyo: Tsukichi Shokan.

————. 1976a. "Gakushini okeru Ōno Entarō no gyōseki" [The achievements of Ōno Entarō in Japanese archaeology]. In *Nihon kōkogaku senshū* [Anthology of Japanese archaeology], vol. 4, 4–10. Tokyo: Tsukichi Shokan.

————. 1976b. "Gakushi ni okeru Yagi Sōzaburō no gyōseki" [The scholarly achievements of Yagi Sōzaburō in Japanese archaeology]. In *Nihon kōkogaku senshū* [Anthology of Japanese archaeology], vol. 4, 96–102. Tokyo: Tsukichi Shokan.

————. 1976c. "Ōno Entarō-ryaku nenpyō" [ōno Entarō chronology]. In *Nihon kōkogaku senshū* [Anthology of Japanese archaeology], vol. 4, 89–91. Tokyo: Tsukichi Shokan.

————. 1976d. "Yagi Sōzaburō shūroku bunken kaisetsu" [Explanations on Yagi Sōzaburō's articles]. In *Nihon kōkogaku senshū* [Anthology of Japanese archaeology], vol. 4, 160–62. Tokyo: Tsukichi Shokan.

————. 1982. *Nihon no hakkutsu* [Excavating Japan]. Tokyo: Tokyo Daigaku Shūppan.

————. 1985. *Kōkogakushi no hitōbitō* [Figures in the history of Japanese archaeology]. Tokyo: Daichi Shobō.

————. 2001. *Nihon kōkogakushi nenpyō* [A chronology of Japanese archaeology]. Tokyo: Gakuseisha.

Sakazume Hideichi. 1997. *Taiheiyō sensō to kōkogaku* [The field of archaeology and the Pacific war]. Tokyo: Yoshikawa Kobunkan Rekishi Bunka Library Series 11.

Sand, Jordan. 2000. "Was Meiji Tastes in Interiors 'Orientalist'?" *Positions* 8 (3): 637–73.

Sanderson, Stephen K. 1990. *Social Evolution: A Critical History*. Cambridge, UK: Blackwell.

Sasaki Kōmei, ed. 1993. *Torii Ryūzō no mita Ajia* [Asia photographed by Torii Ryūzō]. Osaka: Tokushima Kenritsu Hakubutsukan [Tokushima County Museum] / Minpaku [National Museum of Ethnology]/Osaka Kokuritsu Minzoku Hakubutsukan [National Museum of Ethnology].

Satō Dōshin. 1999. *Meiji kindai kokka to bijutsu* [Art and the Meiji modern state]. Tokyo: Kichikawa Kobunkan.

Satow, Ernest, and A. G. S. Hawkes. 1881. *A Handbook for Travelers to Central and Northern Japan*. Yokohama, Japan: Kelly and Walsh.

Schnell, Ivar. 1932. "Prehistoric Finds from the Island World of the Far East, Now Preserved in the Museum of Far Eastern Antiquities, Dedicated to His Royal Highness Crown Prince, Gustaf Adolf." *Museum of Far Eastern Antiquities Bulletin* 4:15–104.

Schwartz, Joan, and James Ryan, eds. 2003. *Picturing Place: Photography and the Geographical Imagination*. London: I. B. Tauris.

Segal, Daniel, ed. 1992. *Crossing Cultures*. Tucson: University of Arizona Press.

Sekino Tadashi. 1904. *Kankoku kenchiku chōsa hōkoku* [Survey reports of Korean architecture]. Tokyo Teikoku Daigaku Kōka Daigaku Gakujutsu Hōkoku [Tokyo Imperial University Department of Engineering] 6. Tokyo: Tokyo Teikoku Daigaku.

————. 1910. *Chōsen keijutsu no kenkyū* [A study of Korean art]. Keijō: Chōsen Sōtokufu.

————. 1929. *The Conservation of Ancient Buildings in Japan*. World Engineering Congress. Paper no. 751, 1–19.

————. 1931. "Ancient Remains and Relics in Korea: Efforts toward Research and Preservation." Paper presented at the Fourth Biannual Conference of the Institute of Pacific Relations, Hangchou.

————. 1932. *Chōsen bijutsushi* [A history of Korean art]. Seoul: Chōsenshi Gakkai.

Sekino Takeshi. 1978. *Sekino Tadashi Exhibition* [A pioneer in the research of Japanese and east Asian art and architecture]. Chōetsu shi: Choetsu-shi Sōgo Hakubutsukan.

Selwyn, Tom, ed. 1996. *The Tourist Image: Myths and Myth Making in Tourism*. Chichester, UK: John Wiley and Sons.

Shapiro, Daniel. 2006. *Pocantico Conference Report*. International symposium, "What Heritage to Preserve?" organized by the International Cultural Property Society at the Pocantico Conference Center for the Rockefeller Brothers' Fund, October 19–21, New York. *International Journal of Cultural Property* 13 (3): 333–60.

Shennan, S. J. 1989. *Archaeological Approaches to Cultural Identity*. London: Unwin Hyman.

Shibata Jōkei. 1908. "Chōsen Kinkai no Kaizuka" [Kimhae shellmound in the Korean peninsula]. *Tokyo Jinrui gakkai zasshi* 24 (273): 95–98.

Shiina Noritaka. 1988. *Nihon Hakubutsukan hattatsu shi* [The historical development of Japanese museums]. Tokyo: Takayama shūppan.

————. 1989. *Meiji Hakkubutsukan koto hajime* [The beginnings of Meiji museums]. Kyoto: Shibungaku Shūppan.

Shiina Shintarō. 1977. *Teisetsu bunkazai hogohō* [A detailed history of cultural properties laws]. Tokyo: Shin Nihon Hogyū Shūppan.

Shim U-sŏng, trans. 1996. *Chosŏn ŭi soban. Chosŏn togi myŏng-ko*. Korean translation of *Chōsen no zen* [Tables of Chōsen], 1935, and *Chōsen toji Meiko* [Nomenclature of the pottery of Chōsen] by Asakawa Takumi. Seoul: Hakkoje.

Shimizu Shigeatsu. 2003. "Kaitei shūri-Nihon no kenzōbutsu ni okeru tentō to kindai no shōkoku" [The rebuilding and preservation of ancient shrines and temples]. *Bunkazai gekkan* 3:32–56.

Shin Gi-wook. 1998. "Nation, History, and Politics: Rhetoric of Minjok in Postwar Korea." In *Nationalism and the Construction of Korean Identity*, edited by Hyung Il Pai and Tim Tangherlini, 148–65. Korea Research Monograph Series 26. Berkeley: University of California East Asia Institute.

Shiratori Kurakichi. 1934. "Waihaku minzoku no yūrai wo nobete: Fuyu, Kōkuri oyobi Kudara no kigen ni oyobu" [On the origins of the Yemaek and their relationship with the origin of Puyŏ, Koguryŏ, and Paekche]. *Shigaku zasshi* 42 (12): 1516–17.

————. 1970. *Shiratori Kurakichi zenshū* [The complete works of Shiratori Kurakichi], vol. 3, edited by Shiratori Sei. Tokyo: Iwanami Shoten.

————. 1986. *Saigai minzokushi kenkyū* [A study of races beyond the borders]. 2 vols. Tokyo: Iwanami shoten.

Shiratori Yoshirō and Ichirō Yawata. 1978. *Nihon minzoku bunka taikei* [A racial and cultural history of Japan]. Vol. 9. Tokyo: Kōdansha.

Shirazu Jōshin. 2002. *Ōtani tankendai to sono jidai* [The expeditions of Ōtani and his times]. Tokyo: Bensei Shūppan.

Shirokorogoff, S. M. 1966. *Social Organization of the Northern Tungus*. Oosterhout, Netherlands: Anthropological Publications.

Shiseki Meishō Tennen Kinenbutsu Hozonkai [Historical sites, famous places, and natural monuments preservation committee], ed. 1942. "Koshajihozonkai no omoidasu: Itō Chuta hakushi o kagomu zadankai" [Remembrances of the preservation of old temples and shrines: A conversation with professor Itō Chuta]. *Shiseki Meishō Tennen Kinenbutsu Hozonkai* 17:659–75.

Shōda Shinya. 2008. "A Brief Introduction to Rescue Archaeology." In *Early Korea*, vol. 1, *Reconsidering Early Korean History through Archaeology*, edited by Early Korea Institute, 201–12. Cambridge, MA: Harvard University.

Siebold, Heinrich von. 1879. *Notes on Japanese Archaeology with Special Reference to the Stone Age*. Yokohama: Typography of C. Levy.

Siegenthaler, Peter. 1999. "The Ningen Kokuhō: A New Symbol for the Japanese Nation." *Andon: Shedding Light on Japanese Art* 62:3–16.

Silberman, Neil A. 1982. *Digging for God and Country: Exploration, Archaeology, and the Secret Struggle for the Holy Land, 1799–1917*. New York: Alfred K. Knopf.

———. 1989. *Between Past and Present: Archaeology, Ideology, and Nationalism in the Modern Middle-East*. New York: Doubleday.

Skya, Walter. 1994. "Emperor Ideology: The Debate over State and Sovereignty in Modern Japan." PhD diss., University of Chicago.

Smith, Anthony D. 1986. *The Ethnic Origins of Nations*. Oxford: Basil Blackwell.

Smith, Valene L., ed. 1977. *Hosts and Guests: The Anthropology of Tourism*. Philadelphia: University of Pennsylvania Press.

Sokei-en. N.d. *Sokei-en annai* [Guide to Ch'anggyŏng wŏn palace]. Tourist brochure. Keijō: Ch'angyŏngwon Palace.

Sōseki Natsume. 2000. *Re-discovering Natsume Sōseki: Celebrating the Centenary of Sōseki's Arrival in England, 1900–1902, with the First English Translation of Travels in Manchuria and Korea*. Introduction and translation by Inger Sigrun Brodey and Sammy I. Tsunematsu. Folkstone: Global Oriental.

Starr, Frederick. 1904. *The Ainu Group at the St. Louis Exposition*. Chicago: Open Court Publishing Company.

Stocking, George W. 1968. *Race, Culture, and Evolutions: Essays in the History of Anthropology*. Free Press: New York.

———. 1985. *Objects and Others: Essays on Museums and Material Culture*. History of Anthropology Series 3. Madison: University of Wisconsin Press.

———. 1988. *Bones, Body, and Behavior: Essays on Biological Anthropology*. History of Anthropology Series 5. Madison: Wisconsin University Press.

———. 1991. *Colonial Situations*. History of Anthropology Series 7. Madison: The University of Wisconsin Press.

Stone, Peter G., and Brian L. Molyneaux. 1994. *The Presented Past: Heritage, Museum, and Education*. One World Archaeology. London: Routledge.

Sugi Ichirōbei, ed. 1910. *Heigō kinen Chōsen shashinjō* [Commemoration photo album of the annexation of Chōsen]. Tokyo: Gengentō Shobō / Keijō: Shinhantō Sha.

Sugihara Sadakichi. 1911. *Chōsen kokuhō taikan* [A survey of Korean cultural treasures]. Seoul: Nikkan Shobō.

Suzuki Hiroyuki. 2003. *Kōkogatachi no jūgyūseiki: Bakumatsu ni okeru "mono" no arukeoroji* [Antiquarians in the nineteenth century: The archaeology of objects at the end of the Tokugawa era]. Tokyo: Yoshikawa Kōbunkan.

Suzuki Ryō and Hiroshi Takagi, eds. 2002. *Bunkazai to kindai Nihon* [Cultural properties and modern Japan]. Tokyo: Yamagawa Shūppan.

Szczesniak, Boleslaw. 1952. "Some Revisions of the Ancient Japanese Chronology Ōjin Tennō Period." *Monumenta Nipponica* 8, no. 1–2.

Takada Ryōshin. 1997. "Hōryūji no rekishi to Kudara Kannon" [The history of Hōryūji and the Paekche Avalokitesvara]. In *Kudara kannon* [The Paekche Avalokitesvara], edited by Tōhaku, 6–11. Tokyo: Asahi Shinbunsha.

Takagi Hiroshi. 1995. "Nihon bijūtsu shi no seiritsu-shiron-kodaibijūtsushi no jidaikubun no seiritsu" [Essay on the making of Japanese art history: A preliminary theory on the periodization scheme in Japanese ancient art history]. *Nihonshi kenkyū* 399 (11): 74–98.

———. 2000. *Kindai tennosei no bunkashideki kenkyū* [A study of modern Japanese imperial cultural policies]. 2nd ed. Tokyo: Kōko Shūppan.

Takagi Yōko. 2002. *Japonisme, in fin de siècle Art in Belgium*. Antwerp: Petraco-Pandora.

Takahashi Kiyoshi. 2003. "Chōsen koseki chōsa ni okeru Oba Tsunekichi" [Oba Tsunekichi's archaeological investigations in the Korean peninsula]. *Nihon kōkogashi kenkyū* 10:37–56.

Takasaki Sōji. 2001. *Chōsen mingei ronshū* [Studies on Chōsen Mingei]. Tokyo: Sofukan.

———. 2002. *Chōsen no dotonatta Nihonjin* [The Japanese who became the Clay of Korea]. 3rd ed. Tokyo: Sofukan.

Takeda Yukio. 1989. "Studies on the King Kwanggae-t'o Inscription and Their Basis." *Memoirs of the Research Department of the Tōyō Bunko* 47:57–87.

Takimoto Jirō. 1928. *Guide-book to Japan, Manchuria, Korea, and China*. Tokyo: Ōbeiryokō Annaisha.

Tamura Kazuhiko. 1990. "Ja-pan Tsu-risto Bū-ro- ni okeru taibaijigyo no tenkai" [The development of the Japan tourist bureau as a ticket agency]. *Nihon kankō gakkai kenkyū* 21:103–9.

Tanaka Migaku. 1982. "Iseki ibutsu ni kansuru hogo kenchiku no gakuritsu katei" [The establishment of principals behind the protection of remains and relics]. In *Kōkogaku ronkō*, edited by Kobayashi Yukio Hakushi Kogi Kinen Kai [Compilation Committee for the Sixtieth Anniversary of Professor Kobayashi Yukio), 765–83. Tokyo: Heibonsha.

Teikoku Kosekishū Chōsakai. 1900–03. Teikoku Kosekishū Chōsa Kaihō [Imperial preservation committee on ancient remains newsletter].

Teikoku Tetsudo-in (JIGR) [Japanese Imperial Government Railways]. 1914. *Japan Pocket Guide: Imperial Government Railways*. Tokyo: Traffic Department.

———. 1922. *Hot Springs of Japan (and the Principal Cold Springs), including Chōsen (Korea), Taiwan (Formosa), and South Manchuria*. Edited by Frederic de Garis. Official English editions of guide book series. Tokyo: Japan Tourist Bureau.

———. 1925. *Travelers Map of Japan, Chōsen (Korea), Taiwan (Formosa)*. Tokyo: Japan Tourist Bureau.

———. 1926. *Pocket Guide to Japan*. Edited by Frederic De Garis. Tokyo: Japan Tourist Bureau/ Japan Hotel Association.

———. 1933. *Some Suggestion for Souvenir Seekers*. Tokyo: Board of Tourist Industry.

Teng Emma J. 2004. *Taiwan's Imagined Geography*. Harvard East Asian Monograph Series. Cambridge, MA: Harvard Asia Center.

Teshigawara Akira. 1995. *Nihon kōkogaku no ayumi* [A historical development of Japanese archaeology]. Tokyo: Meisho Shūppan.

Thomas, Nicholas. 1994. *Colonialism's Culture: Anthropology, Travel, and Government*. Princeton, NJ: Princeton University Press.

Thrasher, William. 1984. "The Beginnings of Chanoyu in America." *Chanoyu Quarterly* 40:7–35. Kyoto: Uranseke Foundation.

Thongchai Winichakul. 1998. *Siam Mapped*. Honolulu: University of Hawai'i Press.

Tokyo Bijutsu, ed. 1990. *Wa-ei Taishō Nihon bijutsu yōgo* [A dictionary of Japanese art terms]. Bilingual Japanese and English editions. Tokyo: Tokyo Bijutsu.

Tōkyō Daigaku Sōgō Kenkyū Shiryōkan. 1991. *Tōkyō Daigaku Sōgō Kenkyū Shiryōkan shōzō Jōmon jidai dogu sono ta dosaihin katalogu* [A catalogue of the Tokyo University museums collections of Jomon clay figurines and other clay objects]. University of Tokyo Material Reports 25. Tokyo: University of Tokyo Museum.

Tokyo Jinrui Gakkai (TJGK). 1895. "Torii Ryūzō shokutaku fuinsho" [Dispatch contract for Torii Ryūzō]. *Tokyo Jinrui Gakkai Zasshi* 10 (112): 148.

Tokyo Kokuritsu Bunkazai Kenkyujō [Tokyo National Institute of Cultural Properties]. 1986. *International Symposium on the Conservation and Restoration of Cultural Property: The Training of Specialists in Various Fields Related to Cultural Properties*. Tokyo: Tokyo National Institute of Cultural Properties.

———. 2004. *Ugoku mono-jikan, kūkan* [Moving objects: Time, space, and context]. The Twenty-Sixth International Symposium on the Preservation of Cultural Property Series. Sponsored by the Tokyo National Research Institute of Cultural Properties. Tokyo: Tōbunken.

Tokyo Kokuritsu Hakubutsukan [Tokyo National Museum], ed. 1976. *Tokyo Kokuritsu Hakubutsukan hyakunenshi* [A hundred-year history of the Tokyo National Museum]. 2 vols. Tokyo: Tokyo Kokuritsu Hakubutsukan.

———. 1992. *Me de miru hyakunijūnen* [Visual records of one hundred and twenty years of the Tokyo National Museum]. Tokyo: Tokyo Bijutsu Publishing.

———. 1997. *Umi o watatta Meiji no bijutsu: Zaiken! 1893 nen Chicago Koronbusu sekai hakubutsukan* [World's Columbian Exposition of 1893 revisited: Nineteenth-century Japanese art shown in Chicago, USA].

———. 2004. *Tokyo Kokuritsu Hakubutsukan zukan mokuroku: Chōsen dokihen* [Illustrated catalogue of Tokyo national museum: Korean ceramics, earthenware, and stoneware]. Tokyo: Tokyo Kokuritsen Hakubutsukan.

———. 2005. *Nen Nihon kokusai hakurankai kaisai kinnen den, seki no saiden hakurankai no bijutsu* [Commemorating the 2005 Aichi World Exposition, arts of East and West from world expositions, 1855–1900, in Paris, Vienna, and Chicago], 154–61. Tokyo: Toppan Shūppan.

Tokyo Teikoku Daigaku, ed. 1915-41. *Mansen chiri rekishi kenkyū hōkoku* [Research Reports of Manchuria-Korea Geography and History]. 16 vols. Tokyo: Tokyo Imperial University, SMR.

Tokyo Teishitsu Hakubutsukan [Imperial Household Museum]. 1901. *Shōhon Nihon Bijutsushi* [First draft of the history of Japanese art]. 1st ed. Nōshōmuchō. Reprinted in 1908, 1909, and 2003. 4th ed. printed by Yumani Shobō.

———. 1938. *Teishitsu hakubutsukan ryakushi* [A short history of the imperial household museum]. Tokyo: Teishitsu Hakubutsukan.

Tomita Shōji. 2003. *Hōterū to Nihon kindai* [The hotel and Japan's modernity]. Tokyo: Seikyūsha.

———. 2005. *Ehagakide miru Nihon kindai* [Japan's modernity seen in picture postcards]. Tokyo: Seikyūsha.

Torii Ryūzō. 1904. "Chōsenjin no taishitsu" [On the physical characteristics of the Chōsenjin]. *Tokyo Jinruigaku Zasshi* 20 (25): 142–48.

———. 1908. "Manshū no sekkijidaiiseki to Chōsen no sekkijidaiiseki to kankei ni tsuite" [The relationship between Korean Stone Age remains and Manchurian Stone Age remains]. In *Nihon Kōkogaku senshū*, vol. 7, edited by Saitō Tadashi, 2–9. Reprint, 1974. Tokyo: Tsukichi Shokan.

———. 1922. "Dorumen ni tsuite" [On Dolmens]. *Dōru-men* 1:14–19.

———. 1923. "Ishiizen ni okeru Chōsen to kino shūi to no kankei" [Korea's relations with its neighbors in prehistory]. *Chōsen* 9:1–28.

———. 1924. "Hamada Umehara ryōshi sho Kinkaizuka hōkoku o yomu" [Book review on the excavation report of Kimhae shellmound by Umehara and Hamada]. In *Nihon kōkogaku senshū 7*, edited by Saitō Tadashi, 92–103. Reprint, 1974. Tokyo: Tsukichi Shokan.

———. 1925a. *Jinruigaku jōyori mitaru waga jōdai no bunka* [Our civilization as seen from an anthropological perspective]. Tokyo: Sōbunkan.

———. 1925b. *Kyokutō minzoku* [Far eastern races], vol. 1. Tōyōjinshū Gakusosho. Tokyo: Bunka-seikatsu Kenkyūkai.

———. 1937. *Ancient Japan in the Light of Anthropology*. Tokyo: Kokusai Bunka Shinkōkai [Society of International Cultural Relations].

———. 1953. *Aru rōgakuto no shūki* [Notes of one old student]. Tokyo: Asahi Shinbunsha.

———. 1976. *Torii Ryūzō zenshū* [The complete works of Torii Ryūzō]. 12 vols. Tokyo: Asahi Shūppan.

Tōyō Kyōkai Chōsabu (Tokyo). 1912. "Setsurin Daidōkō minami no kofun to Rakurō ichi tono kankei" [The relationship between the tombs situated south of the Taedong River and the Wang tombs of Rakurō]. *Tōyō gakuhō* 2 (1): 96–104.

Trigger, Bruce. 1968. *Beyond History: The Methods of Prehistory*. New York: Holt, Rinehart and Winston.

———. 1984. "Alternative Archaeologists: Nationalist, Colonialist, Imperialist." *Man* 19 (3): 355–70.

——. 1989. *A History of Archaeological Thought*. Cambridge: Cambridge University Press.

Tsuboi Shōgorō. 1889. "Nihon kōkogaku kogi sōron" [An overview of Japanese archaeology, parts I and 2]. Reprinted in *Nihon kōkogaku senshū* [A selected anthology of Japanese archaeology], vol. 1, edited by Saitō Tadashi, 15–29. Tokyo: Tsukichi Shokan.

——. 1892. "Kōkogaku to dozokugaku" [The relationship between archaeology and ethnology]. Reprinted in *Nihon kōkogaku senshū* [A selected anthology of Japanese archaeology], vol. 2, edited by Saitō Tadashi, 36–41. Tokyo: Tsukichi shokan, 1972.

——. 1895. Koro-pok-guru Series 1–14. Reprinted in *Nihon kōkogaku senshū* [A selected anthology of Japanese archaeology], vol. 2, edited by Saitō Tadashi, 50–98. Tokyo: Tsukichi Shokan, 1972.

——. 1897. "Seki jidai sōron yōryō" [A summary of the Stone Age]. Reprinted in *Nihon kōkogaku senshū* [A selected anthology of Japanese archaeology], vol. 1, edited by Saitō Tadashi, 44–48. Tokyo: Tsukichi Shokan, 1972.

——. 1903. *Jinshū shi* [History of world races]. Tokyo: Takayama Shinbō.

——. 1905. "Kōkogaku no shinka" [The real value of archaeology]. Reprinted in *Nihon kōkogaku senshū* [A selected anthology of Japanese archaeology], vol. 1, edited by Saitō Tadashi, 30–34. Tokyo: Tsukichi Shokan, 1972.

——. 1907. *Jinruigaku sōwa* [A comprehensive overview of anthropology]. Edited by Shōgorō Tsuboi and Torii Ryūzō. Tokyo: Tokyo Hakubutsukan.

Tylor, Edward B. 1889. *Primitive Culture*. New York: Henry Holt.

Uchida Jun. 2005. "'Brokers of Empire': Japanese Settler Colonialism in Korea, 1910–1937." PhD diss., Harvard University.

Uchida Yoshiaki. 2004. "Kamijidaiseki no shūshū" [Collecting stones of the gods]. In *Ugoku mono-jikan, kūkan* [Moving objects: Time, space, and context], edited by National Research Institute of Cultural Properties Symposium, 55–69. Tokyo: Tōbunken.

Umehara Sueji. 1923. "Kōkogakujō yori mitaru jōdai Nissen no kankei" [The relationship between ancient Korea and Japan from an archaeological perspective]. *Chōsen* 8:138–70.

——. 1969. "Nikkan heigō no kikan ni okonawareta hanto no koseki chōsa to hozon jigyō ni tazusawatta ichi kōkogakuto no kaisōroku" [Remembrances of archaeological investigations and preservations of Korean sites during the Japanese colonial period]. *Chōsen gakuho* 51:95–148.

Umesao Tadao, Angus Lockeyer, and Kenji Yoshida, eds. 2000. *Japanese Civilization in the Modern World: Collection and Representation*. Senri Ethnological Series 16. Osaka: National Museum of Ethnology.

US Department of State. 1949. International Protection of Works of Art and Historical Monuments. International Information and Cultural Series 8:821–71. Reprinted from documents and state papers of June 1949, Division of Publications Office of Public Affairs. Washington, DC: US Department of State.

US Government Alien Property Custodian. 1943. *Yamanaka Dealers' Auction Catalogue*.

Vesey, Alexander. 2004. "For Faith and Prestige: Daimyo Motivations for Buddhist Patronage." *Early Modern Japan* 12 (2): 53–66.

Vlastos, Stephen, ed. 1998. *Mirror of Modernity: Invented Traditions of Modern Japan*. Berkeley: University of California Press.

Vos, Ken. 2001. "The Composition of the Siebold Collection in the National Museum of Ethnology in Leiden." In *Japanese Civilization in the Modern World: Collection and Representation*, edited by Tadao Umesao, Augus Lockeyer, and Kenji Yoshida, 39–48. Senri Ethnological Series 16. Osaka: National Museum of Ethnology.

Wada, Sei. 1938. "Chōsen minzoku no hatten" [The development of the Korean race]. *Nihon rekishi* 30:2–8.

Walsh, Kevin. 1992. *The Representation of the Past: Museums and Heritage in a Post-Modern World*. London: Routledge.

Walraven, Boudewijn. 1999. "The Natives Next Door: Ethnology in Colonial Korea." In *Anthropology and Colonialism in Asia and Oceania*, edited by Jans van Bremen and Akitoshi Shimizu, 266–84. Surrey: Curzon Press.

Warner, Langdon. [1941?]. *List of Monuments in Korea, American Defense-Harvard Group, Committee on the Preservation of Monuments*. Harvard University Rubel Asiatic Library.

Watson, James L., and Evelyn S. Rawski, eds. 1988. *Death Ritual in Late Imperial and Modern China*. Berkeley: University of California Press.

Weiner, Michael, ed. 1997. *Japan's Minorities: The Illusion of Homogeneity*. London: Routledge.

Weisenfeld, Gennifer. 2000. "Touring Japan as Museums: Nippon and other Japanese Imperialist Travelogues." *Positions* 8 (3): 747–93.

Welcome Society of Japan (Kihinkai). 1908. *A Guide Book for Tourists in Japan*. 4th ed. Revised, Head Office, Chamber of Commerce. Tokyo: Tokyo Insatsu.

Wood, Robert E. 1997. "Tourism and the State: Ethnic Options and the Constructions of Otherness." In *Tourism, Ethnicity, and the State in Asian and Pacific Societies*, edited by Michel Picard and Robert E. Wood, 1–34. Honolulu: University of Hawai'i Press.

World Heritage Committee. 1993. *Convention Concerning the Protection of World Cultural and Natural Heritage*. World Heritage Committee Seventeenth Session, December 6–11, Cartegna, Columbia.

Xu Su-bin. 2002. "Tōyō kenchiku shigaku no seiritsu ni miru akademi to nasyonarizumu: Sekino Tadashi to Chūgoku kenchikushi kenkyū" [Nationalism, academia, and the establishment of East Asian architectural history: Sekino Tadashi and the study of Chinese architecture]. *Nihon kenkyū* 26:53–142.

Yagi Shizuyama. 1935. "Meiji kōkogakushi" [A history of Meiji archaeology]. *Dō-rumen* 4 (5): 417–34.

Yagi Sōzaburō. 1894. "Kōkogaku ni okeru Kofun no shinka" [The archaeological significance of Kofun]. In *Nihon kōkogaku senshū* [A selected anthology of Japanese archaeology], vol. 4, edited by Saitō Tadashi, 116–21. Tokyo: Tsukichi Shokan, 1974.

———. 1900. "Kangoku tsushin" [Correspondence from Korea sent to Professor Tsuboi of the medical division of Tokyo University]. *Tokyo Jinuii Gakkai Zasshi* 16 (177): 90–94.

———. 1902. "Chōsen kōkodan" [Korean archaeological stories]. *Kōkogai* 1 (11): 672–73.

Yamaguchi Seiichi. 1982. *Fenōrōsa: Nihon bunka no senyō ni sasageta isshō* [Ernest Fenollosa: A life devoted to the advocacy of Japanese culture]. 3 vols. Tokyo: Sanseidō.

Yamamichi Jōichi. 1910. *Chōsen hanto* [The Korean peninsula]. Seoul: Nikkan Shobōzohan.

Yamamoto Tadanao. 2001. *Eiwa taichō Nihon kōkogaku yōgeiyaku jiden kōhon* [Dictionary of Japanese archaeological terms]. Tokyo: Tokyo Bijutsu.

Yamasaki Shigehisa. 1981. *Chronological Table of Japanese Art*. Tokyo: Geishinsha.

Yanagi Sōetsu. 1922. "For a Korean Architecture about to Be Lost." Translated by Yong-ho Ch'oe. In *Sources of East Asian Tradition*, vol. 2, edited by Theodore De Bary, 552–53. New York: Columbia University Press.

———. 1982. *The Unknown Craftsman*. Tokyo: Kodansha International.

———. 1996. *Chosŏn ŭl saengakhanda* [Thoughts on Chosŏn]. Translated by Sim U-Sŏng. Seoul: Hakkoje.

Yang Da qing. 1999. "Colonial Korea in Japans Imperial Telecommunications Network." In *Colonial Modernity in Korea*, edited by Gi-wook Shin and Michael Robinson, 161–90. Harvard-Hallym Series on Korean Studies. Cambridge, MA: Harvard University Press.

Yi Hong-jik. 1964. "Chaeil Han'guk munhwajae pimangnok" [A memo on Korean cultural relics in Japan]. *Sahak yŏn'gu* 8:791–808.

Yi Ki-baek. 1976. *Han'guksa sillon* [A new history of Korea]. Rev. ed. Seoul: Ilchogak.

———., ed. 1990. *Tan'gun sinhwa nonjip* [Anthology of Tan'gun studies]. Seoul: Saemunsa.

Yi Ku-yŏl. 1996. *Han'guk munhwajae sunansa* [The tortuous history of Korea's cultural relics]. Seoul: Tolbege.

Yi Man-yŏl. 1976. "Ilche kwanhakcha durŭi singminji sakwan" [The colonial historiography of Japanese government scholars]. In *Han'guk ŭi yŏksa insik* [The historical consciousness of Korea], pt. 2, edited by Yi U-sŏng and Kang Man-gil, 500–521. Seoul: Ch'angjak Kwa Pip'yŏngsa.

———. 1979. "Ilche kwanhakcha ŭi Han'guksa sŏsul" [Japanese colonial historical works on Korea]. *Han'guk saron* 6:239–61.

Yi Sŏn-bok. 1993. "Maejang munhwajae kwallijedo kaesŏnŭl wihan chean" [A proposal to reform the regulations of buried remains]. *Yŏngnam kogohak* 12:119–30.

Yi Sŏng-si. 2002. *Mandŭrŏjin kodae* [Manufactured antiquity]. Translated by Park Kyŏng. Seoul: Samin Books.

———. 2004. "Koroniarizumu to kindai rekishigaku" [Colonialism and modern Japanese historiography]. In *Shokuminchishūgi to rekishigaku* [Colonialism and historiography], edited by Terauchi Itarō et al., 71–112. Tokyo: Tosaishobō.

Yi Sun-ja. 2009. *Ilche Kangjŏmki kojŏk chosa yŏngu* [A study of archaeological surveys during the Japanese colonial period]. Seoul: Kyŏngin Munhwasa.

Yokohama Kaikō Shiryokan [The Port of Yokohama Historical Museum], ed. 1987. *F. Beato Bakumatsu Nihon shashinshū* [Catalogue of Felice Beato's photographs dating to the late Tokugawa era]. Yokohama: Benridō.

Yoshida Kenji. 2001. "'Tōhaku' and 'Minpaku' within the History of Modern Japanese Civilization: Museum Collections in Modern Japan." In *Japanese Civilization in the Modern World: Collection and Representation*, edited by Tadao Umesao, Angus Lockeyer, and Kenji Yoshida, 77–102. Senri Ethnological Series 16. Osaka: National Museum of Ethnology.

Yoshida Kenji and John Mack, eds. 1997. *Images of Other Cultures* [Ibunka e no manazashi]: *Reviewing Ethnographic Collections of the British Museum and the National Museum of Ethnology*. Exhibition catalogue. Osaka: NHK Service Center.

Yoshida Tōgo. 1893. *Nikkan koshidan* [Stories of ancient Japan and Korea]. Tokyo: Fukuyama Koshobō.

Yoshii Hideō. 2006. "Shokuminchi ni okeru kōkogakuchōsa no zaikentō" [A review of colonial archaeological surveys in the Korean peninsula]. Kyoto University Graduate School, Archaeology Department Research Report. Kyoto: Kyoto University.

———. 2007. "Ilche kangjŏmgi Sŏkkuram chosa mit haech'e suri wa sajin ch'wallyŏng e taehaesŏ" [A photographic study of the reconstruction of Sŏkkuram during the Japanese colonial period]. In Kyŏngju Silla yujŏk ŭi ŏche wa onŭl: Sŏkkuram, Pulguksa, Namsan [Exhibition catalogue of glass plate photographs of Silla remains in Kyŏngju], vol. 2, edited by Kim T'aesik et al., 198–209. Seoul: Sŏngyunkwan University Museum.

Yoshikawa Kōjirō. 1976. Tōyōgaku no shōshitachi [The founders of east Asian studies]. Tokyo: Kōdansha.

Yoshimura Hidetō. 1999. "Tokyo teigoku daigaku kōkogaku kōza no kaisetsu: Kokka seisaku to gakumon kenkyū no shiza kara" [The establishment of archaeology program at Tokyo Imperial University: From the perspective of state policy advancing academic research]. Nihon Rekishi 608:93–108.

Yoshino Kosaku. 1992. Cultural Nationalism in Modern Japan. London: Routledge.

Young, John. 1958. The Location of Yamato: A Case Study in Japanese Historiography, 720–1945. Ann Arbor: Univeristy of Michigan Press.

———. 1966. The Research Activities of the South Manchuria Railroad Company (1907–1945): A History and Bibliography. New York: Columbia University / East Asia Institute.

Young, Louise. 1998. Japan's Total Empire: Manchuria and the Culture of Wartime Imperialism. Berkeley: University of California Press.

Yu Hong-jun. 1993. Naŭi munhwa yusan tapsaki [My travels to cultural remains]. Seoul: Ch'angjak Kwa Pip'yŏng.

Zimmer, Oliver. 1998. "In Search of National Identity: Alpine Landscape and the Reconstruction of the Swiss Nation." Comparative Studies in Society and History 40 (4): 637–65.

INDEX

www.ingramcontent.com/pod-product-compliance
Lightning Source LLC
Chambersburg PA
CBHW031411270326
41929CB00010BA/1411